Applied Unsupervised Learning with Python

Discover hidden patterns and relationships in unstructured data with Python

Benjamin Johnston, Aaron Jones, and Christopher Kruger

Applied Unsupervised Learning with Python

Authors: Benjamin Johnston, Aaron Jones, and Christopher Kruger

Technical Reviewer: Jay Kim

Managing Editor: Rutuja Yerunkar

Acquisitions Editor: Aditya Date

Production Editor: Nitesh Thakur

Editorial Board: David Barnes, Mayank Bhardwaj, Ewan Buckingham, Simon Cox, Mahesh Dhyani, Taabish Khan, Manasa Kumar, Alex Mazonowicz, Douglas Paterson, Dominic Pereira, Shiny Poojary, Erol Staveley, Ankita Thakur, Mohita Vyas, and Jonathan Wray

First Published: May 2019

Production Reference: 1240519

ISBN: 978-1-78995-229-2

Published by Packt Publishing Ltd.

Livery Place, 35 Livery Street

Birmingham B3 2PB, UK

Table of Contents

Dimension Reduction and PCA 77

Autoencoders 129

t-Distributed Stochastic Neighbor Embedding (t-SNE)   175

Topic Modeling   207

Preface

About

This section briefly introduces the authors, the coverage of this book, the technical skills you'll need to get started, and the hardware and software requirements required to complete all of the included activities and exercises.

About the Book

Unsupervised learning is a useful and practical solution in situations where labeled data is not available.

Applied Unsupervised Learning with Python guides you through the best practices for using unsupervised learning techniques in tandem with Python libraries to extract meaningful information from unstructured data. The book begins by explaining how basic clustering works to find similar data points in a dataset. Once you are well-versed with the k-means algorithm and how it operates, you'll learn what dimensionality reduction is and where to apply it. As you progress, you'll learn various neural network techniques and how they can improve your model. While studying the applications of unsupervised learning, you will also learn how to mine topics that are trending on Twitter. You will complete the book by challenging yourself with various interesting activities, such as performing market basket analysis and identifying relationships between different products.

By the end of this book, you will have the skills you need to confidently build your own models using Python.

About the Authors

Benjamin Johnston is a senior data scientist for one of the world's leading data-driven medtech companies and is involved in the development of innovative digital solutions throughout the entire product development pathway, from problem definition, to solution research and development, through to final deployment. He is currently completing his PhD in machine learning, specializing in image processing and deep convolutional neural networks. He has more than 10 years' experience in medical device design and development, working in a variety of technical roles, and holds first-class honors bachelor's degrees in both engineering and medical science from the University of Sydney, Australia.

Aaron Jones is a full-time senior data scientist at one of America's biggest retailers, as well as a statistical consultant. He has built predictive and inferential models, and numerous data products while working in retail, media, and environmental science. Aaron is based in Seattle, Washington, and has a particular interest in causal modeling, clustering algorithms, natural language processing, and Bayesian statistics.

Christopher Kruger has worked as senior data scientist in the field of advertising. He has designed scalable clustering solutions for clients in a variety of industries. Chris was recently awarded a computer science master's degree from Cornell University, and currently works in the field of computer vision.

Learning Objectives

- Gain an understanding of the basics and importance of clustering
- Build k-means, hierarchical, and DBSCAN clustering algorithms from scratch with built-in packages
- Explore dimensionality reduction and its applications
- Use scikit-learn (sklearn) to implement and analyze principal component analysis (PCA) on the Iris dataset
- Employ Keras to build autoencoder models for the CIFAR-10 dataset
- Apply the Apriori algorithm with machine learning extensions (Mlxtend) to study transaction data

Audience

Applied Unsupervised Learning with Python is designed for developers, data scientists, and machine learning enthusiasts who are interested in unsupervised learning. Some familiarity with Python programming along with basic knowledge of mathematical concepts including exponents, square roots, means, and medians will be beneficial.

Approach

Applied Unsupervised Learning with Python takes a hands-on approach to using Python to reveal the hidden patterns in your unstructured data. It contains multiple activities that use real-life business scenarios for you to practice and apply your new skills in a highly relevant context.

Hardware Requirements

For the optimal student experience, we recommend the following hardware configuration:

- Processor: Intel Core i5 or equivalent
- Memory: 4 GB RAM
- Storage: 5 GB available space

Software Requirements

We also recommend that you have the following software installed in advance:

- OS: Windows 7 SP1 64-bit, Windows 8.1 64-bit, or Windows 10 64-bit; Linux (Ubuntu, Debian, Red Hat, or Suse); or the latest version of OS X

- Python (3.6.5 or later, preferably 3.7; available through https://www.python.org/downloads/release/python-371/)

- Anaconda (This is for the `basemap` module of `mlp_toolkits`; go to https://www.anaconda.com/distribution/, download the 3.7 version, and follow the instructions to install it.)

Conventions

Code words in text, database table names, folder names, filenames, file extensions, pathnames, dummy URLs, user input, and Twitter handles are shown as follows: "There are no prerequisites for using the `math` package, and it is included in all standard installations of Python."

A block of code is set as follows:

```
from sklearn.datasets import make_blobs
import matplotlib.pyplot as plt
import numpy as np
import math
%matplotlib inline
```

New terms and important words are shown in bold. Words that you see on the screen, for example, in menus or dialog boxes, appear in the text like this: "Next, click **Generate file** followed by **Download now** and name the downloaded file `metro-jul18-dec18`."

Installation and Setup

Each great journey begins with a humble step. Our upcoming adventure in the world of unsupervised learning is no exception. Before we can do awesome things with data, we need to be prepared with the most productive environment. Here, we shall see how to do that.

Install Anaconda on Windows

Anaconda is a Python package manager that easily allows you to install and use the libraries needed for this book. To install it on Windows, please follow these steps:

1. Anaconda installation for Windows is very user-friendly. Visit the download page here to get the installation executable: https://www.anaconda.com/distribution/#download-section.

2. Double-click the installer on your computer.

3. Follow the prompts on screen to complete the installation of Anaconda.

4. After installation, you can access Anaconda Navigator, which will be available alongside the rest of your applications as normal.

Install Anaconda on Linux

Anaconda is a Python package manager that easily allows you to install and use the libraries needed for this book. To install it on Linux, please follow these steps:

1. Visit the Anaconda download page here to get the installation shell script: https://www.anaconda.com/distribution/#download-section.

2. To download the shell script directly to your Linux instance use the `curl` or `wget` retrieval libraries. The example here shows how to use `curl` to retrieve the file located at the URL you found on the Anaconda download page:

    ```
    curl -O https://repo.anaconda.com/archive/Anaconda3-2019.03-Linux-x86_64.sh
    ```

3. After downloading the shell script, you can run it with the following command:

    ```
    bash Anaconda3-2019.03-Linux-x86_64.sh
    ```

4. Running the preceding command will move you to a very user-friendly installation process. You will be prompted on where you want to install things and how you wish Anaconda to work. In this case, you should just keep all the standard settings.

5. After Anaconda is installed, you must create environments where you will install packages you wish to use. The great thing about Anaconda environments is that you can build individual environments for specific projects you're working on! To create a new environment, use the following command:

    ```
    conda create --name my_packt_env python=3.7
    ```

6. Once the environment is created, you can activate it using the well-named **activate** command:

```
conda activate my_env
```

That's it! You are now in your own customized environment, which will allow you to install packages as needed for your projects. To exit your environment, you can simply use the **conda deactivate** command.

Install Anaconda on macOS

Anaconda is a Python package manager that allows you to easily install and use the libraries needed for this book. To install it on macOS , please follow these steps:

1. Anaconda installation for Windows is very user-friendly. Visit the download page here to get the installation executable: https://www.anaconda.com/distribution/#download-section.

2. Make sure macOS is selected and double-click the **Download** button for the Python 3 installer.

3. Follow the prompts on screen to complete the installation of Anaconda.

4. After installation, you can access Anaconda Navigator, which will be available alongside the rest of your applications as normal.

Install Python on Windows

1. Find your desired version of Python on the official installation page here: https://www.python.org/downloads/windows/.

2. Ensure that you install the correct "-bit" version depending on your computer system, either 32-bit or 64-bit. You can find out this information in the System Properties window of your OS.

   After you download the installer, simply double-click the file and follow the user-friendly prompts onscreen.

Install Python on Linux

To install Python on Linux, perform the following:

1. Open Command Prompt and verify that Python 3 is not already installed by running **python3 --version**.

2. To install Python 3, run the following:

```
sudo apt-get update
sudo apt-get install python3.6
```

3. If you encounter problems, there are numerous sources online that can help you troubleshoot the issue.

Install Python on macOS X

To install Python on macOS X, perform the following:

1. Open the terminal by holding CMD + *Space*, typing **terminal** in the open search box, and hitting *Enter*.

2. Install Xcode through the command line by running **xcode-select --install**.

3. The easiest way to install Python 3 is with homebrew, which is installed through the command line by running **ruby -e "$(curl -fsSL https://raw.githubusercontent.com/Homebrew/install/master/install)"**

4. Add homebrew to your **PATH** environment variable. Open your profile in the command line by running **sudo nano ~/.profile** and inserting **export PATH="/usr/local/opt/python/libexec/bin:$PATH"** at the bottom.

5. The final step is to install Python. In the command line, run **brew install python**.

6. Note that if you install Anaconda, the latest version of Python will be installed automatically.

Additional Resources

The code bundle for this book is also hosted on GitHub at: https://github.com/TrainingByPackt/Applied-Unsupervised-Learning-with-Python. We also have other code bundles from our rich catalog of books and videos available at https://github.com/PacktPublishing/. Check them out!

We also provide a PDF file that has color images of the screenshots/diagrams used in this book. You can download it here: https://www.packtpub.com/sites/default/files/downloads/9781789952292_ColorImages.pdf.

Introduction to Clustering

Learning Objectives

By the end of this chapter, you will be able to:

- Distinguish between supervised learning and unsupervised learning
- Explain the concept of clustering
- Implement k-means clustering algorithms using built-in Python packages
- Calculate the Silhouette Score for your data

In this chapter, we will have a look at the concept of clustering.

Introduction

Have you ever been asked to take a look at some data and come up empty handed? Maybe you were not familiar with the dataset, or maybe you didn't even know where to start. This may have been extremely frustrating, and even embarrassing, depending on who asked you to take care of the task.

You are not alone, and, interestingly enough, there are many times the data itself is simply too confusing to be made sense of. As you try and figure out what all those numbers in your spreadsheet mean, you're most likely mimicking what many unsupervised algorithms do when they try to find meaning in data. The reality is that many datasets in the real world don't have any rhyme or reason to them. You will be tasked with analyzing them with little background preparation. Don't fret, however – this book will prepare you so that you'll never be frustrated again when dealing with data exploration tasks.

For this book, we have developed some best-in-class content to help you understand how unsupervised algorithms work and where to use them. We'll cover some of the foundations of finding clusters in your data, how to reduce the size of your data so it's easier to understand, and how each of these sides of unsupervised learning can be applied in the real world. We hope you will come away from this book with a strong real-world understanding of unsupervised learning, the problems that it can solve, and those it cannot.

Thanks for joining us and we hope you enjoy the ride!

Unsupervised Learning versus Supervised Learning

Unsupervised learning is one of the most exciting areas of development in machine learning today. If you have explored machine learning bookwork before, you are probably familiar with the common breakout of problems in either supervised or unsupervised learning. **Supervised learning** encompasses the problem set of having a labeled dataset that can be used to either classify (for example, predicting smokers and non-smokers if you're looking at a lung health dataset) or fit a regression line on (for example, predicting the sale price of a home based on how many bedrooms it has). This model most closely mirrors an intuitive human approach to learning.

If you wanted to learn how to not burn your food with a basic understanding of cooking, you could build a dataset by putting your food on the burner and seeing how long it takes (input) for your food to burn (output). Eventually, as you continue to burn your food, you will build a mental model of when burning will occur and avoid it in the future. Development in supervised learning was once fast-paced and valuable, but it has since simmered down in recent years – many of the obstacles to knowing your data have already been tackled:

Unsupervised	Supervised
- No labels provided - Finds structure in unlabeled data - Uses techniques such as clustering or dimensionality reduction.	- Labels provided - Finds patterns in existing structure - Uses techniques such as regression or classification.

Figure 1.1: Differences between unsupervised and supervised learning

Conversely, unsupervised learning encompasses the problem set of having a tremendous amount of data that is unlabeled. Labeled data, in this case, would be data that has a supplied "target" outcome that you are trying to find the correlation to with supplied data (you know that you are looking for whether your food was burned in the preceding example). Unlabeled data is when you do not know what the "target" outcome is, and you only have supplied input data.

Building upon the previous example, imagine you were just dropped on planet Earth with zero knowledge of how cooking works. You are given 100 days, a stove, and a fridge full of food without any instructions on what to do. Your initial exploration of a kitchen could go in infinite directions – on day 10, you may finally learn how to open the fridge; on day 30, you may learn that food can go on the stove; and after many more days, you may unwittingly make an edible meal. As you can see, trying to find meaning in a kitchen devoid of adequate informational structure leads to very noisy data that is completely irrelevant to actually preparing a meal.

Unsupervised learning can be an answer to this problem. By looking back at your 100 days of data, **clustering** can be used to find patterns of similar days where a meal was produced, and you can easily review what you did on those days. However, unsupervised learning isn't a magical answer –simply finding clusters can be just as likely to help you to find pockets of similar yet ultimately useless data.

This challenge is what makes unsupervised learning so exciting. How can we find smarter techniques to speed up the process of finding clusters of information that are beneficial to our end goals?

Clustering

Being able to find groups of similar data that exist in your dataset can be extremely valuable if you are trying to find its underlying meaning. If you were a store owner and you wanted to understand which customers are more valuable without a set idea of what valuable is, clustering would be a great place to start to find patterns in your data. You may have a few high-level ideas of what denotes a valuable customer, but you aren't entirely sure in the face of a large mountain of available data. Through clustering you can find commonalities among similar groups in your data. If you look more deeply at a cluster of similar people, you may learn that everyone in that group visits your website for longer periods of time than others. This can show you what the value is and also provides a clean sample size for future supervised learning experiments.

Identifying Clusters

The following figure shows two scatterplots:

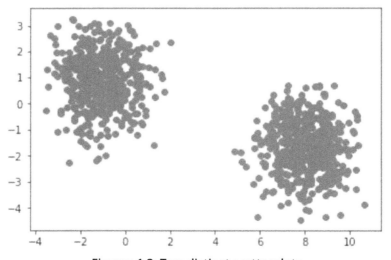

Figures 1.2: Two distinct scatterplots

The following figure separates the scatterplots into two distinct clusters:

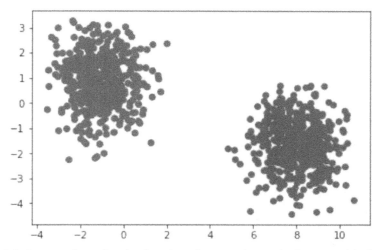

Figure 1.3: Scatterplots clearly showing clusters that exist in a provided dataset

Both figures display randomly generated number pairs (x,y coordinates) pulled from a Gaussian distribution. Simply by glancing at *Figure 1.2*, it should be plainly obvious where the clusters exist in your data – in real life, it will never be this easy. Now that you know that the data can be clearly separated into two clusters, you can start to understand what differences exist between the two groups.

Rewinding a bit from where unsupervised learning fits into the larger machine learning environment, let's begin by understanding the building blocks of clustering. The most basic definition finds clusters simply as groupings of similar data as subsets of a larger dataset. As an example, imagine that you had a room with 10 people in it and each person had a job either in finance or as a scientist. If you told all of the financial workers to stand together and all the scientists to do the same, you would have effectively formed two clusters based on job types. Finding clusters can be immensely valuable in identifying items that are more similar, and, on the other end of the scale, quite different from each other.

Two-Dimensional Data

To understand this, imagine that you were given a simple 1,000-row dataset by your employer that had two columns of numerical data as follows:

```
array([[-0.72690901,  2.76012303],
       [-1.38504876,  2.16558784],
       [-1.12519969,  0.78279526],
       ...,
       [-0.92272983, -0.44782031],
       [ 8.26124228, -0.37099837],
       [-1.01204517,  0.3228703 ]])
```

Figures 1.4: Two-dimensional raw data in a NumPy array

At first glance, this dataset provides no real structure or understanding – confusing to say the least!

A **dimension** in a dataset is another way of simply counting the number of features available. In most organized data tables, you can view the number of features as the number of columns. So, using the 1,000-row dataset example of size (1,000 x 2), you will have 1,000 observations across two dimensions:

You begin by plotting the first column against the second column to get a better idea of what the data structure looks like. There will be plenty of times where the cause of differences between groups will prove to be underwhelming, however the cases that have differences that you can take action on are extremely rewarding!

Exercise 1: Identifying Clusters in Data

You are given two-dimensional plots. Please look at the provided two-dimensional graphs and identify the clusters, to drive the point home that machine learning is important. Without using any algorithmic approaches, identify where the clusters exist in the data.

This exercise will help start to build your intuition of how we identify clusters using our own eyes and thought processes. As you complete the exercises, think of the rationale of why a group of data points should be considered a cluster versus a group that should not be considered a cluster:

1. Identify the clusters in the following scatterplot:

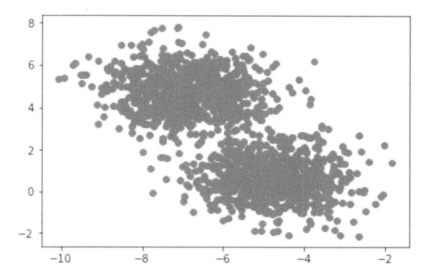

Figure1.5 Two-dimensional scatterplot

The clusters are as follows:

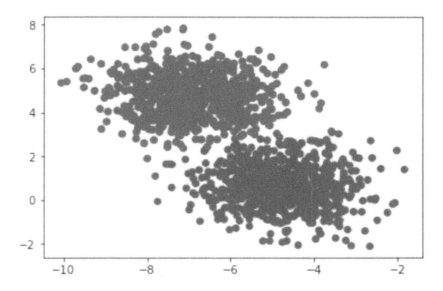

Figure 1.6: Clusters in the scatterplot

2. Identify the clusters in the scatterplot:

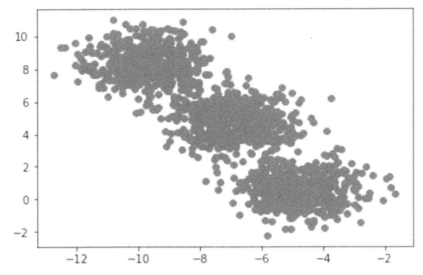

Figure1.7: Two-dimensional scatterplot

The clusters are as follows:

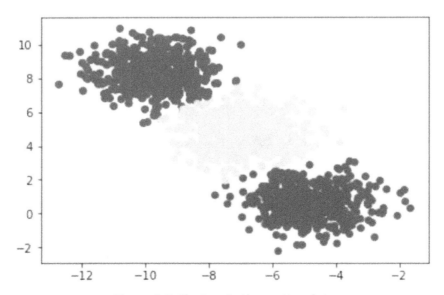

Figure 1.8: Clusters in the scatterplot

3. Identify the clusters in the scatterplot:

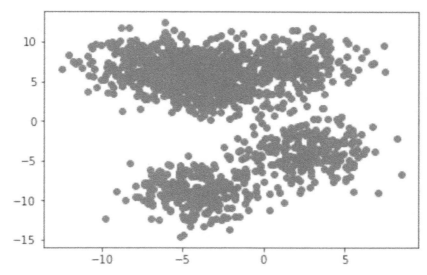

Figure1.9: Two-dimensional scatterplot

The clusters are as follows:

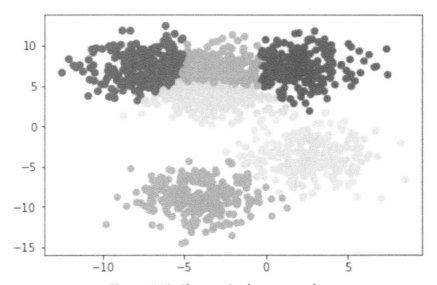

Figure 1.10: Clusters in the scatterplot

Most of these examples were likely quite easy for you to understand – and that's the point! The human brain and eyes are incredible at finding patterns in the real world. Within milliseconds of viewing each plot, you could tell what fitted together and what didn't. While it is easy for you, a computer does not have the ability to see and process plots in the same manner that we do. However, this is not always a bad thing – look back at Figure 1.10. Were you able to find the six discrete clusters in the data just by looking at the plot? You probably found only three to four clusters in this figure, while a computer is able to see all six. The human brain is magnificent, but it also lacks the nuances that come within a strictly logic-based approach. Through algorithmic clustering, you will learn how to build a model that works even better than a human at these tasks!

Let's look at the algorithm in the next section.

Introduction to k-means Clustering

Hopefully, by now, you can see that finding clusters is extremely valuable in a machine learning workflow. However, how can you actually find these clusters? One of the most basic yet popular approaches is by using a cluster analysis called **k-means clustering**. k-means works by searching for K clusters in your data and the workflow is actually quite intuitive – we will start with the no-math introduction to k-means, followed by an implementation in Python.

No-Math k-means Walkthrough

Here is the no-math algorithm of k-means clustering:

1. Pick K centroids (K = expected distinct # of clusters).

2. Randomly place K centroids anywhere amongst your existing training data.

3. Calculate the Euclidean distance from each centroid to all the points in your training data.

4. Training data points get grouped in with their nearest centroid.

5. Amongst the data points grouped into each centroid, calculate the mean data point and move your centroid to that location.

6. Repeat this process until convergence, or when the membership in each group no longer changes.

And that's it! Here is the process laid out step-by-step with a simple cluster example:

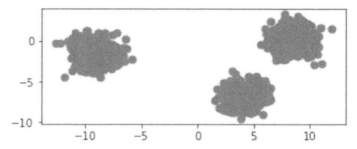

Figure 1.11: Original raw data charted on x,y coordinates

Provided with the original data in Figure 1.11, we can show the iterative process of k-means by showing the predicted clusters in each step:

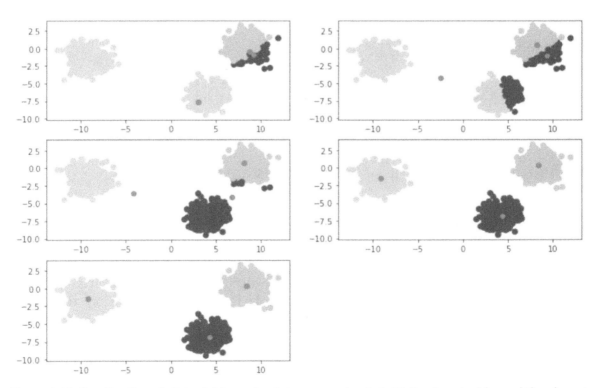

Figure 1.12: Reading from left to right – red points are randomly initialized centroids, and the closest data points are assigned to groupings of each centroid

k-means Clustering In-Depth Walkthrough

To understand k-means at a deeper level, let's walk through the example given in the introductory section again with some of the math that supports k-means. The key component at play is the Euclidean distance formula:

$$d((x, y), (a, b)) = \sqrt{(x - a)^2 + (y - b)^2}$$

Figure 1.13: Euclidean distance formula

Centroids are randomly set at the beginning as points in your n-dimensional space. Each of these centers is fed into the preceding formula as (a,b), and a point in your space is fed in as (x,y). Distances are calculated between each point and the coordinates of every centroid, with the centroid the shortest distance away chosen as the point's group.

The process is as follows:

1. Random Centroids: [(2,5) , (8,3) , (4, 5)]

2. Arbitrary point x: (0, 8)

3. Distance from point to each centroid: [3.61, 9.43, 5.00]

4. Point x is assigned to Centroid 1.

Alternative Distance Metric – Manhattan Distance

Euclidean distance is the most common distance metric for many machine learning applications and is often known colloquially as the distance metric; however, it is not the only, or even the best, distance metric for every situation. Another popular distance metric in use for clustering is **Manhattan distance**.

Manhattan distance is called as such because the intuition behind the metric is as though you were driving a car through a metropolis (such as New York City) that has many square blocks. Euclidean distance relies on diagonals due to it being based on Pythagorean theorem, while Manhattan distance constrains distance to only right angles. The formula for Manhattan distance is as follows:

$$Manhattan\ Distance\ = \sum_{i=1}^{n}|p_i - q_i|$$

Figure 1.14: Manhattan distance formula

Here, $p_i - q_i$ are vectors as in Euclidean distance. Building upon our examples of Euclidean distance, where we want to find the distance between two points, if $p_i = (p_1, p_2)$ and $q_i = (q_1, q_2)$, then the Manhattan distance would equal $q_i = (q_1, q_2)$. This functionality scales to any number of dimensions. In practice, Manhattan distance may outperform Euclidean distance when it comes to higher dimensional data.

Deeper Dimensions

The preceding examples are clear to visualize when your data is only two-dimensional. This is for convenience, to help drive the point home of how k-means works and could lead you into a false understanding of how easy clustering is. In many of your own applications, your data will likely be orders of magnitude larger to the point that it cannot be perceived by visualization (anything beyond three dimensions will be imperceivable to humans). In the previous examples, you could mentally work out a few two-dimensional lines to separate the data into its own groups. At higher dimensions, you will need to be aided by a computer to find an n-dimensional hyperplane that adequately separates the dataset. In practice, this is where clustering methods such as k-means provide significant value.

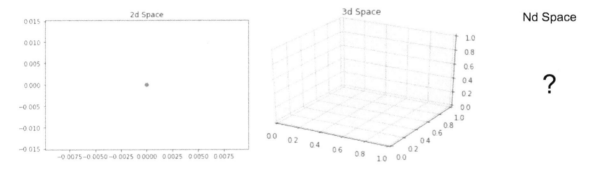

Figure 1.15: Two-dimensional, three-dimensional, and n-dimensional plots

In the next exercise, we will calculate Euclidean distance. We will use the **NumPy** and **Math** packages. **NumPy** is a scientific computing package for Python that pre-packages common mathematical functions in highly-optimized formats. By using a package such as **NumPy** or **Math**, we help cut down the time spent creating custom math functions from scratch and instead focus on developing our solutions.

Exercise 2: Calculating Euclidean Distance in Python

In this exercise, we will create an example point along with three sample centroids to help illustrate how Euclidean distance works. Understanding this distance formula is foundational to the rest of our work in clustering.

By the end of this exercise, we will be able to implement Euclidean distance from scratch and fully understand what it does to points in a feature space.

In this exercise, we will be using the standard Python built-in **math** package. There are no prerequisites for using the **math** package and it is included in all standard installations of Python. As the name suggests, this package is very useful, allowing to use a variety of basic math building blocks off the shelf, such as exponentials, square roots, and others:

1. Open a Jupyter notebook and create a naïve formula that captures the direct math of Euclidean distance, as follows:

   ```python
   import math
   import numpy as np
   def dist(a, b):
       return math.sqrt(math.pow(a[0]-b[0],2) + math.pow(a[1]-b[1],2))
   ```

   This approach is considered naïve because it performs element-wise calculations on your data points (slow) compared to a more real-world implementation using vectors and matrix math to achieve significant performance increases.

2. Create the data points in Python as follows:

   ```python
   centroids = [ (2, 5), (8, 3), (4,5) ]
   x = (0, 8)
   ```

3. Use the formula you created to calculate the Euclidean distance between the example point and each of the three centroids you were provided:

   ```python
   centroid_distances =[]
   for centroid in centroids:
       centroid_distances.append(dist(x,centroid))
   print(centroid_distances)
   print(np.argmin(centroid_distances))
   ```

   The output is as follows:

   ```
   [3.605551275463989, 9.433981132056603, 5.0]
   0
   ```

Since Python is zero-indexed, a position of zero as the minimum in our list of centroid distances signals to us that the example point, x, will be assigned to the number one centroid of three.

This process is repeated for every point in the dataset until each point is assigned to a cluster. After each point is assigned, the mean point is calculated among all of the points within each cluster. The calculation of the mean among these points is the same as calculating a mean between single integers.

Now that you have found clusters in your data using Euclidean distance as the primary metric, think back to how you did this easily in *Exercise 2, Calculating Euclidean Distance in Python*. It is very intuitive for our human minds to see groups of dots on a plot and determine which dots belong to discrete clusters. However, how do we ask a naïve computer to repeat this same task? By understanding this exercise, you help teach a computer an approach to forming clusters of its own with the notion of distance. We will build upon how we use these distance metrics in the next exercise.

Exercise 3: Forming Clusters with the Notion of Distance

By understanding this exercise, you'll help to teach a computer an approach to forming clusters of its own with the notion of distance. We will build upon how we use these distance metrics in this exercise:

1. Store the points [(0,8), (3,8), (3,4)] that are assigned to cluster one:

    ```
    cluster_1_points =[ (0,8), (3,8), (3,4) ]
    ```

2. Calculate the mean point between all of the points to find the new centroid:

    ```
    mean =[ (0+3+3)/3, (8+8+4)/3 ]
    print(mean)
    ```

    The output is as follows:

    ```
    [2.0, 6.666666666666667]
    ```

3. After a new centroid is calculated, you will repeat the cluster membership calculation seen in *Exercise 2, Calculating Euclidean Distance in Python*, and then the previous two steps to find the new cluster centroid. Eventually, the new cluster centroid will be the same as the one you had entering the problem, and the exercise will be complete. How many times this repeats depends on the data you are clustering.

Once you have moved the centroid location to the new mean point of (2, 6.67), you can compare it to the initial list of centroids you entered the problem with. If the new mean point is different than the centroid that is currently in your list, that means you have to go through another iteration of the preceding two exercises. Once the new mean point you calculate is the same as the centroid you started the problem with, you have completed a run of k-means and reached a point called **convergence**.

In the next exercise, we will implement k-means from scratch.

Exercise 4: Implementing k-means from Scratch

In this exercise, we will have a look at the implementation of k-means from scratch. This exercise relies on scikit-learn, an open-source Python package that enables the fast prototyping of popular machine learning models. Within scikit-learn, we will be using the **datasets** functionality to create a synthetic blob dataset. In addition to harnessing the power of scikit-learn, we will also rely on Matplotlib, a popular plotting library for Python that makes it easy for us to visualize our data. To do this, perform the following steps:

1. Import the necessary libraries:

   ```
   from sklearn.datasets import make_blobs
   import matplotlib.pyplot as plt
   import numpy as np
   import math
   %matplotlib inline
   ```

2. Generate a random cluster dataset to experiment on X = coordinate points, y = cluster labels, and define random centroids:

   ```
   X, y = make_blobs(n_samples=1500, centers=3,
                     n_features=2, random_state=800)
   centroids = [[-6,2],[3,-4],[-5,10]]
   ```

3. Print the data:

   ```
   X
   ```

   The output is as follows:

   ```
   array([[-3.83458347,  6.09210705],
          [-4.62571831,  5.54296865],
          [-2.87807159, -7.48754592],
          ...,
   ```

```
[-3.709726  , -7.77993633],
[-8.44553266, -1.83519866],
[-4.68308431,  6.91780744]])
```

4. Plot the coordinate points as follows:

```
plt.scatter(X[:, 0], X[:, 1], s=50, cmap='tab20b')
plt.show()
```

The plot looks as follows:

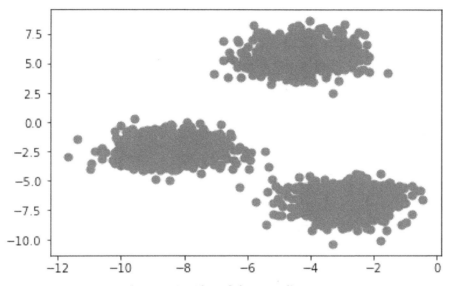

Figure 1.16: Plot of the coordinates

5. Print the array of **y**:

```
y
```

The output is as follows:

```
array([2, 2, 1, ..., 1, 0, 2])
```

6. Plot the coordinate points with the correct cluster labels:

```
plt.scatter(X[:, 0], X[:, 1], c=y,s=50, cmap='tab20b')
plt.show()
```

The plot looks as follows:

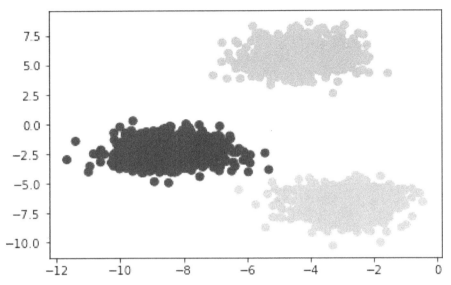

Figure 1.17: Plot of the coordinates with correct cluster labels

Exercise 5: Implementing k-means with Optimization

Let's recreate these results on our own! We will go over an example implementing this with some optimizations. This exercise is built on top of the previous exercise and should be performed in the same Jupyter notebook. For this exercise, we will rely on SciPy, a Python package that allows easy access to highly optimized versions of scientific calculations. In particular, we will be implementing Euclidean distance with **cdist**, the functionally of which replicates the barebones implementation of our distance metric in a much more efficient manner:

1. A non-vectorized implementation of Euclidean distance is as follows:

```
def dist(a, b):
    return math.sqrt(math.pow(a[0]-b[0],2) + math.pow(a[1]-b[1],2))
```

2. Now, implement the optimized Euclidean distance:

```
from scipy.spatial.distance import cdist
```

3. Store the values of X:

```
X[105:110]
```

The output is as follows:

```
array([[-3.09897933,  4.79407445],
       [-3.37295914, -7.36901393],
       [-3.372895  ,  5.10433846],
       [-5.90267987, -3.28352194],
       [-3.52067739,  7.7841276 ]])
```

4. Calculate the distances and choose the index of the shortest distance as a cluster:

```
for x in X[105:110]:
    calcs = []
    for c in centroids:
        calcs.append(dist(x, c))
    print(calcs, "Cluster Membership: ", np.argmin(calcs, axis=0))
```

5. Define the **k_means** function as follows and initialize k-centroids randomly. Repeat the process until the difference between new/old **centroids** equal **0** using the **while** loop:

```
def k_means(X, K):
    # Keep track of history so you can see k-means in action
    centroids_history = []
    labels_history = []
    rand_index = np.random.choice(X.shape[0], K)
    centroids = X[rand_index]
    centroids_history.append(centroids)
    while True:

        # Euclidean distances are calculated for each point relative to
        # centroids, and then np.argmin returns the index location of the
        # minimal distance - which cluster a point is assigned to

        labels = np.argmin(cdist(X, centroids), axis=1)
        labels_history.append(labels)

        # Take mean of points within clusters to find new centroids

        new_centroids = np.array([X[labels == i].mean(axis=0)
                                  for i in range(K)])
```

```
        centroids_history.append(new_centroids)

    # If old centroids and new centroids no longer change, k-means is
    # complete and end. Otherwise continue

        if np.all(centroids == new_centroids):
            break
        centroids = new_centroids

    return centroids, labels, centroids_history, labels_history

centers, labels, centers_hist, labels_hist = k_means(X, 3)
```

Note

Do not break this code, as it might lead to an error.

6. Zip together the historical steps of centers and their labels:

```
for x, y in history:
    plt.figure(figsize=(4,3))
    plt.scatter(X[:, 0], X[:, 1], c=y, s=50, cmap='tab20b');
    plt.scatter(x[:, 0], x[:, 1], c='red')
    plt.show()
```

The first plot is as follows:

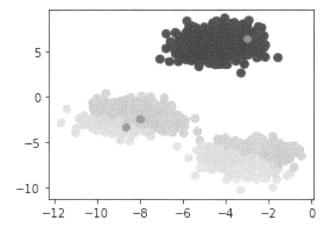

Figure 1.18: First scatterplot

The second plot is as follows:

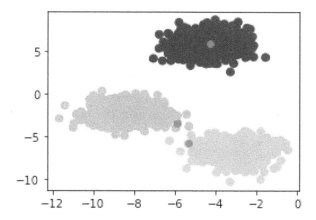

Figure 1.19: Second scatterplot

The third plot is as follows:

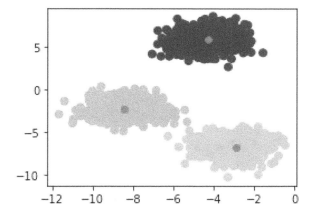

Figure 1.20: Third scatterplot

As you can see in the above figures, k-means takes an iterative approach to refining optimal clusters based on distance. The algorithm starts with random initialization and depending on the complexity of the data, quickly finds the separations that make the most sense.

Clustering Performance: Silhouette Score

Understanding the performance of unsupervised learning methods is inherently much more difficult than supervised learning methods because, often, there is no clear-cut "best" solution. For supervised learning, there are many robust performance metrics – the most straightforward of these being accuracy in the form of comparing model-predicted labels to actual labels and seeing how many the model got correct. Unfortunately, for clustering, we do not have labels to rely on and need to build an understanding of how "different" our clusters are. We achieve this with the Silhouette Score metric. Inherent to this approach, we can also use Silhouette Scores to find optimal "K" numbers of clusters for our unsupervised learning methods.

The Silhouette metric works by analyzing how well a point fits within its cluster. The metric ranges from -1 to 1 – If the average silhouette score across your clustering is one, then you will have achieved perfect clusters and there will be minimal confusion about which point belongs where. If you think of the plots in our last exercise, the Silhouette score will be much closer to one, since the blobs are tightly condensed and there is a fair amount of distance between each blob. This is very rare though – the Silhouette Score should be treated as an attempt at doing the best you can, since hitting one is highly unlikely.

Mathematically, the Silhouette Score calculation is quite straightforward via the Simplified Silhouette Index (SSI), as $SSI_i = \frac{b_i - a_i}{max(a_i, b_i)}$ where a_i is the distance from point i to its own cluster centroid and b_i is the distance from point i to the nearest cluster centroid.

The intuition captured here is that a_i represents how cohesive point i's cluster is as a clear cluster, and b_i represents how far apart the clusters lie. We will use the optimized implementation of `silhouette_score` in scikit-learn for *Activity 1, Implementing k-means Clustering*. Using it is simple and only requires you to pass in the feature array and the predicted cluster labels from your k-means clustering method.

In the next exercise, we will use the pandas library to read a CSV. Pandas is a Python library that makes data wrangling easier through the use of DataFrames. To read data in Python, you will use `variable_name = pd.read_csv('file_name.csv', header=None)`.

Exercise 6: Calculating the Silhouette Score

In this exercise, we're going to learn how to calculate the Silhouette Score of a dataset with a fixed number of clusters. For this, we will use the Iris dataset, which is available at https://github.com/TrainingByPackt/Unsupervised-Learning-with-Python/tree/master/Lesson01/Exercise06.

> **Note**
>
> This dataset was downloaded from https://archive.ics.uci.edu/ml/machine-learning-databases/iris/iris.data. It can be accessed at https://github.com/TrainingByPackt/Unsupervised-Learning-with-Python/tree/master/Lesson01/Exercise06.

1. Load the Iris data file using pandas, a package that makes data wrangling much easier through the use of DataFrames:

    ```python
    import pandas as pd
    import numpy as np
    import matplotlib.pyplot as plt
    from sklearn.metrics import silhouette_score
    from scipy.spatial.distance import cdist
    iris = pd.read_csv('iris_data.csv', header=None)
    iris.columns = ['SepalLengthCm', 'SepalWidthCm', 'PetalLengthCm',
    'PetalWidthCm', 'species']
    ```

2. Separate the **X** features, since we want to treat this as an unsupervised learning problem:

    ```python
    X = iris[['SepalLengthCm', 'SepalWidthCm', 'PetalLengthCm',
    'PetalWidthCm']]
    ```

3. Bring back the **k_means** function we made earlier for reference:

    ```python
    def k_means(X, K):
    #Keep track of history so you can see k-means in action
        centroids_history = []
        labels_history = []
        rand_index = np.random.choice(X.shape[0], K)
        centroids = X[rand_index]
        centroids_history.append(centroids)
        while True:
    # Euclidean distances are calculated for each point relative to
    # centroids, #and then np.argmin returns
    ```

```
# the index location of the minimal distance - which cluster a point
# is #assigned to
        labels = np.argmin(cdist(X, centroids), axis=1)
        labels_history.append(labels)
#Take mean of points within clusters to find new centroids:
        new_centroids = np.array([X[labels == i].mean(axis=0)
                                  for i in range(K)])
        centroids_history.append(new_centroids)

# If old centroids and new centroids no longer change, k-means is
# complete and end. Otherwise continue
        if np.all(centroids == new_centroids):
            break
        centroids = new_centroids

    return centroids, labels, centroids_history, labels_history
```

4. Convert our Iris **X** feature DataFrame to a **NumPy** matrix:

   ```
   X_mat = X.values
   ```

5. Run our **k_means** function on the Iris matrix:

   ```
   centroids, labels, centroids_history, labels_history = k_means(X_mat, 3)
   ```

6. Calculate the Silhouette Score for the **PetalLengthCm** and **PetalWidthCm** columns:

   ```
   silhouette_score(X[['PetalLengthCm','PetalWidthCm']], labels)
   ```

   The output is similar to:

   ```
   0.6214938502379446
   ```

In this exercise, we calculated the Silhouette Score for the **PetalLengthCm** and **PetalWidthCm** columns of the Iris dataset.

Activity 1: Implementing k-means Clustering

Scenario: You are asked in an interview to implement a k-means clustering algorithm from scratch to prove that you understand how it works. We will be using the Iris dataset provided by the UCI ML repository. The Iris dataset is a classic in the data science world and has features that are used to predict Iris species. The download location can be found later in this activity.

For this activity, you are able to use Matplotlib, NumPy, scikit-learn metrics, and pandas.

By loading and reshaping data easily, you can focus more on learning k-means instead of writing dataloader functionality.

Iris data columns are provided as follows for reference:

```
['SepalLengthCm', 'SepalWidthCm', 'PetalLengthCm', 'PetalWidthCm', 'species']
```

Aim: To truly understand how something works, you need to build it from scratch. Take what you have learned in the previous sections and implement k-means from scratch in Python.

Please open your favorite editing platform and try the following:

1. Using `NumPy` or the `math` package and the Euclidean distance formula and write a function that calculates the distance between two coordinates.

2. Write a function that calculates the distance from centroids to each of the points in your dataset and returns the cluster membership.

3. Write a k-means function that takes in a dataset and the number of clusters (K) and returns the final cluster centroids, as well as the data points that make up that cluster's membership. After implementing k-means from scratch, apply your custom algorithm to the Iris dataset, located here: https://github.com/ TrainingByPackt/Unsupervised-Learning-with-Python/tree/master/Lesson01/ Activity01.

> ### Note
>
> This dataset was downloaded from https://archive.ics.uci.edu/ml/machine-learning-databases/iris/iris.data. It can be accessed at https://github.com/ TrainingByPackt/Unsupervised-Learning-with-Python/tree/master/Lesson01/ Activity01.
>
> UCI Machine Learning Repository [http://archive.ics.uci.edu/ml]. Irvine, CA: University of California, School of Information and Computer Science.

4. Remove the classes supplied in this dataset and see if your k-means algorithm can group the different Iris species into their proper groups just based on plant characteristics!

5. Calculate the Silhouette Score using the scikit-learn implementation.

Outcome: By completing this exercise, you will gain hands-on experience of tuning a k-means clustering algorithm for a real-world dataset. The Iris dataset is seen as a classic "hello world" type problem in the data science space and is helpful for testing foundational techniques on. Your final clustering algorithm should do a decent job of finding the three clusters of Iris species types that exist in the data, as follows:

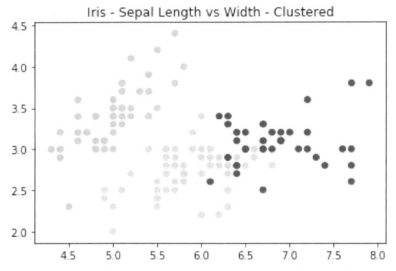

Figure 1.21: Expected plot of three clusters of Iris species

Note

The solution for this activity can be found on page 306.

Summary

In this chapter, we have explored what clustering is and why it is important in a variety of data challenges. Building upon this foundation of clustering knowledge, you implemented k-means, which is one of the simplest yet most popular methods of unsupervised learning. If you have reached this summary and can repeat what k-means does step-by-step to your fellow classmate, good job! If not, please go back and review the previous material – the content only grows in complexity from here. From here, we will be moving on to hierarchical clustering, which, in one configuration, reuses the centroid learning approach that we used in k-means. We will build upon this approach by outlining additional clustering methodologies and approaches in the next chapter.

Hierarchical Clustering

Learning Objectives

By the end of this chapter, you will be able to:

- Implement the hierarchical clustering algorithm from scratch by using packages
- Perform agglomerative clustering
- Compare k-means with hierarchical clustering

In this chapter, we will use hierarchical clustering to build stronger groupings which make more logical sense.

Introduction

In this chapter, we will expand on the basic ideas that we built in *Chapter 1, Introduction to Clustering*, by surrounding clustering with the concept of similarity. Once again, we will be implementing forms of the Euclidean distance to capture the notion of similarity. It is important to bear in mind that the Euclidean distance just happens to be one of the most popular distance metrics and not the only one! Through these distance metrics, we will expand on the simple neighbor calculations that we explored in the previous chapter by introducing the concept of hierarchy. By using hierarchy to convey clustering information we can build stronger groupings that make more logical sense.

Clustering Refresher

Chapter 1, Introduction to Clustering, covered both the high-level intuition and in-depth details of one of the most basic clustering algorithms: k-means. While it is indeed a simple approach, do not discredit it; it will be a valuable addition to your toolkit as you continue your exploration of the unsupervised learning world. In many real-world use cases, companies experience groundbreaking discoveries through the simplest methods, such as k-means or linear regression (for supervised learning). As a refresher, let's quickly walk through what clusters are and how k-means works to find them:

Figure 2.1: The attributes that separate supervised and unsupervised problems

If you were given a random collection of data without any guidance, you would likely start your exploration using basic statistics – for example, what the mean, median, and mode values are of each of the features. Remember that, from a high-level data model that simply exists, knowing whether it is supervised or unsupervised learning is ascribed by the data goals that you have set for yourself or that were set by your manager. If you were to determine that one of the features was actually a label and you wanted to see how the remaining features in the dataset influence it, this would become a supervised learning problem. However, if after initial exploration you realize that the data you have is simply a collection of features without a target in mind (such as a collection of health metrics, purchase invoices from a web store, and so on), then you could analyze it through unsupervised methods.

A classic example of unsupervised learning is finding clusters of similar customers in a collection of invoices from a web store. Your hypothesis is that by understanding which people are most similar, you can create more granular marketing campaigns that appeal to each cluster's interests. One way to achieve these clusters of similar users is through k-means.

k-means Refresher

k-means clustering works by finding "k" number clusters in your data through pairwise Euclidean distance calculations. "K" points (also called centroids) are randomly initialized in your data and the distance is calculated from each data point to each of the centroids. The minimum of these distances designates which cluster a data point belongs to. Once every point has been assigned to a cluster, the mean intra-cluster data point is calculated as the new centroid. This process is repeated until the newly-calculated cluster centroid no longer changes position.

The Organization of Hierarchy

Both the natural and human-made world contain many examples of organizing systems into hierarchies and why, for the most part, it makes a lot of sense. A common representation that is developed from these hierarchies can be seen in tree-based data structures. Imagine that you had a parent node with any number of child nodes that could subsequently be parent nodes themselves. By organizing concepts into a tree structure, you can build an information-dense diagram that clearly shows how things are related to their peers and their larger abstract concepts.

An example from the natural world to help illustrate this concept can be seen in how we view the hierarchy of animals, which goes from parent classes to individual species:

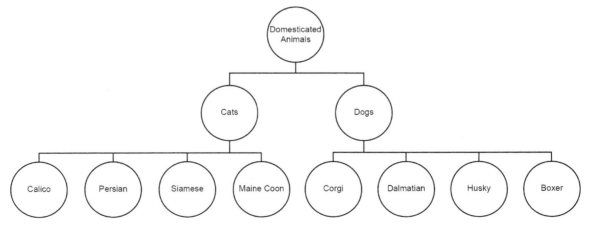

Figure 2.2: Navigating the relationships of animal species in a hierarchical tree structure

In Figure 2.2, you can see an example of how relational information between varieties of animals can be easi y mapped out in a way that both saves space and still transmits a large amount of info mation. This example can be seen as both a tree of its own (showing how cats anc dogs are different but both domesticated animals), and as a potential piece of a l rger tree that shows a breakdown of domesticated versus non-domesticated ani nals.

In the event that most of you are not biologists, let's move back toward the concept of a web store selling prod icts. If you sold a large variety of products, then you would likely want to create a hierarchical system of navigation for your customers. By withholding all of the information i 1 your product catalog, customers will only be exposed to the path down the tree that matches their interests. An example of the hierarchical benefits of navigation can be seen in Figure 2.3:

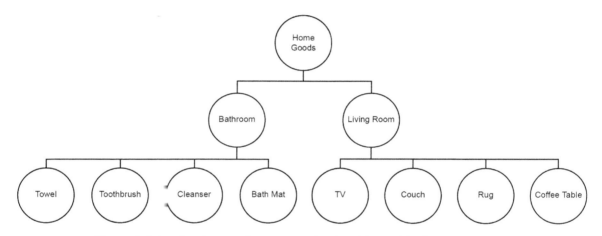

Figure 2.3: Navigating product categories in a hierarchical tree structure

Clearly, the benefits of a hierarchical system of navigation cannot be overstated in terms of improving yc ur customer experience. By organizing information into a hierarchical structure, you can build an intuitive structure out of your data that demonstrates explicit nested relationships. If this sounds like another approach to finding clusters in your data, then you're definitely on the right track! Through the use of similar distance metrics such as the Euclidean distance from k-means, we can develop a tree that shows the many cuts of data that allow a user to subjectively create clusters at their discretion.

Introduction to Hierarchical Clustering

Until this point, we have shown that hierarchies can be excellent structures in which to organize information that clearly show nested relationships among data points. While this is helpful in gaining an understanding of the parent/child relationships between items, it can also be very handy when forming clusters. Expanding on the animal example of the prior section, imagine that you were simply presented with two features of animals: their height (measured from the tip of the nose to the end of the tail) and their weight. Using this information, you then have to recreate the same structure in order to identify which records in your dataset correspond to dogs or cats, as well as their relative subspecies.

Since you are only given animal heights and weights, you won't be able to extrapolate the specific names of each species. However, by analyzing the features that you have been provided, you can develop a structure within the data that serves as an approximation of what animal species exist in your data. This perfectly sets the stage for an unsupervised learning problem that is well solved with hierarchical clustering. In the following plot, you will see the two features that we created on the left: with animal height in the left-hand column and animal weight in the right-hand column. This is then charted on a two-axis plot with the height on the x axis and the weight on the y axis:

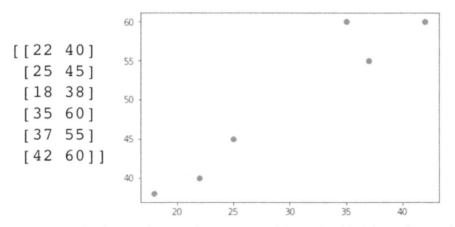

Figure 2.4: An example of a two-feature dataset comprising animal height and animal weight

One way to approach hierarchical clustering is by starting with each data point serving as its own cluster and recursively joining the similar points together to form clusters – this is known as **<u>agglomerative</u>** hierarchical clustering. We will go into more detail about the different ways of approaching hierarchical clustering in a later section.

In the agglomerative hierarchical clustering approach, the concept of data point similarity can be thought of in the paradigm that we saw during k-means. In k-means, we used the Euclidean distance to calculate the distance from the individual points to the centroids of the expected "k" clusters. For this approach to hierarchical clustering, we will reuse the same distance metric to determine the similarity between the records in our dataset.

Eventually, by grouping individual records from the data with their most similar records recursively, you end up building a hierarchy from the bottom up. The individual single-member clusters join together into one single cluster at the top of our hierarchy.

Steps to Perform Hierarchical Clustering

To understand how agglomerative hierarchical clustering works, we can trace the path of a simple toy program as it merges together to form a hierarchy:

1. Given n sample data points, view each point as an individual "cluster" with just that one point as a member.

2. Calculate the pairwise Euclidean distance between the centroids of all the clusters in your data.

3. Group the closest point pairs together.

4. Repeat *Step 2* and *Step 3* until you reach a single cluster containing all the data in your set.

5. Plot a dendrogram to show how your data has come together in a hierarchical structure. A dendrogram is simply a diagram that is used to represent a tree structure, showing an arrangement of clusters from top to bottom.

6. Decide what level you want to create the clusters at.

An Example Walk-Through of Hierarchical Clustering

While slightly more complex than k-means, hierarchical clustering does not change too much from a logistical perspective. Here is a simple example that walks through the preceding steps in slightly more detail:

1. Given a list of four sample data points, view each point as a centroid that is also its own cluster with the point indices from 0 to 3:

    Clusters (4): [(1,7)], [(-5,9)], [(-9,4)] , [(4, -2)]

    Centroids (4): [(1,7)], [(-5,9)], [(-9,4)] , [(4, -2)]

2. Calculate the pairwise Euclidean distance between the centroids of all the clusters. In the matrix displayed in the following diagram, the point indices are between 0 and 3 both horizontally and vertically, showing the distance between the respective points. Along the diagonal are extremely high values to ensure that we do not select a point as its own neighbor (since it technically is the "closest" point). Notice that the values are mirrored across the diagonal:

Point Distances

	(1,7)	(-5,9)	(-9,4)	(4,-2)
(1,7)	[[9.223e+18,	6.325e+00,	1.044e+01,	9.487e+00],
(-5,9)	[6.325e+00,	9.223e+18,	6.403e+00,	1.421e+01],
(-9,4)	[1.044e+01,	6.403e+00,	9.223e+18,	1.432e+01],
(4,-2)	[9.487e+00,	1.421e+01,	1.432e+01,	9.223e+18]]

Figure 2.5: An array of distances

3. Group the closest point pairs together.

   In this case, points [1,7] and [-5,9] join into a cluster since they are closest, with the remaining two points left as single-member clusters:

Point Distances

	(1,7)	(-5,9)	(-9,4)	(4,-2)
(1,7)	[[9.223e+18,	6.325e+00,	1.044e+01,	9.487e+00],
(-5,9)	[6.325e+00,	223e+18,	6.403e+00,	1.421e+01],
(-9,4)	[1.044e+01,	6.403e+00,	9.223e+18,	1.432e+01],
(4,-2)	[9.487e+00,	1.421e+01,	1.432e+01,	9.223e+18]]

Figure 2.6: An array of distances

Here are the resulting three clusters:

```
[ [1,7], [-5,9] ]
[-9,4]
[4,-2]
```

4. Calculate the centroid of the two-member cluster, as follows:

```
mean([ [1,7], [-5,9] ]) = [-2,8]
```

5. Add the centroid to the two single-member centroids and recalculate the distances.

   Clusters (3):

   ```
   [ [1,7], [-5,9] ]
   [-9,4]
   [4,-2]
   ```

   Centroids (3):

   ```
   [-2,8]
   [-9,4]
   [4,-2]
   ```

   The output will be similar to the following diagram, with the shortest distance called using a red arrow:

   Figure 2.7: An array of distances

6. Since it has the shortest distance, point [-9,4] is added to cluster 1:

   Clusters (2):

   ```
   [ [1,7], [-5,9], [-9,4] ]
   [4,-2]
   ```

7. With only point (4,-2) left as the furthest distance away from its neighbors, you can just add it to cluster 1 to unify all the clusters:

   Clusters (1):

   ```
   [ [ [1,7], [-5,9], [-9,4], [4,-2] ] ]
   ```

8. Plot a dendrogram to show the relationship between the points and the clusters:

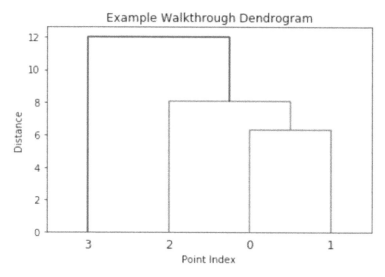

Figure 2.8: A dendrogram showing the relationship between the points and the clusters

At the end of this process you can visualize the hierarchical structure that you created through a dendrogram. This plot shows how data points are similar and will look familiar to the hierarchical tree structures that we discussed earlier. Once you have this dendrogram structure, you can interpret how the data points relate to each other and subjectively decide at which "level" the clusters should exist.

Revisiting the previous animal taxonomy example from that involved dog and cat species, imagine that you were presented with the following dendrogram:

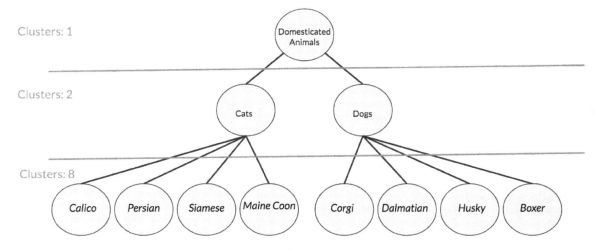

Figure 2.9: An animal taxonomy dendrogram

The great thing about hierarchical clustering and dendrograms is that you can see the entire breakdown of potential clusters to choose from. If you were just interested in grouping your species dataset into dogs and cats, you could stop clustering at the first level of the grouping. However, if you wanted to group all species into domesticated or non-domesticated animals, you could stop clustering at level two.

Exercise 7: Building a Hierarchy

Let's try implementing the preceding hierarchical clustering approach in Python. With the framework for the intuition laid out, we can now explore the process of building a hierarchical cluster with some helper functions provided in **SciPy**. This exercise uses **SciPy**, an open source library that packages functions that are helpful in scientific and technical computing; examples of this include easy implementations of linear algebra and calculus-related methods. In addition to **SciPy**, we will be using Matplotlib to complete this exercise.

1. Generate some dummy data as follows:

```
from scipy.cluster.hierarchy import linkage, dendrogram, fcluster
from sklearn.datasets import make_blobs
import matplotlib.pyplot as plt
%matplotlib inline
# Generate a random cluster dataset to experiment on. X = coordinate
points, y = cluster labels (not needed)
X, y = make_blobs(n_samples=1000, centers=8, n_features=2, random_
state=800)
```

2. Visualize the data as follows:

```
plt.scatter(X[ ,0], X[:,1])
plt.show()
```

The output is as follows:

```
# Generate a random cluster dataset to experiment on. X = coordinate points, y = cluster labels
X, y = make_blobs(n_samples=1000, centers=8, n_features=2, random_state=800)
```

```
# Visualize the data
plt.scatter(X[:,0], X[:,1])
plt.show()
```

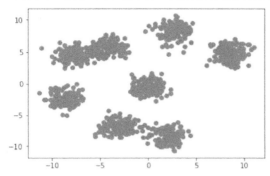

Figure 2.10: A plot of the dummy data

After plotting this simple toy example, it should be pretty clear that our dummy data is comprised of eight clusters.

3. We can easily generate the distance matrix using the built-in **SciPy** package, **'linkage'**:

```
# Generate distance matrix with 'linkage' function
distances = linkage(X, method="centroid", metric="euclidean")
print(distances)
```

The output is as follows:

```
distances = linkage(X, method="centroid", metric="euclidean")
```

```
print(distances)
[[5.720e+02 7.620e+02 7.694e-03 2.000e+00]
 [3.000e+01 1.960e+02 8.879e-03 2.000e+00]
 [5.910e+02 8.700e+02 1.075e-02 2.000e+00]
 ...
 [1.989e+03 1.992e+03 7.812e+00 3.750e+02]
 [1.995e+03 1.996e+03 1.024e+01 7.500e+02]
 [1.994e+03 1.997e+03 1.200e+01 1.000e+03]]]
```

Figure 2.11: A matrix of the distances

In the first situation, you can see that customizing the hyperparameters really drives the performance when finding the ideal linkage matrix. If you recall our previous steps, linkage works by simply calculating the distances between each of the data points. In the **linkage** function, we have the option to select both the metric and the method (we will cover more on this later).

4. After we determine the linkage matrix, we can easily pass it through the dendrogram function provided by **SciPy**:

```
dn = dendrogram(distances)
plt.show()
```

The output is as follows:

Figure 2.12: A dendrogram of the distances

This plot will give us some perspective on the potential breakouts of our data.

5. Using this information, we can wrap up our exercise on hierarchical clustering by using the **fcluster** function from **SciPy**. The number **3** in the

6. following example represents the maximum inter-cluster distance threshold hyperparameter that you will set. This hyperparameter is tunable based on the dataset that you are looking at; however, it is supplied for you as **3** for this exercise:

```
scipy_clusters = fcluster(distances, 3, criterion="distance")
plt.scatter(X[:,0], X[:,1], c=scipy_clusters)
plt.show()
```

The output is as follows:

```
clusters = fcluster(distances, 3, criterion="distance")

plt.scatter(X[:,0], X[:,1], c=clusters)
plt.show()
```

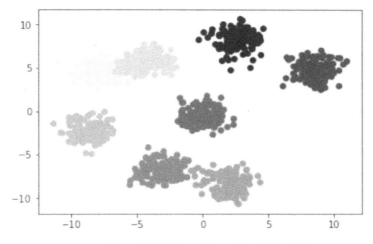

Figure 2.13: A scatter plot of the distances

By simply calling a few helper functions provided by SciPy, you can easily implement agglomerative clustering in just a few lines of code. While SciPy does help with many of the intermediate steps, this is still an example that is a bit more verbose than what you will probably see in your regular work. We will cover more streamlined implementations later.

Linkage

In *Exercise 7, Building a Hierarchy*, you implemented hierarchical clustering using what is known as **Centroid Linkage**. Linkage is the concept of determining how you can calculate the distances between clusters and is dependent on the type of problem you are facing. Centroid linkage was chosen for the first activity as it essentially mirrors the new centroid search that we used in k-means. However, this is not the only option when it comes to clustering data points together. Two other popular choices for determining distances between clusters are single linkage and complete linkage.

Single Linkage works by finding the minimum distance between a pair of points between two clusters as its criteria for linkage. Put simply, it essentially works by combining clusters based on the closest points between the two clusters. This is expressed mathematically as follows:

dist(a,b) = min(dist(a[i]), b[j]))

Complete Linkage is the opposite of single linkage and it works by finding the maximum distance between a pair of points between two clusters as its criteria for linkage. Put simply, it works by combining clusters based on the furthest points between the two clusters. This is mathematically expressed as follows:

dist(a,b) = max(dist(a[i]), b[j]))

Determining what linkage criteria is best for your problem is as much about art as it is about science and it is heavily dependent on your particular dataset. One reason to choose single linkage is that your data is similar in a nearest-neighbor sense, therefore, when there are differences, then the data is extremely dissimilar. Since single linkage works by finding the closest points, it will not be affected by these distant outliers. Conversely, complete linkage may be a better option if your data is distant in terms of inter-cluster, however, it is quite dense intra-cluster. Centroid linkage has similar benefits but falls apart if the data is very noisy and there are less clearly defined "centers" of clusters. Typically, the best approach is to try a few different linkage criteria options and to see which fits your data in a way that's most relevant to your goals.

Activity 2: Applying Linkage Criteria

Recall the dummy data of the eight clusters that we generated in the previous exercise. In the real world, you may be given real data that resembles discrete Gaussian blobs in the same way. Imagine that the dummy data represents different groups of shoppers in a particular store. The store manager has asked you to analyze the shopper data in order to classify the customers into different groups, so that they can tailor marketing materials to each group.

Using the data already generated in the previous exercise, or by generating new data, you are going to analyze which linkage types do the best job of grouping the customers into distinct clusters.

Once you have generated the data, view the documents supplied using SciPy to understand what linkage types are available in the **linkage** function. Then, evaluate the linkage types by applying them to your data. The linkage types you should test are shown in the following list:

```
['centroid', 'single', 'complete', 'average', 'weighted']
```

By completing this activity, you will gain an understanding of the linkage criteria – which is important to understand how effective your hierarchical clustering is. The aim is to gain an understanding of how linkage criteria play a role in different datasets and how it can make a useless clustering into a valid one.

You may realize that we have not covered all of the previously mentioned linkage types – a key part of this activity is to learn how to parse the docstrings provided using packages to explore all of their capabilities.

Here are the steps required to complete this activity:

1. Visualize the dataset that we created in *Exercise 7, Building a Hierarchy*.

2. Create a list with all the possible linkage method hyperparameters.

3. Loop through each of the methods in the list that you just created and display the effect they have on the same dataset.

You should generate a plot for each linkage type and use the plots to comment on which linkage types are most suitable for this data.

The plots that you will generate should look similar to the ones in the following diagram:

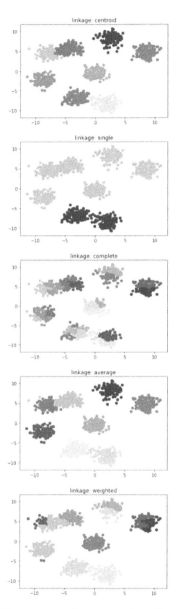

Figure 2.14: The expected scatter plots for all methods

Note

The solution for this activity is on page 310.

Agglomerative versus Divisive Clustering

Our instances of hierarchical clustering so far have all been agglomerative – that is, they have been built from the bottom up. While this is typically the most common approach for this type of clustering, it is important to know that it is not the only way a hierarchy can be created. The opposite hierarchical approach, that is, built from the top up, can also be used to create your taxonomy. This approach is called **Divisive** Hierarchical Clustering and works by having all the data points in your dataset in one massive cluster. Many of the internal mechanics of the divisive approach will prove to be quite similar to the agglomerative approach:

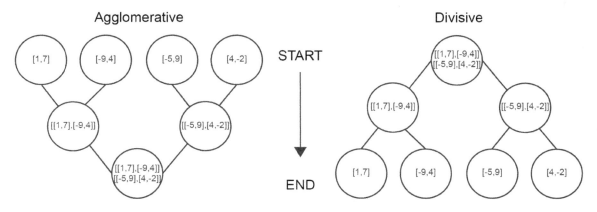

Figure 2.15: Agglomerative versus divisive hierarchical clustering

As with most problems in unsupervised learning, deciding the best approach is often highly dependent on the problem you are faced with solving.

Imagine that you are an entrepreneur who has just bought a new grocery store and needs to stock it with goods. You receive a large shipment of food and drink in a container, but you've lost track of all the shipment information! In order to most effectively sell your products, you must group similar products together (your store will be a huge mess if you just put everything on the shelves in a random order). Setting out on this organizational goal, you can take either a bottom-up or top-down approach. On the bottom-up side, you will go through the shipping container and think of everything as disorganized – you will then pick up a random object and find its most similar product. For example, you may pick up apple juice and realize that it makes sense to group it together with orange juice. With the top-down approach, you will view everything as organized in one large group. Then, you will move through your inventory and split the groups based on the largest differences in similarity. For example, you may originally think that apple juice and tofu go together, but on second thoughts, they are really different. Therefore, you will break them into smaller, dissimilar groups.

In general, it helps to think of agglomerative as the bottom-up approach and divisive as the top-down approach – but how do they trade off in performance? Due to the greedy nature of Agglomerative, it has the potential to be fooled by local neighbors and not see the larger implications of clusters it forms at any given time. On the flip side, the divisive approach has the benefit of seeing the entire data distribution as one from the beginning and choosing the best way to break down clusters. This insight into what the entire dataset looks like is helpful for potentially creating more accurate clusters and should not be overlooked. Unfortunately, a top-down approach, typically, trades off greater accuracy with deeper complexity. In practice, an agglomerative approach works most of the time and should be the preferred starting point when it comes to hierarchical clustering. If, after reviewing the hierarchies, you are unhappy with the results, it may help to take a divisive approach.

Exercise 8: Implementing Agglomerative Clustering with scikit-learn

In most real-world use cases, you will likely find yourself implementing hierarchical clustering with a package that abstracts everything away, such as scikit-learn. Scikit-learn is a free package that is indispensable when it comes to machine learning in Python. It conveniently provides highly optimized forms of the most popular algorithms, such as regression, classification, and, of book, clustering. By using an optimized package such as scikit-learn, your work becomes much easier. However, you should only use it when you fully understand how hierarchical clustering works from the prior sections. The following exercise will compare two potential routes that you can take when forming clusters – using SciPy and scikit-learn. By completing the exercise, you will learn what the pros and cons are of each, and which suits you best from a user perspective:

1. Scikit-learn makes implementation as easy as just a few lines of code:

```
from sklearn.cluster import AgglomerativeClustering
from sklearn.datasets import make_blobs
import matplotlib.pyplot as plt
from scipy.cluster.hierarchy import linkage, dendrogram, fcluster
ac = AgglomerativeClustering(n_clusters = 8, affinity="euclidean",
linkage="average")
X, y = make_blobs(n_samples=1000, centers=8, n_features=2, random_
state=800)
distances = linkage(X, method="centroid", metric="euclidean")
sklearn_clusters = ac.fit_predict(X)
scipy_clusters = fcluster(distances, 3, criterion="distance")
```

First, we assign the model to the **ac** variable, by passing in parameters that we are familiar with, such as **affinity** (the distance function) and **linkage** (explore your options as we did in *Activity 2, Implementing Linkage Criteria*).

2. After instantiating our model into a variable, we can simply pass through the dataset we are interested in in order to determine where the cluster memberships lie using .**fit_predict()** and assigning it to an additional variable.

3. We can then compare how each of the approaches work by comparing the final cluster results through plotting. Let's take a look at the clusters from the scikit-learn approach:

```
plt.figure(figsize=(6,4))
plt.title("Clusters from Sci-Kit Learn Approach")
plt.scatter(X[:, 0], X[:, 1], c = sklearn_clusters ,s=50, cmap='tab20b')
plt.show()
```

Here is the output for the clusters from the scikit-learn approach:

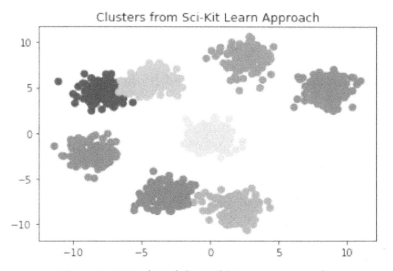

Figure 2.16: A plot of the Scikit-Learn approach

Take a look at the clusters from the SciPy Learn approach:

```
plt.figure(figsize=(6,4))
plt.title("Clusters from SciPy Approach")
plt.scatter(X[:, 0], X[:, 1], c = scipy_clusters ,s=50, cmap='tab20b')
plt.show()
```

The output is as follows:

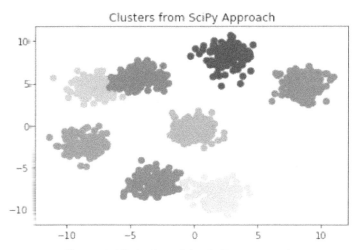

Figure 2.17: A plot of the SciPy approach

As you can see in our example problem, the two converge to basically the same clusters. While this is great from a toy-problem perspective, you will soon learn, in the next activity, that small changes to the input parameters can lead to wildly different results!

Activity 3: Comparing k-means with Hierarchical Clustering

You are managing a store's inventory and receive a large shipment of wine, but the brand labels have fallen off the bottles during transit. Fortunately, your supplier has provided you with the chemical readings for each bottle, along with their respective serial numbers. Unfortunately, you aren't able to open each bottle of wine and taste test the difference – you must find a way to group the unlabeled bottles back together according to their chemical readings! You know from the order list that you ordered three different types of wine and are given only two wine attributes to group the wine types back together. In this activity, we will be using the wine dataset.

> **Note**
>
> The wine dataset can be downloaded from https://archive.ics.uci.edu/ml/machine-learning-databases/wine/. It can be accessed at https://github.com/TrainingByPackt/Applied-Unsupervised-Learning-with-Python/tree/master/Lesson02/Activity03.
>
> UCI Machine Learning Repository [http://archive.ics.uci.edu/ml]. Irvine, CA: University of California, School of Information and Computer Science

The aim of this activity is to implement k-means and hierarchical clustering on the wine dataset and to explore which approach ends up being more accurate or easier for you to use. You can try different combinations of scikit-learn implementations and use helper functions in SciPy and NumPy. You can use the silhouette score to compare the different clustering methods and visualize the clusters on a graph.

Expected Outcome:

After completing this activity, you will have gained an understanding of how k-means and hierarchical clustering work on similar datasets. You will likely notice that one method performs better than the other depending on how the data is shaped. Another key outcome from this activity is gaining an understanding of how important hyperparameters are in any given use case.

Here are the steps to complete this activity:

1. Import the necessary packages from scikit-learn (**KMeans**, **AgglomerativeClustering**, and **silhouette_score**).

2. Read the wine dataset into the pandas DataFrame and print a small sample.

3. Visualize the wine dataset to understand its data structure.

4. Use the sklearn implementation of k-means on the wine dataset, knowing that there are three wine types.

5. Use the sklearn implementation of hierarchical clustering on the wine dataset.

6. Plot the predicted clusters from k-means.

7. Plot the predicted clusters from hierarchical clustering.

8. Compare the silhouette score of each clustering method.

Plot the predicted clusters from the k-means clustering method as follows:

Figure 2.18: The expected clusters from the k-means method

Plot the predicted clusters from the agglomerative clustering method, as follows:

Figure 2.19: The expected clusters from the agglomerative method

Note

The solution for this activity is on page 312.

k-means versus Hierarchical Clustering

Now that we have expanded our understanding of how k-means clustering works, it is important to explore where hierarchical clustering fits into the picture. As mentioned in the linkage criteria section, there is some potential direct overlap when it comes to grouping data points together using centroids. Universal to all of the approaches mentioned so far, is also the use of a distance function to determine similarity. Due to our in-depth exploration in the previous chapter, we have kept using the Euclidean distance, but we understand that any distance function can be used to determine similarity.

In practice, here are some quick highlights for choosing one clustering method over another:

- Hierarchical clustering benefits from not needing to pass in an explicit "k" number of clusters apriori. This means that you can find all the potential clusters and decide which clusters make the most sense after the algorithm has completed.

- k-means clustering benefits from a simplicity perspective – oftentimes, in business use cases, there is a challenge to find methods that can be explained to non-technical audiences but still be accurate enough to generate quality results. k-means can easily fill this niche.

- Hierarchical clustering has more parameters to tweak than k-means clustering when it comes to dealing with abnormally shaped data. While k-means is great at finding discrete clusters, it can falter when it comes to mixed clusters. By tweaking the parameters in hierarchical clustering, you may find better results.

- Vanilla k-means clustering works by instantiating random centroids and finding the closest points to those centroids. If they are randomly instantiated in areas of the feature space that are far away from your data, then it can end up taking quite some time to converge, or it may never even get to that point. Hierarchical clustering is less prone to falling prey to this weakness.

Summary

In this chapter, we discussed how hierarchical clustering works and where it may be best employed. In particular, we discussed various aspects of how clusters can be subjectively chosen through the evaluation of a dendrogram plot. This is a huge advantage compared to k-means clustering if you have absolutely no idea of what you're looking for in the data. Two key parameters that drive the success of hierarchical clustering were also discussed: the agglomerative versus divisive approach and linkage criteria. Agglomerative clustering takes a bottom-up approach by recursively grouping nearby data together until it results in one large cluster. Divisive clustering takes a top-down approach by starting with the one large cluster and recursively breaking it down until each data point falls into its own cluster. Divisive clustering has the potential to be more accurate since it has a complete view of the data from the start; however, it adds a layer of complexity that can decrease the stability and increase the runtime.

Linkage criteria grapples with the concept of how distance is calculated between candidate clusters. We have explored how centroids can make an appearance again beyond k-means clustering, as well as single and complete linkage criteria. Single linkage finds cluster distances by comparing the closest points in each cluster, while complete linkage finds cluster distances by comparing more distant points in each cluster. From the understanding that you have gained in this chapter, you are now able to evaluate how both k-means and hierarchical clustering can best fit the challenge that you are working on. In the next chapter, we will cover a clustering approach that will serve us best in the highly complex data: **DBSCAN** (Density-Based Spatial Clustering of Applications with Noise).

3

Neighborhood Approaches and DBSCAN

Learning Objectives

By the end of this chapter, you will be able to:

- Understand how neighborhood approaches to clustering work from beginning to end

- Implement the DBSCAN algorithm from scratch by using packages

- Identify the best suited algorithm from k-means, hierarchical clustering, and DBSCAN to solve your problem

In this chapter, we will have a look at DBSCAN clustering approach that will serve us best in the highly complex data.

Introduction

So far, we have covered two popular ways of approaching the clustering problem: k-means and hierarchical clustering. Both clustering techniques have pros and cons associated with how they are carried out. Once again, let's revisit where we have been in the first two chapters so we can gain further context to where we will be going in this chapter.

In the challenge space of unsupervised learning, you will be presented with a collection of feature data, but no complementary labels telling you what these feature variables necessarily mean. While you may not get a discrete view into what the target labels are, you can get some semblance of structure out of the data by clustering similar groups together and seeing what is similar within groups. The first approach we covered to achieve this goal of clustering similar data points is k-means.

k-means works best for simpler data challenges where speed is paramount. By simply looking at the closest data points, there is not a lot of computational overhead, however, there is also a greater degree of challenge when it comes to higher-dimensional datasets. k-means is also not ideal if you are unaware of the potential number of clusters you would be looking for. An example we have worked with in *Chapter 2, Hierarchical Clustering,* was looking at chemical profiles to determine which wines belonged together in a disorganized shipment. This exercise only worked well because you knew that three wine types were ordered; however, k-means would have been less successful if you had no intuition on what the original order was made up of.

The second clustering approach we explored was hierarchical clustering. This method can work in multiple ways – either agglomerative or divisive. Agglomerative clustering works with a bottom-up approach, treating each data point as its own cluster and recursively grouping them together with linkage criteria. Divisive clustering works in the opposite direction by treating all data points as one large class and recursively breaking them down into smaller clusters. This approach has the benefit of fully understanding the entire data distribution, as it calculates splitting potential, however, it is typically not done in practice due to its greater complexity. Hierarchical clustering is a strong contender for your clustering needs when it comes to not knowing anything about the data. Using a dendrogram, you can visualize all the splits in your data and consider what number of clusters makes sense after the fact. This can be really helpful in your specific use case; however, it also comes at a higher computational cost that is seen in k-means.

In this chapter, we will cover a clustering approach that will serve us best in the highly complex data: **DBSCAN** (Density-Based Spatial Clustering of Applications with Noise). Canonically, this method has always been seen as a high performer in datasets that have a lot of densely interspersed data. Let's walk through why it does so well in these use cases.

Clusters as Neighborhoods

In the first two chapters, we explored the concept of likeness being described as a function of Euclidean distance – data points that are closer to any one point can be seen as similar, while those that are further away in Euclidean space can be seen as dissimilar. This notion is seen once again in the DBSCAN algorithm. As alluded to by the lengthy name, the DBSCAN approach expands upon basic distance metric evaluation by also incorporating the notion of density. If there are clumps of data points that all exist in the same area as each other, they can be seen as members of the same cluster:

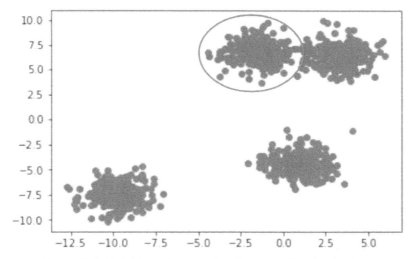

Figure 3.1: Neighbors have a direct connection to clusters

In the preceding example, we can see four neighborhoods.

The density-based approach has a number of benefits when compared to the past approaches we've covered that focus exclusively on distance. If you were just focusing on distance as a clustering threshold, then you may find your clustering makes little sense if faced with a sparse feature space with outliers. Both k-means and hierarchical clustering will automatically group together all data points in the space until no points are left.

While hierarchical clustering does provide a path around this issue somewhat, since you can dictate where clusters are formed using a dendrogram post-clustering run, k-means is the most susceptible to failing, as it is the simplest approach to clustering. These pitfalls are less evident when we begin evaluating neighborhood approaches to clustering:

Figure 3.2: Example dendrogram

By incorporating the notion of neighbor density in DBSCAN, we can leave outliers out of clusters if we choose to, based on the hyperparameters we choose at run time. Only the data points that have close neighbors will be seen as members within the same cluster and those that are farther away can be left as unclustered outliers.

Introduction to DBSCAN

As mentioned in the previous section, the strength of DBSCAN becomes apparent when we analyze the benefits of taking a density-based approach to clustering. DBSCAN evaluates density as a combination of neighborhood radius and minimum points found in a neighborhood deemed a cluster.

This concept can be driven home if we re-consider the scenario where you are tasked with organizing an unlabeled shipment of wine for your store. In the past example, it was made clear that we can find similar wines based off their features, such as scientific chemical traits. Knowing this information, we can more easily group together similar wines and efficiently have our products organized for sale in no time. Hopefully, that is clear by now – but what may not have been clear is the fact that products that you order to stock your store often reflect real-world purchase patterns. To promote variety in your inventory, but still have enough stock of the most popular wines, there is a highly uneven distribution of product types that you have available. Most people love the classic wines, such as white and red, however, you may still carry more exotic wines for your customers who love expensive varieties. This makes clustering more difficult, since there are uneven class distributions (you don't order 10 of every wine available, for example).

DBSCAN differs from k-means and hierarchical clustering because you can build this intuition into how we evaluate the clusters of customers we are interested in forming. It can cut through the noise in an easier fashion and only point out customers who have the highest potential for remarketing in a campaign.

By clustering through the concept of a neighborhood, we can separate out the one-off customers that can be seen as random noise, relative to the more valuable customers that come back to our store time and time again. This approach, of book, calls into question how we establish the best numbers when it comes to neighborhood radius and minimum points per neighborhood.

As a high-level heuristic, we want to have our neighborhood radius small, but not too small. At one end of the extreme, you can have the neighborhood radius be quite high – this can max out at treating all points in the feature space as one massive cluster. On the opposite end of the extreme, you can have a very small neighborhood radius. Too small neighborhood radii can result in no points being clustered together and having a large collection of single member clusters.

Similar logic applies when it comes to the minimum number of points that can make up a cluster. Minimum points can be seen as a secondary threshold that tunes the neighborhood radius a bit depending on what data you have available in your space. If all of the data in your feature space is extremely sparse, minimum points become extremely valuable, in tandem with neighborhood radius, to make sure you don't just have a large number of uncorrelated data points. When you have very dense data, the minimum points threshold becomes less of a driving factor as opposed to neighborhood radius.

As you can see from these two hyperparameter rules, the best options are, as usual, dependent on what your dataset looks like. Oftentimes, you will want to find the perfect "goldilocks" zone of not being too small in your hyperparameters, but also not too large.

DBSCAN In-Depth

To see how DBSCAN works, we can trace the path of a simple toy program as it merges together to form a variety of clusters and noise-labeled data points:

1. Given n unvisited sample data points, move through each point in a loop and mark as visited.

2. From each point, look at the distance to every other point in the dataset.

3. For all points that fall within the neighborhood radius hyperparameter, connect them as neighbors.

4. Check to see whether the number of neighbors is at least as many as the minimum points required.

5. If the minimum point threshold is reached, group together as a cluster. If not, mark the point as noise.

6. Repeat until all data points are categorized in clusters or as noise.

DBSCAN is fairly straightforward in some senses – while there are the new concepts of density through neighborhood radius and minimum points, at its core, it is still just evaluating using a distance metric.

Walkthrough of the DBSCAN Algorithm

Here is a simple example walking through the preceding steps in slightly more detail:

1. Given four sample data points, view each point as its own cluster [(1,7)], [(-8,6)], [(-9,4)], [(4, -2)]:

Figure 3.3: Plot of sample data points

2. Calculate pairwise the Euclidean distance between each of the points:

Point Distances

	(1,7)	(-5,9)	(-9,4)	(4,-2)
(1,7)	[[9.223e+18,	6.325e+00,	1.044e+01,	9.487e+00],
(-5,9)	[6.325e+00,	9.223e+18,	6.403e+00,	1.421e+01],
(-9,4)	[1.044e+01,	6.403e+00,	9.223e+18,	1.432e+01],
(4,-2)	[9.487e+00,	1.421e+01,	1.432e+01,	9.223e+18]]

Figure 3.4: Point distances

3. From each point, expand out a neighborhood size and form clusters. For the purpose of this example, let's imagine we passed through a neighborhood radius of three. This means that any two points will be neighbors if the distance between them is less than three. Points (-8,6) and (-9,4) are now candidates for clustering.

4. Points that have no neighbors are marked as noise and remain unclustered. Points (1,7) and (4,-2) fall out of our frame of interest as being useless in terms of clustering.

5. Points that have neighbors are then evaluated to see whether they pass the minimum points threshold. In this example, if we had passed through a minimum points threshold of two, then points (-8,6) and (-9,4) can formally be grouped together as a cluster. If we had a minimum points threshold of three, then all four data points in this set would be considered superfluous noise.

6. Repeat this process on remaining un-visited data points.

At the end of this process, you will have your entire dataset established as either within clusters or as unrelated noise. Hopefully, as you can tell by walking through the toy example, DBSCAN performance is highly dependent on the threshold hyperparameters you choose a priori. This means that you may have to run DBSCAN a couple of times with different hyperparameter options to get an understanding of how they influence overall performance.

One great thing to notice about DBSCAN is that it does away with concepts of centroids that we saw in both k-means and a centroid-focused implementation of hierarchical clustering. This feature allows DBSCAN to work better for complex datasets, since most data in the wild is not shaped like clean blobs.

Exercise 9: Evaluating the Impact of Neighborhood Radius Size

For this exercise, we will work in reverse of what we have typically seen in previous examples, by first seeing the packaged implementation of DBSCAN in scikit-learn, and then implementing it on our own. This is done on purpose to fully explore how different neighborhood radius sizes drastically impact DBSCAN performance.

By completing this exercise, you will become familiar with how tuning neighborhood radius size can change how well DBSCAN performs. It is important to understand these facets of DBSCAN, as they can save you time in the future by troubleshooting your clustering algorithms efficiently.

1. Generate some dummy data:

```
from sklearn.cluster import DBSCAN
from sklearn.datasets import make_blobs
import matplotlib.pyplot as plt
```

```
%matplotlib inline
# Generate a random cluster dataset to experiment on. X = coordinate
points, #y = cluster labels (not needed)
X, y = make_blobs(n_samples=1000, centers=8, n_features=2, random_
state=800)

# Visualize the data
plt.scatter(X[:,0], X[:,1])
plt.show()
```

The output is as follows:

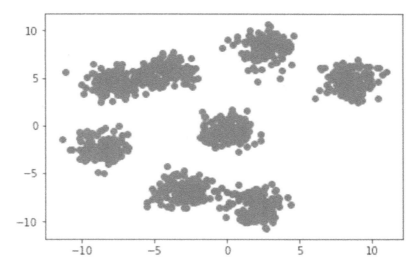

Figure 3.5: Visualized Toy Data Example

2. After plotting the dummy data for this toy problem, you will see that the dataset has two features and approximately seven to eight clusters. To implement DBSCAN using scikit-learn, you will need to instantiate a new scikit-learn class:

```
db = DBSCAN(eps=0.5, min_samples=10, metric='euclidean')
```

Our example DBSCAN instance is stored in the **db** variable, and our hyperparameters are passed through on creation. For the sake of this example, you can see that the neighborhood radius (**eps**) is set to 0.5, while the minimum number of points is set to 10. To keep in line with our past chapters, we will once again be using Euclidean distance as our distance metric.

3. Let's set up a loop that allows us to explore potential neighborhood radius size
    options interactively:

```
eps = [0.2,0.7]
for ep in eps:
    db = DBSCAN(eps=ep, min_samples=10, metric='euclidean')
    plt.scatter(X[:,0], X[:,1], c=db.fit_predict(X))
    plt.title('Toy Problem with eps: ' + str(ep))
    plt.show()
```

The preceding code results in the following two plots:

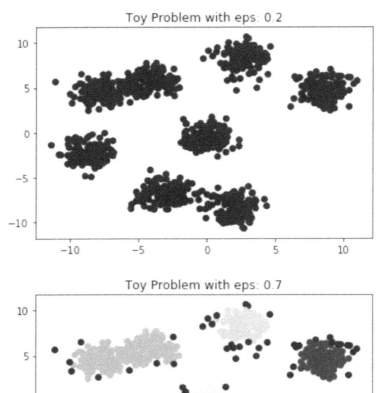

Figure: 3.6: Resulting plots

As you can see from the plots, setting our neighborhood size too small will cause everything to be seen as random noise (purple points). Bumping our neighborhood size up a little bit allows us to form clusters that make more sense. Try recreating the preceding plots and experiment with varying **eps** sizes.

DBSCAN Attributes – Neighborhood Radius

In *Exercise 9, Evaluating the Impact of Neighborhood Radius Size,* you saw how impactful setting the proper neighborhood radius is on the performance of your DBSCAN implementation. If your neighborhood is too small, then you will run into issues where all the data is left unclustered. If you set your neighborhood too large, then all of the data will similarly be grouped together into one cluster and not provide any value. If you explored the preceding exercise further with your own **eps** sizes, you may have noticed that it is very difficult to land on great clustering using only the neighborhood size. This is where a minimum points threshold comes in handy. We will visit that topic later.

To go deeper into the neighborhood concept of DBSCAN, let's take a deeper look at the **eps** hyperparameter you pass at instantiation time. **eps** stands for epsilon and is the distance that your algorithm will look within when searching for neighbors. This epsilon value is converted to a radius that sweeps around any given data point in a circular manner to serve as a neighborhood:

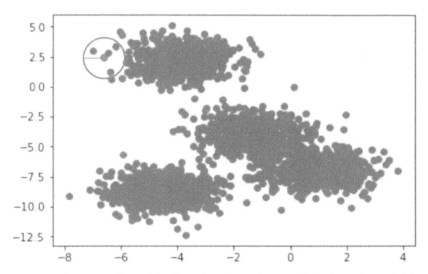

Figure 3.7: Visualization of neighborhood radius where red circle is the neighborhood

In this instance, there will be four neighbors of the center point.

One key aspect to notice here is that the shape formed by your neighborhood search is a circle in two dimensions, and a sphere in three dimensions. This may impact the performance of your model simply based on how the data is structured. Once again, blobs may seem like an intuitive structure to find – this may not always be the case. Fortunately, DBSCAN is well equipped to handle this dilemma of clusters that you may be interested in, yet that do not fit the explicit blob structure:

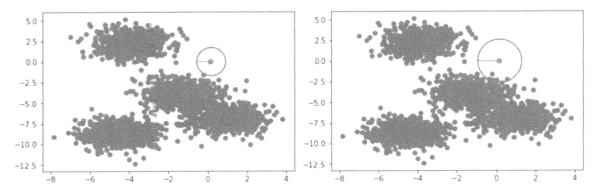

Figure 3.8: Impact of varying neighborhood radius size

On the left, the data point will be classified as random noise. On the right, the data point has multiple neighbors and could be its own cluster.

Activity 4: Implement DBSCAN from Scratch

Using a generated two-dimensional dataset during an interview, you are asked to create the DBSCAN algorithm from scratch. To do this, you will need to code the intuition behind neighborhood searches and have a recursive call that adds neighbors.

Given what you've learned about DBSCAN and distance metrics from prior chapters, build an implementation of DBSCAN from scratch in Python. You are free to use NumPy and SciPy to evaluate distances here.

These steps will help you complete the activity:

1. Generate a random cluster dataset

2. Visualize the data

3. Create functions from scratch that allow you to call DBSCAN on a dataset

4. Use your created DBSCAN implementation to find clusters in the generated dataset. Feel free to use hyperparameters as you see fit, tuning them based on their performance

5. Visualize the clustering performance of your DBSCAN implementation from scratch

The desired outcome of this exercise is for you to understand how DBSCAN works from the ground up before you use the fully packaged implementation in scikit-learn. Taking this approach to any machine learning algorithm from scratch is important, as it helps you "earn" the ability to use easier implementations, while still being able to discuss DBSCAN in depth in the future:

Figure 3.9: Expected outcome

Note

Solution for this activity can be found on page 316.

DBSCAN Attributes – Minimum Points

The other core component to a successful implementation of DBSCAN beyond the neighborhood radius is the minimum number of points required to justify membership within a cluster. As mentioned earlier, it is more obvious that this lower bound benefits your algorithm when it comes to sparser datasets. That's not to say it is a useless parameter when you have very dense data, however – while having single data points randomly interspersed through your feature space can be easily bucketed as noise, it becomes more of a grey area when we have random patches of two to three, for example. Should these data points be their own cluster, or should they also be categorized as noise? Minimum points thresholding helps solve this problem.

In the scikit-learn implementation of DBSCAN, this hyperparameter is seen in the `min_samples` field passed on DBSCAN instance creation. This field is very valuable to play with in tandem with the neighborhood radius size hyperparameter to fully round out your density-based clustering approach:

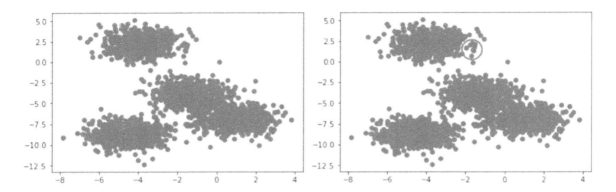

Figure 3.10: Minimum points threshold deciding whether a group of data points is noise or a cluster

On the right, if minimum points threshold is 10 points, it will classify data in this neighborhood as noise.

In real-world scenarios, you can see minimum points being highly impactful when you have truly large amounts of data. Going back to the wine-clustering example, if your store was actually a large wine warehouse, you could have thousands of individual wines with only one or two bottles that can easily be viewed as their own cluster. This may be helpful depending on your use case; however, it is important to keep in mind the subjective magnitudes that come with your data. If you have millions of data points, then random noise can easily be seen as hundreds or even thousands of random one-off sales. However, if your data is on the scale of hundreds or thousands, single data points can be seen as random noise.

Exercise 10: Evaluating the Impact of Minimum Points Threshold

Similar to our *Exercise 9, Evaluating the Impact of Neighborhood Radius Size*, where we explored the value of setting a proper neighborhood radius size, we will repeat the exercise, but instead will change the minimum points threshold on a variety of datasets.

Using our current implementation of DBSCAN, we can easily tune the minimum points threshold. Tune this hyperparameter and see how it performs on generated data.

By tuning the minimum points threshold for DBSCAN, you will understand how it can affect the quality of your clustering predictions.

Once again, let's start with randomly generated data:

1. Generate a random cluster dataset, as follows:

```
from sklearn.cluster import DBSCAN
from sklearn.datasets import make_blobs
import matplotlib.pyplot as plt
%matplotlib inline

X, y = make_blobs(n_samples=1000, centers=8, n_features=2, random_
state=800)
```

2. Visualize the data as follows:

```
# Visualize the data
plt.scatter(X[:,0], X[:,1])
plt.show()
```

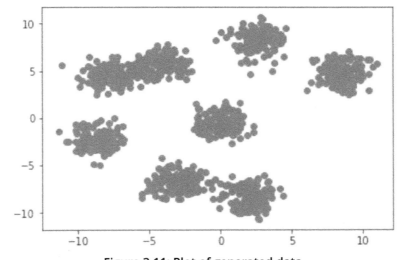

Figure 3.11: Plot of generated data

3. With the same plotted data as before, let's grab one of the better performing neighborhood radius sizes from *Exercise 1, Evaluating the Impact of Neighborhood Radius Size* – **eps** = 0.7:

    ```
    db = DBSCAN(eps=0.7, min_samples=10, metric='euclidean')
    ```

    > **Note**
    >
    > **eps** is a tunable hyperparameter. However, earlier in the same line, we establish that 0.7 comes from previous experimentation, leading us to **eps = 0.7** as the optimal value.

4. After instantiating the DBSCAN clustering algorithm, let's treat the **min_samples** hyperparameter as the variable we wish to tune. We can cycle through a loop to find which minimum number of points works best for our use case:

    ```
    num_samples = [10,19,20]

    for min_num in num_samples:
        db = DBSCAN(eps=0.7, min_samples=min_num, metric='euclidean')
        plt.scatter(X[:,0], X[:,1], c=db.fit_predict(X))
        plt.title('Toy Problem with Minimum Points: ' + str(min_num))
        plt.show()
    ```

    Looking at the first plot generated, we can see where we ended if you followed *Exercise 1, Evaluating the Impact of Neighborhood Radius Size* exactly, using 10 minimum points to mark the threshold for cluster membership:

Figure 3.12: Plot of Toy problem with a minimum of 10 points

The remaining two hyperparameter options can be seen to greatly impact the performance of your DBSCAN clustering algorithm, and show how a shift in one number can greatly influence performance:

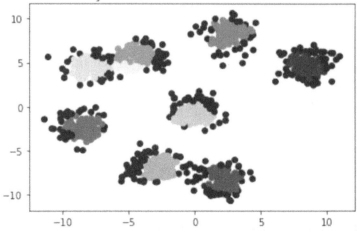

Figure 3.13: Plots of the Toy problem

As you can see, simply changing the number of minimum points from 19 to 20 adds an additional (incorrect!) cluster to our feature space. Given what you've learned about minimum points through this exercise, you can now tweak both epsilon and minimum points thresholding in your scikit-learn implementation to achieve the optimal number of clusters.

> **Note**
>
> In our original generation of the data, we created eight clusters. This points out that small changes in minimum points can add entire new clusters that we know shouldn't be there.

Activity 5: Comparing DBSCAN with k-means and Hierarchical Clustering

You are managing store inventory and have received a large shipment of wine, but the brand labels fell off the bottles during transit. Fortunately, your supplier provided you with the chemical readings for each bottle along with their respective serial numbers. Unfortunately, you aren't able to open each bottle of wine and taste test the difference – you must find a way to group the unlabeled bottles back together according to their chemical readings! You know from the order list that you ordered three different types of wine and are given only two wine attributes to group the wine types back together.

In *Chapter 2, Hierarchical Clustering* we were able to see how k-means and hierarchical clustering performed on the wine dataset. In our best case scenario, we were able to achieve a silhouette score of 0.59. Using scikit-learn's implementation of DBSCAN, let's see if we can get even better clustering.

These steps will help you complete the activity:

1. Import the necessary packages

2. Load the wine dataset and check what the data looks like

3. Visualize the data

4. Generate clusters using k-means, agglomerative clustering, and DBSCAN

5. Evaluate a few different options for DSBSCAN hyperparameters and their effect on the silhouette score

6. Generate the final clusters based on the highest silhouette score

7. Visualize clusters generated using each of the three methods

> **Note**
>
> We have downloaded this dataset from https://archive.ics.uci.edu/ml/datasets/wine. You can access it at https://github.com/TrainingByPackt/Applied-Unsupervised-Learning-with-Python/tree/master/Lesson03/Activity05.
>
> UCI Machine Learning Repository [http://archive.ics.uci.edu/ml]. Irvine, CA: University of California, School of Information and Computer Science.

By completing this activity, you will be recreating a full workflow of a clustering problem. You have already made yourself familiar with the data in *Chapter 2, Hierarchical Clustering*, and, by the end of this activity, you will have performed model selection to find the best model and hyperparameters for your dataset. You will have silhouette scores of the wine dataset for each type of clustering.

> **Note**
>
> The solution for this activity can be found on page 319.

DBSCAN Versus k-means and Hierarchical Clustering

Now that you've reached an understanding of how DBSCAN is implemented and how many different hyperparameters you can tweak to drive performance, let's survey how it compares to the clustering methods we covered in *Chapter 1, Introduction to Clustering* and *Chapter 2, Hierarchical Clustering*.

You may have noticed in *Activity 5, Comparing DBSCAN with k-means and Hierarchical Clustering*, that DBSCAN can be a bit finnicky when it comes to finding the optimal clusters via silhouette score. This is a downside of the neighborhood approach – k-means and hierarchical clustering really excel when you have some idea regarding the number of clusters in your data. In most cases, this number is low enough that you can iteratively try a few different numbers and see how it performs. DBSCAN, instead, takes a more bottom-up approach by working with your hyperparameters and finding the clusters it views as important. In practice, it is helpful to consider DBSCAN when the first two options fail, simply because of the amount of tweaking needed to get it to work properly. That being said, when your DBSCAN implementation is working correctly, it will often immensely outperform k-means and hierarchical clustering. (In practice, this often happens with highly intertwined, yet still discrete data, such as a feature space containing two half-moons).

Compared to k-means and hierarchical clustering, DBSCAN can be seen as being potentially more efficient, since it only has to look at each data point once. Instead of multiple iterations of finding new centroids and evaluating where their nearest neighbors are, once a point has been assigned to a cluster in DBSCAN, it does not change cluster membership. The other key difference that DBSCAN and hierarchical clustering both share, compared to k-means, is not needing to explicitly pass a number of clusters expected at the time of creation. This can be extremely helpful when you have no external guidance on how to break your dataset down.

Summary

DBSCAN takes an interesting approach to clustering compared to k-means and hierarchical clustering. While hierarchical clustering can, in some aspects, be seen as an extension of the nearest neighbors approach seen in k-means, DBSCAN approaches the problem of finding neighbors by applying a notion of density. This can prove extremely beneficial when it comes to highly complex data that is intertwined in a complex fashion. While DBSCAN is very powerful, it is not infallible and can be seen as potentially overkill, depending on what your original data looks like.

Combined with k-means and hierarchical clustering, however, DBSCAN completes a strong toolbox when it comes to the unsupervised learning task of clustering your data. When faced with any problem in this space, it is worthwhile to compare the performance of each method and see which performs best.

With clustering explored, we will now move onto another key piece of rounding out your skills in unsupervised learning: dimensionality reduction. Through smart reduction of dimensions, we can make clustering easier to understand and communicate to stakeholders. Dimensionality reduction is also key to creating all types of machine learning models in the most efficient manner possible.

Dimension Reduction and PCA

Learning Objectives

By the end of this chapter, you will be able to:

- Apply dimension reduction techniques.
- Describe the concepts behind principal components and dimensionality reduction.
- Apply principal component analysis (PCA) when solving problems using scikit-learn.
- Compare manual PCA versus scikit-learn.

In this chapter, we will look at dimension reduction and different dimension reduction techniques.

Introduction

This chapter is the first of a series of three chapters that investigate the use of different feature sets (or spaces) in our unsupervised learning algorithms, and we will start with a discussion around dimensionality reduction, specifically, PCA. We will then extend upon our understanding of the benefits of the different feature spaces through an exploration of two independently powerful machine learning architectures in neural network-based auto-encoders. Neural networks certainly have a well-deserved reputation for being powerful models in supervised learning problems, and, through the use of an autoencoder stage, have been shown to be sufficiently flexible for their application to unsupervised learning problems. Finally, we will build on our neural network implementation and dimensionality reduction as we cover t-distributed nearest neighbors in the final chapter of this micro-series.

What Is Dimensionality Reduction?

Dimensionality reduction is an important tool in any data scientists' toolkit, and, due to its wide variety of use cases, is essentially assumed knowledge within the field. So, before we can consider reducing the dimensionality and why we would want to reduce it, we must first have a good understanding of what dimensionality is. To put it simply, dimensionality is the number of dimensions, features, or variables associated with a sample of data. Often, this can be thought of as a number of columns in a spreadsheet, where each sample is on a new row, and each column describes some attribute of the sample. The following table is an example:

Pressure (hPa)	Temperature (°C)	Humidity (%)
1050	32.2	12
1026	27.8	80

Figure 4.1: Two samples of data with three different features

In *Figure 4.1*, we have two samples of data, each with three independent features or dimensions. Depending upon the problem being solved, or the origin of this dataset, we may want to reduce the number of dimensions per sample without losing the provided information. This is where dimensionality reduction can be helpful.

But how exactly can dimensionality reduction help us in solving problems? We will cover the applications in more detail in the following section; but let's say that we had a very large dataset of time series data, such as echo-cardiogram or ECG (also known as an EKG in some countries) signals as shown in the following figure:

Figure 4.2: Electrocardiogram (ECG or EKG)

These signals were captured from your company's new model of watch, and we need to look for signs of a heart attack or stroke. In looking through the dataset, we can make a few observations:

- Most of the individual heartbeats are very similar.

- There is some noise in the data from the recording system or from the patient moving during the recording.

- Despite the noise, the heartbeat signals are still visible.

- There is a lot of data – too much to be able to process using the hardware available on the watch.

It is in such a situation that dimensionality reduction really shines! By using dimensionality reduction, we are able to remove much of the noise from the signal, which, in turn, will assist with the performance of the algorithms that are applied to the data as well as reduce the size of the dataset to allow for reduced hardware requirements. The techniques that we are going to discuss in this chapter, in particular, PCA and autoencoders, have been well applied in research and industry to effectively process, cluster, and classify such datasets. By the end of this chapter, you will be able to apply these techniques to your own data and hopefully see an increase in the performance of your own machine learning systems.

Applications of Dimensionality Reduction

Before we start a detailed investigation of dimensionality reduction and PCA, we will discuss some of the common applications for these techniques:

- **Pre-processing/feature engineering**: One of the most common implementations is in the pre-processing or feature engineering stages of developing a machine learning solution. The quality of the information provided during the algorithm development, as well as the correlation between the input data and the desired result, is critical in order for a high-performing solution to be designed. In this situation, PCA can provide assistance, as we are able to isolate the most important components of information from the data and provide this to the model so that only the most relevant information is being provided. This can also have a secondary benefit in that we have reduced the number of features being provided to the model, so there can be a corresponding reduction in the number of calculations to be completed. This can reduce the overall training time for the system.

- **Noise reduction**: Dimensionality reduction can also be used as an effective noise reduction/filtering technique. It is expected that the noise within a signal or dataset does not comprise a large component of the variation within the data. Thus, we can remove some of the noise from the signal by removing the smaller components of variation and then restoring the data back to the original dataspace. In the following example, the image on the left has been filtered to the first 20 most significant sources of data, which gives us the image on the right. We can see that the quality of the image has reduced, but the critical information is still there:

Figure 4.3: An image filtered with dimensionality reduction. Left: The original image (Photo by Arthur Brognoli from Pexels), Right: The filtered image

> **Note**
>
> This photograph was taken by Arthur Brognoli from Pexels and is available for free use under https://www.pexels.com/photo-license/.

- **Generating plausible artificial datasets**: As PCA divides the dataset into the components of information (or variation), we can investigate the effects of each components or generate new dataset samples by adjusting the ratios between the eigenvalues. We can scale these components, which, in effect, increases or decreases the importance of that specific component. This is also referred to as **statistical shape modelling**, as one common method is to use it to create plausible variants of shapes. It is also used detect facial landmarks in images in the process of **active shape modelling**.

- **Financial modelling/risk analysis**: Dimensionality reduction provides a useful toolkit for the finance industry, as being able to consolidate a large number of individual market metrics or signals into a smaller number of components allows for faster, and more efficient computations. Similarly, the components can be used to highlight those higher-risk products/companies.

The Curse of Dimensionality

Before we can understand the benefits to using dimensionality reduction techniques, we must first understand why the dimensionality of feature sets need to be reduced at all. The **curse of dimensionality** is a phrase commonly used to describe issues that arise when working with data that has a high number of dimensions in the feature space; for example, the number of attributes that are collected for each sample. Consider a dataset of point locations within a game of *Pac-Man*. Your character, Pac-Man, occupies a position within the virtual world defined by two dimensions or coordinates (x, y). Let's say that we are creating a new computer enemy: an AI-driven ghost to play against, and that it requires some information regarding our character to make its own game logic decisions. For the bot to be effective, we require the player's position (x, y) and their velocity in each of the directions (vx, vy) in addition to the players last five (x, y) positions, the number of remaining hearts, and the number of remaining power-pellets in the maze (power-pellets temporarily allow Pac-Man to eat ghosts). Now, for each moment in time, our bot requires 16 individual features (or dimensions) to make its decisions. This is clearly a lot more than just the two dimensions as provided by the position.

Figure 4.4: Dimensions in a PacMan game

To explain the concept of dimensionality reduction, we will consider a fictional dataset (see *Figure* 4.5) of x and y coordinates as features, giving two dimensions in the feature space. It should be noted that this example is by no means a mathematical proof, but is rather intended to provide a means of visualizing the effect of increased dimensionality. In this dataset, we have six individual samples (or points) and we can visualize the currently occupied volume within the feature space of approximately $(3 - 1)$ x $(4 - 2) = 2$ x $2 = 4$ squared units.

Figure 4.5: Data in a 2D feature space

Suppose, the dataset comprises the same number of points, but with an additional feature (the z coordinate) to each sample. The occupied data volume is now approximately 2 x 2 x 2 = 8 cubed units. So, we now have the same number of samples, but the space enclosing the dataset is now larger. As such, the data takes up less relative volume in the available space and is now sparser. This is the curse of dimensionality; as we increase the number of available features, we increase the sparsity of the data, and, in turn, make statistically valid correlations more difficult. Looking back to our example of creating a video game bot to play against a human player, we have 12 features that are a mix of different feature types: speed, velocity, acceleration, skill level, selected weapon, and available ammunition. Depending on the range of possible values for each of these features and the variance to the dataset provided by each feature, the data could be extremely sparse. Even within the constrained world of Pac-Man, the potential variance of each of the features could be quite large, some much larger than others.

So, without dealing with the sparsity of the dataset, we have more information with the additional feature(s), but may not be able to improve the performance of our machine learning model, as the statistical correlations are more difficult. What we would like to do is keep the useful information provided by the extra features but minimize the negative effect of sparsity. This is exactly what dimensionality reduction techniques are designed to do and these can be extremely powerful in increasing the performance of your machine learning model.

Throughout this chapter, we will discuss a number of different dimensionality reduction techniques and will cover one of the most important and useful methods, PCA, in greater detail with a worked example.

Overview of Dimensionality Reduction Techniques

As discussed in the Introduction section, the goal of any dimensionality reduction technique is to manage the sparsity of the dataset while keeping the useful information that is provided, so dimensionality reduction is typically an important pre-processing step used before a classification stage. Most dimensionality reduction techniques aim to complete this task using a process of **feature projection**, which adjusts the data from the higher dimensional space into a space with fewer dimensions to remove the sparsity from the data. Again, as a means of visualizing the projection process, consider a sphere in a 3D space. We can project the sphere into lower 2D space into a circle with some information loss (the value for the z coordinate) but retaining much of the information that describes its original shape. We still know the origin, radius, and manifold (outline) of the shape, and it is still very clear that it is a circle. So, if we were given just the 2D projection, it would also be possible to re-create the original 3D shape with this information. So, depending upon the problem that we are trying to solve, we may have reduced the dimensionality while retaining the important information:

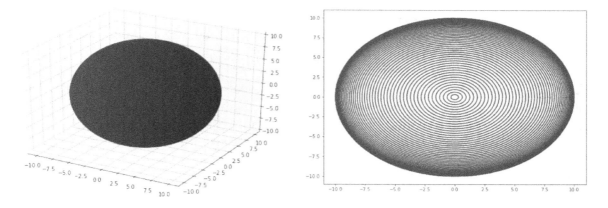

Figure 4.6: A projection of a 3D sphere into a 2D space

The secondary benefit that can be obtained by pre-processing the dataset with a dimensionality reduction stage is the improved computational performance that can be achieved. As the data has been projected into a lower dimensional space, it will contain fewer, but potentially more powerful, features. The fact that there are fewer features means that, during later classification or regression stages, the size of the dataset being processed is significantly smaller. This will potentially reduce the required system resources and processing time for classification/regression, and, in some cases, the dimensionality reduction technique can also be used directly to complete the analysis..

This analogy also introduces one of the important considerations of dimensionality reduction. We are always trying to balance the information loss resulting from the projection into lower dimensional space with reducing the sparsity of the data. Depending upon the nature of the problem and the dataset being used, the correct balance could present itself and be relatively straightforward. In some applications, this decision may rely on the outcome of additional validation methods, such as cross-validation (particularly in supervised learning problems) or the assessment of experts in your problem domain.

One way we like to think about this trade-off in dimensionality reduction is to consider compressing a file or image on a computer for transfer. Dimensionality reduction techniques, such as PCA, are essentially methods of compressing information into a smaller size for transfer, and, in many compression methods, some losses occur as a result of the compression process. Sometimes, these losses are acceptable; if we are transferring a 50 MB image and need to shrink it to 5 MB for transfer, we can expect to still be able to see the main subject of the image, but perhaps some smaller background features will become too blurry to see. We would also not expect to be able to restore the original image to a pixel-perfect representation from the compressed version, but we could expect to restore it with some additional artefacts, such as blurring.

Dimensionality Reduction and Unsupervised Learning

Dimensionality reduction techniques have many uses in machine learning, as the ability to extract the useful information of a dataset can provide performance boosts in many machine learning problems. They are particularly useful in unsupervised learning as opposed to supervised learning methods, as the dataset does not contain any ground truth labels or targets to achieve. In unsupervised learning, the training environment is being used to organize the data in a way that is appropriate for the problem being solved (for example, clustering in a classification problem), which is typically based on the most important information in the dataset. Dimensionality reduction provides an effective means of extracting the important information, and, as there are a number of different methods that we could use, it is beneficial to review some of the available options:

- **Linear Discriminant Analysis** (**LDA**): This is a particularly handy technique that can be used for both classification as well as dimensionality reduction. LDA will be covered in more detail in *Chapter 7: Topic Modeling*.

- **Non-negative matrix factorization** (**NNMF**): Like many of the dimensionality reduction techniques, this relies upon the properties of linear algebra to reduce the number of features in the dataset. NNMF will also be covered in more detail in *Chapter 7, Topic Modeling*.

- **Singular Value Decomposition** (**SVD**): This is somewhat related to PCA (which is covered in more detail in this chapter) and is also a matrix decomposition process not too dissimilar to NNMF.

- **Independant Component Analysis** (**ICA**): This also shares some similarities to SVD and PCA, but relaxing the assumption of the data being a Gaussian distribution allows for non-Gaussian data to be separated.

Each of the methods described so far all use linear separation to reduce the sparsity of the data in their original implementation. Some of these methods also have variants that use non-linear kernel functions in the separation process, providing the ability to reduce the sparsity in a non-linear fashion. Depending on the dataset being used, a non-linear kernel may be more effective at extracting the most useful information from the signal.

PCA

As we described previously, PCA is a commonly used and very effective dimensionality reduction technique, which often forms a pre-processing stage for a number of machine learning models and techniques. For this reason, we will dedicate this section of the book to looking at PCA in more detail than any of the other methods. PCA reduces the sparsity in the dataset by separating the data into a series of components where each component represents a source of information within the data. As its name suggests, the first component produced in PCA, **the principal component** comprises the majority of information or variance within the data. The principal component can often be thought of as contributing the most amount of interesting information in addition to the mean. With each subsequent component, less information, but more subtlety, is contributed to the compressed data. If we consider all of these components together, there will be no benefit from using PCA, as the original dataset will be returned. To clarify this process and the information returned by PCA, we will use a worked example, completing the PCA calculations by hand. But first, we must review some foundational statistical concepts, which are required to execute the PCA calculations.

Mean

The mean, or the average value, is simply the addition of all values divided by the number of values in the set.

Standard Deviation

Often referred to as the spread of the data and related to the variance, the standard deviation is a measure of how much of the data lies within proximity to the mean. In a normally distributed dataset, approximately 68% of the dataset lies within one standard deviation of the mean.

The relationship between the variance and standard deviation is quite a simple one – the variance is the standard deviation squared.

Covariance

Where standard deviation or variance is the spread of the data calculated on a single dimension, the covariance is the variance of one dimension (or feature) against another. When the covariance of a dimension is computed against itself, the result is the same as simply calculating the variance for the dimension.

Covariance Matrix

A covariance matrix is a matrix representation of the possible covariance values that can be computed for a dataset. Other than being particularly useful in data exploration, covariance matrices are also required for executing the PCA of a dataset. To determine the variance of one feature with respect to another, we simply look up the corresponding value in the covariance matrix. Referring to *Figure 4.7* we can see that, in column 1, row 2, the value is the variance of feature or dataset Y with respect to X (*cov(Y, X)*). We can also see that there is a diagonal column of covariance values computed against the same feature or dataset; for example, *cov(X, X)*. In this situation, the value is simply the variance of X.

$$\overline{cov} = \begin{bmatrix} cov(X, X) & cov(X, Y) & cov(X, Z) \\ cov(Y, X) & cov(Y, Y) & cov(Y, Z) \\ cov(Z, X) & cov(Z, Y) & cov(Z, Z) \end{bmatrix}$$

Figure 4.7: The covariance matrix

Typically, the exact values of each of the covariances are not as interesting as looking at the magnitude and relative size of each of the covariances within the matrix. A large value of the covariance of one feature against another would suggest that one feature changes significantly with respect to the other, while a value close to zero would signify very little change. The other interesting aspect of the covariance to look for is the sign associated with the covariance; a positive value indicates that as one feature increases or decreases then so does the other, while a negative covariance indicates that the two features diverge from each other with one increasing as the other decreases or vice versa.

Thankfully, **numpy** and **scipy** provide functions to efficiently make these calculations for you. In the next exercise, we will compute these values in Python.

Exercise 11: Understanding the Foundational Concepts of Statistics

In this exercise, we will briefly review how to compute some of the foundational statistical concepts using both the **numpy** and **pandas** Python packages. In this exercise, we will use dataset of measurements of different Iris flower species, created in 1936 by the British biologist and statistician Sir Ronald Fisher. The dataset, which can be found in the accompanying source code, comprises four individual measurements (sepal width and length, and petal width and length) of three different Iris flower varieties: Iris setosa, Iris versicolor, and Iris virginica.

> **Note**
>
> This dataset is taken from https://archive.ics.uci.edu/ml/machine-learning-databases/iris/. It can be downloaded from https://github.com/TrainingByPackt/Applied-Unsupervised-Learning-with-Python/tree/master/Lesson04/Exercise11.
>
> UCI Machine Learning Repository [http://archive.ics.uci.edu/ml]. Irvine, CA: University of California, School of Information and Computer Science.

The steps to be performed are as follows:

1. Import the **pandas**, **numpy**, and **matplotlib** packages for use:

```
import pandas as pd
import numpy as np
import matplotlib.pyplot as plt
```

2. Load the dataset and preview the first five lines of data:

```
df = pd.read_csv('iris-data.csv')
df.head()
```

The output is as follows:

	Sepal Length	Sepal Width	Petal Length	Petal Width	Species
0	5.1	3.5	1.4	0.2	Iris-setosa
1	4.9	3.0	1.4	0.2	Iris-setosa
2	4.7	3.2	1.3	0.2	Iris-setosa
3	4.6	3.1	1.5	0.2	Iris-setosa
4	5.0	3.6	1.4	0.2	Iris-setosa

Figure 4.8: The head of the data

3. We only require the **Sepal Length** and **Sepal Width** features, so remove the other columns:

```
df = df[['Sepal Length', 'Sepal Width']]
df.head()
```

The output is as follows:

	Sepal Length	Sepal Width
0	5.1	3.5
1	4.9	3.0
2	4.7	3.2
3	4.6	3.1
4	5.0	3.6

Figure 4.9: The head after cleaning the data

4. Visualize the dataset by plotting the **Sepal Length** versus **Sepal Width** values:

```
plt.figure(figsize=(10, 7))
plt.scatter(df['Sepal Length'], df['Sepal Width']);
plt.xlabel('Sepal Length (mm)');
plt.ylabel('Sepal Width (mm)');
plt.title('Sepal Length versus Width');
```

The output is as follows:

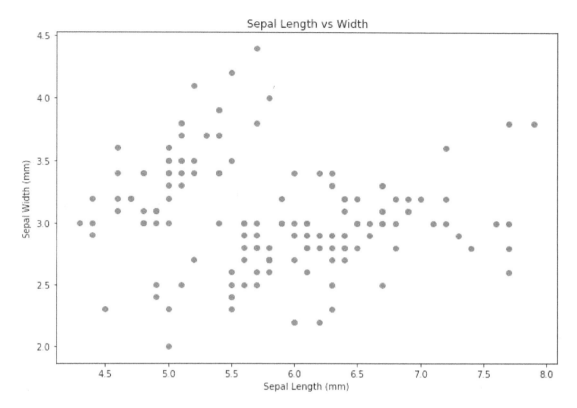

Figure 4.10: Plot of the data

5. Compute the mean value using the **pandas** method:

```
df.mean()
```

The output is as follows:

```
Sepal Length    5.843333
Sepal Width     3.054000
dtype: float64
```

6. Compute the mean value using the **numpy** method:

```
np.mean(df.values, axis=0)
```

The output is as follows:

```
array([5.84333333, 3.054     ])
```

7. Compute the standard deviation value using the **pandas** method:

```
df.std()
```

The output is as follows:

```
Sepal Length    0.828066
Sepal Width     0.433594
dtype: float64
```

8. Compute the standard deviation value using the **numpy** method:

```
np.std(df.values, axis=0)
```

The output is as follows:

```
array([0.8253€129, 0.43214658])
```

9. Compute the variance values using the **pandas** method:

```
df.var()
```

The output is as follows:

```
Sepal Length    0.685694
Sepal Width     0.188004
dtype: float64
```

10. Compute the variance values using the **numpy** method:

```
np.var(df.values, axis=0)
```

The output is as follows:

```
array([0.6811222, 0.18675067])
```

11. Compute the covariance matrix using the **pandas** method:

```
df.cov()
```

The output is as follows:

	Sepal Length	Sepal Width
Sepal Length	0.685694	-0.039268
Sepal Width	-0.039268	0.188004

Figure 4.11: Covariance matrix using the Pandas method

12. Compute the covariance matrix using the **numpy** method:

```
np.cov(df.values.T)
```

The output is as follows:

```
array([[ 0.68569351, -0.03926846],
       [-0.03926846,  0.18800403]])
```

Figure 4.12: The covariance matrix using the NumPy method

Now that we know how to compute the foundational statistic values, we will turn our attention to the remaining components of PCA.

Eigenvalues and Eigenvectors

The mathematical concept of eigenvalues and eigenvectors is a very important one in the fields of physics and engineering, and they also form the final steps in computing the principal components of a dataset. The exact mathematical definition of eigenvalues and eigenvectors is outside the scope of this book, as it is quite involved and requires a reasonable understanding of linear algebra. The linear algebra equation to decompose a dataset (a) into eigenvalues (S) and eigenvectors (U) is as follows:

$$a = USV^T$$

Figure 4.13: An eigenvector/eigenvalue decomposition

In *Figure 4.13*, U and V are related as the left and right values of dataset a. If a has the shape m x n, then U will contain values in the shape m x m and V in the shape n x n.

Put simply, in the context of PCA:

- **Eigenvectors** (U) are the components contributing information to the dataset as described in the first paragraph of this section on principal components. Each eigenvector describes some amount of variability within the dataset.

- **Eigenvalues** (S) are the individual values that describe how much contribution each eigenvector provides to the dataset. As we described previously, the signal eigenvector that describes the largest contribution is referred to as the principal component, and as such, will have the largest eigenvalue. Accordingly, the eigenvector with the smallest eigenvalue contributes the least amount of variance or information to the data.

Exercise 12: Computing Eigenvalues and Eigenvectors

As we discussed previously, deriving and computing the eigenvalues and eigenvectors manually is a little involved and is not in the scope of this book. Thankfully, **numpy** provides all the functionality for us to compute these values. Again, we will use the Iris dataset for this example:

> **Note**
>
> This dataset is taken from https://archive.ics.uci.edu/ml/machine-learning-databases/iris/.
>
> It can be downloaded from https://github.com/TrainingByPackt/Applied-Unsupervised-Learning-with-Python/tree/master/Lesson04/Exercise12.
>
> UCI Machine Learning Repository [http://archive.ics.uci.edu/ml]. Irvine, CA: University of California, School of Information and Computer Science.

1. Import the **pandas** and **numpy** packages:

   ```
   import pandas as pd
   import numpy as np
   ```

2. Load the dataset:

   ```
   df = pd.read_csv('iris-data.csv')
   df.head()
   ```

   The output is as follows:

	Sepal Length	Sepal Width	Petal Length	Petal Width	Species
0	5.1	3.5	1.4	0.2	Iris-setosa
1	4.9	3.0	1.4	0.2	Iris-setosa
2	4.7	3.2	1.3	0.2	Iris-setosa
3	4.6	3.1	1.5	0.2	Iris-setosa
4	5.0	3.6	1.4	0.2	Iris-setosa

   Figure 4.14: The first five rows of the dataset

3. Again, we only require the **Sepal Length** and **Sepal Width** features, so remove the other columns:

```
df = df[['Sepal Length', 'Sepal Width']]
df.head()
```

The output is as follows:

	Sepal Length	Sepal Width
0	5.1	3.5
1	4.9	3.0
2	4.7	3.2
3	4.6	3.1
4	5.0	3.6

Figure 4.15: The Sepal Length and Sepal Width feature

4. From NumPy's linear algebra module, use the single value decomposition function to compute the **eigenvalues** and **eigenvectors**:

```
eigenvectors, eigenvalues, _ = np.linalg.svd(df.values, full_matrices=False)
```

> **Note**
>
> The use of the **full_matrices=False** function argument is a flag for the function to return the eigenvectors in the shape we need; that is, # Samples x # Features.

5. Look at the eigenvalues; we can see that the first value is the largest, so the first eigenvector contributes the most information:

```
eigenvalues
```

The output is as follows:

```
array([81.25483015,  6.96796793])
```

6. It is handy to look at eigenvalues as a percentage of the total variance within the dataset. We will use a cumulative sum function to do this:

```
eigenvalues = np.cumsum(eigenvalues)
eigenvalues
```

The output is as follows:

```
array([81.25413015, 88.22279808])
```

7. Divide by the last or maximum value to convert to a percentage:

```
eigenvalues /= eigenvalues.max()
eigenvalues
```

The output is as follows:

```
array([0.92101851, 1.        ])
```

We can see here that the first (or principal) component comprises 92% of the variation within the data, and thus, most of the information.

8. Now, let's look at the **eigenvectors**:

```
eigenvectors
```

A section of the output is as follows:

```
array([[-0.07553027, -0.11068158],
       [-0.07052087, -0.06007995],
       [-0.06946245, -0.09874988],
       [-0.06780439, -0.09257869],
       [-0.07500106, -0.13001654],
       [-0.08106887, -0.14194824],
       [-0.06949767, -0.13083793],
       [-0.07387221, -0.10451038],
```

Figure 4.16: Eigenvectors

9. Confirm that the shape of the eigenvector matrix is in the for **# Samples x # Features**; that is, **150 x 2**:

```
eigenvectors.shape
```

The output is as follows:

```
(150, 2)
```

10. So, from the eigenvalues, we saw that the principal component was the first eigenvector. Look at the values for the first eigenvector:

```
P = eigenvectors[0]
P
```

The output is as follows:

```
array([-0.07553027, -0.11068158])
```

We have decomposed the dataset down into the principal components, and, using the eigenvectors, we can further reduce the dimensionality of the available data. In the later examples, we will consider PCA and apply this technique to an example dataset.

The Process of PCA

Now we have all of the pieces ready to complete PCA to reduce the number of dimensions in a dataset.

The overall algorithm for completing PCA is as follows:

1. Import the required Python packages (**numpy** and **pandas**).

2. Load the entire dataset.

3. From the available data, select the features that you wish to use in the dimensionality reduction.

> **Note**
>
> If there is a significant difference in the scale between the features of the dataset; for example, one feature ranges in values between 0 and 1, and another between 100 and 1,000, you may need to normalize one of the features, as such differences in magnitude can eliminate the effect of the smaller features. In such a situation, you may need to divide the larger feature into its maximum value.
>
> As an example, have a look at this:
>
> ```
> x1 = [0.1, 0.23, 0.54, 0.76, 0.78]
> ```
>
> ```
> x2 = [121, 125, 167, 104, 192]
> ```
>
> ```
> x2 = x2 / np.max(x2) # Normalise x2 to be between 0 and 1
> ```

4. Compute the **covariance** matrix of the selected (and possibly normalized) data.

5. Compute the eigenvalues and eigenvectors of the **covariance** matrix.

6. Sort the eigenvalues (and corresponding eigenvectors) from highest to lowest value eigenvalue.

7. Compute the eigenvalues as a percentage of the total variance within the dataset.

8. Select the number of eigenvalues (and corresponding eigenvectors) required to comprise a pre-determined value of a minimum composition variance.

> **Note**
>
> At this stage, the sorted eigenvalues represent a percentage of the total variance within the dataset. As such, we can use these values to select the number of eigenvectors required, either for the problem being solved or to sufficiently reduce the size of the dataset being applied in the model. For example, say that we required at least 90% of the variance to be accounted for within the output of PCA. We would then select the number of eigenvalues (and corresponding eigenvectors) that comprise at least 90% of the variance.

9. Multiply the dataset by the selected eigenvectors and you have completed a PCA, reducing the number of features representing the data.

10. Plot the result.

Before moving on to the next exercise, note that **transpose** is a term from linear algebra that means to swap the rows with the columns and vice versa. Say we had a matrix of $X = [1,2,3]$, then the transpose of X would be $x^T = \begin{bmatrix} 1 \\ 2 \\ 3 \end{bmatrix}$.

Exercise 13: Manually Executing PCA

For this exercise, we will be completing PCA manually, again using the Iris dataset. For this example, we want to sufficiently reduce the number of dimensions within the dataset to comprise at least 75% of the available variance:

> **Note**
>
> This dataset is taken from https://archive.ics.uci.edu/ml/machine-learning-databases/iris/. It can be downloaded from https://github.com/TrainingByPackt/Applied-Unsupervised-Learning-with-Python/tree/master/Lesson04/Exercise13.
>
> UCI Machine Learning Repository [http://archive.ics.uci.edu/ml]. Irvine, CA: University of California, School of Information and Computer Science.

1. Import the **pandas** and **numpy** packages:

    ```
    import pandas as pd
    import numpy as np
    import matplotlib.pyplot as plt
    ```

2. Load the dataset:

    ```
    df = pd.read_csv('iris-data.csv')
    df.head()
    ```

    The output is as follows:

	Sepal Length	Sepal Width	Petal Length	Petal Width	Species
0	5.1	3.5	1.4	0.2	Iris-setosa
1	4.9	3.0	1.4	0.2	Iris-setosa
2	4.7	3.2	1.3	0.2	Iris-setosa
3	4.6	3.1	1.5	0.2	Iris-setosa
4	5.0	3.6	1.4	0.2	Iris-setosa

    Figure 4.17: The first five rows of the dataset

3. Again, we only require the **Sepal Length** and **Sepal Width** features, so remove the other columns. In this example, we are not normalizing the selected dataset:

```
df = df[['Sepal Length', 'Sepal Width']]
df.head()
```

The output is as follows:

	Sepal Length	Sepal Width
0	5.1	3.5
1	4.9	3.0
2	4.7	3.2
3	4.6	3.1
4	5.0	3.6

Figure 4.18: The sepal length and sepal width feature

4. Compute the **covariance** matrix for the selected data. Note that we need to take the transpose of the **covariance** matrix to ensure that it is based on the number of features (2) and not samples (150):

```
data = np.cov(cf.values.T)
# The transpose is required to ensure the covariance matrix is
#based on features, not samples data
data
```

The output is as follows:

```
array([[ 0.68569351, -0.03926846],
       [-0.03926846,  0.18800403]])
```

Figure 4.19: The covariance matrix for the selected data

5. Compute the eigenvectors and eigenvalues for the covariance matrix, Again, use the **full_matrices** function argument:

```
eigenvectors, eigenvalues, _ = np.linalg.svd(data, full_matrices=False)
```

6. What are the eigenvalues? These are returned sorted from the highest to lowest value:

```
eigenvalues
```

The output is as follows:

```
array([0.6887728 , 0.18492474])
```

7. What are the corresponding eigenvectors?

```
eigenvectors
```

The output is as follows:

```
array([[-0.99693955,  0.07817635],
       [ 0.07817635,  0.99693955]])
```

Figure 4.20: Eigenvectors

8. Compute the eigenvalues as a percentage of the variance within the dataset:

```
eigenvalues = np.cumsum(eigenvalues)
eigenvalues /= eigenvalues.max()
eigenvalues
```

The output is as follows:

```
array([0.78834238, 1.        ])
```

9. As per the introduction to the exercise, we need to describe the data with at least 75% of the available variance. As per *Step* 7, the principal component comprises 78% of the available variance. As such, we require only the principal component from the dataset. What are the principal components?

```
P = eigenvectors[0]
P
```

The output is as follows:

```
array([-0.99693955,  0.07817635])
```

Now, we can apply the dimensionality reduction process. Execute a matrix multiplication of the principal component with the transpose of the dataset.

> **Note**
>
> The dimensionality reduction process is a matrix multiplication of the selected eigenvectors and the data to be transformed.

10. Without taking the transpose of the **df.values** matrix, multiplication could not occur:

```
x_t_p = P.dot(df.values.T)
x_t_p
```

A section of the output is as follows:

```
array([-4.81077444, -4.65047471, -4.43545153, -4.34357521, -4.70326285,
        -5.07858577, -4.32012231, -4.71889812, -4.15982257, -4.64265708,
        -5.09422104, -4.51951021, -4.55078076, -4.05231098, -5.46954395,
        -5.33857945, -5.07858577, -4.81077444, -5.38548526, -4.78732154,
        -5.11767394, -4.79513917, -4.30448703, -4.82640971, -4.51951021,
        -4.75016867, -4.71889812, -4.9104684 , -4.91828603, -4.43545153,
        -4.54296312, -5.11767394, -4.86356259, -5.15482681, -4.64265708,
        -4.73453339, -5.20955026, -4.64265708, -4.15200494, -4.81859208,
        -4.71108049, -4.30642234, -4.13636967, -4.71108049, -4.78732154,
```

Figure 4.21: The result of matrix multiplication

> **Note**
>
> The transpose of the dataset is required to execute matrix multiplication, as the **inner dimensions of the matrix must be the same** for matrix multiplication to occur. For **A.dot(B)** to be valid, **A** must have the shape $m \times n$ and **B** must have the shape $n \times p$. In this example, the inner dimensions of **A** and **B** are both n.

In the following example, the output of the PCA is a single-column, 150-sample dataset. As such, we have just reduced the size of the initial dataset by half, comprising approximately 79% of the variance within the data:

```
array([-4.81077444, -4.65047471, -4.43545153, -4.34357521, -4.70326285,
        -5.07858577, -4.32012231, -4.71889812, -4.15982257, -4.64265708,
        -5.09422104, -4.51951021, -4.55078076, -4.05231098, -5.46954395,
        -5.33857945, -5.07858577, -4.81077444, -5.38548526, -4.78732154,
        -5.11767394, -4.79513917, -4.30448703, -4.82640971, -4.51951021,
        -4.75016867, -4.71889812, -4.9104684 , -4.91828603, -4.43545153,
        -4.54296312, -5.11767394, -4.86356259, -5.15482681, -4.64265708,
        -4.73453339, -5.20955026, -4.64265708, -4.15200494, -4.81859208,
        -4.71108049, -4.30642234, -4.13636967, -4.71108049, -4.78732154,
        -4.55078076, -4.78732154, -4.33575758, -4.99452708, -4.72671576,
        -6.72841249, -6.13024876, -6.63653617, -5.30336189, -6.26121325,
        -5.46366162, -6.02273717, -4.69738052, -6.35308957, -4.97300948,
        -4.82834502, -5.64741426, -5.80964929, -5.8546198 , -5.35615003,
        -6.43714826, -5.34833239, -5.57117321, -6.0090372 , -5.38742057,
        -5.63177899, -5.86243744, -6.08527825, -5.86243744, -6.15370166,
        -6.34527194, -6.56029512, -6.44496589, -5.75492585, -5.47929689,
        -5.29554425, -5.29554425, -5.57117321, -5.77056112, -5.14804448,
```

Figure 4.22: The output of PCA

11. Plot the values of the principal component:

```
plt.figure(figsize=(10, 7))
plt.plot(x_t_p);
plt.title('Principal Component of Selected Iris Dataset');
plt.xlabel('Sample');
plt.ylabel('Component Value');
```

The output is as follows:

Figure 4.23: The Iris dataset transformed by using a manual PCA

In this exercise, we simply computed the covariance matrix of the dataset without applying any transformations to the dataset beforehand. If the two features have roughly the same mean and standard deviation, this is perfectly fine. However, if one feature is much larger in value (and has a somewhat different mean) than the other, then this feature may dominate the other when decomposing into components. This could have the effect of removing the information provided by the smaller feature altogether. One simple normalization technique before computing the covariance matrix would be to subtract the respective means from the features, thus centering the dataset around zero. We will demonstrate this in *Exercise 15*, *Visualizing Variance Reduction with Manual PCA*.

Exercise 14: Scikit-Learn PCA

Typically, we will not complete PCA manually, especially when scikit-learn provides an optimized API with convenient methods that will allow us to easily transform the data to and from the reduced-dimensional space. In this exercise, we will look at using a scikit-learn PCA on the Iris dataset in more detail:

> **Note**
>
> This dataset is taken from https://archive.ics.uci.edu/ml/machine-learning-databases/iris/.
>
> It can be downloaded from https://github.com/TrainingByPackt/Applied-Unsupervised-Learning-with-Python/tree/master/Lesson04/Exercise14.
>
> UCI Machine Learning Repository [http://archive.ics.uci.edu/ml]. Irvine, CA: University of California, School of Information and Computer Science.

1. Import the **pandas**, **numpy**, and **PCA** modules from the **sklearn** packages:

   ```
   import pandas as pd
   import numpy as np
   import matplotlib.pyplot as plt
   from sklearn.decomposition import PCA
   ```

2. Load the dataset:

   ```
   df = pd.read_csv('iris-data.csv')
   df.head()
   ```

The output is as follows:

	Sepal Length	Sepal Width	Petal Length	Petal Width	Species
0	5.1	3.5	1.4	0.2	Iris-setosa
1	4.9	3.0	1.4	0.2	Iris-setosa
2	4.7	3.2	1.3	0.2	Iris-setosa
3	4.6	3.1	1.5	0.2	Iris-setosa
4	5.0	3.6	1.4	0.2	Iris-setosa

Figure 4.24: The first five rows of the dataset

3. Again, we only require the **Sepal Length** and **Sepal Width** features, so remove the other columns. In this example, we are not normalizing the selected dataset:

```
df = df[['Sepal Length', 'Sepal Width']]
df.head()
```

The output is as follows:

	Sepal Length	Sepal Width
0	5.1	3.5
1	4.9	3.0
2	4.7	3.2
3	4.6	3.1
4	5.0	3.6

Figure 4.25: The Sepal Length and Sepal Width features

4. Fit the data to a scikit-learn PCA model of the covariance data. Using the default values, as we have here, produces the maximum number of eigenvalues and eigenvectors possible for the dataset:

```
model = PCA()
model.fit(df.values)
```

The output is as follows:

```
PCA(copy=True, iterated_power='auto', n_components=None, random_state=None,
    svd_solver='auto', tol=0.0, whiten=False)
```

Figure 4.26: Fitting data to a PCA model

Here, **copy** indicates that the data fit within the model is copied before any calculations are applied. **iterated_power** shows that the **Sepal Length** and **Sepal Width** features is the number of principal components to keep. The default value is **None**, which selects the number of components as one less than the minimum of either the number of samples or number of features. **random_state** allows the user to specify a seed for the random number generator used by the SVD solver. **svd_solver** specifies the SVD solver to be used during PCA. **tol** is the tolerance values used by the SVD solver. With **whiten**, the component vectors are multiplied by the square root of the number of samples. This will remove some information, but can improve the performance of some downstream estimators.

5. The percentage of variance described by the components (eigenvalues) is contained within the **explained_variance_ratio_** property. Display the values for **explained_variance_ratio_**:

```
model.explained_variance_ratio_
```

The output is as follows:

```
array([0.78834238, 0.21165762])
```

6. Display the eigenvectors via the **components_** property:

```
model.components_
```

The output is as follows:

```
array([[ 0.99693955, -0.07817635],
       [ 0.07817635,  0.99693955]])
```

Figure 4.27: Eigenvectors

7. In this exercise, we will again only use the primary component, so we will create a new **PCA** model, this time specifying the number of components (eigenvectors/eigenvalues) to be **1**:

```
model = PCA(n_components=1)
```

8. Use the **fit** method to fit the **covariance** matrix to the **PCA** model and generate the corresponding eigenvalues/eigenvectors:

```
model.fit(df.values)
```

```
PCA(copy=True, iterated_power='auto', n_components=1, random_state=None,
    svd_solver='auto', tol=0.0, whiten=False)
```

Figure 4.28: The maximum number of eigenvalues and eigenvectors

The model is fitted using a number of default parameters, as listed in the preceding output. **copy = True** is the data provided to the **fit** method, which is copied before PCA is applied. **iterated_power='auto'** is used to define the number of iterations by the internal SVD solver. **n_components=1** specifies that the PCA model is to return only the principal component. **random_state=None** specifies the random number generator to be used by the internal SVD solver if required. **svd_solver='auto'** is the type of SVD solver used. **tol=0.0** is the tolerance value for the SVD solver to deem converged. **whiten=False** specifies that the eigenvectors are not to be modified. If set to **True**, whitening further modifies the components by multiplying by the square root of the number of samples and dividing by the singular values. This can help to improve the performance of later algorithm steps.

Typically, you will not need to worry about adjusting any of these parameters, other than the number of components (**n_components**), which you can pass to the **fit** method, for example, **model.fit(data, n_components=2)**.

9. Display the eigenvectors using the **components_** property:

```
model.components_
```

The output is as follows:

```
array([[ 0.99693955, -0.07817635]])
```

10. Transform the Iris dataset into the lower space by using the **fit_transform** method of the model on the dataset. Assign the transformed values to the **data_t** variable.

```
data_t = model.fit_transform(df.values)
```

11. Plot the transformed values to visualize the result:

```
plt.figure(figsize=(10, 7))
plt.plot(data_t);
plt.xlabel('Sample');
plt.ylabel('Transformed Data');
plt.title('The dataset transformed by the principal component');
```

The output is as follows:

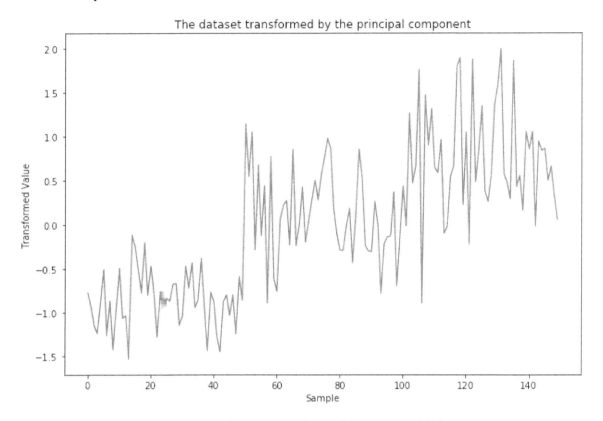

Figure 4.29: The Iris dataset transformed using the scikit-learn PCA

Congratulations! You have just reduced the dimensionality of the Iris dataset using manual PCA, as well as the scikit-learn API. But before we celebrate too early, compare Figure 4.23 and Figure 4.29; these plots should be identical, shouldn't they? We used two separate methods to complete a PCA on the same dataset and selected the principal component for both. In the next activity, we will investigate why there are differences between the two.

Activity 6: Manual PCA versus scikit-learn

Suppose that you have been asked to port some legacy code from an older application executing PCA manually, to a newer application that uses scikit-learn. During the porting process, you notice some differences between the output of the manual PCA versus your port. Why is there a difference between the output of our manual PCA and scikit-learn? Compare the results of the two approaches on the Iris dataset. What are the differences between them?

> **Note**
>
> This dataset is taken from https://archive.ics.uci.edu/ml/machine-learning-databases/iris/. It can be downloaded from https://github.com/TrainingByPackt/Applied-Unsupervised-Learning-with-Python/tree/master/Lesson04/Activity06.
>
> UCI Machine Learning Repository [http://archive.ics.uci.edu/ml]. Irvine, CA: University of California, School of Information and Computer Science.

1. Import the **pandas**, **numpy**, and **matplotlib** plotting libraries and the scikit-learn **PCA** model.

2. Load the dataset and select only the sepal features as per the previous exercises. Display the first five rows of the data.

3. Compute the **covariance** matrix for the data.

4. Transform the data using the scikit-learn API and only the first principal component. Store the transformed data in the **sklearn_pca** variable.

5. Transform the data using the manual PCA and only the first principal component. Store the transformed data in the **manual_pca** variable.

6. Plot the **sklearn_pca** and **manual_pca** values on the same plot to visualize the difference.

7. Notice that the two plots look almost identical, but with some key differences. What are these differences?

8. See whether you can modify the output of the manual PCA process to bring it in line with the scikit-learn version.

> **Note**
>
> As a hint, the scikit-learn API subtracts the mean of the data prior to the transform.

Expected output: By the end of this activity, you will have transformed the dataset using both the manual and scikit-learn PCA methods. You will have produced a plot demonstrating that the two reduced datasets are, in fact, identical, and you should have an understanding of why they initially looked quite different. The final plot should look similar to the following:

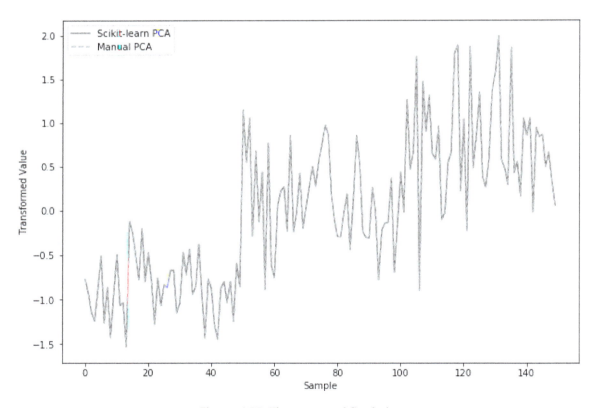

Figure 4.30: The expected final plot

This plot will demonstrate that the dimensionality reduction completed by the two methods are, in fact, the same.

> **Note**
>
> The solution for this activity can be found on page 324.

Restoring the Compressed Dataset

Now that we have covered a few different examples of transforming a dataset into a lower-dimensional space, we should consider what practical effect this transformation has had on the data. Using PCA as a pre-processing step to condense the number of features in the data will result in some of the variance being discarded. The following exercise will walk us through this process so that we can see how much information has been discarded by the transformation.

Exercise 15: Visualizing Variance Reduction with Manual PCA

One of the most important aspects of dimensionality reduction is understanding how much information has been removed from the dataset as a result of the dimensionality reduction process. Removing too much information will add additional challenges to later processing, while not removing enough defeats the purpose of PCA or other techniques. In this exercise, we will visualize the amount of information that has been removed from the Iris dataset as a result of PCA:

> **Note**
>
> This dataset is taken from https://archive.ics.uci.edu/ml/machine-learning-databases/iris/.
>
> It can be downloaded from https://github.com/TrainingByPackt/Applied-Unsupervised-Learning-with-Python/tree/master/Lesson04/Exercise15.
>
> UCI Machine Learning Repository [http://archive.ics.uci.edu/ml]. Irvine, CA: University of California, School of Information and Computer Science.

1. Import the **pandas**, **numpy**, and **matplotlib** plotting libraries:

```
import pandas as pd
import numpy as np
import matplotlib.pyplot as plt
```

2. Read in the **Sepal** features from the Iris dataset:

```
df = pd.read_csv('iris-data.csv')[['Sepal Length', 'Sepal Width']]
df.head()
```

The output is as follows:

	Sepal Length	Sepal Width
0	5.1	3.5
1	4.9	3.0
2	4.7	3.2
3	4.6	3.1
4	5.0	3.6

Figure 4.31: Sepal features

3. Centre the dataset around zero by subtracting the respective means:

> **Note**
>
> As discussed at the end of *Exercise 13, Manually Executing PCA*, here, we are centering the data before computing the covariance matrix.

```
means = np.mean(df.values, axis=0)
means
```

The output is as follows:

```
array([5.84333333, 3.054     ])
```

To calculate the data and print the results, use the following code:

```
data = df.values - means
data
```

A section of the output is as follows:

```
array([[-0.74333333,  0.446     ],
       [-0.94333333, -0.054     ],
       [-1.14333333,  0.146     ],
       [-1.24333333,  0.046     ],
       [-0.84333333,  0.546     ],
       [-0.44333333,  0.846     ],
       [-1.24333333,  0.346     ],
       [-0.84333333,  0.346     ],
```

Figure 4.32: Section of the output

4. Use manual PCA to transform the data on the basis of the first principal component:

```
eigenvectors, eigenvalues, _ = np.linalg.svd(np.cov(data.T), full_
matrices=False)
P = eigenvectors[0]
P
```

The output is as follows:

```
array([-0.99693955,  0.07817635])
```

5. Transform the data into the lower-dimensional space:

```
data_transformed = P.dot(data.T)
```

6. Reshape the principal components for later use:

```
P = P.reshape((-1, 1))
```

7. To compute the inverse transform of the reduced dataset, we need to restore the selected eigenvectors into the higher-dimensional space. To do this, we will invert the matrix. Matrix inversion is another linear algebra technique that we will only cover very briefly. A square matrix, A, is said to be invertible if there exists another square matrix, B, and if AB=BA=I, where I is a special matrix known as an identity matrix, consisting of values of **1** only through the center diagonal:

```
P_transformed = np.linalg.pinv(P)
P_transformed
```

The output is as follows:

```
array([[-0.99693955,  0.07817635]])
```

8. Prepare the transformed data for use in the matrix multiplication:

```
data_transformed = data_transformed.reshape((-1, 1))
```

9. Compute the inverse transform of the reduced data and plot the result to visualize the effect of removing the variance from the data:

```
data_restored = data_transformed.dot(P_transformed)
data_restored
```

A section of the output is as follows:

```
array([[-7.73550366e-01,  6.06589915e-02],
       [-9.33359508e-01,  7.31906401e-02],
       [-1.14772462e+00,  9.00003684e-02],
       [-1.23931976e+00,  9.71829241e-02],
       [-8.80732922e-01,  6.90638556e-02],
       [-5.06558669e-01,  3.97224787e-02],
       [-1.26270089e+00,  9.90163868e-02],
       [-8.65145502e-01,  6.78415472e-02],
       [-1.42251003e+00,  1.11548035e-01],
       [-9.41153218e-01,  7.38017944e-02],
```

Figure 4.33: The inverse transform of the reduced data

10. Add the **means** back to the transformed data:

```
data_restored += means
```

11. Visualize the result by plotting the original dataset and the transformed dataset:

```
plt.figure(figsize=(10, 7))
plt.plot(data_restored[:,0], data_restored[:,1], linestyle=':', label='PCA
restoration');
plt.scatter(df['Sepal Length'], df['Sepal Width'], marker='*',
label='Original');
plt.legend();
plt.xlabel('Sepal Length');
plt.ylabel('Sepal Width');
plt.title('Inverse transform after removing variance');
```

The output is as follows:

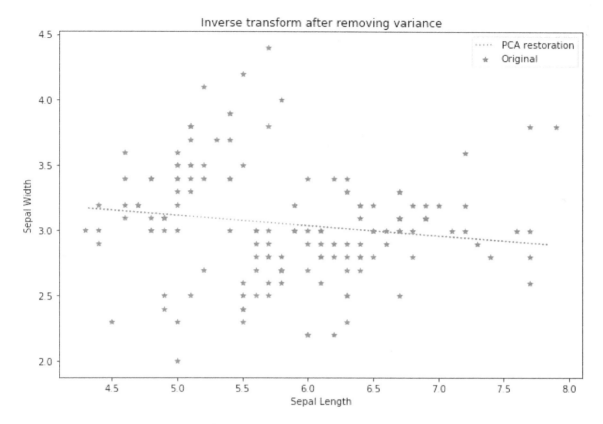

Figure 4.34: The inverse transform after removing variance

12. There are only two components of variation in this dataset. If we do not remove any of the components, what will be the result of the inverse transform? Again, transform the data into the lower-dimensional space, but this time, use all of the eigenvectors:

```
P = eigenvectors
data_transformed = P.dot(data.T)
```

13. Transpose **data_transformed** to put it into the correct shape for matrix multiplication:

```
data_transformed = data_transformed.T
```

14. Now, restore the data back to the higher-dimensional space:

```
data_restored = data_transformed.dot(P)
data_restored
```

A section of the output is as follows:

```
array([[-0.74333333,  0.446      ],
       [-0.94333333, -0.054      ],
       [-1.14333333,  0.146      ],
       [-1.24333333,  0.046      ],
       [-0.84333333,  0.546      ],
       [-0.44333333,  0.846      ],
       [-1.24333333,  0.346      ],
       [-0.84333333,  0.346      ],
```

Figure 4.35: The restored data

15. Add the means back to the restored data:

```
data_restored += means
```

16. Visualize the restored data in the context of the original dataset:

```
plt.figure(figsize=(10, 7))
plt.scatter(data_restored[:,0], data_restored[:,1], marker='d', label='PCA
restoration', c='k');
plt.scatter(df['Sepal Length'], df['Sepal Width'], marker='o',
label='Original', c='k');
plt.legend();
plt.xlabel('Sepal Length');
plt.ylabel('Sepal Width');
plt.title('Inverse transform after removing variance');
```

The output is as follows:

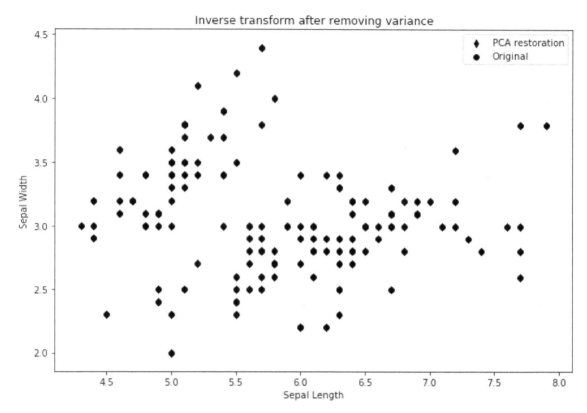

Figure 4.36: The inverse transform after removing the variance

If we compare the two plots produced in this exercise, we can see that the PCA reduced, and the restored dataset is essentially a negative linear trend line between the two feature sets. We can compare this to the dataset restored from all available components, where we have recreated the original dataset as a whole.

Exercise 16: Visualizing Variance Reduction with

In this exercise, we will again visualize the effect of reducing the dimensionality of the dataset; however, this time, we will be using the scikit-learn API. This is this method that you will commonly use in practical applications, due to the power and simplicity of the scikit-learn model:

> **Note**
>
> This dataset is taken from https://archive.ics.uci.edu/ml/machine-learning-databases/iris/. It can be downloaded from https://github.com/TrainingByPackt/Applied-Unsupervised-Learning-with-Python/tree/master/Lesson04/Exercise16.
>
> UCI Machine Learning Repository [http://archive.ics.uci.edu/ml]. Irvine, CA: University of California, School of Information and Computer Science.

1. Import the **pandas**, **numpy**, and **matplotlib** plotting libraries and the **PCA** model from scikit-learn:

```
import pandas as pd
import numpy as np
import matplotlib.pyplot as plt
from sklearn.decomposition import PCA
```

2. Read in the **Sepal** features from the Iris dataset:

```
df = pd.read_csv('iris-data.csv')[['Sepal Length', 'Sepal Width']]
df.head()
```

The output is as follows:

	Sepal Length	Sepal Width
0	5.1	3.5
1	4.9	3.0
2	4.7	3.2
3	4.6	3.1
4	5.0	3.6

Figure 4.37: The Sepal features from the Iris dataset

3. Use the scitkit-learn API to transform the data on the basis of the first principal component:

```
model = PCA(n_components=1)
data_p = model.fit_transform(df.values)
```

The output is as follows:

4. Compute the inverse transform of the reduced data and plot the result to visualize the effect of removing the variance from the data:

```
data = model.inverse_transform(data_p);
plt.figure(figsize=(10, 7))
plt.plot(data[:,0], data[:,1], linestyle=':', label='PCA restoration');
plt.scatter(df['Sepal Length'], df['Sepal Width'], marker='*',
label='Original');
plt.legend();
plt.xlabel('Sepal Length');
plt.ylabel('Sepal Width');
plt.title('Inverse transform after removing variance');
```

The output is as follows:

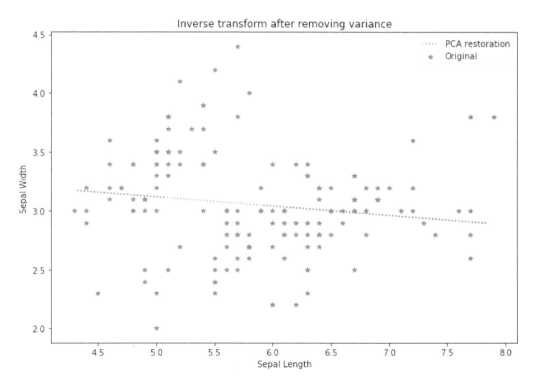

Figure 4.38: The inverse transform after removing the variance

5. There are only two components of variation in this dataset. If we do not remove any of the components, what will the result of the inverse transform be?

```
model = PCA()
data_p = model.fit_transform(df.values)
data = model.inverse_transform(data_p);
plt.figure(figsize=(10, 7))
plt.scatter(data[:,0], data[:,1], marker='d', label='PCA restoration',
c='k');
plt.scatter(df['Sepal Length'], df['Sepal Width'], marker='o',
label='Original', c='k');
plt.legend();
plt.xlabel('Sepal Length');
plt.ylabel('Sepal Width');
plt.title('Inverse transform after removing variance');
```

The output is as follows:

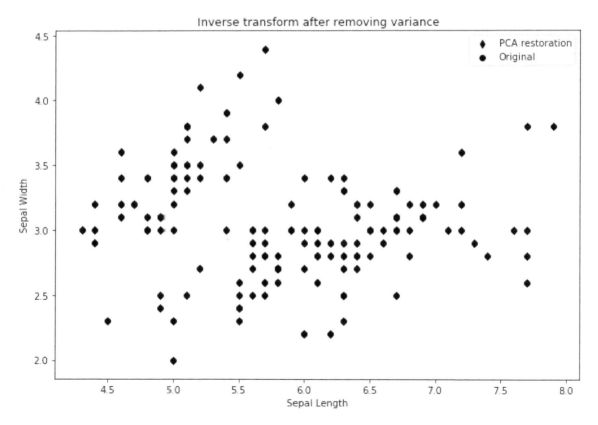

Figure 4.39: The inverse transform after removing the variance

Again, we have demonstrated the effect of removing information from the dataset and the ability to recreate the original data using all the available eigenvectors.

The previous exercises specified the reduction of the dimensionality using PCA to two dimensions, partly to allow the results to be easily visualized. We can, however, use PCA to reduce the dimensions to any value less than that of the original set. The following example demonstrates how PCA can be used to reduce a dataset to three dimensions, allowing visualizations.

Exercise 17: Plotting 3D Plots in Matplotlib

Creating 3D scatter plots in matplotlib are unfortunately not as simple as providing a series of (x, y, z) coordinates to a scatter plot. In this exercise we will work through a simple 3D plotting example, using the Iris dataset:

> **Note**
>
> This dataset is taken from https://archive.ics.uci.edu/ml/machine-learning-databases/iris/.
>
> It can be downloaded from https://github.com/TrainingByPackt/Applied-Unsupervised-Learning-with-Python/tree/master/Lesson04/Exercise17.
>
> UCI Machine Learning Repository [http://archive.ics.uci.edu/ml]. Irvine, CA: University of California, School of Information and Computer Science.

1. Import **pandas** and **matplotlib**. To enable 3D plotting, you will also need to import **Axes3D**:

```
from mpl_toolkits.mplot3d import Axes3D
import pandas as pd
import matplotlib.pyplot as plt
```

2. Read in the dataset and select the **Sepal Length**, **Sepal Width**, and **Petal Width** columns

```
df = pd.read_csv('iris-data.csv')[['Sepal Length', 'Sepal Width', 'Petal Width']]
df.head()
```

The output is as follows:

	Sepal Length	Sepal Width	Petal Width
0	5.1	3.5	0.2
1	4.9	3.0	0.2
2	4.7	3.2	0.2
3	4.6	3.1	0.2
4	5.0	3.6	0.2

Figure 4.40: The first five rows of the data

3. Plot the data in three dimensions and use the **projection='3d'** argument with the **add_subplot** method to create the 3D plot:

```
fig = plt.figure(figsize=(10, 7))
ax = fig.add_subplot(111, projection='3d') # Where Axes3D is required
ax.scatter(df['Sepal Length'], df['Sepal Width'], df['Petal Width']);
ax.set_xlabel('Sepal Length (mm)');
ax.set_ylabel('Sepal Width (mm)');
ax.set_zlabel('Petal Width (mm)');
ax.set_title('Expanded Iris Dataset');
```

The plot will look as follows:

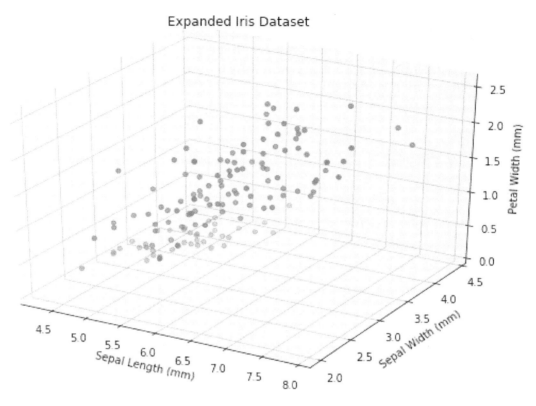

Figure 4.41: The expanded Iris dataset

> **Note**
>
> While the Axes3D was imported but not directly used, it is required for configuring the plot window in three dimensions. If the import of Axes3D was omitted, the **projection='3d'** argument would return an **AttributeError**.

Activity 7: PCA Using the Expanded Iris Dataset

In this activity, we are going to use the complete Iris dataset to look at the effect of selecting a differing number of components in the PCA decomposition. This activity aims to simulate the process that is typically completed in a real-world problem as we try to determine the optimum number of components to select, attempting to balance the extent of dimensionality reduction and information loss. Henceforth, we will be using the scikit-learn PCA model:

> **Note**
>
> This dataset is taken from https://archive.ics.uci.edu/ml/machine-learning-databases/iris/.
>
> It can be downloaded from https://github.com/TrainingByPackt/Applied-Unsupervised-Learning-with-Python/tree/master/Lesson04/Activity07.
>
> UCI Machine Learning Repository [http://archive.ics.uci.edu/ml]. Irvine, CA: University of California, School of Information and Computer Science.

1. Import **pandas** and **matplotlib**. To enable 3D plotting, you will also need to import **Axes3D**.

2. Read in the dataset and select the **Sepal Length**, **Sepal Width**, and **Petal Width** columns.

3. Plot the data in three dimensions.

4. Create a **PCA** model without specifying the number of components.

5. Fit the model to the dataset.

6. Display the eigenvalues or **explained_variance_ratio_**.

7. We want to reduce the dimensionality of the dataset but still keep at least 90% of the variance. What are the minimum number of components required to keep 90% of the variance?

8. Create a new **PCA** model, this time specifying the number of components required to keep at least 90% of the variance.

9. Transform the data using the new model.

10. Plot the transformed data.

11. Restore the transformed data to the original dataspace.

12. Plot the restored data in three dimensions in one subplot and the original data in a second subplot to visualize the effect of removing some of the variance:

```
fig = plt.figure(figsize=(10, 14))

# Original Data
ax = fig.add_subplot(211, projection='3d')

# Transformed Data
ax = fig.add_subplot(212, projection='3d')
```

Expected Output: The final plot will look as follows:

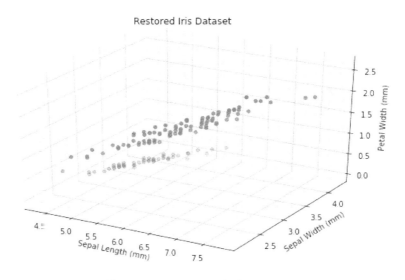

Figure 4.42: Expected plots

Note

The solution for this activity can be found on page 328.

Summary

In this chapter, we covered the process of dimensionality reduction and PCA. We completed a number of exercises and developed the skills to reduce the size of a dataset by extracting only the most important components of variance within the data, using both a manual PCA process and the model provided by scikit-learn. During this chapter, we also returned the reduced datasets back to the original dataspace and observed the effect of removing the variance on the original data. Finally, we discussed a number of potential applications for PCA and other dimensionality reduction processes. In our next chapter, we will introduce neural network-based autoencoders and use the Keras package to implement them.

5

Autoencoders

Learning Objectives

By the end of this chapter, you will be able to do the following:

- Explain where autoencoders can be applied and their use cases

- Understand how artificial neural networks are implemented and used

- Implement an artificial neural network using the Keras framework

- Explain how autoencoders are used in dimensionality reduction and denoising

- Implement an autoencoder using the Keras framework

- Explain and implement an autoencoder model using convolutional neural networks

In this chapter, we will take a look at autoencoders and their applications.

Introduction

This chapter continues our discussion of dimensionality reduction techniques as we turn our attention to autoencoders. Autoencoders are a particularly interesting area of focus as they provide a means of using supervised learning based on artificial neural networks, but in an unsupervised context. Being based on artificial neural networks, autoencoders are an extremely effective means of dimensionality reduction, but also provide additional benefits. With recent increases in the availability of data, processing power, and network connectivity, autoencoders are experiencing a resurgence in usage and study from their origins in the late 1980s. This is also consistent with the study of artificial neural networks, which was first described and implemented as a concept in the 1960s. Presently, you would only need to conduct a cursory internet search to discover the popularity and power of neural nets.

Autoencoders can be used for de-noising images and generating artificial data samples in combination with other methods, such as recurrent or **Long Short-Term Memory** (**LSTM**) architectures, to predict sequences of data. The flexibility and power that arises from the use of artificial neural networks also enables autoencoders to form very efficient representations of the data, which can then be used either directly as an extremely efficient search method, or as a feature vector for later processing.

Consider the use of an autoencoder in an image de-noising application, where we are presented with the image on the left in *Figure 5.1*. We can see that the image is affected by the addition of some random noise. We can use a specially trained autoencoder to remove this noise, as represented by the image on the right in *Figure 5.1*. In learning how to remove this noise, the autoencoder has also learned to encode the important information that composes the image and how to reconstruct (or decode) this information into a clearer version of the original image.

Figure 5.1: Autoencoder de-noising

Note

This image is modified from http://www.freenzphotos.com/free-photos-of-bay-of-plenty/stormy-fishermen/ under CC0.

This example demonstrates one aspect of autoencoders that makes them useful for unsupervised learning (the encoding stage), and one that is useful in generating new images (decoding). Throughout this chapter, we will delve further into these two useful stages of autoencoders and apply the output of the autoencoder to clustering the CIFAR-10 dataset.

Here is a representation of an encoder and decoder:

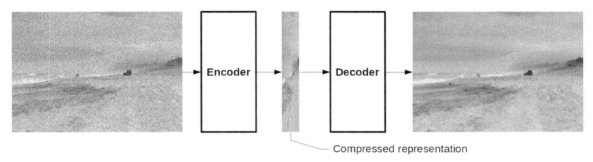

Figure 5.2: Encoder/decoder representation

Fundamentals of Artificial Neural Networks

Given that autoencoders are based on artificial neural networks, an understanding of how neural networks is also critical for understanding autoencoders. This section of the chapter will briefly review the fundamentals of artificial neural networks. It is important to note that there are many aspects of neural nets that are outside of the scope of this book. The topic of neural networks could easily, and has, filled many books on its own, and this section is not to be considered an exhaustive discussion of the topic.

As described earlier, artificial neural networks are primarily used in supervised learning problems, where we have a set of input information, say a series of images, and we are training an algorithm to map the information to a desired output, such as a class or category. Consider the CIFAR-10 dataset (*Figure 5.3*) as an example, which contains images of 10 different categories (airplane, automobile, bird, cat, deer, dog, frog, horse, ship, and truck), with 6,000 images per category. When neural nets are used in a supervised learning context, the images are fed to the network with a representation of the corresponding category labels being the desired output of the network.

The network is then trained to maximize its ability to infer or predict the correct label for a given image.

Figure 5.3: CIFAR-10 dataset

The Neuron

The artificial neural network derives its name from the biological neural networks commonly found in the brain. While the accuracy of the analogy can certainly be questioned, it is a useful metaphor to break down the concept of artificial neural networks and facilitate understanding. As with their biological counterparts, the neuron is the building block on which all neural networks are constructed, connecting a number of neurons in different configurations to form more powerful structures. Each neuron (*Figure* 5.4) is composed of four individual parts: an input value, a tunable weight (theta), an activation function that operates on the input value, and the resulting output value:

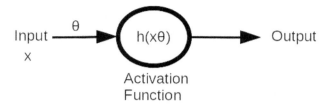

Figure 5.4: Anatomy of a neuron

The activation function is specifically chosen depending upon the objective of the neural network being designed, and there are a number of common functions, including **tanh**, **sigmoid**, **linear**, **sigmoid**, and **ReLU** (rectified linear unit). Throughout this chapter, we will use both the **sigmoid** and **ReLU** activation functions, so let's look at them in a little more detail.

Sigmoid Function

The sigmoid activation function is very commonly used as an output in the classification of neural networks due to its ability to shift the input values to approximate a binary output. The sigmoid function produces the following output:

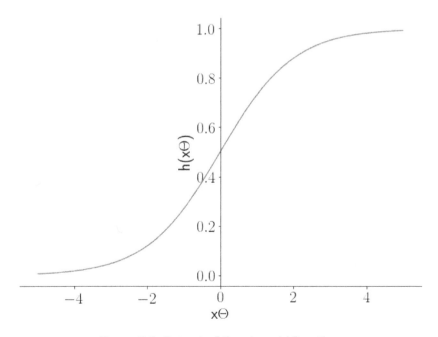

Figure 5.5: Output of the sigmoid function

We can see in *Figure* 5.5 that the output of the sigmoid function asymptotes (approaches but never reaches) 1 as x increases and asymptotes 0 as x moves further away from 0 in the negative direction. This function is used in classification tasks as it provides close to a binary output and is not a member of class (0) or is a member of the class (1).

Rectified Linear Unit (ReLU)

The rectified linear unit is a very useful activation function that's commonly used at intermediary stages of neural networks. Simply put, the value 0 is assigned to values less than 0, and the value is returned for greater than 0.

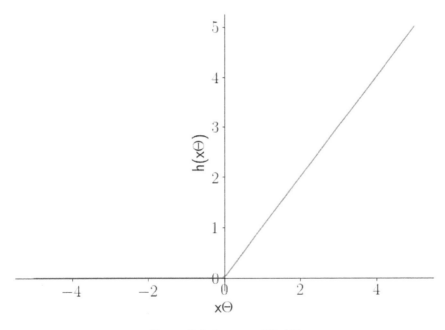

Figure 5.6: Output of ReLU

Exercise 18: Modeling the Neurons of an Artificial Neural Network

In this exercise, we will practically introduce a programmatic representation of the neuron in NumPy using the sigmoid function. We will keep the inputs fixed and adjust the tunable weights to investigate the effect on the neuron. Interestingly, this model is also very close to the supervised learning method of logistic regression. Perform the following steps:

1. Import the **numpy** and matplotlib packages:

```
import numpy as np
import matplotlib.pyplot as plt
```

2. Configure matplotlib to enable the use of Latex to render mathematical symbols in the images:

```
plt.rc('text', usetex=True)
```

3. Define the **sigmoid** function as a Python function:

```
def sigmoid(z):
    return np.exp(z) / (np.exp(z) + 1)
```

> **Note**
>
> Here, we're using the sigmoid function. You could also use the ReLU function. The ReLU activation function, while being powerful in artificial neural networks, is easy to define. It simply needs to return the input value if greater than 0; otherwise, it returns 0:
>
> **def relu(x):**
>
> **return np.max(0, x)**

4. Define the inputs **(x)** and tunable weights **(theta)** for the neuron. In this example, the inputs **(x)** will be 100 numbers linearly spaced between **-5** and **5**. Set **theta= 1**:

```
theta = 1
x = np.linspace(-5, 5, 100)
x
```

A section of the output is as follows:

```
array([-5.        , -4.8989899 , -4.7979798 , -4.6969697 , -4.5959596 ,
       -4.49494949, -4.39393939, -4.29292929, -4.19191919, -4.09090909,
       -3.98989899, -3.88888889, -3.78787879, -3.68686869, -3.58585859,
       -3.48484848, -3.38383838, -3.28282828, -3.18181818, -3.08080808,
       -2.97979798, -2.87878788, -2.77777778, -2.67676768, -2.57575758,
       -2.47474747, -2.37373737, -2.27272727, -2.17171717, -2.07070707,
       -1.96969697, -1.86868687, -1.76767677, -1.66666667, -1.56565657,
```

Figure 5.7: Printing the inputs

5. Compute the outputs **(y)** of the neuron:

```
y = sigmoid(x * theta)
```

6. Plot the output of the neuron versus the input:

```
fig = plt.figure(figsize=(10, 7))
ax = fig.add_subplot(111)

ax.plot(x, y)
ax.set_xlabel('$x$', fontsize=22);
ax.set_ylabel('$h(x\Theta)$', fontsize=22);
ax.spines['left'].set_position(('data', 0));
ax.spines['top'].set_visible(False);
ax.spines['right'].set_visible(False);
ax.tick_params(axis='both', which='major', labelsize=22)
```

The output is as follows:

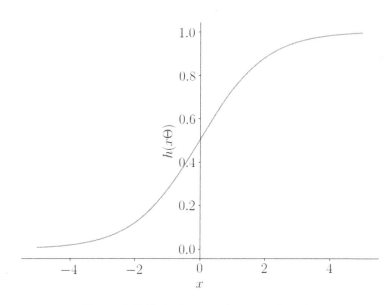

Figure 5.8: Plot of neurons versus inputs

7. Set the tunable parameter, **theta**, to **5**, and recompute and store the output of the neuron:

```
theta = 5
y_2 = sigmoid(x * theta)
```

8. Change the tunable parameter, **theta**, to **0.2**, and recompute and store the output of the neuron:

```
theta = 0.2
y_3 = sigmoid(x * theta)
```

9. Plot the three different output curves of the neuron (**theta** = 1, **theta** = 5, **theta** = 0.2) on one graph:

```
fig = plt.figure(figsize=(10, 7))
ax = fig.add_subplot(111)

ax.plot(x, y, label='$\Theta=1$');
ax.plot(x, y_2, label='$\Theta=5$', linestyle=':');
ax.plot(x, y_3, label='$\Theta=0.2$', linestyle='--');
ax.set_xlabel('$x\Theta$', fontsize=22);
ax.set_ylabel('$h(x\Theta)$', fontsize=22);
ax.spines['left'].set_position(('data', 0));
ax.spines['top'].set_visible(False);
ax.spines['right'].set_visible(False);
ax.tick_params(axis='both', which='major', labelsize=22);
ax.legend(fontsize=22);
```

The output is as follows:

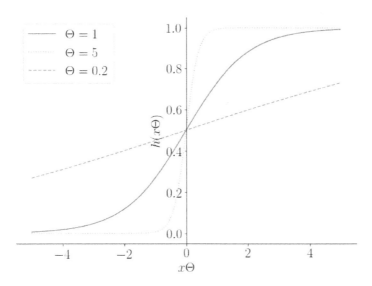

Figure 5.9: Output curves of neurons

In this exercise, we modeled the basic building block of an artificial neural network with a sigmoid activation function. We can see that using the sigmoid function increases the steepness of the gradient and means that only small values of x will push the output to either close to 1 or 0. Similarly, reducing **theta** reduces the sensitivity of the neuron to non-zero values and results in much extreme input values being required to push the result of the output to either 0 or 1, tuning the output of the neuron.

Activity 8: Modeling Neurons with a ReLU Activation Function

In this activity, we will investigate the ReLU activation function and the effect tunable weights have in modifying the output of ReLU units:

1. Import **numpy** and matplotlib.

2. Define the ReLU activation function as a Python function.

3. Define the inputs **(x)** and tunable weights **(theta)** for the neuron. In this example, the inputs **(x)** will be 100 numbers linearly spaced between **-5** and **5**. Set **theta = 1**.

4. Compute the output **(y)**.

5. Plot the output of the neuron versus the input.

6. Now, set **theta = 5**, and recompute and store the output of the neuron.

7. Now, set **theta = 0.2**, and recompute and store the output of the neuron.

8. Plot the three different output curves of the neuron (**theta = 1**, **theta = 5**, and **theta = 0.2**) on one graph.

By the end of this activity, you will have developed a range of response curves for the ReLU activated neuron. You will also be able to describe the effect of changing the value of theta on the output of the neuron. The output will look as follows:

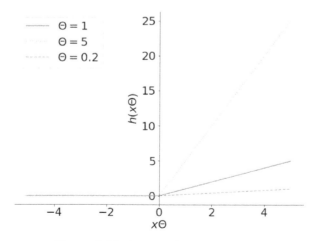

Figure 5.10: Expected output curves

> **Note**
>
> The solution for this activity can be found on page 333.

Neural Networks: Architecture Definition

Individual neurons aren't particularly useful in isolation; they provide an activation function and a means of tuning the output, but a single neuron would have an limited learning ability. Neurons become much more powerful when many of them are combined and connected together in a network structure. By using a number of different neurons and combining the outputs of individual neurons, more complex relationships can be established and more powerful learning algorithms can be built. In this section, we will briefly discuss the structure of a neural network and implement a simple neural network using the Keras machine learning framework (https://keras.io/).

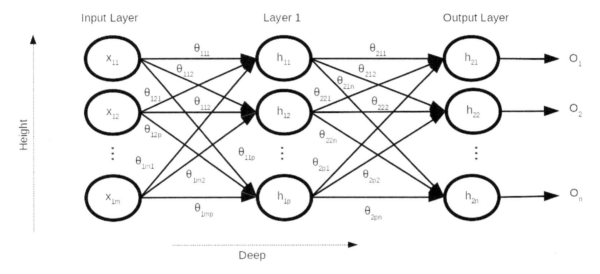

Figure 5.11: Simplified representation of a neural network

Figure 5.11 illustrates the structure of a two-layered, fully-connected neural network. One of the first observations we can make is that there is a lot of information contained within this structure, with a high degree of connectivity as represented by the arrows that point to and from each of the nodes. Working from the left-hand side of the image, we can see the input values to the neural network, as represented by the (x) values. In this example, we have m input values per sample, and only the first sample is being fed into the network, hence, values from X_{11} to X_{1m}. These values are then multiplied by the corresponding weights of the first layer of the neural network ($\theta_{111} - \theta_{1mp}$) before being passed into the activation function of the corresponding neuron. This is known as a **feedforward** neural network. The notation used in *Figure* 5.11 to identify the weights is θ_{ijk}, where i is the layer the weight belongs to, j is the input node number (starting with 1 at the top), and k is the node in the subsequent layer that the weight feeds into.

Looking at the inter-connectivity between the outputs of layer 1 (also known as the **hidden layer**) and the inputs to the output layer, we can see that there is a large number of trainable parameters (weights) that can be used to map the input to the desired output. The network of *Figure 5.11* represents an n class neural network classifier, where the output for each of the n nodes represents the probability of the input belonging to the corresponding class.

Each layer is able to use a different activation function as described by h_1 and h_2, thus allowing different activation functions to be mixed, in which the first layer could use ReLU, the second could use tanh, and the third could use sigmoid, for example. The final output is calculated by taking the sum of the product of the output of the previous layer with the corresponding weights.

If we consider the output of the first node of layer 1, it can be calculated by multiplying the inputs by the corresponding weights, adding the result, and passing it through the activation function:

$$h_{11}(x_{11}\theta_{111} + x_{12}\theta_{121} + \ldots + x_{1m}\theta_{1m1})$$

Figure 5.12: Calculating the output of the last node

As we increase the number of layers between the input and output of the network, we increase the depth of the network. An increase in the depth is also an increase in the number of trainable parameters, as well as the complexity of the relationships within the data, as described by the network. It is, typically, harder to train networks with increased depth because the types of features selected for the input become more critical. Additionally, as we add more neurons to each layer, we increase the height of the neural network. By adding more neurons, the ability of the network to describe the dataset increases as we add more trainable parameters. If too many neurons are added, the network can memorize the dataset but fails to generalize new samples. The trick in constructing neural networks is to find the balance between sufficient complexity to be able to describe the relationships within the data and not be so complicated as to memorize the training samples.

Exercise 19: Defining a Keras Model

In this exercise, we will define a neural network architecture (similar to *Figure 5.11*) using the Keras machine learning framework to classify images for the CIFAR-10 dataset. As each input image is 32 x 32 pixels in size, the input vector will comprise 32*32 = 1,024 values. With 10 individual classes in CIFAR-10, the output of the neural network will be composed of 10 individual values, with each value representing the probability of the input data belonging to the corresponding class.

1. For this exercise, we will require the Keras machine learning framework. Keras is a high-level neural network API that is used on top of an existing library, such as TensorFlow or Theano. Keras makes it easy to switch between lower-level frameworks because the high-level interface it provides remains the same irrespective of the underlying library. In this book, we will be using TensorFlow as the underlying library. If you have yet to install Keras and TensorFlow, do so using **conda**:

```
!conda install tensforflow keras
```

Alternatively, you can install it using **pip**:

```
!pip install tensorflow keras
```

2. We will require the **Sequential** and **Dense** classes from **keras.models** and **keras.layers**, respectively. Import these classes:

```
from keras.models import Sequential
from keras.layers import Dense
```

3. As described earlier, the input layer will receive 1,024 values. The second layer (Layer 1) will have 500 units and, because the network is to classify one of 10 different classes, the output layer will have 10 units. In Keras, a model is defined by passing an ordered list of layers to the **Sequential** model class. This example uses the **Dense** layer class, which is a fully-connected neural network layer. The first layer will use a ReLU activation function, while the output will use the **softmax** function to determine the probability of each class. Define the model:

```
model = Sequential([
    Dense(500, input_shape=(1024,), activation='relu'),
    Dense(10, activation='softmax')
])
```

4. With the model defined, we can use the **summary** method to confirm the structure and the number of trainable parameters (or weights) within the model:

```
model.summary()
```

The output is as follows:

```
Layer (type)                  Output Shape              Param #
=================================================================
dense_1 (Dense)               (None, 500)               512500
_____
dense_2 (Dense)               (None, 10)                5010
=================================================================
Total params: 517,510
Trainable params: 517,510
Non-trainable params: 0
_____
```

Figure 5.13: Structure and count of trainable parameters in the model

This table summarizes the structure of the neural network. We can see that there are the two layers that we specified, with 500 units in the first layer and 10 output units in the second layer. The **Param #** column tells us how many trainable weights are available in that specific layer. The table also tells us that there are 517,510 trainable weights in total within the network.

In this exercise, we created a neural network model in Keras that contains a network of over 500,000 weights that can be used to classify the images of CIFAR-10. In the next section, we will train the model.

Neural Networks: Training

With the neural network model defined, we can begin the training process; at this stage, we will be training the model in a supervised fashion to develop some familiarity with the Keras framework before moving on to training autoencoders. Supervised learning models are trained by providing the model with both the input information as well as the known output; the goal of training is to construct a network that takes the input information and returns the known output using only the parameters of the model.

In a supervised classification example such as CIFAR-10, the input information is an image and the known output is the class that the image belongs to. During training, for each sample prediction, the errors in the feedforward network predictions are calculated using a specified error function. Each of the weights within the model is then tuned in an attempt to reduce the error. This tuning process is known as **back-propagation** because the error is propagated backward through the network from the output to the start of the network.

During back-propagation, each trainable weight is adjusted in proportion to its contribution to the overall error multiplied by a value known as the **learning rate**, which controls the rate of change in the trainable weights. Looking at *Figure 5.14*, we can see that increasing the value of the learning rate can increase the speed at which the error is reduced, but risks not converging on a minimum error as we step over the values. A learning rate that's too small may lead to us running out of patience or simply not having sufficient time to find the global minimum. Thus, finding the correct learning rate is a trial and error process, though starting with a larger learning rate and reducing it can often be a productive method. The following figure represents the selection of the learning rate:

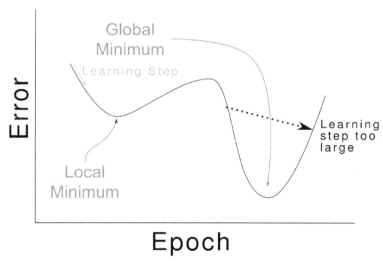

Figure 5.14: Selecting the correct learning rate (one epoch is one learning step)

Training is repeated until the error in the predictions stop reducing or the developer runs out of patience waiting for a result. In order to complete the training process, we first need to make some design decisions, the first being the most appropriate error function. There are a range of error functions available for use, from a simple mean squared difference to more complex options. Categorical cross entropy (which is used in the following exercise) is a very useful error function for classifying more than one class.

With the error function defined, we need to choose the method of updating the trainable parameters using the error function. One of the most memory-efficient and effective update methods is stochastic gradient descent (SGD); there are a number of variants of SGD, all of which involve adjusting each of the weights in accordance with their individual contribution to the calculated error. The final training design decision to be made is the performance metric by which the model is evaluated and the best architecture selected; in a classification problem, this may be the classification accuracy of the model or perhaps the model that produces the lowest error score in a regression problem. These comparisons are generally made using a method of cross-validation.

Exercise 20: Training a Keras Neural Network Model

Thankfully, we don't need to worry about manually programming the components of the neural network, such as backpropagation, because the Keras framework manages this for us. In this exercise, we will use Keras to train a neural network to classify a small subset of the CIFAR-10 dataset using the model architecture defined in the previous exercise. As with all machine learning problems, the first and the most important step is to understand as much as possible about the dataset, and this will be the initial focus of the exercise:

> **Note**
>
> You can download the **data_batch_1** and **batches.meta** files from https://github. com/Train ngByPackt/Applied-Unsupervised-Learning-with-Python/tree/master/ Lesson05/Exercise20.

1. Import **pickle**, **numpy**, **matplotlib** and the **Sequential** class from **keras.models**, and import **Dense** from **keras.layers**:

    ```
    import pickle
    import numpy as np
    import matplotlib.pyplot as plt
    from keras.models import Sequential
    from keras.layers import Dense
    ```

2. Load the sample of the CIFAR-10 dataset that is provided with the accompanying source code in the **data_batch_1** file:

```
with open('data_batch_1', 'rb') as f:
    dat = pickle.load(f, encoding='bytes')
```

3. The data is loaded as a dictionary. Display the keys of the dictionary:

```
dat.keys()
```

The output is as follows:

```
dict_keys([b'batch_label', b'labels', b'data', b'filenames'])
```

4. Note that the keys are stored as binary strings as denoted by **b'**. We are interested in the contents of data and labels. Let's look at labels first:

```
labels = dat[b'labels']
labels
```

The output is as follows:

```
[6,
 9,
 9,
 4,
 1,
 1,
 2,
 7,
 8,
 3,
 4,
 7,
 7
```

Figure 5.15: Displaying the labels

5. We can see that the labels are a list of values 0 – 9, indicating which class each sample belongs to. Now, look at the contents of the **data** key:

    ```
    dat[b'data']
    ```

    The output is as follows:

    ```
    array([[ 59,   43,   50, ...,  140,   84,   72],
           [154,  126,  105, ...,  139,  142,  144],
           [255,  253,  253, ...,   83,   83,   84],
           ...,
           [ 71,   60,   74, ...,   68,   69,   68],
           [250,  254,  211, ...,  215,  255,  254],
           [ 62,   61,   60, ...,  130,  130,  131]], dtype=uint8)
    ```

    Figure 5.16: Content of the data key

6. The data key provides a NumPy array with all the image data stored within the array. What is the shape of the image data?

    ```
    dat[b'data'].shape
    ```

    The output is as follows:

    ```
    (1000, 3072)
    ```

7. We can see that we have 1000 samples, but each sample is a single dimension of 3,072 samples. Aren't the images supposed to be 32 x 32 pixels? Yes, they are, but because the images are color or RGB images, they contain three channels (red, green, and blue), which means the images are 32 x 32 x 3. They are also flattened, providing 3,072 length vectors. So, we can reshape the array and then visualize a sample of images. According to the CIFAR-10 documentation, the first 1,024 samples are red, the second 1,024 are green, and the third 1,024 are blue:

    ```
    images = np.zeros((10000, 32, 32, 3), dtype='uint8')

    for idx, img in enumerate(dat[b'data']):
        images[idx  :, :, 0] = img[:1024].reshape((32, 32)) # Red
        images[idx  :, :, 1] = img[1024:2048].reshape((32, 32)) # Green
        images[idx  :, :, 2] = img[2048:].reshape((32, 32)) # Blue
    ```

8. Display the first 12 images, along with their labels:

```
plt.figure(figsize=(10, 7))
for i in range(12):
    plt.subplot(3, 4, i + 1)
    plt.imshow(images[i])
    plt.title(labels[i])
    plt.axis('off')
```

The output is as follows:

Figure 5.17: The first 12 images

9. What is the actual meaning of the labels? To find out, load the **batches.meta** file:

```
with open('batches.meta', 'rb') as f:
    label_strings = pickle.load(f, encoding='bytes')

label_strings
```

The output is as follows:

```
{b'num_cases_per_batch': 10000,
 b'label_names': [b'airplane',
  b'automobile',
  b'bird',
  b'cat',
  b'deer',
  b'dog',
  b'frog',
  b'horse',
  b'ship',
  b'truck'],
 b'num_vis': 3072}
```

Figure 5.18: Meaning of the labels

10. Decode the binary strings to get the actual labels:

```
actual_labels = [label.decode() for label in label_strings[b'label_
names']]
actual_labels
```

The output is as follows:

```
['airplane',
 'automobile',
 'bird',
 'cat',
 'deer',
 'dog',
 'frog',
 'horse',
 'ship',
 'truck']
```

Figure 5.19: Printing the actual labels

11. Print the labels for the first 12 images:

```
for lab in labels[:12]:
    print(actual_labels[lab], end=', ')
```

The output is as follows:

```
frog, truck, truck, deer, automobile, automobile, bird, horse, ship, cat,
deer, horse,
```

Figure 5.20: Labels of the first 12 images

12. Now we need to prepare the data for training the model. The first step is to prepare the output. Currently, the output is a list of numbers 0 – 9, but we need each sample to be represented as a vector of 10 units as per the previous model. The encoded output will be a NumPy array with a shape of 10000 x 10:

> **Note**
>
> This is known as one hot encoding, where for each sample, there are as many columns as the possible classes, and the identified class is indicated by a 1 in the appropriate column. As an example, say we had the labels [3, 2, 1, 3, 1] with 4 possible classes; the corresponding one hot encoded value would be as follows:
>
> ```
> array([[0., 0., 0., 1.],
>
>        [0., 0., 1., 0.],
>
>        [0., 1., 0., 0.],
>
>        [0., 0., 0., 1 ],
>
>        [0., 0., 1., 0.]])
> ```

```
one_hot_labels = np.zeros((images.shape[0], 10))

for idx, lab in enumerate(labels):
    one_hot_labels[idx, lab] = 1
```

13. Display the one hot encoding values for the first 12 samples:

```
one_hot_labels[:12]
```

The output is as follows:

```
array [[0., 0., 0., 0., 0., 0., 1., 0., 0., 0.],
       [0., 0., 0., 0., 0., 0., 0., 0., 0., 1.],
       [0., 0., 0., 0., 0., 0., 0., 0., 0., 1.],
       [0., 0., 0., 0., 1., 0., 0., 0., 0., 0.],
       [0., 1., 0., 0., 0., 0., 0., 0., 0., 0.],
       [0., 1., 0., 0., 0., 0., 0., 0., 0., 0.],
       [0., 0., 1., 0., 0., 0., 0., 0., 0., 0.],
       [0., 0., 0., 0., 0., 0., 0., 1., 0., 0.],
       [0., 0., 0., 0., 0., 0., 0., 0., 1., 0.],
       [0., 0., 0., 1., 0., 0., 0., 0., 0., 0.],
       [0., 0., 0., 0., 1., 0., 0., 0., 0., 0.],
       [0., 0., 0., 0., 0., 0., 0., 1., 0., 0.]])
```

Figure 5.21: One hot encoding values for first 12 samples

14. The model has 1,024 inputs because it expects a 32 x 32 grayscale image. Take the average of the three channels for each image to convert it to RGB:

```
images = images.mean(axis=-1)
```

15. Display the first 12 images again:

```
plt.figure(figsize=(10, 7))
for i in range(12):
    plt.subplot(3, 4, i + 1)
    plt.imshow(images[i], cmap='gray')
    plt.title(labels[i])
    plt.axis('off')
```

The output is as follows:

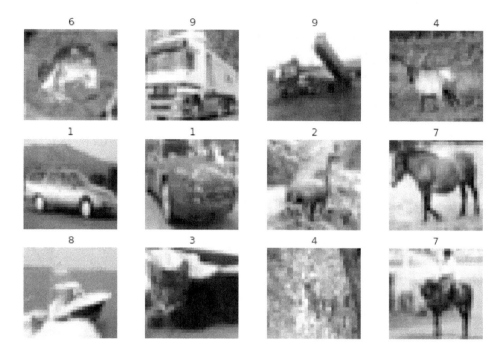

Figure 5.22: Displaying the first 12 images again.

16. Finally, scale the images to be between 0 and 1, which is required for all inputs to a neural network. As the maximum value in an image is 255, we will simply divide by 255:

```
images /= 255.
```

17. We also need the images to be in the shape 10,000 x 1,024:

```
images = images.reshape((-1, 32 ** 2))
```

18. Redefine the model with the same architecture as *Exercise 19*, *Defining a Keras Model*:

```
model = Sequential([
    Dense(500, input_shape=(1024,), activation='relu'),
    Dense(10, activation='softmax')

])
```

19. Now we can train the model in Keras. We first need to compile the method to specify the training parameters. We will be using categorical cross-entropy, with stochastic gradient descent and a performance metric of classification accuracy:

```
model.compile(loss='categorical_crossentropy',
              optimizer='sgd',
              metrics=['accuracy'])
```

20. Train the model using back-propagation for 100 epochs and the **fit** method of the model:

```
model.fit(images, one_hot_labels, epochs=100)
```

The output is as follows:

```
Epoch 97/100
10000/10000 [==============================] - 2s 178us/step - loss: 0.4526 - acc: 0.8824
Epoch 98/100
10000/10000 [==============================] - 2s 176us/step - loss: 0.4488 - acc: 0.8871
Epoch 99/100
10000/10000 [==============================] - 2s 174us/step - loss: 0.4384 - acc: 0.8940
Epoch 100/100
10000/10000 [==============================] - 2s 170us/step - loss: 0.4322 - acc: 0.8955

<keras.callbacks.History at 0x7f12b3c7b978>
```

Figure 5.23: Training the model

21. We achieved approximately 90% classification accuracy for the 1,000 samples using this network. Examine the predictions made for the first 12 samples again:

```
predictions = model.predict(images[:12])
predictions
```

The output is as follows:

```
array([[2.72101886e-03, 2.82521220e-03, 5.80681080e-04, 2.00835592e-03,
        4.87272721e-03, 1.73771027e-02, 9.62930799e-01, 5.69747109e-03,
        7.23911216e-04, 2.62686226e-04],
       [3.00214846e-04, 1.14106536e-01, 4.17048521e-02, 1.38805415e-02,
        4.82545962e-04, 3.11067980e-02, 1.02459533e-04, 2.45292974e-03,
        6.33396162e-03, 7.89529204e-01],
       [1.38785226e-05, 7.90050399e-05, 4.03187078e-05, 1.66309916e-03,
        3.49369337e-04, 3.01616683e-06, 5.77264291e-06, 3.29075777e-03,
        2.98287741e-05, 9.94524956e-01]],
```

Figure 5.24: Printing the predictions

22. We can use the **argmax** method to determine the most likely class for each sample:

```
np.argmax(predictions, axis=1)
```

The output is as follows:

```
array([6, 9, 9, 4, 1, 1, 2, 7, 8, 3, 2, 7])
```

23. Compare with the labels:

```
labels[:12]
```

The output is as follows:

```
[6, 9, 9, 4, 1, 1, 2, 7, 8, 3, 4, 7]
```

The network made one error in these samples, that is, it classified the second last samples as a 2 (bird) instead of a 4 (deer). Congratulations! You have just successfully trained a neural network model in Keras. Complete the next activity to further reinforce your skills in training neural networks.

Activity 9: MNIST Neural Network

In this activity, you will train a neural network to identify images in the MNIST dataset and reinforce your skills in training neural networks. This activity forms the basis of many neural network architectures in different classification problems, particularly in computer vision. From object detection and identification to classification, this general structure is used in a variety of applications.

These steps will help you complete the activity:

1. Import **pickle**, **numpy**, **matplotlib**, and the **Sequential** and **Dense** classes from Keras.

2. Load the **mnist.pkl** file that contains the first 10,000 images and the corresponding labels from the MNIST dataset that are available in the accompanying source code. The MNIST dataset is a series of 28 x 28 grayscale images of handwritten digits, 0 through 9. Extract the images and labels.

> **Note**
>
> You can find the **mnist.pkl** file at https://github.com/TrainingByPackt/Applied-Unsupervised-Learning-with-Python/tree/master/Lesson05/Activity09.

3. Plot the first 10 samples along with the corresponding labels.

4. Encode the labels using one hot encoding.

5. Prepare the images for input into a neural network. As a hint, there are **two** separate steps in this process.

6. Construct a neural network model in Keras that accepts the prepared images and has a hidden layer of 600 units with a ReLU activation function and an output of the same number of units as classes. The output layer uses a **softmax** activation function.

7. Compile the model using multiclass cross-entropy, stochastic gradient descent, and an accuracy performance metric.

8. Train the model. How many epochs are required to achieve at least 95% classification accuracy on the training data?

By completing this activity, you have trained a simple neural network to identify handwritten digits 0 through 9. You have also developed a general framework for building neural networks for classification problems. With this framework, you can extend upon and modify the network for a range of other tasks.

> **Note**
>
> The solution for his activity can be found on page 335.

Autoencoders

Now that we are comfortable developing supervised neural network models in Keras, we can return our attention to unsupervised learning and the main subject of this chapter—autoencoders. Autoencoders are a specifically designed neural network architecture that aims to compress the input information into lower dimensional space in an efficient yet descriptive manner. Autoencoder networks can be decomposed into two individual sub-networks or stages: an **encoding** stage and a **decoding** stage. The first, or encoding, stage takes the input information and compresses it through a subsequent layer that has fewer units than the size of the input sample. The latter stage, that is, the decoding stage, then expands the compressed form of the image and aims to return the compressed data to its original form. As such, the inputs and desired outputs of the network are the same; the network takes, say, an image in the CIFAR-10 dataset and tries to return the same image. This network architecture is shown in *Figure 5.25*; in this image, we can see that the encoding stage of the autoencoder reduces the number of neurons to represent the information, while the decoding stage takes the compressed format and returns it to its original state. The use of the decoding stage helps to ensure that the encoder has correctly represented the information, because the compressed representation is all that is provided to restore the image in its original state. We will now work through a simplified autoencoder model using the CIFAR-10 dataset:

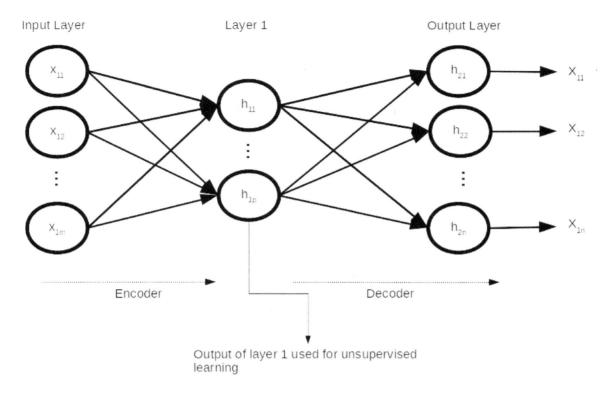

Figure 5.25: Simple autoencoder network architecture

Exercise 21: Simple Autoencoder

In this exercise, we will construct a simple autoencoder for the sample of the CIFAR-10 dataset, compressing the information stored within the images for later use.

> **Note**
>
> You can download the **data_batch_1** file from https://github.com/TrainingByPackt/ Applied-Unsupervised-Learning-with-Python/tree/master/Lesson05/Exercise21.

1. Import **pickle**, **numpy**, and **matplotlib**, as well as the **Model** class from **keras.models**, and import **Input** and **Dense** from **keras.layers**:

```
import pickle
import numpy as np
import matplotlib.pyplot as plt
from keras.models import Model
from keras.layers import Input, Dense
```

2. Load the data:

```
with open('data_batch_1', 'rb') as f:
    dat = pickle.load(f, encoding='bytes')
```

3. As this is an unsupervised learning method, we are only interested in the image data. Load the image data as per the previous exercise:

```
images = np.zeros((10000, 32, 32, 3), dtype='uint8')

for idx, img in enumerate(dat[b'data']):
    images[idx, :, :, 0] = img[:1024].reshape((32, 32)) # Red
    images[idx, :, :, 1] = img[1024:2048].reshape((32, 32)) # Green
    images[idx, :, :, 2] = img[2048:].reshape((32, 32)) # Blue
```

4. Convert the image to grayscale, scale between 0 and 1, and flatten each to a single 1,024 length vector:

```
images = images.mean(axis=-1)
images = images / 255.0
images = images.reshape((-1, 32 ** 2))
images
```

5. Define the autoencoder model. As we need access to the output of the encoder stage, we will need to define the model using a slightly different method to that previously used. Define an input layer of **1024** units:

```
input_layer = Input(shape=(1024,))
```

6. Define a subsequent **Dense** layer of **256** units (a compression ratio of 1024/256 = 4) and a ReLU activation function as the encoding stage. Note that we have assigned the layer to a variable and passed the previous layer to a call method for the class:

```
encoding_stage = Dense(256, activation='relu')(input_layer)
```

7. Define a subsequent decoder layer using the sigmoid function as an activation function and the same shape as the input layer. The sigmoid function has been selected because the input values to the network are only between 0 and 1:

```
decoding_stage = Dense(1024, activation='sigmoid')(encoding_stage)
```

8. Construct the model by passing the first and last layers of the network to the **Model** class:

```
autoencoder = Model(input_layer, decoding_stage)
```

9. Compile the autoencoder using a binary cross-entropy loss function and adadelta gradient descent:

```
autoencoder.compile(loss='binary_crossentropy',
                    optimizer='adadelta')
```

> **Note**
>
> **adadelta** is a more sophisticated version of stochastic gradient descent where the learning rate is adjusted on the basis of a window of recent gradient updates. Compared to the other methods of modifying the learning rate, this prevents the gradient of very old epochs from influencing the learning rate.

10. Now, let's fit the model; again, we pass the images as the training data and as the desired output. Train for 100 epochs:

```
autoencoder.fit(images, images, epochs=100)
```

The output is as follows:

```
Epoch 95/100
10000/10000 [==============================] - 4s 416us/step - loss: 0.5779
Epoch 96/100
10000/10000 [==============================] - 4s 418us/step - loss: 0.5777
Epoch 97/100
10000/10000 [==============================] - 4s 434us/step - loss: 0.5778
Epoch 98/100
10000/10000 [==============================] - 4s 428us/step - loss: 0.5776
Epoch 99/100
10000/10000 [==============================] - 4s 438us/step - loss: 0.5775
Epoch 100/100
10000/10000 [==============================] - 4s 404us/step - loss: 0.5775

<keras.callbacks.History at 0x7fb44d6fe8d0>
```

Figure 5.26: Training the model

11. Calculate and store the output of the encoding stage for the first five samples:

```
encoder_output = Model(input_layer, encoding_stage).predict(images[:5])
```

12. Reshape the encoder output to 16 x 16 (16 x 16 = 256) pixels and multiply by 255:

```
encoder_output = encoder_output.reshape((-1, 16, 16)) * 255
```

13. Calculate and store the output of the decoding stage for the first five samples:

```
decoder_output = autoencoder.predict(images[:5])
```

14. Reshape the output of the decoder to 32 x 32 and multiply by 255:

```
decoder_output = decoder_output.reshape((-1, 32,32)) * 255
```

15. Reshape the original images:

```
images = images.reshape((-1, 32, 32))
plt.figure(figsize=(10, 7))
for i in range(5):
    plt.subplot(3, 5, i + 1)
    plt.imshow(images[i], cmap='gray')
    plt.axis('off')

    plt.subplot(3, 5, i + 6)
    plt.imshow(encoder_output[i], cmap='gray')
    plt.axis('off')

    plt.subplot(3, 5, i + 11)
    plt.imshow(decoder_output[i], cmap='gray')
    plt.axis('off')
```

The output is as follows:

Figure 5.27: Output of simple autoencoder

In *Figure* 5.27, we can see three rows of images. The first row is the original grayscale image, the second row is the corresponding autoencoder output for the original image, and finally, the third row is the reconstruction of the original image from the encoded input. We can see that the decoded images in the third row contain information about the basic shape of the image; we can see the main body of the frog and the deer, as well as the outline of the trucks and cars in the sample. Given that we only trained the model for 100 samples, this exercise would also benefit from an increase in the number of training epochs to further improve the performance of both the encoder and decoder. Now that we have the output of the autoencoder stage trained, we can use it as the feature vector for other unsupervised algorithms, such as K-means or K nearest neighbors.

Activity 10: Simple MNIST Autoencoder

In this activity, you will create an autoencoder network for the MNIST dataset contained within the accompanying source code. An autoencoder network such as the one built in this activity can be an extremely useful in the pre-processing stage of unsupervised learning. The encoded information produced by the network can be used in clustering or segmentation analysis, such as image-based web searches:

1. Import **pickle**, **numpy**, and **matplotlib**, and the **Model**, **Input**, and **Dense** classes from Keras.

2. Load the images from the supplied sample of the MNIST dataset that is provided with the accompanying source code (**mnist.pkl**).

> **Note**
>
> You can download the **mnist.pklP-code** file from https://github.com/ TrainingByPackt/Applied-Unsupervised-Learning-with-Python/tree/master/ Lesson05/Activity10.

3. Prepare the images for input into a neural network. As a hint, there are **two** separate steps in this process.

4. Construct a simple autoencoder network that reduces the image size to 10 x 10 after the encoding stage.

5. Compile the autoencoder using a binary cross-entropy loss function and **adadelta** gradient descent.

6. Fit the encoder model.

7. Calculate and store the output of the encoding stage for the first five samples.

8. Reshape the encoder output to 10 x 10 (10 x 10 = 100) pixels and multiply by 255.

9. Calculate and store the output of the decoding stage for the first five samples.

10. Reshape the output of the decoder to 28 x 28 and multiply by 255.

11. Plot the original image, the encoder output, and the decoder.

In completing this activity, you will have successfully trained an autoencoder network that extracts the critical information from the dataset, preparing it for later processing. The output will be similar to the following:

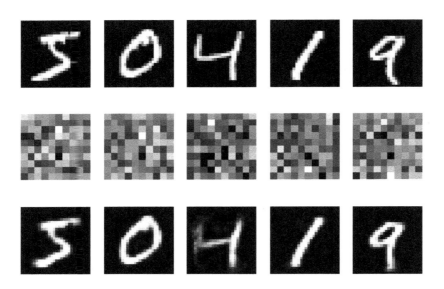

Figure 5.28: Expected plot of original image, the encoder output, and the decoder

Note

The solution for this activity can be found on page 338.

Exercise 22: Multi-Layer Autoencoder

In this exercise, we will construct a multi-layer autoencoder for the sample of the CIFAR-10 dataset, compressing the information stored within the images for later use:

> **Note**
>
> You can download the **data_batch_1** file from https://github.com/TrainingByPackt/Applied-Unsupervised-Learning-with-Python/tree/master/Lesson05/Exercise22.

1. Import **pickle**, **numpy**, and **matplotlib**, as well as the **Model** class from **keras.models**, and import **Input** and **Dense** from **keras.layers**:

```
import pickle
import numpy as np
import matplotlib.pyplot as plt
from keras.models import Model
from keras.layers import Input, Dense
```

2. Load the data:

```
with open('data_batch_1', 'rb') as f:
    dat = pickle.load(f, encoding='bytes')
```

3. As this is an unsupervised learning method, we are only interested in the image data. Load the image data as per the previous exercise:

```
images = np.zeros((10000, 32, 32, 3), dtype='uint8')

for idx, img in enumerate(dat[b'data']):
    images[idx, :, :, 0] = img[:1024].reshape((32, 32)) # Red
    images[idx, :, :, 1] = img[1024:2048].reshape((32, 32)) # Green
    images[idx, :, :, 2] = img[2048:].reshape((32, 32)) # Blue
```

4. Convert the image to grayscale, scale between 0 and 1, and flatten each to a single 1,024 length vector:

```
images = images.mean(axis=-1)
images = images / 255.0
images = images.reshape((-1, 32 ** 2))
images
```

5. Define the multi-layer autoencoder model. We will use the same shape input as the simple autoencoder model:

```
input_layer = Input(shape=(1024,))
```

6. We will add another layer before the 256 autoencoder stage, this time with 512 neurons:

```
hidden_encoding = Dense(512, activation='relu')(input_layer)
```

7. Using the same size autoencoder as the previous exercise, but the input to the layer is the **hidden_encoding** layer this time:

```
encoding_stage = Dense(256, activation='relu')(hidden_encoding)
```

8. Add a decoding hidden layer:

```
hidden_decoding = Dense(512, activation='relu')(encoding_stage)
```

9. Use the same output stage as in the previous exercise, this time connected to the hidden decoding stage:

```
decoding_stage = Dense(1024, activation='sigmoid')(hidden_decoding)
```

10. Construct the model by passing the first and last layers of the network to the **Model** class:

```
autoencoder = Model(input_layer, decoding_stage)
```

11. Compile the autoencoder using a binary cross-entropy loss function and **adadelta** gradient descent:

```
autoencoder.compile(loss='binary_crossentropy',
                 optimizer='adadelta')
```

12. Now, let's fit the model; again, we pass the images as the training data and as the desired output. Train for 100 epochs:

```
autoencoder.fit(images, images, epochs=100)
```

The output is as follows:

```
Epoch 93/100
10000/10000 [==============================] - 9s 945us/step - loss: 0.5805
Epoch 94/100
10000/10000 [==============================] - 10s 965us/step - loss: 0.5806
Epoch 95/100
10000/10000 [==============================] - 10s 969us/step - loss: 0.5807
Epoch 96/100
10000/10000 [==============================] - 10s 968us/step - loss: 0.5804
Epoch 97/100
10000/10000 [==============================] - 10s 1ms/step - loss: 0.5803
Epoch 98/100
10000/10000 [==============================] - 10s 971us/step - loss: 0.5804
Epoch 99/100
10000/10000 [==============================] - 10s 970us/step - loss: 0.5802
Epoch 100/100
10000/10000 [==============================] - 10s 972us/step - loss: 0.5799
```

Figure 5.29: Training the model

13. Calculate and store the output of the encoding stage for the first five samples:

```
encoder_output = Model(input_stage, encoding_stage).predict(images[:5])
```

14. Reshape the encoder output to 10 x 10 (10 x 10 = 100) pixels and multiply by 255:

```
encoder_output = encoder_output.reshape((-1, 10, 10)) * 255
```

15. Calculate and store the output of the decoding stage for the first five samples:

```
decoder_output = autoencoder.predict(images[:5])
```

16. Reshape the output of the decoder to 28 x 28 and multiply by 255:

```
decoder_output = decoder_output.reshape((-1, 28, 28)) * 255
```

17. Plot the original image, the encoder output, and the decoder:

```
images = images.reshape((-1, 28, 28))
plt.figure(figsize=(10, 7))
for i in range(5):
    plt.subplot(3, 5, i + 1)
    plt.imshow(images[i], cmap='gray')
    plt.axis('off')
```

```
plt.subplot(3, 5, i + 6)
plt.imshow(encoder_output[i], cmap='gray')
plt.axis('off')

plt.subplot(3, 5, i + 11)
plt.imshow(decoder_output[i], cmap='gray')
plt.axis('off')
```

The output is as follows:

Figure 5.30: Output of multi-layer autoencoder

By looking at the error score produced by both the simple and multilayer autoencoders and by comparing *Figure* 5.27 and *Figure* 5.30, we can see that there is little difference between the output of the two encoder structures. The middle row of both figures show that the features learned by the two models are, in fact, different. There are a number of options we can use to improve both of these models, such as training for more epochs, using a different number of units or neurons in the layers, or using varying numbers of layers. This exercise was constructed to demonstrate how to build and use an autoencoder, but optimization is often a process of systematic trial and error. We encourage you to adjust some of the parameters of the model and investigate the different results for yourself.

Convolutional Neural Networks

In constructing all of our previous neural network models, you would have noticed that we removed all the color information when converting the image to grayscale, and then flattened each image into a single vector of length 1,024. In doing so, we essentially threw out a lot of information that may be of use to us. The colors in the images may be specific to the class or objects in the image; additionally, we lost a lot of our spatial information about the image, for example, the position of the trailer in the truck image relative to the cab or the legs of the deer relative to the head. Convolutional neural networks do not suffer from this information loss. This is because rather than using a flat structure of trainable parameters, they store the weights in a grid or matrix, which means that each group of parameters can have many layers in their structure. By organizing the weights in a grid, we prevent the loss of spatial information because the weights are applied in a sliding fashion across the image. Also, by having many layers, we can retain the color channels associated with the image.

In developing convolutional neural-network-based autoencoders, the MaxPooling2D and Upsampling2D layers are very important. The MaxPooling 2D layer downsamples or reduces the size of an input matrix in two dimensions by selecting the maximum value within a window of the input. Say we had a 2 x 2 matrix, where three cells have a value of 1 and one single cell has a value of 2:

1	1
1	2

Figure 5.31: Demonstration of sample matrix

If provided to the MaxPooling2D layer, this matrix would return a single value of 2, thus reducing the size of the input in both directions by one half.

The UpSampling2D layer has the opposite effect as that of the MaxPooling2D layer, increasing the size of the input rather than reducing it. The upsampling process repeats the rows and columns of the data, thus doubling the size of the input matrix.

Exercise 23: Convolutional Autoencoder

In this exercise, we will develop a convolutional neural-network-based autoencoder and compare the performance to the previous fully-connected neural network autoencoder:

> **Note**
>
> You can download the **data_batch_1** file from https://github.com/TrainingByPackt/ Applied-Unsupervised-Learning-with-Python/tree/master/Lesson05/Exercise23.

1. Import **pickle**, **numpy**, and **matplotlib**, as well as the **Model** class from **keras.models**, and import **Input**, **Conv2D**, **MaxPooling2D**, and **UpSampling2D** from **keras.layers**:

```
import pickle
import numpy as np
import matplotlib.pyplot as plt
from keras.models import Model
from keras.layers import Input, Conv2D, MaxPooling2D, UpSampling2D
```

2. Load the data:

```
with open('data_batch_1', 'rb') as f:
    dat = pickle.load(f, encoding='bytes')
```

3. As this is an unsupervised learning method, we are only interested in the image data. Load the image data as per the previous exercise:

```
images = np.zeros((10000, 32, 32, 3), dtype='uint8')

for idx, img in enumerate(dat[b'data']):
    images[idx, :, :, 0] = img[:1024].reshape((32, 32)) # Red
    images[idx, :, :, 1] = img[1024:2048].reshape((32, 32)) # Green
    images[idx, :, :, 2] = img[2048:].reshape((32, 32)) # Blue
```

4. As we are using a convolutional network, we can use the images with only rescaling:

```
images = images / 255.
```

5. Define the convolutional autoencoder model. We will use the same shape input as an image:

```
input_layer = Input(shape=(32, 32, 3,))
```

6. Add a convolutional stage with 32 layers or filters, a 3 x 3 weight matrix, a ReLU activation function, and using the same padding, which means the output has the same length as the input image:

> **Note**
>
> Conv2D convolutional layers are the two-dimensional equivalent of weights in a fully-connected neural network. The weights exist in a series of 2D weight filters or layers, which are then convolved with the input of the layer.

```
hidden_encoding = Conv2D(
    32, # Number of layers or filters in the weight matrix
    (3, 3), # Shape of the weight matrix
    activation='relu',
    padding='same', # How to apply the weights to the images
)(input_layer)
```

7. Add a max pooling layer to the encoder with a 2 x 2 kernel. **MaxPooling** looks at all the values in an image, scanning through with a 2 x 2 matrix. The maximum value in each 2 x 2 area is returned, thus reducing the size of the encoded layer by a half:

```
encoded = MaxPooling2D((2, 2))(hidden_encoding)
```

8. Add a decoding convolutional layer (this layer should be identical to the previous convolutional layer):

```
hidden_decoding = Conv2D(
    32, # Number of layers or filters in the weight matrix
    (3, 3), # Shape of the weight matrix
    activation='relu',
    padding='same', # How to apply the weights to the images
)(encoded)
```

9. Now we need to return the image to its original size, for which we will upsample by the same size as **MaxPooling2D**:

```
upsample_decoding = UpSampling2D((2, 2))(hidden_decoding)
```

10. Add the final convolutional stage using three layers for the RGB channels of the images:

```
decoded = Conv2D(
    3, # Number of layers or filters in the weight matrix
    (3, 3), # Shape of the weight matrix
    activation='sigmoid',
    padding='same', # How to apply the weights to the images
)(upsample_decoding)
```

11. Construct the model by passing the first and last layers of the network to the **Model** class:

```
autoencoder = Model(input_layer, decoded)
```

12. Display the structure of the model:

```
autoencoder.summary()
```

Note that we have far fewer trainable parameters as compared to the previous autoencoder examples. This has been a specific design decision to ensure that the example runs on a wide variety of hardware. Convolutional networks typically require a lot more processing power and often special hardware such as Graphical Processing Units (GPUs).

13. Compile the autoencoder using a binary cross-entropy loss function and **adadelta** gradient descent:

```
autoencoder.compile(loss='binary_crossentropy',
            optimizer='adadelta')
```

14. Now, let's fit the model; again, we pass the images as the training data and as the desired output. Train for 20 epochs, because convolutional networks take a lot longer to compute:

```
autoencoder.fit(images, images, epochs=20)
```

The output is as follows:

```
Epoch 1/20
10000/10000 [==============================] - 21s 2ms/step - loss: 0.5934
Epoch 2/20
10000/10000 [==============================] - 21s 2ms/step - loss: 0.5687
Epoch 3/20
10000/10000 [==============================] - 22s 2ms/step - loss: 0.5633
Epoch 4/20
10000/10000 [==============================] - 21s 2ms/step - loss: 0.5602
Epoch 5/20
10000/10000 [==============================] - 21s 2ms/step - loss: 0.5590:
Epoch 6/20
10000/10000 [==============================] - 21s 2ms/step - loss: 0.5581
Epoch 7/20
10000/10000 [==============================] - 21s 2ms/step - loss: 0.5578
Epoch 8/20
10000/10000 [==============================] - 21s 2ms/step - loss: 0.5572
Epoch 9/20
10000/10000 [==============================] - 21s 2ms/step - loss: 0.5566
Epoch 10/20
10000/10000 [==============================] - 21s 2ms/step - loss: 0.5557
Epoch 11/20
10000/10000 [==============================] - 21s 2ms/step - loss: 0.5553
Epoch 12/20
10000/10000 [==============================] - 21s 2ms/step - loss: 0.5552
Epoch 13/20
10000/10000 [==============================] - 21s 2ms/step - loss: 0.5551
Epoch 14/20
10000/10000 [==============================] - 22s 2ms/step - loss: 0.5543
Epoch 15/20
10000/10000 [==============================] - 22s 2ms/step - loss: 0.5544
Epoch 16/20
10000/10000 [==============================] - 22s 2ms/step - loss: 0.5548
Epoch 17/20
10000/10000 [==============================] - 22s 2ms/step - loss: 0.5541
Epoch 18/20
10000/10000 [==============================] - 22s 2ms/step - loss: 0.5539
Epoch 19/20
10000/10000 [==============================] - 22s 2ms/step - loss: 0.5538
Epoch 20/20
10000/10000 [==============================] - 22s 2ms/step - loss: 0.5539
```

Figure 5.32: Training the model

Note that the error was already less than in the previous autoencoder exercise after the second epoch, suggesting a better encoding/decoding model. This reduced error can be mostly attributed to the fact that the convolutional neural network did not discard a lot of data, and the encoded images are 16 x 16 x 32, which is significantly larger than the previous 16 x 16 size. Additionally, we have not compressed the images per se as they now contain fewer pixels (16 x 16 x 32 = 8,192), but with more depth (32 x 32 x 3,072) than before. This information has been rearranged to allow more effective encoding/decoding processes.

15. Calculate and store the output of the encoding stage for the first five samples:

```
encoder_output = Model(input_layer, encoded).predict(images[:5])
```

16. Each encoded image has a shape of 16 x 16 x 32 due to the number of filters selected for the convolutional stage. As such, we cannot visualize them without modification. We will reshape them to be 256 x 32 in size for visualization:

```
encoder_output = encoder_output.reshape((-1, 256, 32))
```

17. Get the output of the decoder for the first five images:

```
decoder_output = autoencoder.predict(images[:5])
```

18. Plot the original image, the mean encoder output, and the decoder:

```
plt.figure(figsize=(10, 7))
for i in range(5):
    plt.subplot(3, 5, i + 1)
    plt.imshow(images[i], cmap='gray')
    plt.axis('off')

    plt.subplot(3, 5, i + 6)
    plt.imshow(encoder_output[i], cmap='gray')
    plt.axis('off')

    plt.subplot(3, 5, i + 11)
    plt.imshow(decoder_output[i])
    plt.axis('off')
```

The output is as follows:

Figure 5.33: The original image, the encoder output, and the decoder

Activity 11: MNIST Convolutional Autoencoder

In this activity, we will reinforce our knowledge of convolutional autoencoders using the MNIST dataset. Convolutional autoencoders typically achieve significantly improved performance when working with image-based datasets of a reasonable size. This is particularly useful when using autoencoders to generate artificial image samples:

1. Import **pickle**, **numpy**, and **matplotlib**, as well as the **Model** class from **keras.models**, and import **Input**, **Conv2D**, **MaxPooling2D**, and **UpSampling2D** from **keras.layers**.

2. Load the **mnist.pkl** file, which contains the first 10,000 images and corresponding labels from the MNIST dataset, which are available in the accompanying source code.

> **Note**
>
> You can download the **mnist.pkl** file from https://github.com/TrainingByPackt/Applied-Unsupervised-Learning-with-Python/tree/master/Lesson05/Activity11.

3. Rescale the images to have values between 0 and 1.

4. We need to reshape the images to add a single depth channel for use with convolutional stages. Reshape the images to have a shape of 28 x 28 x 1.

5. Define an input layer. We will use the same shape input as an image.

6. Add a convolutional stage, with 16 layers or filters, a 3 x 3 weight matrix, a ReLU activation function, and using same padding, which means the output has the same length as the input image.

7. Add a max pooling layer to the encoder with a 2 x 2 kernel.

8. Add a decoding convolutional layer.

9. Add an upsampling layer.

10. Add the final convolutional stage using 1 layer as per the initial image depth.

11. Construct the model by passing the first and last layers of the network to the **Model** class.

12. Display the structure of the model.

13. Compile the autoencoder using a binary cross-entropy loss function and **adadelta** gradient descent.

14. Now, let's fit the model; again, we pass the images as the training data and as the desired output. Train for 20 epochs as convolutional networks take a lot longer to compute.

15. Calculate and store the output of the encoding stage for the first five samples.

16. Reshape the encoder output for visualization, where each image is X*Y in size.

17. Get the output of the decoder for the first five images.

18. Reshape the decoder output to be 28 x 28 in size.

19. Reshape the original images back to be 28 x 28 in size.

20. Plot the original image, the mean encoder output, and the decoder.

At the end of this activity, you will have developed an autoencoder comprising convolutional layers within the neural network. Note the improvements made in the decoder representations. The output will be similar to the following:

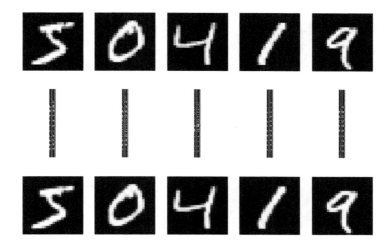

Figure 5.34: Expected original image, the encoder output, and the decoder

> **Note**
>
> The solution for this activity can be found on page 340.

Summary

In this chapter, we started with an introduction to artificial neural networks, how they are structured, and the processes by which they learn to complete a particular task. Starting with a supervised learning example, we built an artificial neural network classifier to identify objects within the CIFAR-10 dataset. We then progressed to the autoencoder architecture of neural networks and learned how we can use these networks to prepare a dataset for use in an unsupervised learning problem. Finally, we completed this investigation with autoencoders, looking at convolutional neural networks and the benefits these additional layers can provide. This chapter prepared us well for the final instalment in dimensionality reduction, as we look at using and visualizing the encoded data with t-distributed nearest neighbors (t-SNE). T-distributed nearest neighbors provides an extremely effective method of visualizing high-dimensional data even after applying reduction techniques such as PCA. T-SNE is particularly useful method for unsupervised learning.

t-Distributed Stochastic Neighbor Embedding (t-SNE)

Learning Objectives

By the end of this chapter, you will be able to:

- Describe and understand the motivation behind t-SNE
- Describe the derivation of SNE and t-SNE
- Implement t-SNE models in scikit-learn
- Explain the limitations of t-SNE

In this chapter, we will discuss Stochastic Neighbor Embedding (SNE) and t-Distributed Stochastic Neighbor Embedding (t-SNE) as a means of visualizing high-dimensional datasets.

Introduction

This chapter is the final instalment in the micro-series on dimensionality reduction techniques and transformations. Our previous chapters in this series have described a number of different methods for reducing the dimensionality of a dataset as a means of either cleaning the data, reducing its size for computational efficiency, or for extracting the most important information available within the dataset. While we have demonstrated many methods for reducing high-dimensional datasets, in many cases, we are unable to reduce the number of dimensions to a size that can be visualized, that is, two or three dimensions, without excessively degrading the quality of the data. Consider the MNIST dataset that we used in *Chapter* 5, *Autoencoders*, which is a collection of digitized handwritten digits of the numbers 0 through 9. Each image is 28 x 28 pixels in size, providing 784 individual dimensions or features. If we were to reduce these 784 dimensions down to 2 or 3 for visualization purposes, we would lose almost all the available information.

In this chapter, we will discuss Stochastic Neighbor Embedding (SNE) and t-Distributed Stochastic Neighbor Embedding (t-SNE) as a means of visualizing high-dimensional datasets. These techniques are extremely helpful in unsupervised learning and the design of machine learning systems because the visualization of data is a powerful tool. Being able to visualize data allows relationships to be explored, groups to be identified, and results to be validated. t-SNE techniques have been used to visualize cancerous cell nuclei that have over 30 characteristics of interest, whereas data from documents can have over thousands of dimensions, sometimes even after applying techniques such as PCA.

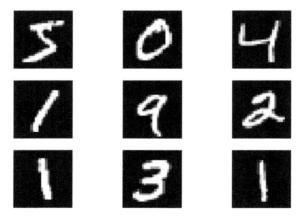

Figure 6.1: MNIST data sample

Throughout this chapter, we will explore SNE and t-SNE using the MNIST dataset provided with the accompanying source code as the basis of practical examples. Before we continue, we will quickly review MNIST and the data that is within it. The complete MNIST dataset is a collection of 60,000 training and 10,000 test examples of handwritten digits of the numbers 0 to 9, represented as black and white (or grayscale) images 28 x 28 pixels in size (giving 784 dimensions or features) with equal numbers of each type of digit (or class) in the dataset. Due to its size and the quality of the data, MNIST has become one of the quintessential datasets in machine learning, often being used as the reference dataset for many research papers in machine learning. One of the advantages of using MINST to explore SNE and t-SNE compared to other datasets is that while the samples contain a high number of dimensions, they can be visualized even after dimensionality reduction because they can be represented as an image. *Figure 6.1* shows a sample of the MNIST dataset, and *Figure 6.2* shows the same sample, reduced to 30 components using PCA:

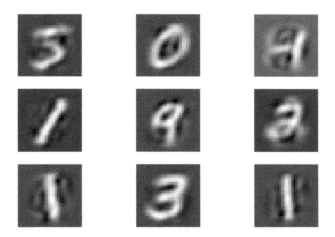

Figure 6.2: MNST reduced using PCA to 30 components

Stochastic Neighbor Embedding (SNE)

Stochastic Neighbor Embedding (SNE) is one of a number of different methods that fall within the category of **manifold learning**, which aims to describe high-dimensional spaces within low-dimensional manifolds or bounded areas. At first thought, this seems like an impossible task; how can we reasonably represent data in two dimensions if we have a dataset with at least 30 features? As we work through the derivation of SNE, it is hoped that you will see how it is possible. Don't worry, we will not be covering the mathematical details of this process in great depth as it is outside of the scope of this chapter. Constructing an SNE can be divided into the following steps:

1. Convert the distances between datapoints in the high-dimensional space to conditional probabilities. Say we had two points, x_i and x_j, in high-dimensional space, and we wanted to determine the probability ($p_{i|j}$) that x_j would be picked as a neighbor of x_i. To define this probability, we use a Gaussian curve, and we see that the probability is high for nearby points, while it is very low for distant points.

2. We need to determine the width of the Gaussian curve as this controls the rate of probability selection. A wide curve would suggest that many points are far away, while a narrow curve suggests that they are tightly compacted.

3. Once we project the data into the low-dimensional space, we can also determine the corresponding probability ($q_{i|j}$) between the corresponding low-dimensional data, y_i and y_j.

4. What SNE aims to do is position the data in the lower dimensions to minimize the differences between $p_{i|j}$ and $q_{i|j}$ over all the data points using a cost function (C) known as the Kullback-Leibler (KL) divergence:

$$C = \sum_i \sum_j p_{i|j} \log \frac{p_{i|j}}{q_{i|j}}$$

Figure 6.3: Kullback-Leibler divergence.

> **Note**
>
> For Python code to construct a Gaussian distribution, refer to the `GaussianDist.ipynb` Jupyter notebook at https://github.com/TrainingByPackt/Applied-Unsupervised-Learning-with-Python/blob/master/Lesson06/GaussianDist.ipynb.

Gaussian distribution maps the data into low-dimensional space. To do this, SNE uses a process of gradient descent to minimize C using the standard parameters of learning rate and epochs as we covered in the previous chapter, looking at neural networks and autoencoders. SNE implements an additional term in the training process—**perplexity**. Perplexity is a selection of the effective number of neighbors used in the comparison and is relatively stable for the values of perplexity between 5 and 50. In practice, a process of trial and error using perplexity values within this range is recommended.

SNE provides an effective way of visualizing high-dimensional data in a low-dimensional space, though it still suffers from an issue known as **the crowding problem**. The crowding problem can occur if we have some points positioned approximately equidistantly within a region around a point i. When these points are visualized in the lower-dimensional space, they crowd around each other, making visualization difficult. The problem is exacerbated if we try to put some more space between these crowded points, because any other points that are further away will then be placed very far away within the low-dimensional space. Essentially, we are trying to balance being able to visualize close points while not losing information provided by points that are further away.

t-Distributed SNE

t-SNE aims to address the crowding problem using a modified version of the KL divergence cost function and by substituting the Gaussian distribution with the Student's t-distribution in the low-dimensional space. Student's t-distribution is a continuous distribution that is used when one has a small sample size and unknown population standard deviation. It is often used in the Student's t-test.

The modified KL cost function considers the pairwise distances in the low-dimensional space equally, while the student's distribution employs a heavy tail in the low-dimensional space to avoid the crowding problem. In the higher-dimensional probability calculation, the Gaussian distribution is still used to ensure that a moderate distance in the higher dimensions is still represented as such in the lower dimensions. This combination of different distributions in the respective spaces allows the faithful representation of datapoints separated by small and moderate distances.

> **Note**
>
> For example code of how to reproduce the Student's t Distribution in Python refer to the Jupyter notebook at https://github.com/TrainingByPackt/Applied-Unsupervised-Learning-with-Python/blob/master/Lesson06/StudentTDist.ipynb.

Thankfully, we don't need to worry about implementing t-SNE by hand, because scikit-learn provides a very effective implementation in its straightforward API. What we need to remember is that both SNE and t-SNE determine the probability of two points being neighbors in both high- and low-dimensionality space and aim to minimize the difference in the probability between the two spaces.

Exercise 24: t-SNE MNIST

In this exercise, we will use the MNIST dataset (provided in the accompanying source code) to explore the scikit-learn implementation to t-SNE. As described earlier, using MNIST allows us to visualize the high-dimensional space in a way that is not possible in other datasets such as the Boston Housing Price or Iris dataset:

1. For this exercise, import **pickle**, **numpy**, **PCA**, and **TSNE** from scikit-learn, as well as **matplotlib**:

```
import pickle
import numpy as np
import matplotlib.pyplot as plt
from sklearn.decomposition import PCA
from sklearn.manifold import TSNE
```

2. Load and visualize the MNIST dataset that is provided with the accompanying source code:

> **Note**
>
> You can find the **mnist.pkl** file at https://github.com/TrainingByPackt/Applied-Unsupervised-Learning-with-Python/tree/master/Lesson06/Exercise24.

```
with open('mnist.pkl', 'rb') as f:
    mnist = pickle.load(f)

plt.figure(figsize=(10, 7))
for i in range(9):
    plt.subplot(3, 3, i + 1)
    plt.imshow(mnist['images'][i], cmap='gray')
    plt.title(mnist['labels'][i])
    plt.axis('off')
plt.show()
```

The output is as follows:

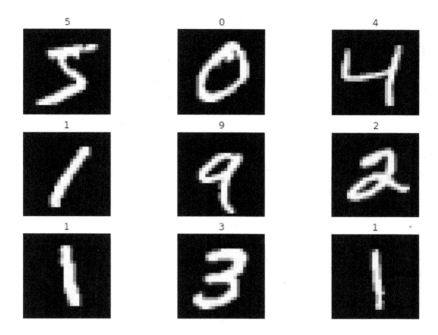

Figure 6.4: Output after loading the dataset

This demonstrates that MNIST has been successfully loaded.

3. In this exercise, we will use PCA on the dataset to reduce extract only the first 30 components.

> **Note**
>
> The scikit-learn PCA API requires that the data passed to the fit method is in the form required (number of samples, number of features). As such, we first need to reshape the MNIST images as they are in the form (number of samples, feature 1, feature 2). Hence, we will use of the **reshape** method in the following source code.

```
model_pca = PCA(n_components=30)
mnist_pca = model_pca.fit(mnist['images'].reshape((-1, 28 ** 2)))
```

4. Visualize the effect of reducing the dataset to 30 components. To do this, we must first transform the dataset into the lower-dimensional space and then use the **inverse_transform** method to return the data to its original size for plotting. We will, of book, need to reshape the data before and after the transform process:

```
mnist_30comp = model_pca.transform(mnist['images'].reshape((-1, 28 ** 2)))
mnist_30comp_vis = model_pca.inverse_transform(mnist_30comp)
mnist_30comp_vis = mnist_30comp_vis.reshape((-1, 28, 28))

plt.figure(figsize=(10, 7))
for i in range(9):
    plt.subplot(3, 3, i + 1)
    plt.imshow(mnist_30comp_vis[i], cmap='gray')
    plt.title(mnist['labels'][i])
    plt.axis('off')
plt.show()
```

The output is as follows:

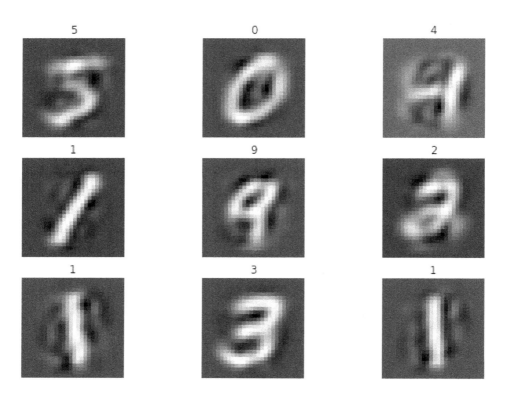

Figure 6.5: Visualizing the effect of reducing the dataset

Note that while we have lost some clarity in the images, for the most part, the numbers are still pretty clearly visible due to the dimension reduction process. It is interesting to note, however, that the number four (4) seems to have been the most visually affected by this process. Perhaps much of the discarded information from the PCA process contained information specific to the samples of four (4).

5. Now, we will apply t-SNE to the PCA-transformed data to visualize the 30 components in two-dimensional space. We can construct a t-SNE model in scikit-learn using the standard model API interface. We will start off using the default values that specify that we are embedding the 30 dimensions into two for visualization, using a perplexity of 30, a learning rate of 200, and 1,000 iterations. We will specify a **random_state** value of 0 and set **verbose** to 1:

```
model_tsne = TSNE(random_state=0, verbose=1)
model_tsne
```

The output is as follows:

```
TSNE(angle=0.5, early_exaggeration=12.0, init='random', learning_rate=200.0,
    method='barnes_hut', metric='euclidean', min_grad_norm=1e-07,
    n_components=2, n_iter=1000, n_iter_without_progress=300,
    perplexity=30.0, random_state=None, verbose=0)
```

Figure 6.6: Applying t-SNE to PCA-transformed data

In the previous screenshot, we can see a number of configuration options available for the t-distributed stochastic neighbor embedding model with some more important than the others. We will focus on the values of **learning_rate**, **n_components**, **n_iter**, **perplexity**, **random_state**, and **verbose**. For **learning_rate**, as discussed previously, t-SNE uses stochastic gradient descent to project the high-dimensional data in low-dimensional space. The learning rate controls the speed at which the process is executed. If learning rate is too high, the model may fail to converge on a solution or if too slow may take a very long time to reach it (if at all). A good rule of thumb is to start with the default; if you find the model producing NaNs (not a number values), you may need to reduce the learning rate. Once you are happy with the model, it is also wise to reduce the learning rate and let it run for longer (**increase n_iter**) as; you may in fact get a slightly better result. **n_components** is the number of dimensions in the embedding (or visualization space). More often than not, you would like a two-dimensional plot of the data, hence you just need the default value of **2**. **n_iter** is the maximum number of iterations of gradient descent. **perplexity**, as discussed in the previous section, is the number of neighbors to use in the visualizing the data.

Typically, a value between 5 and 50 will be appropriate, knowing that larger datasets typically require more perplexity than smaller ones. `random_state` is an important variable for any model or algorithm that initializes its values randomly at the start of training. The random number generators provided within computer hardware and software tools are not, in fact, truly random; they are actually pseudo-random number generators. They give a good approximation of randomness, but are not truly random. Random numbers within computers start with a value known as a seed and are then produced in a complicated manner after that. By providing the same seed at the start of the process, the same "random numbers" are produced each time the process is run. While this sounds counter-intuitive, it is great for reproducing machine learning experiments as you won't see any difference in performance solely due to the initialization of the parameters at the start of training. This can provide more confidence that a change in performance is due to the considered change to the model or training, for example, the architecture of the neural network.

> **Note**
>
> Producing true random sequences is actually one of the hardest tasks to achieve with a computer. Computer software and hardware is designed such that the instructions provided are executed in exactly the same way each time it is run so that you get the same result. Random differences in execution, while being ideal for producing sequences of random numbers, would be a nightmare in terms of automating tasks and debugging problems.

verbose is the verbosity level of the model and describes the amount of information printed to the screen during the model fitting process. A value of 0 indicates no output, while 1 or greater indicates increasing levels of detail in the output.

6. Use t-SNE to transform the decomposed dataset of MNIST:

```
mnist_tsne = model_tsne.fit_transform(mnist_30comp)
```

The output is as follows:

```
[t-SNE] Computing 91 nearest neighbors...
[t-SNE] Indexed 10000 samples in 0.016s...
[t-SNE] Computed neighbors for 10000 samples in 5.454s...
[t-SNE] Computed conditional probabilities for sample 1000 / 10000
[t-SNE] Computed conditional probabilities for sample 2000 / 10000
[t-SNE] Computed conditional probabilities for sample 3000 / 10000
[t-SNE] Computed conditional probabilities for sample 4000 / 10000
[t-SNE] Computed conditional probabilities for sample 5000 / 10000
[t-SNE] Computed conditional probabilities for sample 6000 / 10000
[t-SNE] Computed conditional probabilities for sample 7000 / 10000
[t-SNE] Computed conditional probabilities for sample 8000 / 10000
[t-SNE] Computed conditional probabilities for sample 9000 / 10000
[t-SNE] Computed conditional probabilities for sample 10000 / 10000
[t-SNE] Mean sigma: 304.998835
[t-SNE] KL divergence after 250 iterations with early exaggeration: 85.546951
[t-SNE] KL divergence after 1000 iterations: 1.696535
```

Figure 6.7: Transforming the decomposed dataset

The output provided during the fitting process provides an insight into the calculations being completed by scikit-learn. We can see that it is indexing and computing neighbors for all the samples and is then determining the conditional probabilities of being neighbors for the data in batches of 10. At the end of the process, it provides a mean standard deviation (variance) value of 304.9988 with KL divergence after 250 and 1,000 iterations of gradient descent.

7. Now, visualize the number of dimensions in the returned dataset:

```
mnist_tsne.shape
```

The output is as follows:

```
1000,2
```

So, we have successfully reduced the 784 dimensions down to 2 for visualization, so what does it look like?

8. Create a scatter plot of the two-dimensional data produced by the model:

```
plt.figure(figsize=(10, 7))
plt.scatter(mnist_tsne[:,0], mnist_tsne[:,1], s=5)
plt.title('Low Dimensional Representation of MNIST');
```

The output is as follows:

Figure 6.8: 2D representation of MNIST (no labels).

In *Figure 6.8*, we can see that we have represented the MNIST data in two dimensions, but we can also see that it seems to be grouped together. There are a number of different clusters or clumps of data congregated together and separated from other clusters by some white space. There also seem to be about nine different groups of data. All these observations suggest that there is some relationship within and between the individual clusters.

9. Plot the two-dimensional data grouped by the corresponding image label, and use markers to separate the individual labels. Along with the data, add the image labels to the plot to investigate the structure of the embedded data:

```
MARKER = ['o', 'v', '1', 'p' ,'*', '+', 'x', 'd', '4', '.']
plt.figure(figsize=(10, 7))
plt.title('Low Dimensional Representation of MNIST');
for i in range(10):
    selections = mnist_tsne[mnist['labels'] == i]
    plt.scatter(selections[:,0], selections[:,1], alpha=0.2,
```

```
marker=MARKER[i], s=5);
    x, y = selections.mean(axis=0)
    plt.text(x, y, str(i), fontdict={'weight': 'bold', 'size': 30})
plt.show()
```

The output is as follows:

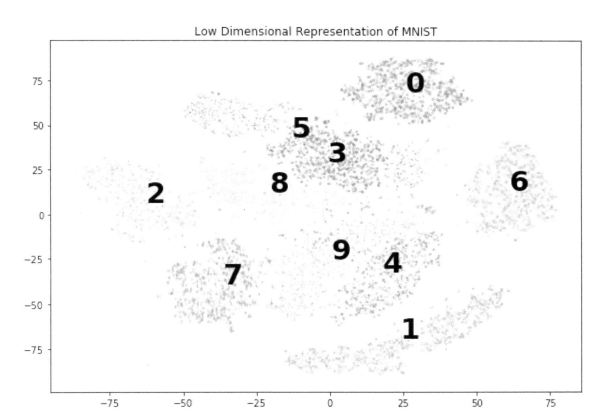

Figure 6.9: 2D representation of MNIST with labels.

Figure 6.9 is very interesting! We can see here that the clusters correspond with each of the different image classes (zero through nine) within the dataset. In an unsupervised fashion, that is, without providing the labels in advance, a combination of PCA and t-SNE has been able to separate and group the individual classes within the MNIST dataset. What is particularly interesting is that there seems to be some confusion within the data regarding the number four images and the number nine images, as well as the five and three images; the two clusters somewhat overlap. This makes sense if we look at the number nine and number four PCA images extracted from *Step 4, Exercise 24, t-SNE MNIST*:

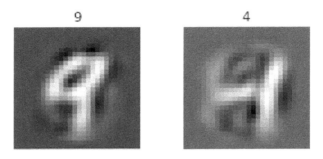

Figure 6.10: PCA images of nine.

They do, in fact, look quite similar; perhaps it is due to the uncertainty in the shape of the number four. Looking at the image that follows, we can see in the four on the left-hand side that the two vertical lines almost join, while the four on the right-hand side has the two lines parallel:

Figure 6.11: Shape of number four

The other interesting feature to note in *Figure* 6.9 are the edge cases, better shown in color in the Jupyter notebooks. We can see around the edges of each cluster that some samples would be misclassified in the traditional supervised learning sense but represent samples that may have more in common with other clusters than their own. Let's take a look at an example; there are a number of samples of the number three that are quite far from the correct cluster.

10. Get the index of all the number threes in the dataset:

```
threes = np.where(mnist['labels'] == 3)[0]
threes
```

The output is as follows:

```
array([   7,   10,   12, ..., 9974, 9977, 9991])
```

Figure 6.12: Index of threes in the dataset.

11. Find the threes that were plotted with an **x** value of less than 0:

```
tsne_threes = mnist_tsne[threes]
far_threes = np.where(tsne_threes[:,0]< 0)[0]
far_threes
```

The output is as follows:

```
array([   0,    1,    6,   11,   13,   14,   17,   18,   19,   21,   22,
         23,   25,   29,   30,   31,   32,   34,   35,   37,   38,   39,
         41,   42,   43,   45,   50,   51,   52,   54,   55,   56,   57,
         58,   59,   60,   61,   62,   63,   66,   67,   68,   71,   72,
```

Figure 6.13: The threes with x value less than zero.

12. Display the coordinates to find one that is reasonably far from the three cluster:

```
tsne_threes[far_threes]
```

The output is as follows:

```
array([[-16.126516 ,  35.23472  ],
       [ -4.217844 ,  31.871649 ],
       [ -2.3769686,  35.472614 ],
       ...,
       [ -6.4078546,  38.2851   ],
       [-10.40415  ,  45.599823 ],
       [ -8.813534 ,  39.997196 ]], dtype=float32)
```

Figure 6.14: Coordinates away from the three cluster

13. Chose a sample with a reasonably high negative value as an **x** coordinate. In this example, we will select the fourth sample, which is sample 10. Display the image for the sample:

```
plt.imshow(mnist['images'][10], cmap='gray')
plt.axis('off');
plt.show()
```

The output is as follows:

Figure 6.15: Image of sample ten

Looking at this sample image and the corresponding t-SNE coordinates, approximately (-8, 47), it is not surprising that this sample lies near the cluster of eights and fives as there are quite a few features that are common to both of those numbers in this image. In this example, we applied a simplified SNE, demonstrating some of its efficiencies as well as possible sources of confusion and the output of unsupervised learning.

> **Note**
>
> Even with providing a random number seed, t-SNE does not guarantee identical outputs each time it is executed because it is based upon selection probabilities. As such, you may notice some differences in the specifics between the example provided in the content and your implementation. While the specifics may differ, the overall principals and techniques still apply. From a real-world application perspective, it is recommended that the process is repeated multiple times to discern the significant information from the data.

Activity 12: Wine t-SNE

In this activity, we will reinforce our knowledge of t-SNE using the Wine dataset. By completing this activity, you will be able to build-SNE models for your own custom applications. The Wine dataset (https://archive.ics.uci.edu/ml/datasets/Wine) is a collection of attributes regarding the chemical analysis of wine from Italy from three different producers, but the same type of wine for each producer. This information could be used as an example to verify the validity of a bottle of wine made from the grapes from a specific region in Italy. The 13 attributes are Alcohol, Malic acid, Ash, Alcalinity of ash, Magnesium, Total phenols, Flavanoids, Nonflavanoid phenols, Proanthocyanins, Color intensity, Hue, OD280/OD315 of diluted wines, and Proline.

Each sample contains a class identifier (1 – 3).

> **Note**
>
> This dataset is taken from https://archive.ics.uci.edu/ml/machine-learning-databases/wine/. It can be downloaded from https://github.com/TrainingByPackt/Applied-Unsupervised-Learning-with-Python/tree/master/Lesson06/Activity12.
>
> UCI Machine Learning Repository [http://archive.ics.uci.edu/ml]. Irvine, CA: University of California, School of Information and Computer Science.

These steps will help you complete the activity:

1. Import **pandas**, **numpy**, **matplotlib**, and the **t-SNE** and **PCA** models from scikit-learn.

2. Load the Wine dataset using the **wine.data** file included in the accompanying source code and display the first five rows of data.

> **Note**
>
> You can delete columns within Pandas DataFrames through use of the **del** keyword. Simply pass **del** the DataFrame and the selected column within square root.

3. The first column contains the labels; extract this column and remove it from the dataset.

4. Execute PCA to reduce the dataset to the first six components.

5. Determine the amount of variance within the data described by these six components.

6. Create a t-SNE model using a specified random state and a **verbose** value of 1.

7. Fit the PCA data to the t-SNE model.

8. Confirm that the shape of the t-SNE fitted data is two dimensional.

9. Create a scatter plot of the two-dimensional data.

10. Create a secondary scatter plot of the two-dimensional data with the class labels applied to visualize any clustering that may be present.

At the end of this activity, you will have constructed a t-SNE visualization of the Wine dataset described using its six components and identified some relationships in the location of the data within the plot. The final plot will look similar to the following:

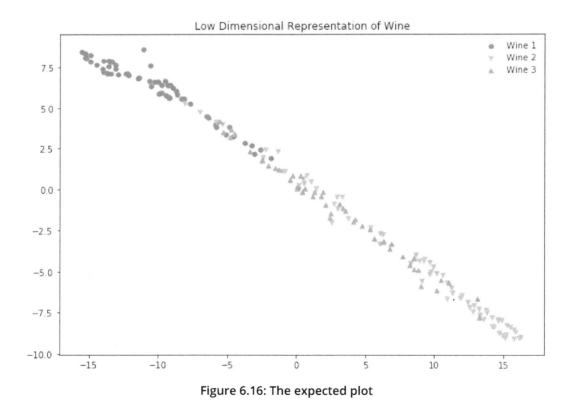

Figure 6.16: The expected plot

> **Note**
>
> The solution for this activity can be found on page 345.

In this section, we covered the basics of generating SNE plots. The ability to represent high-dimensional data in low-dimensional space is critical, especially for developing a thorough understanding of the data at hand. Occasionally, these plots can be tricky to interpret as the exact relationships are sometimes contradictory, leading at times to misleading structures.

Interpreting t-SNE Plots

Now that we are able to use t-distributed SNE to visualize high-dimensional data, it is important to understand the limitations of such plots and what aspects are important in interpreting and generating them. In this section of the chapter, we will highlight some of the important features of t-SNE and demonstrate how care should be taken when using the visualization technique.

Perplexity

As described in the introduction to t-SNE, the perplexity values specify the number of nearest neighbors to be used in computing the conditional probability. The selection of this value can make a significant difference to the end result; with a low value of perplexity, local variations in the data dominate because a small number of samples are used in the calculation. Conversely, a large value of perplexity considers more global variations as many more samples are used in the calculation. Typically, it is worth trying a range of different values to investigate the effect of perplexity. Again, values between 5 and 50 tend to work quite well.

Exercise 25: t-SNE MNIST and Perplexity

In this exercise, we will try a range of different values for perplexity and look at the effect in the visualization plot:

1. Import **pickle**, **numpy**, **matplotlib**, and **PCA** and **t-SNE** from scikit-learn:

    ```
    import pickle
    import numpy as np
    import matplotlib.pyplot as plt
    from sklearn.decomposition import PCA
    from sklearn.manifold import TSNE
    ```

2. Load the MNIST dataset:

> **Note**
>
> You can find the **mnist.pkl** file at https://github.com/TrainingByPackt/Applied-Unsupervised-Learning-with-Python/tree/master/Lesson06/Exercise25.

```
with open('mnist.pkl', 'rb') as f:
    mnist = pickle.load(f)
```

3. Using PCA, select only the first 30 components of variance from the image data:

```
model_pca = PCA(n_components=30)
mnist_pca = model_pca.fit_transform(mnist['images'].reshape((-1, 28 ** 2)))
```

4. In this exercise, we are investigating the effect of perplexity on the t-SNE manifold. Iterate through a model/plot loop with a perplexity of 3, 30, and 300:

```
MARKER = ['o', 'v', '1', 'p' ,'*', '+', 'x', 'd', '4', '.']
for perp in [3, 30, 300]:
    model_tsne = TSNE(random_state=0, verbose=1, perplexity=perp)
    mnist_tsne = model_tsne.fit_transform(mnist_pca)

    plt.figure(figsize=(10, 7))
    plt.title(f'Low Dimensional Representation of MNIST (perplexity =
{perp})');
    for i in range(10):
        selections = mnist_tsne[mnist['labels'] == i]
        plt.scatter(selections[:,0], selections[:,1], alpha=0.2,
marker=MARKER[i], s=5);
        x, y = selections.mean(axis=0)
        plt.text(x, y, str(i), fontdict={'weight': 'bold', 'size': 30})
```

The output is as follows:

```
[t-SNE] Computing 10 nearest neighbors...
[t-SNE] Indexed 10000 samples in 0.018s...
[t-SNE] Computed neighbors for 10000 samples in 3.438s...
[t-SNE] Computed conditional probabilities for sample 1000 / 10000
[t-SNE] Computed conditional probabilities for sample 2000 / 10000
[t-SNE] Computed conditional probabilities for sample 3000 / 10000
[t-SNE] Computed conditional probabilities for sample 4000 / 10000
[t-SNE] Computed conditional probabilities for sample 5000 / 10000
[t-SNE] Computed conditional probabilities for sample 6000 / 10000
[t-SNE] Computed conditional probabilities for sample 7000 / 10000
[t-SNE] Computed conditional probabilities for sample 8000 / 10000
[t-SNE] Computed conditional probabilities for sample 9000 / 10000
[t-SNE] Computed conditional probabilities for sample 10000 / 10000
[t-SNE] Mean sigma: 165.134196
[t-SNE] KL divergence after 250 iterations with early exaggeration: 96.804878
[t-SNE] KL divergence after 1000 iterations: 1.850921
[t-SNE] Computing 91 nearest neighbors...
[t-SNE] Indexed 10000 samples in 0.014s...
[t-SNE] Computed neighbors for 10000 samples in 5.129s...
[t-SNE] Computed conditional probabilities for sample 1000 / 10000
[t-SNE] Computed conditional probabilities for sample 2000 / 10000
[t-SNE] Computed conditional probabilities for sample 3000 / 10000
[t-SNE] Computed conditional probabilities for sample 4000 / 10000
[t-SNE] Computed conditional probabilities for sample 5000 / 10000
[t-SNE] Computed conditional probabilities for sample 6000 / 10000
[t-SNE] Computed conditional probabilities for sample 7000 / 10000
[t-SNE] Computed conditional probabilities for sample 8000 / 10000
[t-SNE] Computed conditional probabilities for sample 9000 / 10000
[t-SNE] Computed conditional probabilities for sample 10000 / 10000
[t-SNE] Mean sigma: 283.586365
[t-SNE] KL divergence after 250 iterations with early exaggeration: 85.399399
[t-SNE] KL divergence after 1000 iterations: 1.696069
[t-SNE] Computing 901 nearest neighbors...
[t-SNE] Indexed 10000 samples in 0.013s...
[t-SNE] Computed neighbors for 10000 samples in 7.993s...
[t-SNE] Computed conditional probabilities for sample 1000 / 10000
[t-SNE] Computed conditional probabilities for sample 2000 / 10000
[t-SNE] Computed conditional probabilities for sample 3000 / 10000
[t-SNE] Computed conditional probabilities for sample 4000 / 10000
[t-SNE] Computed conditional probabilities for sample 5000 / 10000
[t-SNE] Computed conditional probabilities for sample 6000 / 10000
[t-SNE] Computed conditional probabilities for sample 7000 / 10000
[t-SNE] Computed conditional probabilities for sample 8000 / 10000
[t-SNE] Computed conditional probabilities for sample 9000 / 10000
[t-SNE] Computed conditional probabilities for sample 10000 / 10000
[t-SNE] Mean sigma: 393.939776
[t-SNE] KL divergence after 250 iterations with early exaggeration: 67.932961
[t-SNE] KL divergence after 1000 iterations: 1.193975
[t-SNE] Computing 9001 nearest neighbors...
```

Figure 6.17: Iterating through a model

Note the KL divergence in each of the three different perplexity values, along with the increase in the average standard deviation (variance). Looking at the three following t-SNE plots with class labels, we can see that with a low perplexity value, the clusters are nicely contained with relatively few overlaps. However, there is almost no space between the clusters. As we increase the perplexity, the space between the clusters improves with reasonably clear distinctions at a perplexity of 30. As the perplexity increases to 300, we can see that the clusters of eight and five, along with nine, four, and seven, are starting to converge.

Start with a low perplexity value:

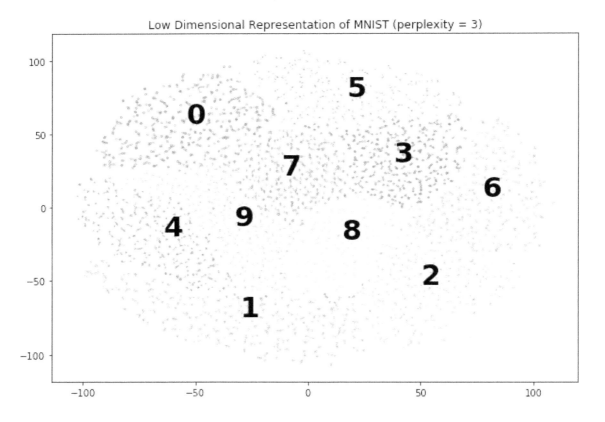

Figure 6.18: Plot of low perplexity value

Increasing the perplexity by a factor of 10 shows much clearer clusters:

Figure 6.19: Plot after increasing perplexity by a factor of 10

By increasing the perplexity to 300, we start to merge more of the labels together:

Figure 6.20: Increasing the perplexity value to 300

In this exercise, we developed our understanding of the effect of perplexity and the sensitivity of this value to the overall result. A small perplexity value can lead to a more homogenous mix of locations with very little space between them. Increasing the perplexity separates the clusters more effectively, but an excessive value leads to overlapping clusters.

Activity 13: t-SNE Wine and Perplexity

In this activity, we will use the Wine dataset to further reinforce the influence of perplexity on the t-SNE visualization process. In this activity, we are trying to determine whether we can identify the source of the wine based on its chemical composition. The t-SNE process provides an effective means of representing and possibly identifying the sources.

> **Note**
>
> This dataset is taken from https://archive.ics.uci.edu/ml/machine-learning-databases/wine/. It can be downloaded from https://github.com/TrainingByPackt/Applied-Unsupervised-Learning-with-Python/tree/master/Lesson06/Activity13.
>
> UCI Machine Learning Repository [http://archive.ics.uci.edu/ml]. Irvine, CA: University of California, School of Information and Computer Science.

1. Import **pandas**, **numpy**, **matplotlib**, and the **t-SNE** and **PCA** models from scikit-learn.

2. Load the Wine dataset and inspect the first five rows.

3. The first column provides the labels; extract these from the DataFrame and store them in a separate variable. Ensure that the column is removed from the DataFrame.

4. Execute PCA on the dataset and extract the first six components.

5. Construct a loop that iterates through the perplexity values (1, 5, 20, 30, 80, 160, 320). For each loop, generate a t-SNE model with the corresponding perplexity and print a scatter plot of the labeled wine classes. Note the effect of different perplexity values.

By the end of this activity, you will have generated a two-dimensional representation of the Wine dataset and inspected the resulting plot for clusters or groupings of data.

> **Note**
>
> The solution for this activity can be found on page 348.

Iterations

The final parameter we will experimentally investigate is that of iterations, which, as per our investigation in autoencoders, is simply the number of training epochs to apply to gradient descent. Thankfully, the number of iterations is a reasonably simple parameter to adjust and often requires only a certain amount of patience as the position of the points in the low-dimensional space stabilize in their final locations.

Exercise 26: t-SNE MNIST and Iterations

In this exercise, we will look at the influence of a range of different iteration parameters applied to the t-SNE model and highlight some indicators that perhaps more training is required. Again, the value of these parameters is highly dependent on the dataset and the volume of data available for training. Again, we will use MNIST in this example:

1. Import **pickle**, **numpy**, **matplotlib**, and **PCA** and **t-SNE** from scikit-learn:

   ```
   import pickle
   import numpy as np
   import matplotlib.pyplot as plt
   from sklearn.decomposition import PCA
   from sklearn.manifold import TSNE
   ```

2. Load the MNIST dataset:

   > **Note**
   >
   > You can find the **mnist.pkl** file at https://github.com/TrainingByPackt/Applied-Unsupervised-Learning-with-Python/tree/master/Lesson06/Exercise25.

   ```
   with open('mnist.pkl', 'rb') as f:
       mnist = pickle.load(f)
   ```

3. Using PCA, select only the first 30 components of variance from the image data:

   ```
   model_pca = PCA(n_components=30)
   mnist_pca = model_pca.fit_transform(mnist['images'].reshape((-1, 28 ** 2)))
   ```

4. In this exercise, we are investigating the effect of iterations on the t-SNE manifold. Iterate through a model/plot loop with iteration and iteration with progress values of **250**, **500**, and **1000**:

   ```
   MARKER = ['o', 'v', '1', 'p' ,'*', '+', 'x', 'd', '4', '.']
   for iterations in [250, 500, 1000]:
   ```

```
model_tsne = TSNE(random_state=0, verbose=1, n_iter=iterations, n_
iter_without_progress=iterations)
model_tsne = model_tsne.fit_transform(mnist_pca)
```

5. Plot the results:

```
plt.figure(figsize=(10, 7))
plt.title(f'Low Dimensional Representation of MNIST (iterations =
{iterations})');
for i in range(10):
    selections = mnist_tsne[mnist['labels'] == i]
    plt.scatter(selections[:,0], selections[:,1], alpha=0.2,
marker=MARKER[i], s=5);
    x, y = selections.mean(axis=0)
    plt.text(x, y, str(i), fontdict={'weight': 'bold', 'size': 30})
```

A reduced number of iterations limits the extent to which the algorithm can find relevant neighbors, leading to ill-defined clusters:

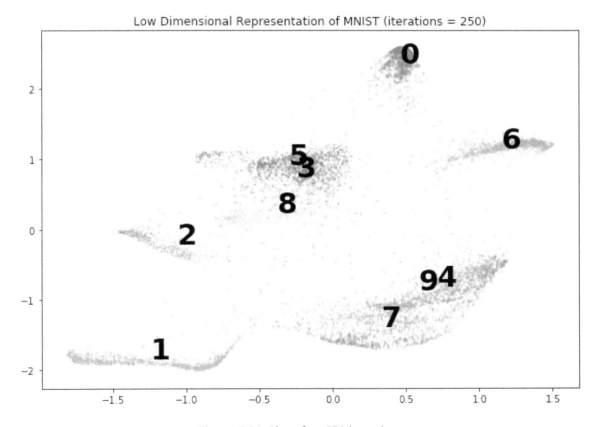

Figure 6.21: Plot after 250 iterations

Increasing the number of iterations provides the algorithm with sufficient time to adequately project the data:

Figure 6.22: Plot after increasing the iterations to 500

Once the clusters have settled, increased iterations have an extremely small effect and essentially lead to increased training time:

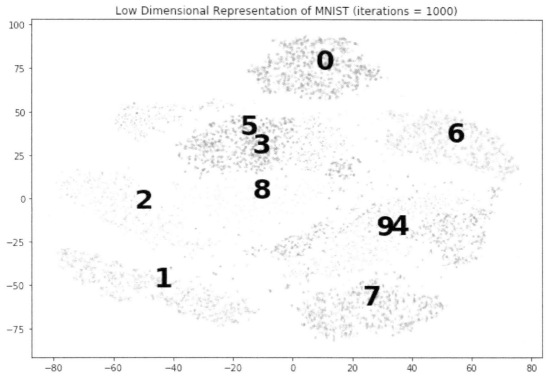

Figure 6.23: Plot after 1,000 iterations

Looking at the previous plots, we can see that the cluster positions with iteration values of 500 and 1,000 are stable and relatively unchanged between the plots. The most interesting plot is that of an iteration value of 250, where it seems as though the clusters are still in a process of motion, making their way to the final positions. As such, there is sufficient evidence to suggest an iteration value of 500 is sufficient.

Activity 14: t-SNE Wine and Iterations

In this activity, we will investigate the effect of the number of iterations on the visualization of the Wine dataset. This is a process that's commonly used during the exploration phase of data processing, cleaning, and understanding the relationships in the data. Depending on the dataset and the type of analysis, we may need to try a number of different iterations, such as those completed in this activity.

> **Note**
>
> This dataset is taken from https://archive.ics.uci.edu/ml/machine-learning-databases/wine/. It can be downloaded from https://github.com/TrainingByPackt/Applied-Unsupervised-Learning-with-Python/tree/master/Lesson06/Activity14.
>
> UCI Machine Learning Repository [http://archive.ics.uci.edu/ml]. Irvine, CA: University of California, School of Information and Computer Science.

These steps will help you complete the activity:

1. Import **pandas**, **numpy**, **matplotlib**, and the **t-SNE** and **PCA** models from scikit-learn.

2. Load the Wine dataset and inspect the first five rows.

3. The first column provides the labels; extract these from the DataFrame and store them in a separate variable. Ensure that the column is removed from the DataFrame.

4. Execute PCA on the dataset and extract the first six components.

5. Construct a loop that iterates through the iteration values (**250**, **500**, **1000**). For each loop, generate a t-SNE model with the corresponding number of iterations and an identical number of iterations without progress values.

6. Construct a scatter plot of the labeled wine classes. Note the effect of different iteration values.

By completing this activity, we will have investigated the effect of modifying the iteration parameter of the model. This is an important parameter in ensuring that the data has settled into a somewhat final position in the low-dimensional space.

> **Note**
>
> The solution for this activity can be found on page 353.

Final Thoughts on Visualizations

As we conclude our chapter on t-Distributed Stochastic Neighbor Embeddings, there are a couple of important aspects to note regarding the visualizations. The first is that the size of the clusters or the relative space between clusters may not actually provide any real indication of proximity. As we discussed earlier in the chapter, a combination of Gaussian and Student's t-distributions is used to represent high-dimensional data in a low-dimensional space. As such, there is no guarantee of a linear relationship in distance, as t-SNE balances the positions of localized and global data structures. The actual distance between points in local structures may be visually very close within the representation, but still might be some distance away in high-dimensional space.

This property also has additional consequences in that sometimes, random data can be present as if it had some structure, and that it is often required to generate multiple visualizations using differing values of perplexity, learning rate, number of iterations, and random seed values.

Summary

In this chapter, we were introduced to t-Distributed Stochastic Neighbor Embeddings as a means of visualizing high-dimensional information that may have been produced from prior processes such as PCA or autoencoders. We discussed the means by which t-SNEs produce this representation and generated a number of them using the MNIST and Wine datasets and scikit-learn. In this chapter, we were able to see some of the power of unsupervised learning because PCA and t-SNE were able to cluster the classes of each image without knowing the ground truth result. In the next chapter, we will build on this practical experience as we look into the applications of unsupervised learning, including basket analysis and topic modeling.

Topic Modeling

Learning Objectives

By the end of this chapter, you'll be able to:

- Perform basic cleaning techniques for textual data
- Evaluate latent Dirichlet allocation models
- Execute non-negative matrix factorization models
- Interpret the results of topic models
- Identify the best topic model for the given scenario

In this chapter, we will see how topic modeling provides insights into the underlying structure of documents.

Introduction

Topic modeling is one facet of **<u>natural language processing</u>** (**<u>NLP</u>**), the field of computer science exploring the relationship between computers and human language, which has been increasing in popularity with the increased availability of textual datasets. NLP can deal with language in almost any form, including text, speech, and images. Besides topic modeling, sentiment analysis, object character recognition, and lexical semantics are noteworthy NLP algorithms. Nowadays, the data being collected and needing analysis less frequently comes in standard tabular forms and more frequently coming in less structured forms, including documents, images, and audio files. As such, successful data science practitioners need to be fluent in methodologies used for handling these diverse datasets.

Here is a demonstration of identifying words in a text and assigning them to topics:

Figure 7.1: Example of identifying words in a text and assigning them to topics

Your immediate question is probably *what are topics*? Let's answer that question with an example. You could imagine, or perhaps have noticed, that on days when major events take place, such as national elections, natural disasters, or sport championships, the posts on social media websites tend to focus on those events. Posts generally reflect, in some way, the day's events, and they will do so in varying ways. Posts can and will have a number of divergent viewpoints. If we had tweets about the World Cup final, the topics of those tweets could cover divergent viewpoints, ranging from the quality of the refereeing to fan behavior. In the United States, the president delivers an annual speech in mid to late January called the State of the Union. With sufficient numbers of social media posts, we would be able to infer or predict high-level reactions – topics – to the speech from the social media community by grouping posts using the specific keywords contained in them.

Topic Models

Topic models fall into the unsupervised learning bucket because, almost always, the topics being identified are not known in advance. So, no target exists on which we can perform regression or classification modeling. In terms of unsupervised learning, topic models most resemble clustering algorithms, specifically k-means clustering. You'll recall that, in k-means clustering, the number of clusters is established first and then the model assigns each data point to one of the predetermined number of clusters. The same is generally true in topic models. We select the number of topics at the start and then the model isolates the words that form that number of topics. This is a great jumping-off point for a high-level topic modeling overview.

Before that, let's check that the correct environment and libraries are installed and ready for use. The following table lists the required libraries and their main purposes:

Library	Use
`langdetect`	Used to detect the language of any text.
`matplotlib.pyplot`	Used to do basic plotting.
`nltk`	Used to do a variety of natural language processing tasks.
`numpy`	Used to work with arrays and matrices.
`pandas`	Used to work with data frames.
`pyLDAvis`	Used to visualize the results of Latent Dirichlet Allocation models.
`pyLDAvis.sklearn`	Used to run `pyLDAvis` with `sklearn` models.
`regex`	Used to write and execute regular expressions.
`sklearn`	Used to build machine learning models.

Figure 7.2: Table showing different libraries and their use

Exercise 27: Setting Up the Environment

To check whether the environment is ready for topic modeling, we will perform several steps. The first of which involves loading all the libraries that will be needed in this chapter:

> **Note**
>
> If any or all of these libraries are not currently installed, install the required packages via the command line using **pip**. For example, **pip install langdetect**, if not installed already.

1. Open a new Jupyter notebook.

2. Import the requisite libraries:

```
import langdetect
import matplotlib.pyplot
import nltk
import numpy
import pandas
import pyLDAvis
import pyLDAvis.sklearn
import regex
import sklearn
```

Note that not all of these packages are used for cleaning the data; some of them are used in the actual modeling, but it is nice to import all of the required libraries at once, so let's take care of all library importing now.

3. Libraries not yet installed will return the following error:

```
---------------------------------------------------------------------------
ModuleNotFoundError                       Traceback (most recent call last)
<ipython-input-3-a62286ae48f9> in <module>
      4 import numpy
      5 import pandas
----> 6 import pyLDAvis
      7 import pyLDAvis.sklearn
      8 import regex

ModuleNotFoundError: No module named 'pyLDAvis'
```

Figure 7.3: Library not installed error

If this error is returned, install the relevant libraries via the command line as previously discussed. Once successfully installed, rerun the library import process using **import**.

4. Certain textual data cleaning and preprocessing processes require word dictionaries (more to come). In this step, we will install two of these dictionaries. If the **nltk** library is imported, the following code can be executed:

```
nltk.download('wordnet')
nltk.download('stopwords')
```

The output is as follows:

```
[nltk_data] Downloading package wordnet to
[nltk_data]     C:\Users\rutujay\AppData\Roaming\nltk_data...
[nltk_data]   Unzipping corpora\wordnet.zip.
[nltk_data] Downloading package stopwords to
[nltk_data]     C:\Users\rutujay\AppData\Roaming\nltk_data...
[nltk_data]   Unzipping corpora\stopwords.zip.

True
```

Figure 7.4: Importing libraries and downloading dictionaries

5. Run the **matplotlib** magic and specify inline so that the plots print inside the notebook:

```
%matplotlib inline
```

The notebook and environment are now set and ready for data loading.

A High-Level Overview of Topic Models

When it comes to analyzing large volumes of potentially related text data, topic models are one go-to approach. By related, we mean that the documents ideally come from the same source. That is, survey results, tweets, and newspaper articles would not normally be analyzed simultaneously in the same model. It is certainly possible to analyze them together, but the results are liable to be very vague and therefore meaningless. To run any topic model, the only data requirement is the documents themselves. No additional data, meta or otherwise, is required.

In the simplest terms, topic models identify the abstract topics (also known as themes) in a collection of documents, referred to as a **corpus**, using the words contained in the documents. That is, if a sentence contains the words salary, employee, and meeting, it would be safe to assume that that sentence is about, or that its topic is, work. It is of note that the documents making up the corpus need not be documents as traditionally defined – think letters or contracts. A document could be anything containing text, including tweets, news headlines, or transcribed speech.

Topic models assume that words in the same document are related and use that assumption to define abstract topics by finding groups of words that repeatedly appear in close proximity. In this way, these models are classic pattern recognition algorithms where the patterns being detected are made up of words. The general topic modeling algorithm has four main steps:

1. Determine the number of topics.

2. Scan the documents and identify co-occurring words or phrases.

3. Auto-learn groups (or clusters) of words characterizing the documents.

4. Output abstract topics characterizing the corpus as word groupings.

As step 1 notes, the number of topics needs to be selected before fitting the model. Selecting an appropriate number of topics can be tricky, but, as is the case with most machine learning models, this parameter can be optimized by fitting several models using different numbers of topics and selecting the best model based on some performance metric. We'll dive into this process again later.

The following is the generic topic modeling workflow:

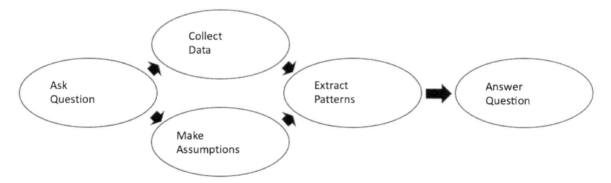

Figure 7.5: The generic topic modeling workflow

It is important to select the best number of topics possible, as this parameter can majorly impact topic coherence. This is because the model finds groups of words that best fit the corpus under the constraint of a predefined number of topics. If the number of topics is too high, the topics become inappropriately narrow. Overly specific topics are referred to as **over-cooked**. Likewise, if the number of topics is too low, the topics become generic and vague. These types of topics are considered **under-cooked**. Over-cooked and under-cooked topics can sometimes be fixed by decreasing or increasing the number of topics, respectively. A frequent and unavoidable result of topic models is that, frequently, at least one topic will be problematic.

A key aspect of topic models is that they do not produce specific one-word or one-phrase topics, but rather collections of words, each of which represents an abstract topic. Recall the imaginary sentence about work from before. The topic model built to identify the topics of some hypothetical corpus to which that sentence belongs would not return the word work as a topic. It would instead return a collection of words, such as paycheck, employee, and boss; words that describe the topic and from which the one-word or one-phrase topic could be inferred. This is because topic models understand word **proximity**, not context. The model has no idea what paycheck, employee, and boss mean; it only knows that these words, generally, whenever they appear, appear in close proximity to one another:

Figure 7.6: Inferring topics from word groupings

Topic models can be used to predict the topic(s) belonging to unseen documents, but, if you are going to make predictions, it is important to recognize that topic models only know the words used to train them. That is, if the unseen documents have words that were not in the training data, the model will not be able to process those words even if they link to one of the topics identified in the training data. Because of this fact, topic models tend to be used more for exploratory analysis and inference more so than for prediction.

Each topic model outputs two matrices. The first matrix contains words against topics. It lists each word related to each topic with some quantification of the relationship. Given the number of words being considered by the model, each topic is only going to be described by a relatively small number of words. Words can either be assigned to one topic or to multiple topics at differing quantifications. Whether words are assigned to one or multiple topics depends on the algorithm. Similarly, the second matrix contains documents against topics. It lists each document related to a topic with some quantification of how related each document is to that topic.

When discussing topic modeling, it is important to continually reinforce the fact that the word groups representing topics are not related conceptually, only by proximity. The frequent proximity of certain words in the documents is enough to define topics because of an assumption stated previously, which is that all words in the same document are related. However, this assumption may either not be true or the words may be too generic to form coherent topics. Interpreting abstract topics involves balancing the innate characteristics of text data with the generated word groupings. Text data, and language in general, is highly variable, complex, and has context, which means any generalized result needs to be consumed cautiously. This is not to downplay or invalidate the results of the model. Given thoroughly cleaned documents and an appropriate number of topics, word groupings, as we will see, can be a good guide as to what is contained in a corpus and can effectively be incorporated into larger data systems.

We have discussed some of the limitations of topic models already, but there are some additional points to consider. The noisy nature of text data can lead topic models to assign words unrelated to one of the topics to that topic. Again, consider the sentence about work from before. The word meeting could appear in the word grouping representing the topic work. It is also possible that the word long could be in that group, but the word long is not directly related to work. Long may be in the group because it frequently appears in close proximity to the word meeting. Therefore, long would probably be considered to be spuriously correlated to work and should probably be removed from the topic grouping, if possible. Spuriously correlated words in word groupings can cause significant problems when analyzing data.

This is not necessarily a flaw in the model, it is, instead, a characteristic of the model that, given noisy data, could extract quirks from the data that might negatively impact the results. Spurious correlations could be the result of how, where, or when the data was collected. If the documents were collected only in some specific geographic region, words associated with that region could be incorrectly, albeit accidentally, linked to one or many of the word groupings output from the model. Note that, with additional words in the word group, we could be attaching more documents to that topic than should be attached. It should be straightforward that, if we shrink the number of words belonging to a topic, then that topic will be assigned to fewer documents. Keep in mind that this is not a bad thing. We want each word grouping to contain only words that make sense so that we assign the appropriate topics to the appropriate documents.

There are many topic modeling algorithms, but perhaps the two best known are **Latent Dirichlet Allocation** and **Non-Negative Matrix Factorization**. We will discuss both in detail later on.

Business Applications

Despite its limitations, topic modeling can provide actionable insights that drive business value if used correctly and in the appropriate context. Let's now review one of the biggest applications of topic models.

One of the use cases is exploratory data analysis on new text data where the underlying structure of the dataset is unknown. This is the equivalent to plotting and computing summary statistics for an unseen dataset featuring numeric and categorical variables whose characteristics need to be understood before more sophisticated analyses can be reasonably performed. With the results of topic modeling, the usability of this dataset in future modeling exercises is ascertainable. For example, if the topic model returns clear and distinct topics, then that dataset would be a great candidate for further clustering-type analyses.

Effectively, what determining topics does is to create an additional variable that can be used to sort, categorize, and/or chunk data. If our topic model returns cars, farming, and electronics as abstract topics, we could filter our large text dataset down to just the documents with farming as a topic. Once filtered, we could perform further analyses, including sentiment analysis, another round of topic modeling, or any other analysis we could think up. Beyond defining the topics present in a corpus, topic modeling returns a lot of other information indirectly that could also be used to break a large dataset down and understand its characteristics.

A representation of sorting documents is shown here:

Figure 7.7: Sorting/categorizing documents

Among those characteristics is topic prevalence. Think about performing an analysis on an open response survey that is designed to gauge the response to a product. We could imagine the topic model returning topics in the form of sentiment. One group of words might be good, excellent, recommend, and quality, while the other might be garbage, broken, poor, and disappointing. Given this style of survey, the topics themselves may not be that surprising, but what would be interesting is that we could count the number of documents containing each topic. From the counts, we could say things like x-percent of the survey respondents had a positive reaction to the product, while only y-percent of the respondents had a negative reaction. Essentially, what we would have created is a rough version of a sentiment analysis.

Currently, the most frequent use for a topic model is as a component of a recommendation engine. The emphasis today is on personalization – delivering products to customers that are specifically designed and curated for individual customers. Take websites, news or otherwise, devoted to the propagation of articles. Companies such as Yahoo and Medium need customers to keep reading in order to stay in business, and one way to keep customers reading is to feed them articles that they would be more inclined to read. This is where topic modeling comes in. Using a corpus made up of articles previously read by an individual, a topic model would essentially tell us what types of articles said subscriber likes to read. The company could then go to its inventory and find articles with similar topics and send them to the individual either via their account page or email. This is custom curation to facilitate simplicity and ease of use while also maintaining engagement.

Before we get into prepping data for our model, let's quickly load and explore the data.

Exercise 28: Data Loading

In this exercise we will load the data from a dataset and format it. The dataset for this and all the subsequent exercises in this chapter comes from the Machine Learning Repository, hosted by the University of California, Irvine (UCI). To find the data, go to https://github.com/TrainingByPackt/Applied-Unsupervised-Learning-with-Python/tree/master/Lesson07/Exercise27-Exercise%2038.

> **Note**
>
> This data is downloaded from https://archive.ics.uci.edu/ml/datasets/News+Popularity+in+Multiple+Social+Media+Platforms. It can be accessed at https://github.com/TrainingByPackt/Applied-Unsupervised-Learning-with-Python/tree/master/Lesson07/Exercise27-Exercise%2038. Nuno Moniz and LuÃs Torgo (2018), Multi-Source Social Feedback of Online News Feeds, CoRR UCI Machine Learning Repository [http://archive.ics.uci.edu/ml]. Irvine, CA: University of California, School of Information and Computer Science.

This is the only file that is required for this exercise. Once downloaded and saved locally, the data can be loaded into the notebook:

> **Note**
>
> Execute the exercises of this chapter in the same notebook.

1. Define the path to the data and load it using **pandas**:

    ```
    path = "News_Final.csv"
    df = pandas.read_csv(path, header=0)
    ```

> **Note**
>
> Add the file on the same path where you have opened your notebook.

2. Examine the data briefly by executing the following code:

```
def dataframe_quick_look(df, nrows):
    print("SHAPE:\n{shape}\n".format(shape=df.shape))
    print("COLUMN NAMES:\n{names}\n".format(names=df.columns))
    print("HEAD:\n{head}\n".format(head=df.head(nrows)))


dataframe_quick_look(df, nrows=2)
```

This user-defined function returns the shape of the data (number of rows and columns), the column names, and the first two rows of the data.

```
SHAPE:
(93239, 11)

COLUMN NAMES:
Index(['IDLink', 'Title', 'Headline', 'Source', 'Topic', 'PublishDate',
       'SentimentTitle', 'SentimentHeadline', 'Facebook', 'GooglePlus',
       'LinkedIn'],
      dtype='object')

HEAD:
    IDLink                                             Title  \
0  99248.0    Obama Lays Wreath at Arlington National Cemetery
1  10423.0           A Look at the Health of the Chinese Economy

                                            Headline      Source     Topic  \
0  Obama Lays Wreath at Arlington National Cemete...  USA TODAY     obama
1  Tim Haywood, investment director business-unit...  Bloomberg   economy

            PublishDate  SentimentTitle  SentimentHeadline  Facebook  \
0  2002-04-02 00:00:00        0.000000          -0.053300        -1
1  2008-09-20 00:00:00        0.208333          -0.156386        -1

   GooglePlus  LinkedIn
0          -1        -1
1          -1        -1
```

Figure 7.8: Raw data

This is a much larger dataset in terms of features than is needed to run the topic models.

3. Notice that one of the columns, named **Topic**, actually contains the information that topic models are trying to ascertain. Let's briefly look at the provided topic data, so that when we finally generate our own topics, the results can be compared. Run the following line to print the unique topic values and their number of occurrences:

```
print("TOPICS:\n{topics}\n".format(topics=df["Topic"].value_counts()))
```

The output is as follows:

```
TOPICS:
economy      33928
obama        28610
microsoft    21858
palestine     8843
Name: Topic, dtype: int64
```

4. Now, we extract the headline data and transform the extracted data into a list object. Print the first five elements of the list and the list length to confirm that the extraction was successful:

```
raw = df["Headline"].tolist()
print("HEADLINES:\n{lines}\n".format(lines=raw[:5]))
print("LENGTH:\n{length}\n".format(length=len(raw)))
```

```
HEADLINES:
['Obama Lays Wreath at Arlington National Cemetery. President Barack Obama has laid a wreath at the Tomb of the Unknowns to hon
or', 'Tim Haywood, investment director business-unit head for fixed income at Gam, discusses the China beige book and the state
of the economy.', "Nouriel Roubini, NYU professor and chairman at Roubini Global Economics, explains why the global economy is
n't facing the same conditions", "Finland's economy expanded marginally in the three months ended December, after contracting i
n the previous quarter, preliminary figures from Statistics Finland showed Monday. ", 'Tourism and public spending continued to
boost the economy in January, in light of contraction in private consumption and exports, according to the Bank of Thailand dat
a. ']

LENGTH:
93239
```

Figure 7.9: A list of headlines

With the data now loaded and correctly formatted, let's talk about textual data cleaning and then jump into some actual cleaning and preprocessing. For instructional purposes, the cleaning process will initially be built and executed on only one headline. Once we have established the process and tested it on the example headline, we will go back and run the process on every headline.

Cleaning Text Data

A key component of all successful modeling exercises is a clean dataset that has been appropriately and sufficiently preprocessed for the specific data type and analysis being performed. Text data is no exception, as it is virtually unusable in its raw form. It does not matter what algorithm is being run: if the data isn't properly prepared, the results will be at best meaningless and at worst misleading. As the saying goes, "*garbage in, garbage out.*" For topic modeling, the goal of data cleaning is to isolate the words in each document that could be relevant by removing everything that could be obstructive.

Data cleaning and preprocessing is almost always specific to the dataset, meaning that each dataset will require a unique set of cleaning and preprocessing steps selected to specifically handle the issues in the dataset being worked on. With text data, cleaning and preprocessing steps can include language filtering, removing URLs and screen names, lemmatizing, and stop word removal, among others. In the forthcoming exercises, a dataset featuring news headlines is cleaned for topic modeling.

Data Cleaning Techniques

To reiterate a previous point, the goal of cleaning text for topic modeling is to isolate the words in each document that could be relevant to finding the abstract topics of the corpus. This means removing common words, short words (generally more common), numbers, and punctuation. No hard and fast process exists for cleaning data, so it is important to understand the typical problem points in the type of data being cleaned and to do extensive exploratory work.

Let's now discuss some of the text data cleaning techniques that we will employ. One of the first things that needs to be done when doing any modeling task involving text is to determine the language(s) of the text. In this dataset, most of the headlines are English, so we will remove the non-English headlines for simplicity. Building models on non-English text data requires additional skill sets, the least of which is fluency in the particular language being modeled.

The next crucial step in data cleaning is to remove all elements of the documents that are either not relevant to word-based models or are potential sources of noise that could obscure the results. Elements needing removal could include website addresses, punctuation, numbers, and stop words. Stop words are basically simple, everyday words, including we, are, and the. It is important to note that there is no definitive dictionary of stop words; instead, every dictionary varies slightly. Despite the differences, each dictionary represents a number of common words that are assumed to be topic agnostic. Topic models try to identify words that are both frequent and infrequent enough to be descriptive of an abstract topic.

The removal of website addresses has a similar motivation. Specific website addresses will appear very rarely, but even if one specific website address appears enough to be linked to a topic, website addresses are not interpretable in the same way as words. Removing irrelevant information from the documents reduces the amount of noise that could either prevent model convergence or obscure results.

Lemmatization, like language detection, is an important component of all modeling activities involving text. It is the process of reducing words to their base form as a way to group words that should all be the same but are not. Consider the words running, runs, and ran. All three of these words have the base form of run. A great aspect of lemmatizing is that it looks at all the words in a sentence, or in other words it considers the context, before determining how to alter each word. Lemmatization, like most of the preceding cleaning techniques, simply reduces the amount of noise in the data, so that we can identify clean and interpretable topics.

Now, with basic knowledge of textual cleaning techniques, let's apply it to real-world data.

Exercise 29: Cleaning Data Step by Step

In this exercise, we will learn how to implement some key techniques for cleaning text data. Each technique will be explained as we work through the exercise. After every cleaning step, the example headline is output using **print**, so we can watch the evolution from raw data to modeling-ready data:

1. Select the fifth headline as the example on which we will build and test the cleaning process. The fifth headline is not a random choice; it was selected because it contains specific problems that will be addressed during the cleaning process:

   ```
   example = raw[5]
   print(example)
   ```

   The output is as follows:

   ```
   Over 100 attendees expected to see latest version of Microsoft Dynamics SL and Dynamics GP (PRWeb February 29, 2016) Read the f
   ull story at http://www.prweb.com/releases/2016/03/prweb13238571.htm
   ```

   Figure 7.10: The fifth headline

2. Use the **langdetect** library to detect the language of each headline. If the language is anything other than English ("**en**"), remove that headline from the dataset:

```
def do_language_identifying(txt):
    try: the_language = langdetect.detect(txt)
    except: the_language = 'none'
    return the_language

print("DETECTED LANGUAGE:\n{lang}\n".format(lang=do_language_
identifying(example)
))
```

The output is as follows:

```
DETECTED LANGUAGE:
en
```

Figure 7.11: Detected language

3. Split the string containing the headline into pieces, called **tokens**, using the white spaces. The returned object is a list of words and numbers that make up the headline. Breaking the headline string into tokens makes the cleaning and preprocessing process simpler:

```
example = example.split(" ")
print(example)
```

The output is as follows:

```
['Over', '100', 'attendees', 'expected', 'to', 'see', 'latest', 'version', 'of', 'Microsoft', 'Dynamics', 'SL', 'and', 'Dynamic
s', 'GP', '(PRWeb', 'February', '29,', '2016)', 'Read', 'the', 'full', 'story', 'at', 'http://www.prweb.com/releases/2016/03/pr
web13238571.htm', '']
```

Figure 7.12: String split using white spaces

4. Identify all URLs using a regular expression search for tokens containing **http://** or **https://**. Replace the URLs with the '**URL**' string:

```
example = ['URL' if bool(regex.search("http[s]?://", i))else i for i in
example]
print(example)
```

The output is as follows:

```
['Over', '100', 'attendees', 'expected', 'to', 'see', 'latest', 'version', 'of', 'Microsoft', 'Dynamics', 'SL', 'and', 'Dynamic
s', 'GP', '(PRWeb', 'February', '29,', '2016)', 'Read', 'the', 'full', 'story', 'at', 'URL', '']
```

Figure 7.13: URLs replaced with the URL string

5. Replace all punctuation and newline symbols (**\n**) with empty strings using regular expressions:

```
example = [regex.sub("[^\\w\\s]|\n", "", i) for i in example]
print(example)
```

The output is as follows:

```
['Over', '100', 'attendees', 'expected', 'to', 'see', 'latest', 'version', 'of', 'Microsoft', 'Dynamics', 'SL', 'and', 'Dynamic
s', 'GP', 'PRWeb', 'February', '29', '2016', 'Read', 'the', 'full', 'story', 'at', 'URL', '']
```

Figure 7.14: Punctuation replaced with newline character

6. Replace all numbers with empty strings using regular expressions:

```
example = [regex.sub("^[0-9]*$", "", i) for i in example]
print(example)
```

The output is as follows:

```
['Over', '', 'attendees', 'expected', 'to', 'see', 'latest', 'version', 'of', 'Microsoft', 'Dynamics', 'SL', 'and', 'Dynamics',
'GP', 'PRWeb', 'February', '', '', 'Read', 'the', 'full', 'story', 'at', 'URL', '']
```

Figure 7.15: Numbers replaced with empty strings

7. Change all uppercase letters to lowercase. Converting everything to lowercase is not a mandatory step, but it does help reduce complexity. With everything lowercase, there is less to keep track of and therefore less chance of error:

```
example = [i.lower() if i not in "URL" else i for i in example]
print(example)
```

The output is as follows:

```
['over', '', 'attendees', 'expected', 'to', 'see', 'latest', 'version', 'of', 'microsoft', 'dynamics', 'sl', 'and', 'dynamics',
'gp', 'prweb', 'february', '', '', 'read', 'the', 'full', 'story', 'at', 'URL', '']
```

Figure 7.16: Uppercase letters converted to lowercase

8. Remove the **"URL"** string that was added as a placeholder in *step* 4. The previously added **"URL"** string is not actually needed for modeling. If it seems harmless to leave it in, consider that the **"URL"** string could appear naturally in a headline and we do not want to artificially boost its number of appearances. Also, the **"URL"** string does not appear in every headline, so by leaving it in we could be unintentionally creating a connection between the **"URL"** strings and a topic:

```
example = [i for i in example if i not in "URL"]
print(example)
```

The output is as follows:

```
['over', 'attendees', 'expected', 'to', 'see', 'latest', 'version', 'of', 'microsoft', 'dynamics', 'sl', 'and', 'dynamics', 'g
p', 'prweb', 'february', 'read', 'the', 'full', 'story', 'at']
```

Figure 7.17: String URL removed

9. Load in the **stopwords** dictionary from **nltk** and print it:

```
list_stop_words = nltk.corpus.stopwords.words("English")
list_stop_words = [regex.sub("[^\\w\\s]", "", i) for i in list_stop_words]
print(list_stop_words)
```

The output is as follows:

```
['i', 'me', 'my', 'myself', 'we', 'our', 'ours', 'ourselves', 'you', 'youre', 'youve', 'youll', 'youd', 'your', 'yours', 'yours
elf', 'yourselves', 'he', 'him', 'his', 'himself', 'she', 'shes', 'her', 'hers', 'herself', 'it', 'its', 'its', 'itself', 'the
y', 'them', 'their', 'theirs', 'themselves', 'what', 'which', 'who', 'whom', 'this', 'that', 'thatll', 'these', 'those', 'am',
'is', 'are', 'was', 'were', 'be', 'been', 'being', 'have', 'has', 'had', 'having', 'do', 'does', 'did', 'doing', 'a', 'an', 'th
e', 'and', 'but', 'if', 'or', 'because', 'as', 'until', 'while', 'of', 'at', 'by', 'for', 'with', 'about', 'against', 'betwee
n', 'into', 'through', 'during', 'before', 'after', 'above', 'below', 'to', 'from', 'up', 'down', 'in', 'out', 'on', 'off', 'ov
er', 'under', 'again', 'further', 'then', 'once', 'here', 'there', 'when', 'where', 'why', 'how', 'all', 'any', 'both', 'each',
'few', 'more', 'most', 'other', 'some', 'such', 'no', 'nor', 'not', 'only', 'own', 'same', 'so', 'than', 'too', 'very', 's',
't', 'can', 'will', 'just', 'don', 'dont', 'should', 'shouldve', 'now', 'd', 'll', 'm', 'o', 're', 've', 'y', 'ain', 'aren', 'a
rent', 'couldn', 'couldnt', 'didn', 'didnt', 'doesn', 'doesnt', 'hadn', 'hadnt', 'hasn', 'hasnt', 'haven', 'havent', 'isn', 'is
nt', 'ma', 'mightn', 'mightnt', 'mustn', 'mustnt', 'needn', 'neednt', 'shan', 'shant', 'shouldn', 'shouldnt', 'wasn', 'wasnt',
'weren', 'werent', 'won', 'wont', 'wouldn', 'wouldnt']
```

Figure 7.18: List of stop words

Before using the dictionary, it is important to reformat the words to match the formatting of our headlines. That involves confirming that everything is lowercase and without punctuation.

10. Now that we have correctly formatted the **stopwords** dictionary, use it to remove all stop words from the headline:

```
example = [i for i in example if i not in list_stop_words]
print(example)
```

The output is as follows:

```
['attendees', 'expected', 'see', 'latest', 'version', 'microsoft', 'dynamics', 'sl', 'dynamics', 'gp', 'prweb', 'february', 're
ad', 'full', 'story']
```

Figure 7.19: Stop words removed from the headline

11. Perform lemmatization by defining a function that can be applied to each headline individually. Lemmatizing requires loading the wordnet dictionary:

```
def do_lemmatizing(wrd):
    out = nltk.corpus.wordnet.morphy(wrd)
    return (wrd if out is None else out)


example = [do_lemmatizing(i) for i in example]
print(example)
```

The output is as follows:

```
['attendee', 'expect', 'see', 'latest', 'version', 'microsoft', 'dynamics', 'sl', 'dynamics', 'gp', 'prweb', 'february', 'rea
d', 'full', 'story']
```

Figure 7.20: Output after performing lemmatization

12. Remove all words with a length of four of less from the list of tokens. The assumption around this step is that short words are, in general, more common and therefore will not drive the types of insights we are looking to extract from the topic models. This is the final step of data cleaning and preprocessing:

```
example = [i for i in example if len(i) >= 5]
print(example)
```

The output is as follows:

```
['attendee', 'expect', 'latest', 'version', 'microsoft', 'dynamics', 'dynamics', 'prweb', 'february', 'story']
```

Figure 7.21: Headline number five post-cleaning

Now that we have worked through the cleaning and preprocessing steps individually on one headline, we need to apply those steps to every one of the nearly 100,000 headlines. Applying the steps to every headline the way we applied them to the single headline, which is in a manual way, is not feasible.

Exercise 30: Complete Data Cleaning

In this exercise, we will consolidate steps 2 through 12 from *Exercise 29, Cleaning Data Step-by-Step*, into one function that we can apply to every headline. The function will take one headline in string format as an input and output one cleaned headline as a list of tokens. The topic models require that documents be formatted as strings instead of as lists of tokens, so, in *step 4*, the lists of tokens are converted back into strings:

1. Define a function that contains all the individual steps of the cleaning process from *Exercise 29, Cleaning Data Step-by-step*:

```python
def do_headline_cleaning(txt):
    # identify language of tweet
    # return null if language not English
    lg = do_language_identifying(txt)
    if lg != 'en':
        return None
    # split the string on whitespace
    out = txt.split(" ")
    # identify urls
    # replace with URL
    out = ['URL' if bool(regex.search("http[s]?://", i)) else i for i in out]
    # remove all punctuation
    out = [regex.sub("[^\\w\\s]|\n", "", i) for i in out]
    # remove all numerics
    out = [regex.sub("^[0-9]*$", "", i) for i in out]
    # make all non-keywords lowercase
    out = [i.lower() if i not in "URL" else i for i in out]
    # remove URL
    out = [i for i in out if i not in "URL"]
    # remove stopwords
    list_stop_words = nltk.corpus.stopwords.words("English")
    list_stop_words = [regex.sub("[^\\w\\s]", "", i) for i in list_stop_words]
    out = [i for i in out if i not in list_stop_words]
    # lemmatizing
    out = [do_lemmatizing(i) for i in out]
    # keep words 5 or more characters long
    out = [i for i in out if len(i) >= 5]
    return out
```

2. Execute the function on each headline. The **map** function in Python is a nice way to apply a user-defined function to each element of a list. Convert the **map** object to a list and assign it to the **clean** variable. The **clean** variable is a list of lists:

```
clean = list(map(do_headline_cleaning, raw))
```

3. In **do_headline_cleaning**, **None** is returned if the language of the headline is detected as being any language other than English. The elements of the final cleaned list should only be lists, not **None**, so remove all **None** types. Use **print** to display the first five cleaned headlines and the length of the **clean** variable:

```
clean = list(filter(None.__ne__, clean))
print("HEADLINES:\n{lines}\n".format(lines=clean[:5]))
print("LENGTH:\n{length}\n".format(length=len(clean)))
```

The output is as follows:

```
HEADLINES:
[['obama', 'wreath', 'arlington', 'national', 'cemetery', 'president', 'barack', 'obama', 'wreath', 'unknown', 'honor'], ['hayw
ood', 'investment', 'director', 'businessunit', 'income', 'discus', 'china', 'beige', 'state', 'economy'], ['nouriel', 'roubin
i', 'professor', 'chairman', 'roubini', 'global', 'economics', 'explain', 'global', 'economy', 'facing', 'conditions'], ['finla
nd', 'economy', 'expand', 'marginally', 'three', 'month', 'december', 'contracting', 'previous', 'quarter', 'preliminary', 'fig
ure', 'statistics', 'finland', 'monday'], ['tourism', 'public', 'spending', 'continue', 'boost', 'economy', 'january', 'light',
'contraction', 'private', 'consumption', 'export', 'accord', 'thailand']]

LENGTH:
92948
```

Figure 7.22: Headline and its length

4. For every individual headline, concatenate the tokens using a white space separator. The headlines should now be an unstructured collection of words, nonsensical to the human reader, but ideal for topic modeling:

```
clean_sentences = [" ".join(i) for i in clean]
print(clean_sentences[0:10])
```

The cleaned headlines should resemble the following:

```
['obama wreath arlington national cemetery president barack obama wreath unknown honor', 'haywood investment director businessu
nit income discus china beige state economy', 'nouriel roubini professor chairman roubini global economics explain global econo
my facing conditions', 'finland economy expand marginally three month december contracting previous quarter preliminary figure
statistics finland monday', 'tourism public spending continue boost economy january light contraction private consumption expor
t accord thailand', 'attendee expect latest version microsoft dynamics dynamics prweb february story', 'ramallah february pales
tine liberation organization sectretarygeneral erekat thursday express concern kenyan president uhuru kenyattas visit jerusalem
jordan valley', 'first michelle obama speak state white house washington wednesday interactive student workshop musical legacy
charles student school community organization across country participate quotin performance white housequot series', 'hancock c
ounty early monday morning family years', 'delhi feb29 technology giant microsoft target rival apple series focusing windows gr
oss windows machine']
```

Figure 7.23: Headlines cleaned for modeling

To recap, what the cleaning and preprocessing work effectively does is strip out the noise from the data, so that the model can hone in on elements of the data that could actually drive insights. For example, words that are agnostic to any topic (or stop words) should not be informing topics, but, by accident alone if left in, could be informing topics. In an effort to avoid what we could call "*fake signals*," we remove those words. Likewise, since topic models cannot discern context, punctuation is irrelevant and is therefore removed. Even if the model could find the topics without removing the noise from the data, the uncleaned data could have thousands to millions of extra words and random characters to parse, depending on the number of documents in the corpus, which could significantly increase the computational demands. So, data cleaning is an integral part of topic modeling.

Activity 15: Loading and Cleaning Twitter Data

In this activity, we will load and clean Twitter data for modeling done in subsequent activities. Our usage of the headline data is ongoing, so let's complete this activity in a separate Jupyter notebook, but with all the same requirements and imported libraries.

The goal is to take the raw tweet data, clean it, and produce the same output that we did in *Step* 4 of the previous exercise. That output should be a list whose length is similar to the number of rows in the raw data file. The length is similar to, meaning potentially not equal to, the number of rows, because tweets can get dropped in the cleaning process for reasons including that the tweet might not be in English. Each element of the list should represent one tweet and should contain just the words in the tweet that might be relevant to topic formation.

Here are the steps to complete the activity:

1. Import the necessary libraries.

2. Load the LA Times health Twitter data (latimeshealth.txt) from https://github.com/TrainingByPackt/Applied-Unsupervised-Learning-with-Python/tree/master/Lesson07/Activity15-Activity17.

> **Note**
>
> This dataset is downloaded from https://archive.ics.uci.edu/ml/datasets/Health+News+in+Twitter. We have uploaded it on GitHub and it can be downloaded from https://github.com/TrainingByPackt/Applied-Unsupervised-Learning-with-Python/tree/master/Lesson07/Activity15-Activity17. Karami, A., Gangopadhyay, A., Zhou, B., & Kharrazi, H. (2017). Fuzzy approach topic discovery in health and medical corpora. International Journal of Fuzzy Systems. UCI Machine Learning Repository [http://archive.ics.uci.edu/ml]. Irvine, CA: University of California, School of Information and Computer Science.

3. Run a quick exploratory analysis to ascertain data size and structure.

4. Extract the tweet text and convert it to a list object.

5. Write a function to perform language detection, tokenization on whitespaces, and replace screen names and URLs with **SCREENNAME** and **URL**, respectively. The function should also remove punctuation, numbers, and the SCREENNAME and URL replacements. Convert everything to lowercase, except SCREENNAME and URL. It should remove all stop words, perform lemmatization, and keep words with five or more letters.

6. Apply the function defined in *step 5* to every tweet.

7. Remove elements of the output list equal to **None**.

8. Turn the elements of each tweet back into a string. Concatenate using white space.

9. Keep the notebook open for future modeling.

> **Note**
>
> All the activities in this chapter need to be performed in the same notebook.

10. The output will be as follows:

```
['running shoes extra', 'class crunch intense workout pulley system', 'thousand natural product', 'natural product ex
plore beauty supplement', 'fitness weekend south beach spark activity', 'kayla harrison sacrifice', 'sonic treatment
alzheimers disease', 'ultrasound brain restore memory alzheimers needle onlyso farin mouse', 'apple researchkit reall
y medical research', 'warning chantix drink taking might remember']
```

Figure 7.24: Tweets cleaned for modeling

> **Note**
>
> The solution for this activity can be found on page 357.

Latent Dirichlet Allocation

In 2003, David Biel, Andrew Ng, and Michael Jordan published their article on the topic modeling algorithm known as **Latent Dirichlet Allocation** (**LDA**). LDA is a generative probabilistic model. This means that we assume the process, which is articulated in terms of probabilities, by which the data was generated is known and then work backward from the data to the parameters that generated it. In this case, it is the topics that generated the data that are of interest. The process discussed here is the most basic form of LDA, but for learning, it is also the most comprehensible.

For each document in the corpus, the assumed generative process is:

1. Select $N \sim Poisson(\lambda)$, where N is the number of words.

2. Select $\theta \sim Dirichlet(\alpha)$, where θ is the distribution of topics.

3. For each of the N words w_n, select topic $z_n \sim Multinomial(\theta)$, and select word w_n from $P(w_n|z_n, \beta)$.

Let's go through the generative process in a bit more detail. The preceding three steps repeat for every document in the corpus. The initial step is to choose the number of words in the document by sampling from, in most cases, the *Poisson* distribution. It is important to note that, because N is independent of the other variables, the randomness associated with its generation is mostly ignored in the derivation of the algorithm. Coming after the selection of N is the generation of the topic mixture or distribution of topics, which is unique to each document. Think of this as a per-document list of topics with probabilities representing the amount of the document represented by each topic. Consider three topics: A, B, and C. An example document could be 100% topic A, 75% topic B, and 25% topic C, or an infinite number of other combinations. Lastly, the specific words in the document are selected via a probability statement conditioned on the selected topic and the distribution of words for that topic. Note that documents are not really generated in this way, but it is a reasonable proxy.

This process can be thought of as a distribution over distributions. A document is selected from the collection (distribution) of documents, and from that document one topic is selected, via the multinomial distribution, from the probability distribution of topics for that document generated by the Dirichlet distribution:

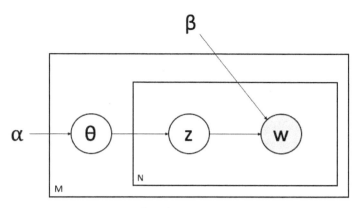

Figure 7.25: Graphical representation of LDA

The most straightforward way to build the formula representing the LDA solution is through a graphical representation. This particular representation is referred to as a plate notation graphical model, as it uses plates to represent the two iterative steps in the process. You will recall that the generative process was executed for every document in the corpus, so the outermost plate, labeled M, represents iterating over each document. Similarly, the iteration over words in *step 3* is represented by the innermost plate of the diagram, labeled N. The circles represent the parameters, distributions, and results. The shaded circle, labeled *w*, is the selected word, which is the only known piece of data and, as such, is used to reverse-engineer the generative process. Besides *w*, the other four variables in the diagram are defined as follows:

- α: Hyperparameter for the topic-document Dirichlet distribution

- β: Distribution of words for each topic

- Z: This is the latent variable for the topic

- θ: This is the latent variable for the distribution of topics for each document

α and β control the frequency of topics in documents and of words in topics. If α increases, the documents become increasingly similar as the number of topics in each document increases. On the other hand, if α decreases, the documents become increasingly dissimilar as the number of topics in each document decreases. The β parameter behaves similarly.

Variational Inference

The big issue with LDA is that the evaluation of the conditional probabilities, the distributions, is unmanageable, so instead of computing them directly, the probabilities are approximated. Variational inference is one of the simpler approximation algorithms, but it has an extensive derivation that requires significant knowledge of probability. In order to spend more time on the application of LDA, this section will give some high-level details on how variational inference is applied in this context, but will not fully explore the algorithm.

Let's take a moment to work through the variational inference algorithm intuitively. Start by randomly assigning each word in each document in the corpus to one of the topics. Then, for each document and each word in each document separately, calculate two proportions. Those proportions would be the proportion of words in the document that are currently assigned to the topic, $P(Topic|Document)$, and the proportion of assignments across all documents of a specific word to the topic, $P(Word|Topic)$. Multiply the two proportions and use the resulting proportion to assign the word to a new topic. Repeat this process until a steady state, where topic assignments are not changing significantly, is reached. These assignments are then used to estimate the within-document topic mixture and the within-topic word mixture.

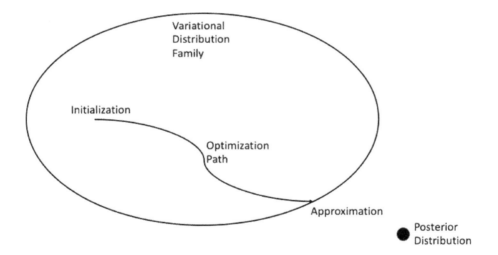

Figure 7.26: The variational inference process

The thought process behind variational inference is that, if the actual distribution is intractable, then a simpler distribution, let's call it the variational distribution, very close to initial distribution, which is tractable, should be found so that inference becomes possible.

To start, select a family of distributions, q, conditioned on new variational parameters. The parameters are optimized so that the original distribution, which is actually the posterior distribution for those people familiar with Bayesian statistics, and the variational distribution are as close as possible. The variational distribution will be close enough to the original posterior distribution to be used as a proxy, making any inference done on it applicable to the original posterior distribution. The generic formula for the family of distributions, q, is as follows:

$$q(\theta, z | \gamma, \phi) = q(\theta | \gamma) \prod_{n=1}^{N} q(z_n | \phi_n)$$

Figure 7.27: Formula for the family of distributions, q

There is a large collection of potential variational distributions that can be used as an approximation for the posterior distribution. An initial variational distribution is selected from the collection, which acts as the starting point for an optimization process that iteratively moves closer and closer to the optimal distribution. The optimal parameters are the parameters of the distribution that best approximate the posterior.

The similarity of the two distributions is measured using the **Kullback-Leibler** (KL) divergence. KL divergence is also known as relative entropy. Again, finding the best variational distribution, q, for the original posterior distribution, p, requires minimizing the KL divergence. The default method for finding the parameters that minimize the divergence is the iterative fixed-point method, which we will not dig into here.

Once the optimal distribution has been identified, which means the optimal parameters have been identified, it can be leveraged to produce the output matrices and do any required inference.

Bag of Words

Text cannot be passed directly into any machine learning algorithm; it first needs to be encoded numerically. A straightforward way of working with text in machine learning is via a bag-of-words model, which removes all information around the order of the words and focuses strictly on the degree of presence, meaning count or frequency, of each word. The Python **sklearn** library can be leveraged to transform the cleaned vector created in the previous exercise into the structure that the LDA model requires. Since LDA is a probabilistic model, we do not want to do any scaling or weighting of the word occurrences; instead, we opt to input just the raw counts.

The input of the bag-of-words model will be the list of cleaned strings that were returned from *Exercise 4, Complete Data Cleaning*. The output will be the document number, the word as its numeric encoding, and the count of times that word appears in that document. These three items will be presented as a tuple and an integer. The tuple will be something like (0, 325), where 0 is the document number and 325 is the numerically encoded word. Note that 325 would be the encoding of that word across all documents. The integer would then be the count. The bag-of-words models we will be running in this chapter are from **sklearn** and are called **CountVectorizer** and **TfIdfVectorizer**. The first model returns the raw counts and the second returns a scaled value, which we will discuss a bit later.

A critical note is that the results of both topic models being covered in this chapter can vary from run to run, even when the data is the same, because of randomness. Neither the probabilities in LDA nor the optimization algorithms are deterministic, so do not be surprised if your results differ slightly from the results shown from here on out.

Exercise 31: Creating a Bag-of-Words Model Using the Count Vectorizer

In this exercise, we will run the **CountVectorizer** in **sklearn** to convert our previously created cleaned vector of headlines into a bag-of-words data structure. In addition, we will define some variables that will be used through the modeling process.

1. Define **number_words**, **number_docs**, and **number_features**. The first two variables control the visualization of the LDA results. More to come later. The **number_features** variable controls the number of words that will be kept in the feature space:

```
number_words = 10
number_docs = 10
number_features = 1000
```

2. Run the count vectorizer and print the output. There are three crucial inputs, which are **max_df**, **min_df**, and **max_features**. These parameters further filter the number of words in the corpus down to those that will most likely influence the model. Words that only appear in a small number of documents are too rare to be attributed to any topic, so **min_df** is used to throw away words that appear in less than the specified number of documents. Words that appear in too many documents are not specific enough to be linked to specific topics, so **max_df** is used to throw away words that appear in more than the specified percentage of documents. Lastly, we do not want to overfit the model, so the number of words used to fit the model is limited to the most frequently occurring specified number (**max_features**) of words:

```
vectorizer1 = sklearn.feature_extraction.text.CountVectorizer(
    analyzer="word",
```

```
        max_df=0.5,
        min_df=20,
        max_features=number_features
    )
    clean_vec1 = vectorizer1.fit_transform(clean_sentences)
    print(clean_vec1[0])
```

The output is as follows:

```
(0, 407)        1
(0, 88)         1
(0, 643)        1
(0, 557)        1
(0, 572)        2
```

Figure 7.28: The bag-of-words data structure

3. Extract the feature names and the words from the vectorizer. The model is only fed the numerical encodings of the words, so having the feature names vector to merge with the results will make interpretation easier:

```
feature_names_vec1 = vectorizer1.get_feature_names()
```

Perplexity

Models generally have metrics that can be leveraged to evaluate their performance. Topic models are no different, although performance in this case has a slightly different definition. In regression and classification, predicted values can be compared to actual values from which clear measures of performance can be calculated. With topic models, prediction is less reliable, because the model only knows the words it was trained on and new documents may not contain any of those words, despite featuring the same topics. Due to that difference, topic models are evaluated using a metric specific to language models called **perplexity**. Perplexity, abbreviated to PP, measures the number of different equally most probable words that can follow any given word on average. Let's consider two words as an example: the and announce. The word the can preface an enormous number of equally most probable words, while the number of equally most probable words that can follow the word announce is significantly less – albeit still a large number.

The idea is that words that, on average, can be followed by a smaller number of equally most probable words are more specific and can be more tightly tied to topics. As such, lower perplexity scores imply better language models. Perplexity is very similar to entropy, but perplexity is typically used because it is easier to interpret. As we will see momentarily, it can be used to select the optimal number of topics. With m being the number of words in the sequence of words, perplexity is defined as:

$$PP = \hat{P}(w_1, \ldots, w_m)^{-1/m}$$

Figure 7.29: Formula of perplexity

Exercise 32: Selecting the Number of Topics

As stated previously, LDA has two required inputs. The first are the documents themselves and the second is the number of topics. Selecting an appropriate number of topics can be very tricky. One approach to finding the optimal number of topics is to search over several numbers of topics and select the number of topics that corresponds to the smallest perplexity score. In machine learning, this approach is referred to as grid search.

In this exercise, we use the perplexity scores for LDA models fit on varying numbers of topics to determine the number of topics with which to move forward. Keep in mind that the original dataset had the headlines sorted into four topics. Let's see whether this approach returns four topics:

1. Define a function that fits an LDA model on various numbers of topics and computes the perplexity score. Return two items: a data frame that has the number of topics with its perplexity score and the number of topics with the minimum perplexity score as an integer:

    ```
    def perplexity_by_ntopic(data, ntopics):
        output_dict = {
            "Number Of Topics": [],
            "Perplexity Score": []
        }

        for t in ntopics:
            lda = sklearn.decomposition.LatentDirichletAllocation(
                n_components=t,
                learning_method="online",
                random_state=0
            )
    ```

```
lda.fit(data)

output_dict["Number Of Topics"].append(t)
output_dict["Perplexity Score"].append(lda.perplexity(data))

output_df = pandas.DataFrame(output_dict)

index_min_perplexity = output_df["Perplexity Score"].idxmin()
output_num_topics = output_df.loc[
    index_min_perplexity,  # index
    "Number Of Topics"  # column
]

return (output_df, output_num_topics)
```

2. Execute the function defined in *step 1*. The **ntopics** input is a list of numbers of topics that can be of any length and contain any values. Print out the data frame:

```
df_perplexity, optimal_num_topics = perplexity_by_ntopic(
    clean_vec1,
    ntopics=[1, 2, 3, 4, 6, 8, 10]
)
print(df_perplexity)
```

The output is as follows:

	Number Of Topics	Perplexity Score
0	1	510.011710
1	2	464.310162
2	3	413.054650
3	4	431.545934
4	6	511.728157
5	8	542.678576
6	10	572.124718

Figure 7.30: Data frame containing number of topics and perplexity score

3. Plot the perplexity scores as a function of the number of topics. This is just another way to view the results contained in the data frame from *step 2*:

```
df_perplexity.plot.line("Number Of Topics", "Perplexity Score")
```

The plot looks as follows:

```
<matplotlib.axes._subplots.AxesSubplot at 0x1ebe05b15f8>
```

Figure 7.31: Line plot view of perplexity as a function of the number of topics

As the data frame and plot show, the optimal number of topics using perplexity is three. Having the number of topics set to four yielded the second-lowest perplexity, so, while the results did not exactly match with the information contained in the original dataset, the results are close enough to engender confidence in the grid search approach to identifying the optimal number of topics. There could be several reasons that the grid search returned three instead of four, which we will dig into in future exercises.

Exercise 33: Running Latent Dirichlet Allocation

In this exercise, we implement LDA and examine the results. LDA outputs two matrices. The first is the topic-document matrix and the second is the word-topic matrix. We will look at these matrices as returned from the model and as nicely formatted tables that are easier to digest:

1. Fit an LDA model using the optimal number of topics found in *Exercise 32, Selecting the Number of Topics*:

```
lda = sklearn.decomposition.LatentDirichletAllocation(
    n_components=optimal_num_topics,
    learning_method="online",
    random_state=0
)
lda.fit(clean_vec1)
```

The output is as follows:

```
LatentDirichletAllocation(batch_size=128, doc_topic_prior=None,
            evaluate_every=-1, learning_decay=0.7,
            learning_method='online', learning_offset=10.0,
            max_doc_update_iter=100, max_iter=10, mean_change_tol=0.001,
            n_components=3, n_jobs=None, n_topics=None, perp_tol=0.1,
            random_state=0, topic_word_prior=None,
            total_samples=1000000.0, verbose=0)
```

Figure 7.32: LDA model

2. Output the topic-document matrix and its shape to confirm that it aligns with the number of topics and the number of documents. Each row of the matrix is the per-document distribution of topics:

```
lda_transform = lda.transform(clean_vec1)
print(lda_transform.shape)
print(lda_transform)
```

The output is as follows:

```
(92948, 3)
[[0.90423071 0.04761949 0.0481498 ]
 [0.0449056  0.04292327 0.91217113]
 [0.0435693  0.0441942  0.91223649]
 ...
 [0.20977116 0.03942095 0.75080789]
 [0.09239268 0.07121637 0.83639094]
 [0.20062764 0.41458136 0.384791  ]]
```

Figure 7.33: Topic-document matrix and its dimensions

3. Output the word-topic matrix and its shape to confirm that it aligns with the number of features (words) specified in *Exercise 31, Creating Bag-of-Words Model Using the Count Vectorizer*, and the number of topics input. Each row is basically the counts (although not counts exactly) of assignments to that topic of each word, but those quasi-counts can be transformed into the per-topic distribution of words:

```
lda_components = lda.components_
print(lda_components.shape)
print(lda_components)
```

The output is as follows:

```
(3, 1000)
[[3.67812459e-01 3.83046413e-01 3.79939561e-01 ... 3.48448881e-01
  1.18665576e+02 4.62012727e+02]
 [3.36269915e-01 2.72144107e+02 2.61257455e+01 ... 3.35946774e-01
  2.05558903e+02 3.94048139e-01]
 [2.74795972e+02 4.27720110e-01 1.89390109e+02 ... 2.31713244e+02
  1.79236579e+02 4.10569467e-01]]
```

Figure 7.34: Word-topic matrix and its dimensions

4. Define a function that formats the two output matrices into easy-to-read tables:

```
def get_topics(mod, vec, names, docs, ndocs, nwords):
    # word to topic matrix
    W = mod.components_
    W_norm = W / W.sum(axis=1)[:, numpy.newaxis]
    # topic to document matrix
    H = mod.transform(vec)
    W_dict = {}
    H_dict = {}
    for tpc_idx, tpc_val in enumerate(W_norm):
        topic = "Topic{}".format(tpc_idx)
        # formatting w
        W_indices = tpc_val.argsort()[::-1][:nwords]
        W_names_values = [
            (round(tpc_val[j], 4), names[j])
            for j in W_indices
        ]
```

```
            W_dict[topic] = W_names_values
            # formatting h
            H_indices = H[:, tpc_idx].argsort()[::-1][:ndocs]
            H_names_values = [
                (round(H[:, tpc_idx][j], 4), docs[j])
                for j in H_indices
            ]
            H_dict[topic] = H_names_values
        W_df = pandas.DataFrame(
            W_dict,
            index=["Word" + str(i) for i in range(nwords)]
        )
        H_df = pandas.DataFrame(
            H_dict,
            index=["Doc" + str(i) for i in range(ndocs)]
        )
        return (W_df, H_df)
```

The function may be tricky to navigate, so let's walk through it. Start by creating the W and H matrices, which includes converting the assignment counts of W into the per-topic distribution of words. Then, iterate over the topics. Inside each iteration, identify the top words and documents associated with each topic. Convert the results into two data frames.

5. Execute the function defined in *step* 4:

```
W_df, H_df = get_topics(
    mod=lda,
    vec=clean_vec1,
    names=feature_names_vec1,
    docs=raw,
    ndocs=number_docs,
    nwords=number_words
)
```

6. Print out the word-topic data frame. It shows the top-10 words, by distribution value, that are associated with each topic. From this data frame, we can identify the abstract topics that the word groupings represent. More on abstract topics to come:

```
print(W_df)
```

The output is as follows:

```
                        Topic0              Topic1                 Topic2
Word0       (0.1009, obama)    (0.1025, microsoft)      (0.0874, economy)
Word1   (0.0874, president)     (0.0235, windows)      (0.0301, economic)
Word2      (0.0502, barack)      (0.0229, company)     (0.0161, palestine)
Word3      (0.0157, obamas)   (0.0185, microsofts)       (0.0152, growth)
Word4  (0.015, washington)      (0.0155, announce)       (0.0129, global)
Word5        (0.014, state)        (0.014, today)   (0.0126, palestinian)
Word6        (0.013, house)      (0.0105, release)    (0.011, government)
Word7       (0.0119, white)      (0.0088, business)     (0.0103, minister)
Word8 (0.0117, administration)     (0.0088, update)       (0.0101, world)
Word9       (0.0087, visit)      (0.0075, surface)          (0.01, china)
```

Figure 7.35: Word-topic table

7. Print out the topic-document data frame. It shows the 10 documents to which each topic is most closely related. The values are from the per-document distribution of topics:

```
print(H_df)
```

The output is as follows:

```
                                                    Topic0  \
Doc0   (0.9776, March 13 marked the 75th anniversary ...
Doc1   (0.9776, Preying on the minds of financial mar...
Doc2   (0.9772, Obama has narrowed his list to 3 nomi...
Doc3   (0.9768, Member nations of the Organization of...
Doc4   (0.9767, Malia Obama is 17 and probably wants ...
Doc5   (0.9765, Democratic presidential front-runner ...
Doc6   (0.9758, Chinese Premier Li Keqiang pledged th...
Doc7   (0.9756, UNITED NATIONS """ France said Friday...
Doc8   (0.9756, French Foreign Minister Laurent Fabiu...
Doc9   (0.9755, KANSAS CITY """ Missouri Republican a...

                                                    Topic1  \
Doc0   (0.9776, That appears to be the thinking behin...
Doc1   (0.9764, Arundhati Bhattacharya recognises tha...
Doc2   (0.9757, France's fragile economy has cooled i...
Doc3   (0.9755, Software maker Microsoft Corp is sell...
Doc4   (0.9755, WASHINGTON (AP) — President Barack Ob...
Doc5   (0.9754, France's Palestine peace plan is part...
Doc6   (0.9752, Patent trolls drain $1.5 billion a we...
Doc7   (0.9751, Rancho Mirage, California (CNN) Presi...
Doc8   (0.975, 2 economy could be sucked into a Japan...
Doc9   (0.975, Economist with the University of Ghana...

                                                    Topic2
Doc0   (0.9783, President Barack Obama drinks water a...
Doc1   (0.9781, Ifo economist Klaus Wohlrabe told Reu...
Doc2   (0.978, Microsoft's latest Windows Phone, the ...
Doc3   (0.978, Microsoft CEO Satya Nadella discussed ...
Doc4   (0.9779, People's Bank of China Governor Zhou ...
Doc5   (0.9778, President Obama welcomed the Super Bo...
Doc6   (0.9778, The UK is facing a digital skills cri...
Doc7   (0.9778, Microsoft said Monday that it is buyi...
Doc8   (0.9778, Microsoft has been on the acquisition...
Doc9   (0.9777, Twitter, Microsoft, Facebook and YouT...
```

Figure 7.36: Topic-document table

The results of the word-topic data frame show that the abstract topics are Barack Obama, the economy, and Microsoft. What is interesting is that the word grouping describing the economy contains references to Palestine. All four topics specified in the original dataset are represented in the word-topic data frame output, but not in the fully distinct manner expected. We could be facing one of two problems. First, the topic referencing both the economy and Palestine could be under-cooked, which means increasing the number of topics may fix the issue. The other potential problem is that LDA does not handle correlated topics well. In *Exercise 35, Trying Four Topics*, we will try expanding the number of topics, which will give us a better idea of why one of the word groupings is seemingly a mixture of topics.

Exercise 34: Visualize LDA

Visualization is a helpful tool for exploring the results of topic models. In this exercise, we will look at three different visualizations. Those visualizations are basic histograms and specialty visualizations using t-SNE and PCA.

To create some of the visualizations, we are going to use the **pyLDAvis** Library. This library is flexible enough to take in topic models built using several different frameworks. In this case, we will use the **sklearn** framework. This visualization tool returns a histogram showing the words that are the most closely related to each topic and a biplot, frequently used in PCA, where each circle corresponds to a topic. From the biplot, we know how prevalent each topic is across the whole corpus, which is reflected by the area of the circle, and the similarity of the topics, which is reflected by the closeness of the circles. The ideal scenario is to have the circles spread throughout the plot and be of reasonable size. That is, we want the topics to be distinct and to appear consistently across the corpus:

1. Run and display **pyLDAvis**. This plot is interactive. Clicking on each circle updates the histogram to show the top words related to that specific topic. The following is one view of this interactive plot:

    ```
    lda_plot = pyLDAvis.sklearn.prepare(lda, clean_vec1, vectorizer1, R=10)
    pyLDAvis.display(lda_plot)
    ```

The plot looks as follows:

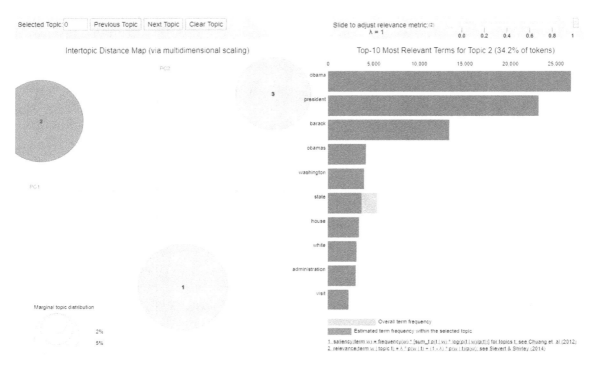

Figure 7.37: A histogram and biplot for the LDA model

2. Define a function that fits a t-SNE model and then plots the results:

```
def plot_tsne(data, threshold):
    # filter data according to threshold
    index_meet_threshold = numpy.amax(data, axis=1) >= threshold
    lda_transform_filt = data[index_meet_threshold]
    # fit tsne model
    # x-d -> 2-d, x = number of topics
    tsne = sklearn.manifold.TSNE(
        n_components=2,
        verbose=0,
        random_state=0,
        angle=0.5,
        init='pca'
    )
    tsne_fit = tsne.fit_transform(lda_transform_filt)
    # most probable topic for each headline
    most_prob_topic = []
    for i in range(tsne_fit.shape[0]):
```

```
            most_prob_topic.append(lda_transform_filt[i].argmax())
    print("LENGTH:\n{}\n".format(len(most_prob_topic)))
    unique, counts = numpy.unique(
        numpy.array(most_prob_topic),
        return_counts=True
    )
    print("COUNTS:\n{}\n".format(numpy.asarray((unique, counts)).T))
    # make plot
    color_list = ['b', 'g', 'r', 'c', 'm', 'y', 'k']
    for i in list(set(most_prob_topic)):
        indices = [idx for idx, val in enumerate(most_prob_topic) if val
  == i]
        matplotlib.pyplot.scatter(
            x=tsne_fit[indices, 0],
            y=tsne_fit[indices, 1],
            s=0.5,
            c=color_list[i],
            label='Topic' + str(i),
            alpha=0.25
        )
    matplotlib.pyplot.xlabel('x-tsne')
    matplotlib.pyplot.ylabel('y-tsne')
    matplotlib.pyplot.legend(markerscale=10)
```

The function starts by filtering down the topic-document matrix using an input threshold value. There are tens of thousands of headlines and any plot incorporating all the headlines is going to be difficult to read and therefore not helpful. So, this function only plots a document if one of the distribution values is greater than or equal to the input threshold value. Once the data is filtered down, we run t-SNE, where the number of components is two, so we can plot the results in two dimensions. Then, create a vector with an indicator of which topic is most related to each document. This vector will be used to color-code the plot by topic. To understand the distribution of topics across the corpus and the impact of threshold filtering, the function returns the length of the topic vector as well as the topics themselves with the number of documents to which that topic has the largest distribution value. The last step of the function is to create and return the plot.

3. Execute the function:

```
plot_tsne(data=lda_transform, threshold=0.75)
```

The output is as follows:

```
LENGTH:
56455

COUNTS:
[[     0 18477]
 [     1 15766]
 [     2 22212]]
```

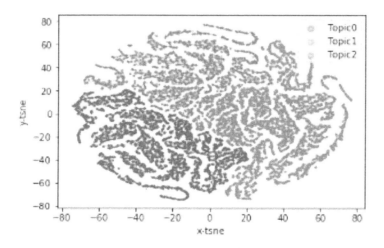

Figure 7.38: t-SNE plot with metrics around the distribution of the topics across the corpus

The visualizations show that the LDA model with three topics is producing good results overall. In the biplot, the circles are of a medium size, which suggests that the topics appear consistently across the corpus and the circles have good spacing. The t-SNE plot shows clear clusters supporting the separation between the circles represented in the biplot. The only glaring issue, which was previously discussed, is that one of the topics has words that do not seem to belong to that topic. In the next exercise, let's rerun the LDA using four topics.

Exercise 35: Trying Four Topics

In this exercise, LDA is run with the number of topics set to four. The motivation for doing this is to try and solve what might be an under-cooked topic from the three-topic LDA model that has words related to both Palestine and the economy. We will run through the steps first and then explore the results at the end:

1. Run an LDA model with the number of topics equal to four:

```
lda4 = sklearn.decomposition.LatentDirichletAllocation(
    n_components=4,  # number of topics data suggests
    learning_method="online",
    random_state=0
)
lda4.fit(clean_vec1)
```

The output is as follows:

```
LatentDirichletAllocation(batch_size=128, doc_topic_prior=None,
          evaluate_every=-1, learning_decay=0.7,
          learning_method='online', learning_offset=10.0,
          max_doc_update_iter=100, max_iter=10, mean_change_tol=0.001,
          n_components=4, n_jobs=None, n_topics=None, perp_tol=0.1,
          random_state=0, topic_word_prior=None,
          total_samples=1000000.0, verbose=0)
```

Figure 7.39: LDA model

2. Execute the **get_topics** function, defined in the preceding code, to produce the more readable word-topic and topic-document tables:

```
W_df4, H_df4 = get_topics(
    mod=lda4,
    vec=clean_vec1,
    names=feature_names_vec1,
    docs=raw,
    ndocs=number_docs,
    nwords=number_words
)
```

3. Print the word-topic table:

```
print(W_df4)
```

The output is as follows:

```
                         Topic0                    Topic1                     Topic2  \
Word0     (0.0344, palestine)         (0.1332, obama)         (0.1062, economy)
Word1    (0.0283, washington)     (0.1155, president)        (0.0365, economic)
Word2   (0.0269, palestinian)        (0.0664, barack)          (0.0185, growth)
Word3         (0.0244, house)        (0.0208, obamas)            (0.017, world)
Word4         (0.0225, white)  (0.0154, administration)        (0.0157, global)
Word5       (0.0214, tuesday)         (0.0122, state)        (0.0126, minister)
Word6        (0.0185, people)         (0.0107, trump)           (0.0122, china)
Word7      (0.0162, american)    (0.0102, republican)        (0.0114, percent)
Word8         (0.0149, unite)         (0.0087, union)     (0.0106, government)
Word9         (0.0146, state)         (0.0087, visit)          (0.0103, market)

                         Topic3
Word0     (0.1155, microsoft)
Word1       (0.0265, windows)
Word2       (0.0259, company)
Word3    (0.0209, microsofts)
Word4      (0.0171, announce)
Word5         (0.0158, today)
Word6       (0.0115, release)
Word7        (0.0099, update)
Word8      (0.0091, business)
Word9       (0.0084, surface)
```

Figure 7.40: The word-topic table using the four-topic LDA model

4. Print the document-topic table:

```
print(H_df4)
```

The output is as follows:

```
                                                    Topic0  \
Doc0    (0.9618, President Barack Obama on Friday will...
Doc1    (0.9494, NEW YORK (Reuters) - Facing a hostile...
Doc2    (0.9459, The Personalization Gallery offers a ...
Doc3    (0.9459, In the budget he plans to release tom...
Doc4    (0.9458, When Microsoft introduced its new on-...
Doc5    (0.9369, President Barack Obama speaks at the ...
Doc6    (0.9369, In an email interview, Adam Fforde, p...
Doc7    (0.9358, A panel of Fox Business pundits excor...
Doc8    (0.9317, President Obama talked about efforts ...
Doc9    (0.9315, An Israeli soldier takes aim during c...


                                                    Topic1  \
Doc0    (0.9686, Artists including Missy Elliott, Kell...
Doc1    (0.9686, President Barack Obama has chosen a n...
Doc2    (0.9686, WASHINGTON — President Barack Obama h...
Doc3    (0.9671, Plouffe, who managed President Obama'...
Doc4    (0.9671,  is dragging the economy through the ...
Doc5    (0.967, President Obama challenged the content...
Doc6    (0.9578, While many people opt for social medi...
Doc7    (0.9558, WASHINGTON """ President Barack Obama...
Doc8    (0.9558, KIEV, March 16. /TASS/. Overwhelming ...
Doc9    (0.9557, Premier Li Keqiang said Wednesday tha...


                                                    Topic2  \
Doc0    (0.9739, WASHINGTON """ President Obama on Sat...
Doc1    (0.9739, TULKARM, November 29, 2015 (WAFA) """...
Doc2    (0.9729, Chris Christie boasted that he banned...
Doc3    (0.9729, CHANTILLY, Va. """ President Barack O...
Doc4    (0.9728, As Microsoft's mobile platform contin...
Doc5    (0.9714, Its growth estimate for 2015-16 has j...
Doc6    (0.9709, The rivalry between Sony and Microsof...
Doc7    (0.9706, Kuwait's economy contracted last year...
Doc8    (0.9706, Kuwait's economy contracted last year...
Doc9    (0.9698, The economic situation in Europe is l...


                                                    Topic3
Doc0    (0.9749, US President Barack Obama has been at...
Doc1    (0.9729, US President Barack Obama on Wednesda...
Doc2    (0.9721, 2 economy could be sucked into a Japa...
Doc3    (0.9721, """When I began working on this conce...
Doc4    (0.9721, The Estonian economy was also positiv...
Doc5    (0.9718, Japan's surprise, albeit modest, meas...
Doc6    (0.9711, The importance of a first good impres...
Doc7    (0.971, The Obama administration on Friday ask...
Doc8    (0.9698, REDMOND, Wash., Dec. 9, 2015 /PRNewsw...
Doc9    (0.9696, The controversial move by Brazil's pr...
```

Figure 7.41: The document-topic table using the four-topic LDA model

5. Display the results of the LDA model using **pyLDAvis**:

```
lda4_plot = pyLDAvis.sklearn.prepare(lda4, clean_vec1, vectorizer1, R=10)
pyLDAvis.display(lda4_plot)
```

The plot is as follows:

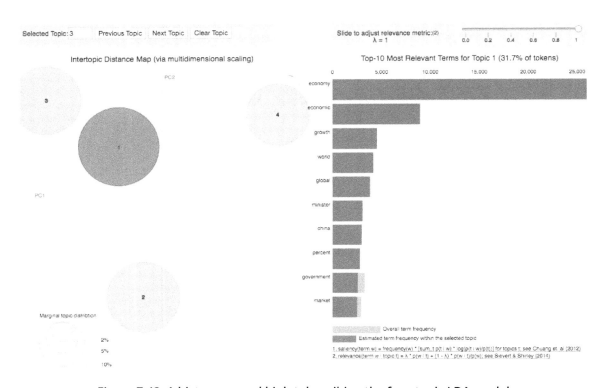

Figure 7.42: A histogram and biplot describing the four-topic LDA model

Looking at the word-topic table, we see that the four topics found by this model align with the four topics specified in the original dataset. Those topics are Barack Obama, Palestine, Microsoft, and the economy. The question now is, why did the model built using four topics have a higher perplexity score than the model with three topics? That answer comes from the visualization produced in *step* 5. The biplot has circles of reasonable size, but two of those circles are quite close together, which suggests that those two topics, Microsoft and the economy, are very similar. In this case, the similarity actually makes intuitive sense. Microsoft is a major global company that impacts and is impacted by the economy. A next step, if we were to make one, would be to run the t-SNE plot to check whether the clusters in the t-SNE plot overlap. Let's now apply our knowledge of LDA to another dataset.

Activity 16: Latent Dirichlet Allocation and Health Tweets

In this activity, we apply LDA to the health tweets data loaded and cleaned in *Activity 15, Loading and Cleaning Twitter Data*. Remember to use the same notebook used in *Activity 15, Loading and Cleaning Twitter Data*. Once the steps have been executed, discuss the results of the model. Do these word groupings make sense?

For this activity, let's imagine that we are interested in acquiring a high-level understanding of the major public health topics. That is, what people are talking about in the world of health. We have collected some data that could shed light on this inquiry. The easiest way to identify the major topics in the dataset, as we have discussed, is topic modeling.

Here are the steps to complete the activity:

1. Specify the **number_words**, **number_docs**, and **number_features** variables.

2. Create a bag-of-words model and assign the feature names to another variable for use later on.

3. Identify the optimal number of topics.

4. Fit the LDA model using the optimal number of topics.

5. Create and print the word-topic table.

6. Print the document-topic table.

7. Create a biplot visualization.

8. Keep the notebook open for future modeling.

The output will be as follows:

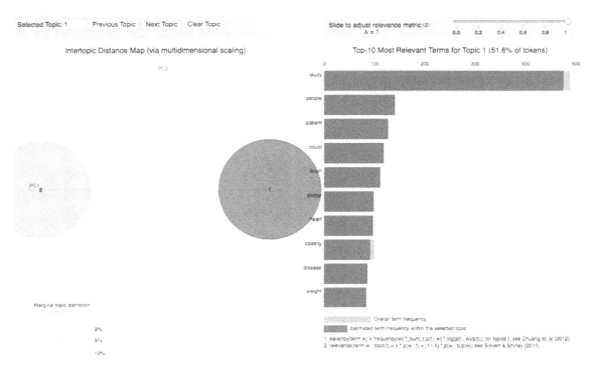

Figure 7.43: A histogram and biplot for the LDA model trained on health tweets

> **Note**
>
> The solution for this activity can be found on page 360.

Bag-of-Words Follow-Up

When running LDA models, the count vectorizer bag-of-words model was used, but that is not the only bag-of-words model. Term Frequency – Inverse Document Frequency (TF-IDF) is similar to the count vectorizer used in the LDA algorithm, except that instead of returning raw counts, TF-IDF returns a weight that reflects the importance of a given word to a document in the corpus. The key component of this weighting scheme is that there is a normalization component for how frequently a given word appears across the entire corpus. Consider the word have.

The word have may occur several times in a single document, suggesting that it could be important for isolating the topic of that document, but have will occur in many documents, if not most, in the corpus, potentially rendering it unless for isolating topics. Essentially, this scheme goes one step further than just returning the raw counts of the words in the document in an effort to initially identify words that may help identify abstract topics. The TF-IDF vectorizer is executed using **sklearn** via **TfidfVectorizer**.

Exercise 36: Creating a Bag-of-Words Using TF-IDF

In this exercise, we will create a bag-of-words using TF-IDF:

1. Run the TF-IDF vectorizer and print out the first few rows:

```
vectorizer2 = sklearn.feature_extraction.text.TfidfVectorizer(
    analyzer="word",
    max_df=0.5,
    min_df=20,
    max_features=number_features,
    smooth_idf=False
)
clean_vec2 = vectorizer2.fit_transform(clean_sentences)
print(clean_vec2[0])
```

The output is as follows:

```
(0,  572)       0.4507592105469774
(0,  557)       0.4666029379072775
(0,  643)       0.2348310160024775
(0,  88)        0.2807099986206347
(0,  407)       0.667198713308869
```

Figure 7.44: Output of the TF-IDF vectorizer

2. Return the feature names, the actual words in the corpus dictionary, to use when analyzing the output. You recall that we did the same thing when we ran the **CountVectorizer** in *Exercise 31, Creating Bag-of-Words Model Using the Count Vectorizer*:

```
feature_names_vec2 = vectorizer2.get_feature_names()
feature_names_vec2
```

A section of the output is as follows:

```
['abbas',
 'ability',
 'accelerate',
 'accept',
 'access',
 'accord',
 'account',
 'accused',
 'achieve',
 'acknowledge',
 'acquire',
 'acquisition',
 'across',
 'action',
 'activist',
 'activity',
 'actually',
```

Non-Negative Matrix Factorization

Unlike LDA, non-negative matrix factorization (NMF) is not a probabilistic model. It is instead, as the name implies, an approach involving linear algebra. Using matrix factorization as an approach to topic modeling was introduced by Daniel D. Lee and H. Sebastian Seung in 1999. The approach falls into the decomposition family of models that includes PCA, the modeling technique introduced in *Chapter 4, An Introduction to Dimensionality Reduction & PCA*.

The major differences between PCA and NMF are that PCA requires components to be orthogonal while allowing them to be either positive or negative. NMF requires matrix components be non-negative, which should make sense if you think of this requirement in the context of the data. Topics cannot be negatively related to documents and words cannot be negatively related to topics. If you are not convinced, try to interpret a negative weight associating a topic with a document. It would be something like, topic T makes up -30% of document D; but what does that even mean? It is nonsensical, so NMF has non-negative requirements for every part of matrix factorization.

Let's define the matrix to be factorized, call it X, as a term-document matrix where the rows are words and the columns are documents. Each element of matrix X is either the number of occurrences of word i (the ith row) in document j (the jth column) or some other quantification of the relationship between word i and document j. The matrix, X, is naturally a sparse matrix as most elements in the term-document matrix will be zero, since each document only contains a limited number of words. There will be more on creating this matrix and deriving the quantifications later:

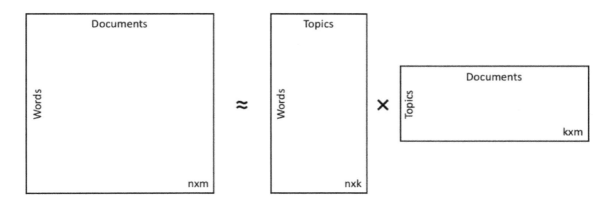

Figure 7.45: The matrix factorization

The matrix factorization takes the form $X_{nxm} \approx W_{nxk} H_{kxm}$, where the two component matrices, W and H, represent the topics as collections of words and the topic weights for each document, respectively. More specifically, W_{nxk} is a word by topic matrix, H_{kxm} is a topic by document matrix, and, as stated earlier, X_{nxm} is a word by document matrix. A nice way to think of this factorization is as a weighted sum of word groupings defining abstract topics. The equivalency symbol in the formula for the matrix factorization is an indicator that the factorization WH is an approximation and thus the product of those two matrices will not reproduce the original term-document matrix exactly. The goal, as it was with LDA, is to find the approximation that is closest to the original matrix. Like X, both W and H are sparse matrices as each topic is only related to a few words and each document is a mixture of only a small number of topics – one topic in many cases.

Frobenius Norm

The goal of solving NMF is the same as that of LDA: find the best approximation. To measure the distance between the input matrix and the approximation, NMF can use virtually any distance measure, but the standard is the Frobenius norm, also known as the Euclidean norm. The Frobenius norm is the sum of the element-wise squared errors mathematically expressed as $\|A\|_F = \sqrt{\sum_{i=1}^{m} \sum_{j=1}^{n} |a|}$.

With the measure of distance selected, the next step is defining the objective function. The minimization of the Frobenius norm will return the best approximation of the original term-document matrix and thus the most reasonable topics. Note that the objective function is minimized with respect to W and H so that both matrices are non-negative. It is expressed as $min_{w \geq 0, H \geq 0} |X - WH|_F^2$.

Multiplicative Update

The optimization algorithm used to solve NMF by Lee and Seung in their 1999 paper is the Multiplicative Update algorithm and it is still one of the most commonly used solutions. It will be implemented in the exercises and activities later in the chapter. The update rules, for both W and H, are derived by expanding the objective function and taking the partial derivatives with respect to W and H. The derivatives are not difficult but do require fairly extensive linear algebra knowledge and are time-consuming, so let's skip the derivatives and just state the updates. Note that, in the update rules, i is the current iteration and T means the transpose of the matrix. The first update rule is as follows:

$$H^{i+1} \leftarrow H^i \frac{(W^i)^T X}{(W^i)^T W^i H^i}$$

Figure 7.46: First update rule

The second update rule is as follows:

$$w^{i+1} \leftarrow w^i \frac{X(H^{i+1})^T}{W^i H^{i+1}(H^{i+1})^T}$$

Figure 7.47: Second update rule

W and H are updated iteratively until the algorithm converges. The objective function can also be shown to be non-increasing. That is, with each iterative update of W and H, the objective function gets closer to the minimum. Note that the multiplicative update optimizer, if the update rules are reorganized, is a rescaled gradient descent algorithm.

The final component of building a successful NMF algorithm is initializing the W and H component matrices so that the multiplicative update works quickly. A popular approach to initializing matrices is Singular Value Decomposition (SVD), which is a generalization of Eigen decomposition. In the implementation of NMF done in the forthcoming exercises, the matrices are initialized via non-negative Double Singular Value Decomposition, which is basically a more advanced version of SVD that is strictly non-negative. The full details of these initialization algorithms are not important to understanding NMF. Just note that initialization algorithms are used as a starting point for the optimization algorithms and can drastically speed up convergence.

Exercise 37: Non-negative Matrix Factorization

In this exercise, we fit the NMF algorithm and output the same two result tables we did with LDA previously. Those tables are the word-topic table, which shows the top-10 words associated with each topic, and the document-topic table, which shows the top-10 documents associated with each topic. There are two additional parameters in the NMF algorithm function that we have not previously discussed, which are **alpha** and **l1_ratio**. If an overfit model is of concern, these parameters control how (**l1_ratio**) and the extent to which (**alpha**) regularization is applied to the objective function. More details can be found in the documentation for the scikit-learn library (https://scikit-learn.org/stable/modules/generated/sklearn.decomposition.NMF.html):

1. Define the NMF model and call the **fit** function using the output of the TF-IDF vectorizer:

```
nmf = sklearn.decomposition.NMF(
    n_components=4,
    init="nndsvda",
    solver="mu",
    beta_loss="frobenius",
    random_state=0,
    alpha=0.1,
    l1_ratio=0.5
)
nmf.fit(clean_vec2)
```

The output is as follows:

```
NMF(alpha=0.1, beta_loss='frobenius', init='nndsvda', l1_ratio=0.5,
    max_iter=200, n_components=4, random_state=0, shuffle=False, solver='mu',
    tol=0.0001, verbose=0)
```

Figure 7.48: Defining the NMF model

2. Run the **get_topics** functions to produce the two output tables:

```
W_df, H_df = get_topics(
    mod=nmf,
    vec=clean_vec2,
    names=feature_names_vec2,
    docs=raw,
    ndocs=number_docs,
    nwords=number_words
)
```

3. Print the **W** table:

```
print(W_df)
```

The output is as follows:

```
                         Topic0              Topic1               Topic2  \
Word0          (0.0696, obama)     (0.0628, economy)    (0.0869, microsoft)
Word1      (0.0646, president)    (0.0212, economic)     (0.0306, windows)
Word2         (0.0484, barack)      (0.0179, growth)     (0.0196, company)
Word3     (0.0157, washington)      (0.0144, global)    (0.0162, announce)
Word4          (0.0149, house)       (0.0128, china)  (0.0124, microsofts)
Word5          (0.0144, white)     (0.0111, percent)      (0.0118, update)
Word6         (0.0127, obamas)       (0.0109, world)     (0.0106, release)
Word7          (0.0109, state)     (0.0097, quarter)         (0.01, today)
Word8 (0.0096, administration)      (0.0093, market)     (0.0096, surface)
Word9          (0.0081, first)     (0.0086, country)       (0.0085, cloud)

                         Topic3
Word0      (0.0881, palestine)
Word1    (0.0766, palestinian)
Word2        (0.0309, israeli)
Word3         (0.0278, israel)
Word4          (0.0172, state)
Word5  (0.0094, international)
Word6       (0.0092, ramallah)
Word7       (0.0089, minister)
Word8         (0.0079, unite)
Word9         (0.0078, force)
```

Figure 7.49: The word-topic table containing probabilities

4. Print the **H** table:

```
print(H_df)
```

```
                                                Topic0  \
Doc0    (0.0844, NCRI - The Iranian regime's former Mi...
Doc1    (0.0844, South Africa's economy shrank sharply...
Doc2    (0.0844, Horacio Gutierrez, Microsoft's genera...
Doc3    (0.0844, A Microsoft recruiting event at the U...
Doc4    (0.0844, The Federal Reserve's recent rate hik...
Doc5    (0.0844, President Barack Obama received a chi...
Doc6    (0.0844, President Obama met with gun control ...
Doc7    (0.0844, (CNN) """Leaders gathered in Paris to...
Doc8    (0.0844, Fears have returned that China's debt...
Doc9    (0.0844, Russia is not ready to share US Presi...

                                                Topic1  \
Doc0    (0.0677, Both China's central bank and a respe...
Doc1    (0.0677, TAMPA -- Sen. Marco Rubio (R-Fla.) sa...
Doc2    (0.0677, WASHINGTON - President Barack Obama i...
Doc3    (0.0677, The U.S. Supreme Court on Friday agre...
Doc4    (0.0677, WASHINGTON""President Barack Obama w...
Doc5    (0.0677, One of the challenges for writing app...
Doc6    (0.0677, President Barack Obama speaks during ...
Doc7       (0.0677, The U.S. economy is humming again. )
Doc8    (0.0677, WASHINGTON — President Barack Obama s...
Doc9    (0.0677, Microsoft to shut down portal site MS...

                                                Topic2  \
Doc0    (0.0836, Colin Fenton, managing partner at Bla...
Doc1    (0.0836, As I study in Canada, I am exposed to...
Doc2    (0.0836, Ban Ki Mun: Sramota me zbog Izraela i...
Doc3    (0.0836, But the argument that Microsoft is wi...
Doc4    (0.0836, 6:55 p.m. On the heels of Donald Trum...
Doc5    (0.0836, Colorado's economy had the fourth str...
Doc6    (0.0836, Back in September 2014 I wrote an art...
Doc7    (0.0836, During its developer conference, Micr...
Doc8    (0.0836, Speaking in Japan after a summit with...
Doc9    (0.0836, Korea's exports marked the worst slum...

                                                Topic3
Doc0    (0.1078, SYDNEY, April 18 (Xinhua) -- Australi...
Doc1    (0.1078, It's both fascinating and ironic how ...
Doc2    (0.0856, German government spending on refugee...
Doc3    (0.0852, President Barack Obama, center, walks...
Doc4    (0.0842, The gig economy tends to divide opini...
Doc5    (0.0828, I hope the Committee on the Future Ec...
Doc6    (0.0815, President Obama has spent the last se...
Doc7    (0.0815, OTTAWA -- Barack Obama has arrived in...
Doc8    (0.0815, For Max Wolff, chief economist at Man...
Doc9    (0.0815, Just over a year ago, Microsoft annou...
```

Figure 7.50: The document-topic table containing probabilities

The word-topic table contains word groupings that suggest the same abstract topics that the four-topic LDA model produced in *Exercise 35, Trying four topics*. However, the interesting part of the comparison is that some of the individual words contained in these groupings are new or in a new place in the grouping. This is not surprising given that the methodologies are distinct. Given the alignment with the topics specified in the original dataset, we have shown that both of these methodologies are effective tools for extracting the underlying topic structure of the corpus.

Exercise 38: Visualizing NMF

The purpose of this exercise is to visualize the results of NMF. Visualizing the results gives insights into the distinctness of the topics and the prevalence of each topic in the corpus. In this exercise, we do the visualizing using t-SNE, which was discussed fully in *Chapter 6, t-Distributed Stochastic Neighbor Embedding (t-SNE)*:

1. Run **transform** on the cleaned data to get the topic-document allocations. Print both the shape and an example of the data:

```
nmf_transform = nmf.transform(clean_vec2)
print(nmf_transform.shape)
print(nmf_transform)
```

The output is as follows:

```
(92948, 4)
[[5.12543656e-02 3.63195740e-15 3.10455307e-34 7.82654193e-16]
 [7.41162473e-04 2.04135415e-02 6.83519643e-15 2.13620923e-03]
 [2.96652472e-15 1.94116773e-02 4.78856726e-21 1.20646716e-18]
 ...
 [9.58970155e-06 3.41045363e-03 6.15591120e-04 3.23909905e-02]
 [6.37006094e-07 1.31884850e-07 3.39453370e-08 6.14080053e-02]
 [4.46386338e-05 1.15780717e-04 1.84769162e-02 2.00666640e-03]]
```

Figure 7.51: Shape and example of data

2. Run the **plot_tsne** function to fit a t-SNE model and plot the results:

```
plot_tsne(data=nmf_transform, threshold=0)
```

The plot looks as follows:

```
LENGTH:
92946

COUNTS:
[[      0 28977]
 [      1 32946]
 [      2 22146]
 [      3  8877]]
```

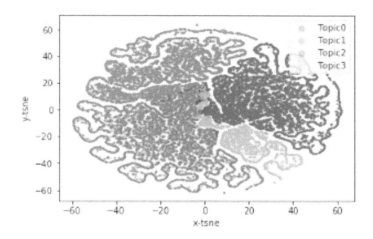

Figure 7.52: t-SNE plot with metrics summarizing the topic distribution across the corpus

The t-SNE plot, with no threshold specified, shows some topic overlap and a clear discrepancy in the topic frequency across the corpus. These two facts explain why, when using perplexity, the optimal number of topics is three. There seems to be some correlation between topics that the model can't fully accommodate. Even with the correlation between topics, the model is finding the topics it should when the number of topics is set to four.

To recap, NMF is a non-probabilistic topic model that seeks to answer the same question LDA is trying to answer. It uses a popular concept of linear algebra known as matrix factorization, which is the process of breaking a large and intractable matrix down into smaller and more easily interpretable matrices that can be leveraged to answer many questions about the data. Remember that the non-negative requirement is not rooted in mathematics, but in the data itself. It does not make sense for the components of any documents to be negative. In many cases, NMF does not perform as well as LDA, because LDA incorporates prior distributions that add an extra layer of information to help inform the topic word groupings. However, we know that there are cases, especially when the topics are highly correlated, when NMF is the better performer. One of those cases was the headline data on which all the exercises were based.

Activity 17: Non-Negative Matrix Factorization

This activity is the summation of the topic modeling analysis done on the health Twitter data loaded and cleaned in activity one, and on which LDA was done in activity two. The execution of NMF is straightforward and requires limited coding, so I suggest taking this opportunity to play with the parameters of the model while thinking about the limitations and benefits of NMF.

Here are the steps to complete the activity:

1. Create the appropriate bag-of-words model and output the feature names as another variable.

2. Define and fit the NMF algorithm using the number of topics (**n_components**) value from activity two.

3. Get the topic-document and word-topic result tables. Take a few minutes to explore the word groupings and try to define the abstract topics. Can you quantify the meanings of the word groupings? Do the word groupings make sense? Are the results similar to those produced using LDA?

4. Adjust the model parameters and rerun *step* 3 and *step* 4. How do the results change?

The output will be as follows:

```
                        Topic0                      Topic1
Word0      (0.3726, study)       (0.5974, latfit)
Word1      (0.0259, cancer)      (0.0477, steps)
Word2      (0.0208, people)      (0.0448, today)
Word3      (0.0185, health)      (0.0404, exercise)
Word4     (0.0184, obesity)     (0.0274, healthtips)
Word5      (0.0182, brain)       (0.0257, workout)
Word6     (0.0173, suggest)      (0.0204, getting)
Word7      (0.0167, weight)      (0.0193, fitness)
Word8      (0.0159, woman)       (0.0143, great)
Word9      (0.0131, death)       (0.0132, morning)
```

Figure 7.53: The word-topic table with probabilities

> **Note**
>
> The solution for this activity can be found on page 364.

Summary

When faced with the task of extracting information from an as yet unseen large collection of documents, topic modeling is a great approach, as it provides insights into the underlying structure of the documents. That is, topic models find word groupings using proximity, not context. In this chapter, we have learned how to apply two of the most common and most effective topic modeling algorithms: latent Dirichlet allocation and non-negative matrix factorization. We should now feel comfortable cleaning raw text documents using several different techniques; techniques that can be utilized in many other modeling scenarios. We continued by learning how to convert the cleaned corpus into the appropriate data structure of per-document raw word counts or word weights by applying bag-of-words models. The main focus of the chapter was fitting the two topic models, including optimizing the number of topics, converting the output to easy-to-interpret tables, and visualizing the results. With this information, you should be able to apply fully functioning topic models to derive value and insights for your business.

In the next chapter, we will change directions entirely. We will deep dive into market basket analysis.

8

Market Basket Analysis

Learning Objectives

By the end of this chapter, you will be able to:

- Work with transaction-level data
- Use market basket analysis in the appropriate context
- Run the Apriori algorithm and build association rules
- Perform basic visualizations on association rules
- Interpret the key metrics of market basket analysis

In this chapter, we will explore a foundational and reliable algorithm for analyzing transaction data.

Introduction

In this chapter, we are going to change direction entirely. The previous chapter, which explored topic models, focused on natural language processing, text data, and applying relatively recently developed algorithms. Most data science practitioners would agree that natural language processing, including topic models, is toward the cutting edge of data science and is an active research area. We now understand that topic models can, and should, be leveraged wherever text data could potentially drive insights or growth, including in social media analysis, recommendation engines, and news filtering.

This chapter takes us into the retail space to explore a foundational and reliable algorithm for analyzing transaction data. While this algorithm might not be on the cutting edge or in the catalog of the most popular machine learning algorithms, it is ubiquitous and undeniably impactful in the retail space. The insights it drives are easily interpretable, immediately actionable, and instructive for determining analytical next steps. If you work in the retail space or with transaction data, you would be well-served to dive deep into market basket analysis.

Market Basket Analysis

Imagine you work for a retailer that sells dozens of products and your boss comes to you and asks the following questions:

- What products are purchased together most frequently?

- How should the products be organized and positioned in the store?

- How do we identify the best products to discount via coupons?

You might reasonably respond with complete bewilderment, as those questions are very diverse and do not immediately seem answerable using a single algorithm and dataset. However, the answer to all those questions and many more is **market basket analysis**. The general idea behind market basket analysis is to identify and quantify which items, or groups of items, are purchased together frequently enough to drive insight into customer behavior and product relationships.

Before we dive into the analytics, it is worth defining the term market basket. A market basket is a permanent set of products in an economic system. In this case, permanent does not necessarily mean permanent in the traditional sense. It means that until such time as the product is taken out of the catalog, it will consistently be available for purchase. The product referenced in the preceding definition is any good, service, or element of a group, including a bicycle, having your house painted, or a website. Lastly, an economic system could be a company, a collection of activities, or a country. The easiest example of a market basket is a grocery store, which is a system made up of a collection of food and drink items.

The Economic System: Butcher Shop

The Permanent Set of Items:

Chicken Wings	Ribs
Sausage	Leg of Lamb
Pork Chop	Strip Steak
Ground Bison	Meatballs
Filet Mignon	...

Figure 8.1: An example market basket where the economic system is the butcher shop and the permanent set of items is all the meat products offered by the butcher

Even without using any models or analyses, certain product relationships are obvious. Let's take the relationship between meat and vegetables. Typically, market basket analysis models return relationships more specific than meat and vegetables, but, for argument's sake, we will generalize to meat and vegetables. Okay, there is a relationship between meat and vegetables. So what? Well, we know these are staple items that are frequently purchased together. We can leverage this information by putting the vegetables and meats on opposite sides of the store, which you will notice is often the positioning of those two items, forcing customers to walk the full distance of the store, and thereby increasing the likelihood that they will buy additional items that they might not have bought if they did not have to traverse the whole store.

One of the things retail companies struggle with is how to discount items effectively. Let's consider another obvious relationship: peanut butter and jelly. In the United States, peanut butter and jelly sandwiches are incredibly popular, especially among children. When peanut butter is in a shopping basket, the chance jelly is also there can be assumed to be quite high. Since we know peanut butter and jelly are purchased together, it does not make sense to discount them both. If we want customers to buy both items, we can just discount one of the items, knowing that if we can get the customers to buy the discounted item, they will probably buy the other item too, even if it is full price.

Figure 8.2: A visualization of market basket analysis

Just like the topic models in the previous chapter, market basket analysis is all about identifying frequently occurring groups. Here, we are looking for frequently occurring groups of products, whereas in topic models, we were looking for frequently occurring groups of words. Thus, as it was to topic models, the word clustering could be applied to market basket analysis. The major differences are that the clusters in market basket analysis are micro, only a few products per cluster, and the order of the items in the cluster matters when it comes to computing probabilistic metrics. We will dive much deeper into these metrics and how they are calculated later in this chapter.

What has clearly been implied by the previous two examples is that, in market basket analysis, retailers can discover the relationships – obvious and surprising – between the products that customers buy. Once uncovered, the relationships can be used to inform and improve the decision-making process. A great aspect of market basket analysis is that while this analysis was developed in relation to, discussed in terms of, and mostly applied to the retail world, it can be applied to many diverse types of businesses.

The only requirement for performing this type of analysis is that the data is a list of collections of items. In the retail case, this would be a list of transactions where each transaction is a group of purchased products. One example of an alternative application is analyzing website traffic. With website traffic, we consider the products to be websites, so each element of the list is the collection of websites visited by an individual over a specified time period. Needless to say, the applications of market basket analysis extend well beyond the principal retail application.

Use Cases

There are three principal use cases in the traditional retail application: pricing enhancement, coupon and discount recommendation, and store layout. As was briefly mentioned previously, by using the product associations uncovered by the model, retailers can strategically place products in their stores to get customers to buy more items and thus spend more money. If any relationship between two or more products is sufficiently strong, meaning the product grouping occurs often in the dataset and the individual products in the grouping appear separate from the group infrequently, then the products could be placed far away from one another in the store without significantly jeopardizing the odds of the customer purchasing both products. By forcing the customer to traverse the whole store to get both products, the retailer increases the chances that the customer will notice and purchase additional products. Likewise, retailers can increase the chances of customers purchasing two weakly related or non-staple products by placing the two items next to each other. Obviously, there are a lot of factors that drive store layout, but market basket analysis is definitely one of those factors:

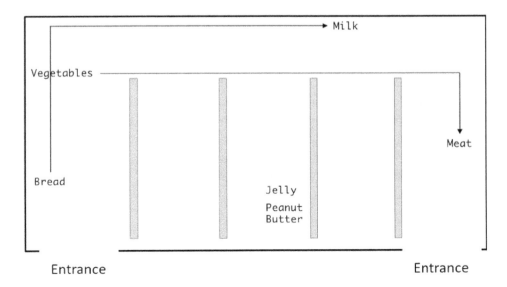

Figure 8.3: How product associations can help inform efficient and lucrative store layouts

Pricing enhancement and coupon and discount recommendation are two sides of the same coin. They can simply be interpreted as where to raise and where to lower prices. Consider the case of two strongly related items. These two items are most likely going to be purchased in the same transaction, so one way to increase the profitability of that transaction would be to increase the price of one of the items. If the association between the two items is sufficiently strong, the price increase can be made with little to no risk of the customer not purchasing both items. In a similar way, retailers can encourage customers to purchase an item weakly associated with another through discounting or couponing.

For example, retailers could compare the purchase history of individual customers with the results of market basket analysis done on all transactions and find where some of the items certain customers are purchasing are weakly associated to items those customers are not currently purchasing. Using this comparison, retailers could offer discounts to the customers for the as-yet-unpurchased items the model suggested were related to the items previously purchased by those customers. If you have ever had coupons print out with your receipt at the end of a transaction, the chances are high that those items were found to be related to the items involved in your just-completed transaction.

A non-traditional, but viable, use of market basket analysis would be to enhance online advertising and search engine optimization. Imagine we had access to lists of websites visited by individuals. Using market basket analysis, we could find relationships between websites and use those relationships to both strategically order and group the websites resulting from a search engine query. In many ways, this is similar to the store layout use case.

With a general sense of what market basket analysis is all about and a clear understanding of its use cases, let's dig into the data used in these models.

Important Probabilistic Metrics

Market basket analysis is built upon the computation of several probabilistic metrics. The five major metrics covered here are support, confidence, lift, leverage, and conviction. Before digging into transaction data and the specific market basket analysis models, including the **Apriori algorithm** and **association rules**, we should spend some time defining and exploring these metrics using a small, made-up set of transactions. We start by making up some data to use.

Exercise 39: Creating Sample Transaction Data

Since this is the first exercise of the chapter, let's set the environment. This chapter will use the same environment requirements that were used in *Chapter 7, Topic Modeling*. If any of the packages do not load, as happened in the previous chapter, use **pip** to install them via the command line. One of the libraries we will use is **mlxtend**, which may be unfamiliar to you. It is a machine learning extensions library that contains useful supplemental tools, including ensembling, stacking, and, of book, market basket analysis models. This exercise does not have any real output. We will simply create a sample transaction dataset for use in subsequent exercises.

1. Open a Jupyter notebook with Python 3.

2. Install the following libraries: **matplotlib.pyplot**, which is used to plot the results of the models, **mlxtend.frequent_patterns**, which is used to run the models, **mlxtend.preprocessing**, which is used to encode and prep the data for the models, **numpy**, which is used to work with arrays, and **pandas**, which is used to work with DataFrames:

> **Note**
>
> To install **mlxtend**, go to the Anaconda prompt and execute **pip install mlxtend**.

```
import matplotlib.pyplot as plt
import mlxtend.frequent_patterns
import mlxtend.preprocessing
import numpy
import pandas
```

3. Create 10 fake transactions featuring grocery store items. The data will take the form of a list of lists, a data structure that will be relevant later when discussing formatting transaction data for the models:

```
example = [
    ['milk', 'bread', 'apples', 'cereal', 'jelly',
     'cookies', 'salad', 'tomatoes'],
    ['beer', 'milk', 'chips', 'salsa', 'grapes',
     'wine', 'potatoes', 'eggs', 'carrots'],
    ['diapers', 'baby formula', 'milk', 'bread',
     'chicken', 'asparagus', 'cookies'],
    ['milk', 'cookies', 'chicken', 'asparagus',
     'broccoli', 'cereal', 'orange juice'],
    ['steak', 'asparagus', 'broccoli', 'chips',
     'salsa', 'ketchup', 'potatoes', 'salad'],
```

```
        ['beer', 'salsa', 'asparagus', 'wine', 'cheese',
         'crackers', 'strawberries', 'cookies'],
        ['chocolate cake', 'strawberries', 'wine', 'cheese',
         'beer', 'milk', 'orange juice'],
        ['chicken', 'peas', 'broccoli', 'milk', 'bread',
         'eggs', 'potatoes', 'ketchup', 'crackers'],
        ['eggs', 'bread', 'cheese', 'turkey', 'salad',
         'tomatoes', 'wine', 'steak', 'carrots'],
        ['bread', 'milk', 'tomatoes', 'cereal', 'chicken',
         'turkey', 'chips', 'salsa', 'diapers']
    ]
```

This simple dataset will make explaining and interpreting the probabilistic metrics much easier.

Support

Support is simply the probability that the item set appears in the data, which can be calculated by counting the number of transactions in which the item set appears and dividing that count by the total number of transactions. Note that an item set can be a single item or a group of items. Support is an important metric, despite being very simple, as it is one of the primary metrics used to determine the believability and strength of association between groups of items. For example, it is possible to have two items that only occur with each other, suggesting that their association is very strong, but in a dataset containing 100 transactions, only appearing twice is not very impressive. Because the item set appears in only 2% of the transactions, and 2% is small in terms of the raw number of appearances, the association cannot be considered significant and, thus, is probably unusable in decision making.

Note that since support is a probability, it will fall in the range [0,1]. The formula takes the following form if the item set is two items, X and Y, and N is the total number of transactions.

$$Support(X \Rightarrow Y) = Support(X,Y) = P(X,Y) = \frac{Frequency(X,Y)}{N}$$

Figure 8.4: Formula for support

Let's return momentarily to the made-up data from *Exercise 39, Creating Sample Transaction Data* and define an item set as being milk and bread. We can easily look through the 10 transactions and count the number of transactions in which this milk and bread item set occurs – that would be 4 times. Given that there are 10 transactions, the support of milk and bread is 4 divided by 10, or 0.4. Whether this is large enough support depends on the dataset itself, which we will get into in a later section.

Confidence

The **confidence** metric can be thought of in terms of conditional probability, as it is basically the probability that product B is purchased given the purchase of product A. Confidence is typically notated as A $\Rightarrow$ B, and expressed as the proportion of transactions containing A that also contain B. Hence, confidence is found by filtering the full set of transactions down to those containing A, and then computing the proportion of those transactions that contain B. Like support, confidence is a probability, so its range is [0,1]. Using the same variable definitions from the support section, the following is the formula for confidence:

$$Confidence(X \Rightarrow Y) = P(Y|X) = \frac{Support(X,Y)}{P(X)} = \frac{\frac{Frequency(X,Y)}{N}}{\frac{Frequency(X)}{N}}$$

Figure 8.5: Formula for confidence

To demonstrate confidence, we will use the items beer and wine. Specifically, let's compute the confidence of Beer $\Rightarrow$ Wine. To start, we need to identify the transactions that contain beer. There are 3 of them, and they are transactions 2, 6, and 7. Now, of those transactions, how many contain wine? The answer is all of them. Thus, the confidence of Beer $\Rightarrow$ Wine is 1. Every time a customer bought beer, they also bought wine. It might be obvious, but for identifying actionable associations, higher confidence values are better:

Lift and Leverage

We will discuss the next two metrics, lift and leverage, simultaneously, since despite being calculated differently, both seek to answer the same question. Like confidence, **lift** and **leverage** are notated as A $\Rightarrow$ B. The question to which we seek an answer is, can one item, say A, be used to determine anything about another item, say B? Stated another way, if product A is bought by an individual, can we say anything about whether they will or will not purchase product B with some level of confidence? These questions are answered by comparing the support of A and B under the standard case when A and B are not assumed to be independent with the case where the two products are assumed to be independent. Lift calculates the ratio of these two cases, so its range is [0, Infinity]. When lift equals one, the two products are independent and, hence, no conclusions can be made about product B when product A is purchased:

$$Lift(X \Rightarrow Y) = \frac{Support(X,Y)}{Support(X) * Support(Y)} = \frac{P(X,Y)}{P(X) * P(Y)}$$

Figure 8.6: Formula for lift

Leverage calculates the difference between the two cases, so its range is [-1, 1]. Leverage equaling zero can be interpreted the same way as lift equaling one:

$$Leverage(X \Rightarrow Y) = Support(X, Y) - \big(Support(X) * Support(Y)\big) = P(X, Y) - \big(P(X) * P(Y)\big)$$

Figure 8.7: Formula for leverage

The values of the metrics measure the strength and direction of the relationship between the items. If the lift value is 0.1, we could say the relationship between the two items is strong in the negative direction. That is, it could be said that when one product is purchased, the chance the second product is purchased is diminished. The positive and negative associations are separated by the points of independence, which, as stated earlier, are 1 for lift and 0 for leverage, and the further away the value gets from these points, the stronger the association.

Conviction

The last metric to be discussed is conviction, which is a bit less intuitive than the other metrics. Conviction is the ratio of the expected frequency that X occurs without Y, given that X and Y are independent to the frequency of incorrect predictions. The frequency of incorrect predictions is defined as 1 minus the confidence of X $\Rightarrow$ Y. Remember that confidence can be defined as $P(Y|X)$, which means $.1 - P(Y|X) = P(Not\ Y|X)$. The numerator could also be thought of as $1 - P(Y|X) = P(Not\ Y|X)$. The only difference between the two is that the numerator has the assumption of independence between X and Y, while the denominator does not. A value greater than 1 is ideal because that means the association between products or item sets X and Y is incorrect more often if the association between X and Y is random chance (in other words, X and Y are independent). To reiterate, this stipulates that the association between X and Y is meaningful. A value of 1 applies independence, and a value of less than 1 signifies that the random chance X and Y relationship is correct more often than the X and Y relationship that has been defined as X $\Rightarrow$ Y. Under this situation, the relationship might go the other way (in other words, Y $\Rightarrow$ X). Conviction has the range [0, Inf] and the following form:

$$Conviction(X \Rightarrow Y) = \frac{1 - Support(Y)}{1 - Confidence(X \Rightarrow Y)}$$

Figure 8.8: Formula for conviction

Let's again return to the products beer and wine, but for this explanation, we will consider the opposite association of Wine ⇒ Beer. Support(Y) or, in this case, Support(Beer) is 3/10 and Confidence X ⇒ Y, or, in this case, Confidence(Wine ⇒ Beer), is 3/4. Thus, the Conviction(Wine ⇒ Beer) is (1-3/10) / (1-3/4) = (7/10) * (4/1). We can conclude by saying that Wine ⇒ Beer would be incorrect 2.8 times as often if wine and beer were independent. Thus, the previously articulated association between wine and beer is legitimate.

Exercise 40: Computing Metrics

In this exercise, we use the fake data in *Exercise 39, Creating Sample Transaction Data* to compute the five previously described metrics, which we will use again in the covering of the Apriori algorithm and association rules. The association on which these metrics will be evaluated is Milk ⇒ Bread.

> **Note**
>
> All exercises in this chapter need to be performed in the same Jupyter notebook.

1. Define and print the frequencies that are the basis of all five metrics, which would be Frequency(Milk), Frequency(Bread), and Frequency(Milk, Bread). Also, define N as the total number of transactions in the dataset:

```
N = len(example)
f_x = sum(['milk' in i for i in example]) # milk
f_y = sum(['bread' in i for i in example]) # bread
f_x_y = sum([
    all(w in i for w in ['milk', 'bread'])
    for i in example
])

print(
    "N = {}\n".format(N) +
    "Freq(x) = {}\n".format(f_x) +
    "Freq(y) = {}\n".format(f_y) +
    "Freq(x, y) = {}".format(f_x_y)
)
```

The output is as follows:

```
N = 10
Freq(x) = 7
Freq(y) = 5
Freq(x, y) = 4
```

Figure 8.9: Screenshot of the frequencies

2. Calculate and print Support(Milk $\Rightarrow$ Bread):

```
support = f_x_y / N
print("Support = {}".format(round(support, 4)))
```

The support of **x** to **y** is **0.4**. From experience, if we were working with a full transaction dataset, this support value would be considered very large in many cases.

3. Calculate and print Confidence(Milk $\Rightarrow$ Bread):

```
confidence = support / (f_x / N)
print("Confidence = {}".format(round(confidence, 4)))
```

The confidence of **x** to **y** is **0.5714**. This means that the probability of Y being purchased given that **x** was purchased is just slightly higher than 50%.

4. Calculate and print Lift(Milk $\Rightarrow$ Bread):

```
lift = confidence / (f_y / N)
print("Lift = {}".format(round(lift, 4)))
```

The lift of **x** to **y** is **1.1429**.

5. Calculate and print Leverage(Milk $\Rightarrow$ Bread):

```
leverage = support - ((f_x / N) * (f_y / N))
print("Leverage = {}".format(round(leverage, 4)))
```

The leverage of **x** to **y** is **0.05**. Both lift and leverage can be used to say that the association **x** to **y** is positive (in other words, **x** implies **y**), but weak. That is, the values are close to 1 and 0, respectively.

6. Calculate and print Conviction(Milk $\Rightarrow$ Bread):

```
conviction = (1 - (f_y / N)) / (1 - confidence)
print("Conviction = {}".format(round(conviction, 4)))
```

The conviction value of **1.1667** can be interpreted by saying the Milk $\Rightarrow$ Bread association would be incorrect **1.1667** times as often if milk and bread were independent.

Before diving into the Apriori algorithm and association rule learning on actual data, we will explore transaction data and get some retail data loaded and prepped for modeling.

Characteristics of Transaction Data

The data used in market basket analysis is transaction data or any type of data that resembles transaction data. In its most basic form, transaction data has some sort of transaction identifier, such as an invoice or transaction number, and a list of products associated with said identifier. It just so happens that these two base elements are all that is needed to perform market basket analysis. However, transaction data rarely – it is probably even safe to say never – comes in this basic form. Transaction data typically includes pricing information, dates and times, and customer identifiers, among many other things:

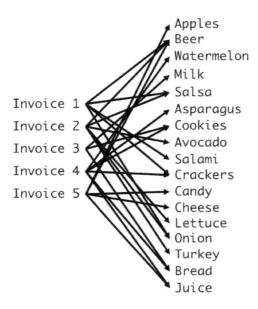

Figure 8.10: Each available product is going to map back to multiple invoice numbers

Due to the complexity of transaction data, data cleaning is crucial. The goal of data cleaning in the context of market basket analysis is to filter out all the unnecessary information, which includes removing variables in the data that are not relevant, and filtering out problematic transactions. The techniques used to complete these two cleaning steps vary, depending on the particular transaction data file. In an attempt to not get bogged down in data cleaning, the exercises from here on out will use a subset of an online retail dataset from the UCI Machine Learning Repository, and the activities will use the whole dataset. This both limits the data cleaning discussion, but also gives us an opportunity to discuss how the results change when the size of the dataset changes. This is important because if you work for a retailer and run market basket analysis, it will be important to understand and be able to clearly articulate the fact that, as more data is received, product relationships can, and most likely will, shift. Before discussing the specific cleaning process required for this dataset, let's load the online retail dataset.

Exercise 41: Loading Data

In this exercise, we will load and view an example online retail dataset. This dataset is originally from the UCI Machine Learning Repository and can be found at https://github.com/TrainingByPackt/Applied-Unsupervised-Learning-with-Python/tree/master/Lesson08/Exercise39-Exercise45. Once you have downloaded the dataset, save it and note the path. Now, let's proceed with the exercise. The output of this exercise is the transaction data that will be used in future modeling exercises and some exploratory figures to help us better understand the data with which we are working.

> **Note**
>
> This dataset is taken from http://archive.ics.uci.edu/ml/datasets/online+retail#. It can be downloaded from https://github.com/TrainingByPackt/Applied-Unsupervised-Learning-with-Python/tree/master/Lesson08/Exercise39-Exercise45. Daqing Chen, Sai Liang Sain, and Kun Guo, Data mining for the online retail industry: A case study of RFM model-based customer segmentation using data mining, Journal of Database Marketing and Customer Strategy Management, Vol. 19, No. 3, pp. 197-208, 2012.
>
> UCI Machine Learning Repository [http://archive.ics.uci.edu/ml]. Irvine, CA: University of California, School of Information and Computer Science.

1. Using the **read_excel** function from **pandas**, load the data. Note that the first row of the Excel file contains the column names:

```
online = pandas.read_excel(
    io="~/Desktop/Online Retail.xlsx",
    sheet_name="Online Retail",
    header=0
)
```

> **Note**
>
> The path to **Online Retail.xlsx** should be changed as per the location of the file on your system.

2. Print out the first 10 rows of the DataFrame. Notice that the data contains some columns that will not be relevant to market basket analysis:

```
online.head(10)
```

The output is as follows:

	InvoiceNo	StockCode	Description	Quantity	InvoiceDate	UnitPrice	CustomerID	Country
0	536365	85123A	WHITE HANGING HEART T-LIGHT HOLDER	6	2010-12-01 08:26:00	2.55	17850.0	United Kingdom
1	536365	71053	WHITE METAL LANTERN	6	2010-12-01 08:26:00	3.39	17850.0	United Kingdom
2	536365	84406B	CREAM CUPID HEARTS COAT HANGER	8	2010-12-01 08:26:00	2.75	17850.0	United Kingdom
3	536365	84029G	KNITTED UNION FLAG HOT WATER BOTTLE	6	2010-12-01 08:26:00	3.39	17850.0	United Kingdom
4	536365	84029E	RED WOOLLY HOTTIE WHITE HEART.	6	2010-12-01 08:26:00	3.39	17850.0	United Kingdom
5	536365	22752	SET 7 BABUSHKA NESTING BOXES	2	2010-12-01 08:26:00	7.65	17850.0	United Kingdom
6	536365	21730	GLASS STAR FROSTED T-LIGHT HOLDER	6	2010-12-01 08:26:00	4.25	17850.0	United Kingdom
7	536366	22633	HAND WARMER UNION JACK	6	2010-12-01 08:28:00	1.85	17850.0	United Kingdom
8	536366	22632	HAND WARMER RED POLKA DOT	6	2010-12-01 08:28:00	1.85	17850.0	United Kingdom
9	536367	84879	ASSORTED COLOUR BIRD ORNAMENT	32	2010-12-01 08:34:00	1.69	13047.0	United Kingdom

Figure 8.11: The raw online retail data

3. Print out the data type for each column in the DataFrame. This information will come in handy when trying to perform specific cleaning tasks:

```
online.dtypes
```

The output is as follows:

```
InvoiceNo                    object
StockCode                    object
Description                  object
Quantity                      int64
InvoiceDate         datetime64[ns]
UnitPrice                   float64
CustomerID                  float64
Country                      object
dtype: object
```

Figure 8.12: Data type for each column in the dataset

4. Get the dimensions of the DataFrame, as well as the number of unique invoice numbers and customer identifications:

```
print(
    "Data dimension (row count, col count): {dim}"
    .format(dim=online.shape)
)
print(
    "Count of unique invoice numbers: {cnt}"
    .format(cnt=online.InvoiceNo.nunique())
)
print(
    "Count of unique customer ids: {cnt}"
    .format(cnt=online.CustomerID.nunique())
)
```

The output is as follows:

```
Data dimension (row count, col count): (541909, 8)
Count of unique invoice numbers: 25900
Count of unique customer ids: 4372
```

In this exercise, we have loaded the data and performed some exploratory work.

Data Cleaning and Formatting

With the dataset now loaded, let's delve into the specific data cleaning processes to be performed. Since we are going to filter the data down to just the invoice numbers and items, we focus the data cleaning on these two columns of the dataset. Remember that market basket analysis looks to identify associations between the items purchased by all customers over time. As such, the main focus of the data cleaning involves removing transactions with non-positive numbers of items. This could happen when the transaction involves voiding another transaction, when items are returned, or when the transaction is some administrative task. These types of transactions will be filtered out in two ways. The first is that canceled transactions have invoice numbers that are prefaced with "C," so we will identify those specific invoice numbers and remove them from the data. The other approach is to remove all transactions with either zero or negative numbers of items. After performing these two steps, the data will be subset down to just the invoice number and item description columns, and any row of the now two-column dataset with at least one missing value is removed.

The next stage of the data cleaning exercise involves putting the data in the appropriate format for modeling. In this and subsequent exercises, we will use a subset of the full data. The subset will be done by taking the first 5,000 unique invoice numbers. Once we have cut the data down to the first 5,000 unique invoice numbers, we change the data structure to that needed to run the models. Note that the data is currently in long format, where each item is on its own row. The desired format is a list of lists, like the made-up data from earlier in the chapter. Each subset list represents a unique invoice number, so in this case, the outer list should contain 5,000 sub-lists. The elements of the sub-lists are all the items belonging to the invoice number that that sub-list represents. With the cleaning process described, let's proceed to the exercise.

Exercise 42: Data Cleaning and Formatting

In this exercise, we will perform the cleaning steps described previously. As we work through the process, the evolution of the data will be monitored by printing out the current state of the data and computing some basic summary metrics. Be sure to perform data cleaning in the same notebook in which the data is loaded.

1. Create an indicator column stipulating whether the invoice number begins with "C":

```
online['IsCPresent'] = (
    online['InvoiceNo']
    .astype(str)
    .apply(lambda x: 1 if x.find('C') != -1 else 0)
)
```

2. Filter out all transactions having either zero or a negative number of items, remove all invoice numbers starting with "C" using the column created in step one, subset the DataFrame down to **InvoiceNo** and **Description**, and lastly, drop all rows with at least one missing value. Rename the DataFrame **online1**:

```
online1 = (
    online
    # filter out non-positive quantity values
    .loc[online["Quantity"] > 0]
    # remove InvoiceNos starting with C
    .loc[online['IsCPresent'] != 1]
    # column filtering
    .loc[:, ["InvoiceNo", "Description"]]
    # dropping all rows with at least one missing value
    .dropna()
)
```

3. Print out the first 10 rows of the filtered DataFrame, **online1**:

```
online1.head(10)
```

	InvoiceNo	Description
0	536365	WHITE HANGING HEART T-LIGHT HOLDER
1	536365	WHITE METAL LANTERN
2	536365	CREAM CUPID HEARTS COAT HANGER
3	536365	KNITTED UNION FLAG HOT WATER BOTTLE
4	536365	RED WOOLLY HOTTIE WHITE HEART.
5	536365	SET 7 BABUSHKA NESTING BOXES
6	536365	GLASS STAR FROSTED T-LIGHT HOLDER
7	536366	HAND WARMER UNION JACK
8	536366	HAND WARMER RED POLKA DOT
9	536367	ASSORTED COLOUR BIRD ORNAMENT

Figure 8.13: The cleaned online retail dataset

4. Print out the dimensions of the cleaned DataFrame and the number of unique invoice numbers:

```
print(
    "Data dimension (row count, col count): {dim}"
    .format(dim=online1.shape)
)
print(
```

```
"Count of unique invoice numbers: {cnt}"
.format(cnt=online1.InvoiceNo.nunique())
)
```

The output is as follows:

```
Data dimension (row count, col count): (530693, 2)
Count of unique invoice numbers: 20136
```

Notice that we have already removed approximately 10,000 rows and 5,800 invoice numbers.

5. Extract the invoice numbers from the DataFrame as a list. Remove duplicate elements to create a list of unique invoice numbers. Confirm that the process was successful by printing the length of the list of unique invoice numbers. Compare with the output of *Step 4*:

```
invoice_no_list = online1.InvoiceNo.tolist()
invoice_no_list = list(set(invoice_no_list))
print(
    "Length of list of invoice numbers: {ln}"
    .format(ln=len(invoice_no_list))
)
```

The output is as follows:

```
Length of list of invoice numbers: 20136
```

6. Take the list from step five and cut it to only include the first 5,000 elements. Print out the length of the new list to confirm that it is, in fact, the expected length of 5,000:

```
subset_invoice_no_list = invoice_no_list[0:5000]
print(
    "Length of subset list of invoice numbers: {ln}"
    .format(ln=len(subset_invoice_no_list))
)
```

The output is as follows:

```
Length of subset list of invoice numbers: 5000
```

7. Filter the **online1** DataFrame down by only keeping the invoice numbers in the list from the previous step:

```
online1 = online1.loc[online1["InvoiceNo"].isin(subset_invoice_no_list)]
```

8. Print out the first 10 rows of **online1**:

    ```
    online1.head(10)
    ```

    The output is as follows:

	InvoiceNo	Description
229435	557056	SET OF 4 KNICK KNACK TINS DOILEY
229436	557057	RED POLKADOT BEAKER
229437	557057	BLUE POLKADOT BEAKER
229438	557057	DAIRY MAID TOASTRACK
229439	557057	BLUE EGG SPOON
229440	557057	RED EGG SPOON
229441	557057	MODERN FLORAL STATIONERY SET
229442	557057	FLORAL FOLK STATIONERY SET
229443	557057	CERAMIC BOWL WITH LOVE HEART DESIGN
229444	557057	WOOD STAMP SET THANK YOU

    Figure 8.14: The cleaned dataset with only 5,000 unique invoice numbers

9. Print out the dimensions of the DataFrame and the number of unique invoice numbers to confirm that the filtering and cleaning process was successful:

    ```
    print(
        "Data dimension (row count, col count): {dim}"
        .format(dim=online1.shape)
    )
    print(
        "Count of unique invoice numbers: {cnt}"
        .format(cnt=online1.InvoiceNo.nunique())
    )
    ```

    The output is as follows:

    ```
    Data dimension (row count, col count): (129815, 2)
    Count of unique invoice numbers: 5000
    ```

10. Transform the data in **online1** into the aforementioned list of lists called **invoice_item_list**. The process for doing this is to iterate over the unique invoice numbers and, at each iteration, extract the item descriptions as a list and append that list to the larger **invoice_item_list** list. Print out elements one through four of the list:

    ```
    invoice_item_list = []
    for num in list(set(online1.InvoiceNo.tolist())):
    ```

```
# filter dataset down to one invoice number
tmp_df = online1.loc[online1['InvoiceNo'] == num]
# extract item descriptions and convert to list
tmp_items = tmp_df.Description.tolist()
# append list invoice_item_list
invoice_item_list.append(tmp_items)

print(invoice_item_list[1:5])
```

The output is as follows:

```
[['RED POLKADOT BEAKER ', 'BLUE POLKADOT BEAKER ', 'DAIRY MAID TOASTRACK', 'BLUE EGG SPOON', 'RED  EGG  SPOON', 'MODERN FLORAL
STATIONERY SET', 'FLORAL FOLK STATIONERY SET', 'CERAMIC BOWL WITH LOVE HEART DESIGN', 'WOOD STAMP SET THANK YOU', 'WOOD STAMP S
ET HAPPY BIRTHDAY', 'PENS ASSORTED SPACEBALL', 'PENS ASSORTED FUNNY FACE', 'PENS ASSORTED FUNKY JEWELED ', 'SCOTTIE DOGS BABY B
IB', 'CHARLIE AND LOLA TABLE TINS', 'CHARLIE & LOLA WASTEPAPER BIN FLORA', 'CHARLIE & LOLA WASTEPAPER BIN BLUE', 'CHARLIE AND L
OLA FIGURES TINS', 'TV DINNER TRAY DOLLY GIRL', 'SET/20 RED RETROSPOT PAPER NAPKINS ', 'MINT KITCHEN SCALES', 'RED KITCHEN SCAL
ES', '36 FOIL HEART CAKE CASES', '36 FOIL STAR CAKE CASES ', 'ILLUSTRATED CAT BOWL ', 'POTTING SHED TEA MUG', 'CERAMIC STRAWBER
RY DESIGN MUG', 'RED RETROSPOT SHOPPER BAG', 'BUTTON BOX ', 'MINI CAKE STAND  HANGING STRAWBERY', 'LUNCH BAG DOILEY PATTERN ',
'JUMBO BAG STRAWBERRY', 'STRAWBERRY SHOPPER BAG', 'SUKI  SHOULDER BAG', 'JUMBO BAG ALPHABET', 'SKULL SHOULDER BAG', 'LUNCH BAG
BLACK SKULL.', 'TRADITIONAL WOODEN CATCH CUP GAME ', '10 COLOUR SPACEBOY PEN', 'JUMBO BAG SPACEBOY DESIGN', 'LUNCH BAG SPACEBOY
DESIGN ', "CHILDREN'S APRON DOLLY GIRL ", 'LUNCH BAG DOLLY GIRL DESIGN', 'TEATIME ROUND PENCIL SHARPENER ', 'SILVER HEARTS TABL
E DECORATION', 'PARISIENNE KEY CABINET ', 'PARISIENNE JEWELLERY DRAWER ', 'BUNDLE OF 3 SCHOOL EXERCISE BOOKS ', 'JUMBO BAG DOI
LEY PATTERNS', 'DOILEY STORAGE TIN', 'SET OF 4 KNICK KNACK TINS POPPIES', 'SET OF 4 KNICK KNACK TINS DOILEY ', 'SET OF 3 REGENC
Y CAKE TINS', 'SET OF 3 WOODEN HEART DECORATIONS', 'SPACEBOY CHILDRENS BOWL', 'DOLLY GIRL CHILDRENS CUP', 'DOLLY GIRL CHILDRENS
BOWL', 'SPACE BOY CHILDRENS CUP', 'GARDENERS KNEELING PAD CUP OF TEA ', 'GARDENERS KNEELING PAD KEEP CALM ', 'CARTOON  PENCIL S
HARPENERS', 'POPART RECT PENCIL SHARPENER ASST', 'PIECE OF CAMO STATIONERY SET', 'POPART WOODEN PENCILS ASST', 'ORIGAMI VANILLA
INCENSE/CANDLE SET ', 'ORIGAMI JASMINE INCENSE/CANDLE SET', 'FRENCH FLORAL CUSHION COVER ', 'FRENCH LATTICE CUSHION COVER '],
['SET OF TEA COFFEE SUGAR TINS PANTRY', 'SET OF 3 CAKE TINS PANTRY DESIGN '], ['JUMBO BAG PINK VINTAGE PAISLEY', 'JUMBO  BAG BA
ROQUE BLACK WHITE', 'RIBBON REEL STRIPES DESIGN ', 'RIBBON REEL LACE DESIGN ', 'RIBBON REEL POLKADOTS ', 'TRAVEL CARD WALLET TR
ANSPORT', 'TRAVEL CARD WALLET FLOWER MEADOW', 'TRAVEL CARD WALLET VINTAGE LEAF', 'TRAVEL CARD WALLET VINTAGE TICKET', 'VINTAGE
2 METER FOLDING RULER', 'IVORY WICKER HEART LARGE', 'BUNDLE OF 3 ALPHABET EXERCISE BOOKS', 'BUNDLE OF 3 RETRO NOTE BOOKS', '20
DOLLY PEGS RETROSPOT', 'CLOTHES PEGS RETROSPOT PACK 24 ', 'VICTORIAN  METAL POSTCARD SPRING', 'ROLL WRAP VINTAGE CHRISTMAS', 'R
OLL WRAP VINTAGE SPOT ', 'ENAMEL MEASURING JUG CREAM', 'JUMBO BAG VINTAGE CHRISTMAS ', 'JUMBO BAG 50'S CHRISTMAS ", 'SET OF 4 K
NICK KNACK TINS DOILY ', 'SET OF 4 KNICK KNACK TINS POPPIES', 'IVORY WICKER HEART LARGE', 'JINGLE BELL HEART ANTIQUE GOLD', 'SE
T OF 4 NAPKIN CHARMS CUTLERY', 'SET OF 4 NAPKIN CHARMS HEARTS', 'SET OF 4 KNICK KNACK TINS LEAF', 'MADRAS NOTEBOOK MEDIUM', 'SE
T OF 3 WOODEN HEART DECORATIONS', 'FAMILY ALBUM WHITE PICTURE FRAME', 'REX CASH+CARRY JUMBO SHOPPER'], ['COFFEE MUG PEARS  DESI
GN', 'TRAVEL CARD WALLET VINTAGE TICKET', 'AIRLINE BAG VINTAGE JET SET RED', 'AIRLINE BAG VINTAGE JET SET WHITE', 'GREY HEART H
OT WATER BOTTLE', 'LOVE HOT WATER BOTTLE', 'TRAVEL CARD WALLET I LOVE LONDON', 'KNITTED UNION FLAG HOT WATER BOTTLE', 'HOT WATE
R BOTTLE I AM SO POORLY', 'AIRLINE BAG VINTAGE WORLD CHAMPION ', 'AIRLINE BAG VINTAGE TOKYO 78', 'HOT WATER BOTTLE TEA AND SYMP
ATHY', 'BLUE PAISLEY POCKET BOOK', 'ABSTRACT CIRCLES POCKET BOOK', 'HAND WARMER RED RETROSPOT', 'PLASTERS IN TIN WOODLAND ANIMA
LS', 'PLASTERS IN TIN VINTAGE PAISLEY', 'HAND WARMER SCOTTY DOG DESIGN', 'HAND WARMER BIRD DESIGN', 'PLASTERS IN TIN STRONGMA
N', 'PLASTERS IN TIN CIRCUS PARADE ']]
```

Figure 8.15: Four elements of the list of lists, where each sub-list contains all the items belonging to an individual invoice

> **Note**
>
> This step can take some minutes to complete.

Data Encoding

While cleaning the data is crucial, the most important part of the data preparation process is molding the data into the correct form. Before running the models, the data, currently in the list of lists form, needs to be encoded and recast as a DataFrame. To do this, we will leverage **TransactionEncoder** from the **preprocessing** module of **mlxtend**. Outputted from the encoder is a multidimensional array, where each row is the length of the total number of unique items in the transaction dataset and the elements are Boolean variables, indicating whether that particular item is linked to the invoice number that row represents. With the data encoded, we can recast it as a DataFrame where the rows are the invoice numbers and the columns are the unique items in the transaction dataset.

In the following exercise, the data encoding will be done using **mlxtend**, but it is very easy to encode the data without using any package. The first step is to unlist the list of lists and return one list with every value from the original list of lists. Next, the duplicate products are filtered out and, if preferred, the data is sorted in alphabetical order. Before doing the actual encoding, we initialize the final DataFrame by having all elements equal to false, a number of rows equal to the number of invoice numbers in the dataset, and column names equal to the non-duplicated list of product names.

In this case, we have 5,000 transactions and over 3,100 unique products. Thus, the DataFrame has over 15,000,000 elements. The actual encoding is done by looping over each transaction and each item in each transaction. Change the row i and column j cell values in the initialized dataset from false to true if the ith transaction contains the jth product. This double loop is not fast as we need to iterate over 15,000,000 cells. There are ways to improve performance, including some that have been implemented in **mlxtend**, but to better understand the process, it is helpful to work through the double loop methodology. The following is an example function to do the encoding from scratch without the assistance of any package other than **pandas**:

```
def manual_encoding(ll):
    # unlist the list of lists input
    # result is one list with all the elements of the sublists
    list_dup_unsort_items = [element for sub in ll for element in sub]
    # two cleaning steps:
    #     1. remove duplicate items, only want one of each item in list
```

```
#      2. sort items in alphabetical order
list_nondup_sort_items = sorted(list(set(list_dup_unsort_items)))


# initialize DataFrame with all elements having False value
# name the columns the elements of list_dup_unsort_items
manual_df = pandas.DataFrame(
    False,
    index=range(len(ll)),
    columns=list_dup_unsort_items
)


# change False to True if element is in individual transaction list
# each row is represents the contains of an individual transaction
# (sublist from the original list of lists)
for i in range(len(ll)):
    for j in ll[i]:
        manual_df.loc[i, j] = True


# return the True/False DataFrame
return manual_df
```

Exercise 43: Data Encoding

In this exercise, we continue the data preparation process by taking the list of lists generated in the previous exercise and encoding the data in the specific way required to run the models.

1. Initialize and fit the transaction encoder. Print out an example of the resulting data:

```
online_encoder = mlxtend.preprocessing.TransactionEncoder()
online_encoder_array = online_encoder.fit_transform(invoice_item_list)
print(online_encoder_array)
```

The output is as follows:

```
[[False False False ... False False False]
 [False False False ... False False False]
 [False False False ... False False False]
 ...
 [False False False ... False False False]
 [False False False ... False False False]
 [False False False ... False False False]]
```

Figure 8.16: The multi-dimensional array containing the Boolean variables indicating product presence in each transaction

2. Recast the encoded array as a DataFrame named **online_encoder_df**. Print out a predefined subset of the DataFrame that features both true and false values:

```
online_encoder_df = pandas.DataFrame(
    online_encoder_array,
    columns=online_encoder.columns_
)

# this is a very big table, so for more
# easy viewing only a subset is printed
online_encoder_df.loc[
    4970:4979,
    online_encoder_df.columns.tolist()[0:8]
]
```

The output will be similar to the following:

	4 PURPLE FLOCK DINNER CANDLES	50'S CHRISTMAS GIFT BAG LARGE	DOLLY GIRL BEAKER	I LOVE LONDON MINI BACKPACK	NINE DRAWER OFFICE TIDY	OVAL WALL MIRROR DIAMANTE	RED SPOT GIFT BAG LARGE	SET 2 TEA TOWELS I LOVE LONDON
4970	False	False	False	False	False	False	False	False
4971	False	False	True	False	False	False	False	False
4972	False	False	False	False	False	False	False	False
4973	False	False	False	False	False	False	False	False
4974	False	False	False	False	False	False	False	False
4975	False	False	False	False	False	False	False	False
4976	False	False	False	False	False	False	False	False
4977	False	False	False	False	False	False	False	False
4978	False	False	False	False	False	False	False	False
4979	False	False	False	False	False	False	False	False

Figure 8.17: A small section of the encoded data recast as a DataFrame

3. Print out the dimensions of the encoded DataFrame. It should have 5,000 rows because the data used to generate it was previously filtered down to 5,000 unique invoice numbers:

```
print(
    "Data dimension (row count, col count): {dim}"
    .format(dim=online_encoder_df.shape)
)
```

The output will be similar to the following:

```
Data dimension (row count, col count): (5000, 3334)
```

The data is now prepped for modeling. In the next section, we will explore the Apriori algorithm.

Activity 18: Loading and Preparing Full Online Retail Data

In this activity, we are charged with loading and preparing a large transaction dataset for modeling. The final output will be an appropriately encoded dataset that has one row for each unique transaction in the dataset, and one column for each unique item in the dataset. If an item appears in an individual transaction, that element of the DataFrame will be marked true.

This activity will largely repeat the last few exercises, but will use the complete online retail dataset file. No new downloads need to be executed, but you will need the path to the file downloaded previously. Perform this activity in a separate Jupyter notebook.

The following steps will help you to complete the activity:

1. Load the online retail dataset file:

> **Note**
>
> This dataset is taken from http://archive.ics.uci.edu/ml/datasets/online+retail#. It can be downloaded from https://github.com/TrainingByPackt/Applied-Unsupervised-Learning-with-Python/tree/master/Lesson08/Activity18-Activity20. Daqing Chen, Sai Liang Sain, and Kun Guo, Data mining for the online retail industry: A case study of RFM model-based customer segmentation using data mining, Journal of Database Marketing and Customer Strategy Management, Vol. 19, No. 3, pp. 197-208, 2012.
>
> UCI Machine Learning Repository [http://archive.ics.uci.edu/ml]. Irvine, CA: University of California, School of Information and Computer Science.

2. Clean and prep the data for modeling, including turning the cleaned data into a list of lists.

3. Encode the data and recast it as a DataFrame:

> **Note**
>
> The solution for this activity can be found on page 366.

The output will be similar to the following:

	6 CHOCOLATE LOVE HEART T-LIGHTS	6 EGG HOUSE PAINTED WOOD	6 GIFT TAGS 50'S CHRISTMAS	6 GIFT TAGS VINTAGE CHRISTMAS	6 RIBBONS ELEGANT CHRISTMAS	6 RIBBONS EMPIRE	6 RIBBONS RUSTIC CHARM	6 RIBBONS SHIMMERING PINKS	6 ROCKET BALLOONS	60 CAKE CASES DOLLY GIRL DESIGN
20125	False	False	False	False	False	False	False	False	False	False
20126	False	False	False	False	False	False	False	False	False	False
20127	False	False	False	False	False	False	False	False	False	False
20128	False	False	False	False	False	False	False	False	False	False
20129	False	False	False	False	False	False	False	False	False	False
20130	False	False	False	False	False	False	False	False	False	False
20131	False	False	False	False	False	False	False	False	False	False
20132	False	False	False	False	False	False	False	False	False	False
20133	False	False	False	False	False	False	False	False	False	False
20134	False	False	False	False	False	False	False	False	False	False
20135	False	False	False	False	False	False	False	False	False	False

Figure 8.18: A subset of the cleaned, encoded, and recast DataFrame built from the complete online retail dataset

Apriori Algorithm

The **Apriori** algorithm is a data mining methodology for identifying and quantifying frequent item sets in transaction data, and is the foundational component of association rule learning. Extending the results of the Apriori algorithm to association rule learning will be discussed in the next section. The minimum value to qualify as frequent in the Apriori algorithm is an input into the model and, as such, is adjustable. Frequency is quantified here as support, so the value inputted into the model is the minimum support acceptable for the analysis being done. The model then identifies all item sets whose support is greater than, or equal to, the minimum support provided to the model. Note that the minimum support parameter is not a parameter that can be optimized via a grid search because there is no evaluation metric for the Apriori algorithm. Instead, the minimum support parameter is set based on the data, the use case, and domain expertise.

The main idea behind the Apriori algorithm is the Apriori principle: any subset of a frequent item set must itself be frequent.

Another aspect worth mentioning is the corollary: no superset of an infrequent item set can be frequent.

Let's take some examples. If the item set {hammer, saw, and nail} is frequent, then, according to the Apriori principle and what is hopefully obvious, any less complex item set, say {hammer, saw}, is also frequent. On the contrary, if that same item set, {hammer, saw, nail}, is infrequent, then adding complexity, such as incorporating wood in the item set {hammer, saw, nail, wood}, is not going to result in the item set becoming frequent.

It might seem straightforward to calculate the support value for every item set in a transactional database and only return those item sets whose support is greater than or equal to the prespecified minimum support threshold, but it is not because of the number of computations that need to happen. For example, take an item set with 10 unique items. This would result in 1,023 individual item sets for which support would need to be calculated. Now, try to extrapolate out to our working dataset that has 3,135 unique items. That is going to be an enormous number of item sets for which we need to compute a support value. Computational efficiency is a major issue:

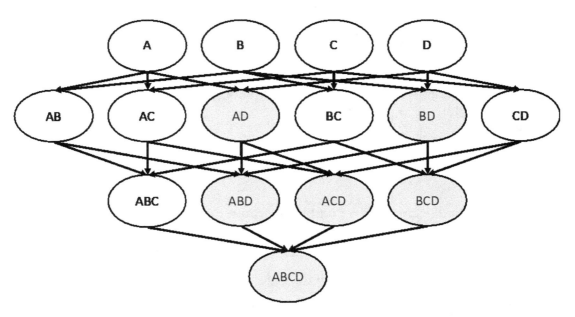

Figure 8.19: A mapping of how item sets are built and how the Apriori principle can greatly decrease the computational requirements (all the grayed-out nodes are infrequent)

In order to address the computational demands, the Apriori algorithm is defined as a bottom-up model that has two steps. These steps involve generating candidate item sets by adding items to already existing frequent item sets and testing these candidate item sets against the dataset to determine whether these candidate datasets are also frequent. No support value is computed for item sets that contain infrequent item sets. This process repeats until no further candidate item sets exist:

Figure 8.20: Assuming a minimum support threshold of 0.4, the diagram shows the general Apriori algorithm structure

The preceding structure includes establishing an item set, computing support values, filtering out infrequent item sets, creating new item sets, and repeating the process.

There is a clear tree-like structure that serves as the path for identifying candidate item sets. The specific search technique used, which was built for traversing tree-like data structures, is called a breadth-first search, which means that each step of the search process focuses on completely searching one level of the tree before moving on instead of searching branch by branch.

The high-level steps of the algorithm are to:

1. Define the set of frequent items. To start, this is typically the set of individual items.

2. Derive candidate item sets by combining frequent item sets together. Move up in size one item at a time. That is, go from item sets with one item to two, two to three, and so on.

3. Compute the support value for each candidate item set.

4. Create a new frequent item set made up of the candidate item sets whose support value exceeded the specified threshold.

Repeat *Steps* 1 to 4 until there are no more frequent item sets; that is, until we have worked through all the combinations.

The pseudo code for the Apriori algorithm is as follows:

```
L₁ = {frequent items}


For k = 1 and L₁ != empty set do
    C_{k+1} = candidate item sets derived from L_k


    For each transaction t in the dataset do
        Increment the count of the candidates in C_{k+1} that appear in t


    Compute the support for the candidates in C_{k+1} using the appearance counts
    L_{k+1} = the candidates in C_{k+1} meeting the minimum support requirement
        End


Return L = U_k L_k = all frequent item sets with corresponding support values
```

Despite the Apriori principle, this algorithm can still face significant computational challenges depending on the size of the transaction dataset. There are several strategies currently accepted to further reduce the computational demands.

Computational Fixes

Transaction reduction is an easy way to reduce the computational load. Note that after each candidate set of item sets is generated, the entirety of the transaction data needs to be scanned in order to count the number of appearances of each candidate item set. If we could shrink the size of the transaction dataset, the size of the dataset scans would decrease dramatically. The shrinking of the transaction dataset is done by realizing that any transaction containing no frequent item sets in the *ith* iteration is not going to contain any frequent item sets in subsequent iterations. Therefore, once each transaction contains no frequent item sets, it can be removed from the transaction dataset used for future scans.

Sampling the transaction dataset and testing each candidate item set against it is another approach to reducing the computational requirements associated with scanning the transaction dataset to calculate the support of each item set. When this approach is implemented it is important to lower the minimum support requirement to guarantee that no item sets that should be present in the final data are left out. Given that the sampled transaction dataset will naturally cause the support values to be smaller, leaving the minimum support at its original value will incorrectly remove what should be frequent item sets from the output of the model.

A similar approach is partitioning. In this case, the dataset is partitioned into several individual datasets on which the evaluation of each candidate item set is executed. Item sets are deemed frequent in the full transaction dataset if frequent in one of the partitions. Each partition is scanned consecutively until frequency for an item set is established.

Regardless of whether or not one of these techniques is employed, the computational requirements are always going to be fairly substantial when it comes to the Apriori algorithm. As should now be clear, the essence of the algorithm, the computation of support, is not as complex as other models discussed in this text.

Exercise 44: Executing the Apriori algorithm

The execution of the Apriori algorithm is made easy with **mlxtend**. As a result, this exercise will focus on how to manipulate the outputted dataset and to interpret the results. You will recall that the cleaned and encoded transaction data was defined as **online_encoder_df**. Perform this exercise in the same notebook that all previous exercises were run as we will continue using the environment, data, and results already established in that notebook. (So, you should be using the notebook that contains the reduced dataset of 5,000 entries, not the full dataset as used in the activity.)

1. Run the Apriori algorithm using **mlxtend** without changing any of the default parameter values:

```
mod = mlxtend.frequent_patterns.apriori(online_encoder_df)
mod
```

The output is an empty DataFrame. The default minimum support value is set to 0.5, so since an empty DataFrame was returned, we know that all item sets have a support of less than 0.5. Depending on the number of transactions and the diversity of available items, having no item set with a plus 0.5 support is not unusual.

2. Rerun the Apriori algorithm, but with the minimum support set to 0.01. This minimum support value is the same as saying that when analyzing 5,000 transactions, we need an item set to appear 50 times to be considered frequent. As mentioned previously, the minimum support can be set to any value in the range [0,1]. There is no best minimum support value; the setting of this value is entirely subjective. Many businesses have their own specific thresholds for significance, but there is no industry standard or method for optimizing this value:

```
mod_minsupport = mlxtend.frequent_patterns.apriori(
    online_encoder_df,
    min_support=0.01
)
mod_minsupport.loc[0:6]
```

The output will be similar to the following:

	support	itemsets
0	0.0168	(2)
1	0.0150	(10)
2	0.0116	(15)
3	0.0144	(18)
4	0.0210	(19)
5	0.0144	(20)
6	0.0138	(21)

Figure 8.21: Basic output of the Apriori algorithm run using mlxtend

Notice that the item sets are designated numerically in the output, which makes the results hard to interpret.

3. Rerun the Apriori algorithm with the same minimum support as in *Step 2*, but this time set **use_colnames** to True. This will replace the numerical designations with the actual item names:

```
mod_colnames_minsupport = mlxtend.frequent_patterns.apriori(
    online_encoder_df,
    min_support=0.01,
    use_colnames=True
)
mod_colnames_minsupport.loc[0:6]
```

The output will be similar to the following:

	support	itemsets
0	0.0168	(DOLLY GIRL BEAKER)
1	0.0150	(10 COLOUR SPACEBOY PEN)
2	0.0116	(12 MESSAGE CARDS WITH ENVELOPES)
3	0.0144	(12 PENCILS SMALL TUBE SKULL)
4	0.0210	(12 PENCILS TALL TUBE POSY)
5	0.0144	(12 PENCILS TALL TUBE RED RETROSPOT)
6	0.0138	(12 PENCILS TALL TUBE SKULLS)

Figure 8.22: The output of the Apriori algorithm with the actual item names instead of numerical designations

This DataFrame contains every item set whose support value is greater than the specified minimum support value. That is, these item sets occur with sufficient frequency to potentially be meaningful and therefore actionable.

4. Add an additional column to the output of *Step 3* that contains the size of the item set, which will help with filtering and further analysis:

```
mod_colnames_minsupport['length'] = (
    mod_colnames_minsupport['itemsets'].apply(lambda x: len(x))
)
mod_colnames_minsupport.loc[0:6]
```

The output will be similar to the following:

	support	itemsets	length
0	0.0168	(DOLLY GIRL BEAKER)	1
1	0.0150	(10 COLOUR SPACEBOY PEN)	1
2	0.0116	(12 MESSAGE CARDS WITH ENVELOPES)	1
3	0.0144	(12 PENCILS SMALL TUBE SKULL)	1
4	0.0210	(12 PENCILS TALL TUBE POSY)	1
5	0.0144	(12 PENCILS TALL TUBE RED RETROSPOT)	1
6	0.0138	(12 PENCILS TALL TUBE SKULLS)	1

Figure 8.23: The Apriori algorithm output plus an additional column containing the lengths of the item sets

5. Find the support of the item set containing '10 COLOUR SPACEBOY PEN':

```
mod_colnames_minsupport[
    mod_colnames_minsupport['itemsets'] == frozenset(
        {'10 COLOUR SPACEBOY PEN'}
    )
]
```

The output is as follows:

	support	itemsets	length
1	0.015	(10 COLOUR SPACEBOY PEN)	1

Figure 8.24: The output DataFrame filtered down to a single item set

This single row DataFrame gives us the support value for this specific item set that contains one item. The support value says that this specific item set appears in 1.5% of the transactions.

6. Return all item sets of length 2 whose support is in the range [0.02, 0.021]

```
mod_colnames_minsupport[
    (mod_colnames_minsupport['length'] == 2) &
    (mod_colnames_minsupport['support'] >= 0.02) &
    (mod_colnames_minsupport['support'] < 0.021)
]
```

The output will be similar to the following:

	support	itemsets	length
837	0.0202	(ALARM CLOCK BAKELIKE IVORY, ALARM CLOCK BAKEL...	2
956	0.0202	(LUNCH BAG APPLE DESIGN, CHARLOTTE BAG APPLES ...	2
994	0.0200	(LUNCH BAG PINK POLKADOT, CHARLOTTE BAG PINK P...	2
1026	0.0206	(CHARLOTTE BAG SUKI DESIGN, LUNCH BAG BLACK S...	2
1032	0.0206	(CHARLOTTE BAG SUKI DESIGN, LUNCH BAG RED RETR...	2
1131	0.0200	(JUMBO SHOPPER VINTAGE RED PAISLEY, DOTCOM POS...	2
1298	0.0208	(HEART OF WICKER LARGE, HEART OF WICKER SMALL)	2
1305	0.0200	(HEART OF WICKER SMALL, SMALL WHITE HEART OF W...	2
1316	0.0204	(JAM MAKING SET PRINTED, JAM MAKING SET WITH J...	2
1349	0.0208	(SET OF 3 REGENCY CAKE TINS, JAM MAKING SET PR...	2
1440	0.0200	(JUMBO BAG ALPHABET, LUNCH BAG ALPHABET DESIGN)	2
1464	0.0206	(JUMBO BAG APPLES, JUMBO BAG DOILEY PATTERNS)	2
1471	0.0202	(JUMBO BAG SCANDINAVIAN BLUE PAISLEY, JUMBO BA...	2
1472	0.0202	(JUMBO BAG SPACEBOY DESIGN, JUMBO BAG APPLES)	2
1479	0.0204	(JUMBO BAG APPLES, JUMBO STORAGE BAG SKULLS)	2
1575	0.0200	(JUMBO BAG PINK POLKADOT, JUMBO BAG OWLS)	2
1583	0.0208	(JUMBO BAG WOODLAND ANIMALS, JUMBO BAG OWLS)	2

Figure 8.25: The Apriori algorithm output DataFrame filtered by length and support

This DataFrame contains all the item sets (pairs of items bought together) whose support value is in the range specified at the start of the step. Each of these item sets appears in between 2.0% and 2.1% of transactions.

Note that when filtering on **support**, it is wise to specify a range instead of a specific value since it is quite possible to pick a value for which there are no item sets. The preceding output has 18 item sets. Keep note of that and the particular items in the item sets because we will be running this same filter when we scale up to the full data and we will want to execute a comparison.

7. Plot the support values. Note that this plot will have no support values less than 0.01 because that was the value used as the minimum support:

```
mod_colnames_minsupport.hist("support", grid=False, bins=30)
plt.title("Support")
```

The output will be similar to the following plot:

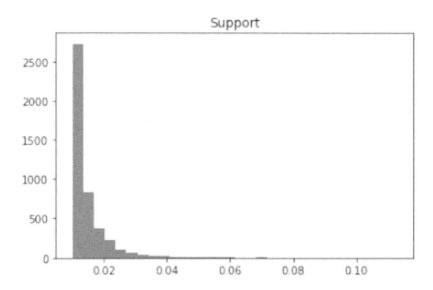

Figure 8.26: Distribution of the support values returned by the Apriori algorithm

The maximum support value is approximately 0.14, which is approximately 700 transactions. What might appear to be a small value may not be given the number of products available. Larger numbers of products tend to result in lower support values because the variability of item combinations increases.

Hopefully, you can think of more ways in which this data could be used and with a view to supporting retail businesses. We will generate even more useful information in the next section by using the Apriori algorithm results to generate association rules.

Activity 19: Apriori on the Complete Online Retail Dataset

Imagine you work for an online retailer. You are given all the transaction data from the last month and told to find all the item sets appearing in at least 1% of the transactions. Once the qualifying item sets are identified, you are subsequently told to identify the distribution of the support values. The distribution of support values will tell all interested parties whether groups of items exist that are purchased together with high probability as well as the mean of the support values. Let's collect all the information for the company leadership and strategists.

In this activity, you will run the Apriori algorithm on the full online retail dataset.

> **Note**
>
> This dataset is taken from http://archive.ics.uci.edu/ml/datasets/online+retail#. It can be downloaded from https://github.com/TrainingByPackt/Applied-Unsupervised-Learning-with-Python/tree/master/Lesson08/Activity18-Activity20. Daqing Chen, Sai Liang Sain, and Kun Guo, Data mining for the online retail industry: A case study of RFM model-based customer segmentation using data mining, Journal of Database Marketing and Customer Strategy Management, Vol. 19, No. 3, pp. 197-208, 2012.
>
> UCI Machine Learning Repository [http://archive.ics.uci.edu/ml]. Irvine, CA: University of California, School of Information and Computer Science.

Ensure that you complete this activity in the same notebook as the previous activity (in other words, the notebook that uses the full dataset, not the notebook that uses the subset of 5,000 items that you're using for the exercises).

This will also provide you with an opportunity to compare the results with those generated using only 5,000 transactions. This is an interesting activity, as it provides some insight into the ways in which the data may change as more data is collected, as well as some insight into how support values change when the partitioning technique is employed. Note that what was done in the exercises is not a perfect representation of the partitioning technique because 5,000 was an arbitrary number of transactions to sample.

> **Note**
>
> All the activities in this chapter need to be performed in the same notebook.

The following steps will help you to complete the activity:

1. Run the Apriori algorithm on the full data with reasonable parameter settings.

2. Filter the results down to the item set containing **10 COLOUR SPACEBOY PEN**. Compare the support value to that of *Exercise 44, Executing the Apriori algorithm.*

3. Add another column containing the item set length. Then, filter down to those item sets whose length is two and whose support is in the range [0.02, 0.021]. Compare this to the result from *Exercise 44, Executing the Apriori algorithm.*

4. Plot the **support** values.

> **Note**
>
> The solution for this activity can be found on page 367.

The output of this activity will be similar to the following:

```
Text(0.5, 1.0, 'Support')
```

Figure 8.27: Distribution of support values

Association Rules

Association rule learning is a machine learning model that seeks to unearth the hidden patterns (in other words, relationships) in transaction data that describe the shopping habits of the customers of any retailer. The definition of an association rule was hinted at when the common probabilistic metrics were defined and explained previously.

Consider the imaginary frequent item set {Milk, Bread}. Two association rules can be formed from that item set: Milk $\Rightarrow$ Bread and Bread $\Rightarrow$ Milk. For simplicity, the first item set in the association rule is referred to as the antecedent, while the second item set in the association rule is referred to as the consequent. Once the association rules have been identified, all the previously discussed metrics can be computed to evaluate the validity of the association rules determining whether or not the rules can be leveraged in the decision-making process.

The establishment of an association rule is based on support and confidence. Support, as we discussed in the last section, identifies which item sets are frequent, while confidence measures the frequency of truthfulness for a particular rule. Confidence is typically referred to as the measure of interestingness, as it is the metric that determines whether an association should be formed. Thus, the establishment of an association rule is a two-step process. Identify frequent datasets and then evaluate the confidence of a candidate association rule and, if that confidence value exceeds some arbitrary threshold, the result is an association rule.

A major issue of association rule learning is the discovery of spurious associations, which are highly likely given the huge numbers of potential rules. Spurious associations are defined as associations that occur with surprising regularity in the data given that the association occurs entirely by chance. To clearly articulate the idea, assume we are in a situation where we have 100 candidate rules. If we run a statistical test for independence at the 0.05 significance level, we are still faced with a 5% chance that an association is found when no association exists. Let's further assume that all 100 candidate rules are not valid associations. Given the 5% chance, we should still expect to find 5 valid association rules. Now scale the imaginary candidate rule list up to millions or billions, so that that 5% amounts to an enormous number of associations. This problem is not unlike the issue of statistical significance and error faced by virtually every model. It is worth calling out that some techniques exist to combat the spurious association issue, but they are neither consistently incorporated in the frequently used association rule libraries nor in the scope of this chapter.

Let's now apply our working knowledge of association rule learning to the online retail dataset.

Exercise 45: Deriving Association Rules

In this exercise, we will derive association rules for the online retail dataset and explore the associated metrics. Ensure that you complete this exercise in the same notebook as the previous exercises (in other words, the notebook that uses the 5,000-item subset, not the full dataset from the activities).

1. Use the **mlxtend** library to derive association rules for the online retail dataset. Use confidence as the measure of interestingness, set the minimum threshold to 0.6, and return all the metrics, not just support. Count the number of returned association rules:

```
rules = mlxtend.frequent_patterns.association_rules(
    mod_colnames_minsupport,
    metric="confidence",
    min_threshold=0.6,
    support_only=False
)
rules.loc[0:6]
```

The output is similar to the following:

	antecedents	consequents	antecedent support	consequent support	support	confidence	lift	leverage	conviction
0	(DOLLY GIRL BEAKER)	(SPACEBOY BEAKER)	0.0168	0.0172	0.0126	0.750000	43.604651	0.012311	3.931200
1	(SPACEBOY BEAKER)	(DOLLY GIRL BEAKER)	0.0172	0.0168	0.0126	0.732558	43.604651	0.012311	3.676313
2	(ALARM CLOCK BAKELIKE CHOCOLATE)	(ALARM CLOCK BAKELIKE GREEN)	0.0208	0.0580	0.0160	0.769231	13.262599	0.014794	4.082000
3	(ALARM CLOCK BAKELIKE CHOCOLATE)	(ALARM CLOCK BAKELIKE RED)	0.0208	0.0498	0.0142	0.682692	13.708681	0.013164	2.994570
4	(ALARM CLOCK BAKELIKE IVORY)	(ALARM CLOCK BAKELIKE GREEN)	0.0302	0.0580	0.0202	0.668874	11.532313	0.018448	2.844840
5	(ALARM CLOCK BAKELIKE ORANGE)	(ALARM CLOCK BAKELIKE GREEN)	0.0282	0.0580	0.0212	0.751773	12.961604	0.019564	3.794914
6	(ALARM CLOCK BAKELIKE PINK)	(ALARM CLOCK BAKELIKE GREEN)	0.0380	0.0580	0.0254	0.668421	11.524501	0.023196	2.840952

Figure 8.28: The first 7 rows of the association rules generated using only 5,000 transactions

2. Print the number of associations as follows:

```
print("Number of Associations: {}".format(rules.shape[0]))
```

5,070 association rules were found.

> **Note**
>
> The number of association rules may differ.

3. Try running another version of the model. Choose any minimum threshold and any measure of interestingness. Count and explore the returned rules:

```
rules2 = mlxtend.frequent_patterns.association_rules(
    mod_colnames_minsupport,
    metric="lift",
    min_threshold=50,
    support_only=False
)
rules2.loc[0:6]
```

The output is as follows:

	antecedents	consequents	antecedent support	consequent support	support	confidence	lift	leverage	conviction
0	(POPPY'S PLAYHOUSE KITCHEN, POPPY'S PLAYHOUSE ...	(POPPY'S PLAYHOUSE LIVINGROOM)	0.0136	0.0148	0.0102	0.750000	50.675676	0.009999	3.940800
1	(POPPY'S PLAYHOUSE LIVINGROOM)	(POPPY'S PLAYHOUSE KITCHEN, POPPY'S PLAYHOUSE ...	0.0148	0.0136	0.0102	0.689189	50.675676	0.009999	3.173635
2	(DOLLY GIRL CHILDRENS BOWL, SPACEBOY CHILDRENS...	(DOLLY GIRL CHILDRENS CUP, SPACEBOY CHILDRENS ...	0.0136	0.0140	0.0120	0.882353	63.025210	0.011810	8.381000
3	(DOLLY GIRL CHILDRENS CUP, SPACEBOY CHILDRENS ...	(DOLLY GIRL CHILDRENS BOWL, SPACEBOY CHILDRENS...	0.0140	0.0136	0.0120	0.857143	63.025210	0.011810	6.904800
4	(REGENCY TEA PLATE ROSES , GREEN REGENCY TEACU...	(REGENCY TEA PLATE GREEN , PINK REGENCY TEACUP...	0.0160	0.0138	0.0112	0.700000	50.724638	0.010979	3.287333
5	(REGENCY TEA PLATE GREEN , PINK REGENCY TEACUP...	(REGENCY TEA PLATE ROSES , GREEN REGENCY TEACU...	0.0138	0.0160	0.0112	0.811594	50.724638	0.010979	5.222769
6	(REGENCY TEA PLATE PINK, GREEN REGENCY TEACUP ...	(ROSES REGENCY TEACUP AND SAUCER , REGENCY TEA...	0.0124	0.0166	0.0106	0.854839	51.496308	0.010394	6.774533

Figure 8.29: The first 7 rows of the association rules

4. Print the number of associations as follows:

```
print("Number of Associations: {}".format(rules2.shape[0]))
```

The number of association rules found using the metric lift and the minimum threshold value of 50 is 26, which is significantly lower than in *Step* 2. We will see in the following that 50 is quite a high threshold value, so it is not surprising that we returned fewer association rules.

5. Plot confidence against support and identify specific trends in the data:

```
rules.plot.scatter("support", "confidence", alpha=0.5, marker="*")
plt.xlabel("Support")
plt.ylabel("Confidence")
plt.title("Association Rules")
plt.show()
```

The output is as follows:

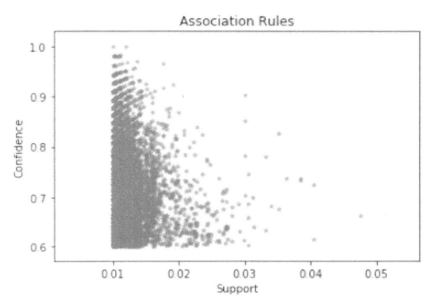

Figure 8.30: A plot of confidence against support

Notice that there are not any association rules with both extremely high confidence and extremely high support. This should hopefully make sense. If an item set has high support, the items are likely to appear with many other items, making the chances of high confidence very low.

6. Look at the distribution of confidence:

```
rules.hist("confidence", grid=False, bins=30)
plt.title("Confidence")
```

The output is as follows:

```
Text(0.5, 1.0, 'Confidence')
```

Figure 8.31: The distribution of confidence values

7. Now, look at the distribution of lift:

```
rules.hist("lift", grid=False, bins=30)
plt.title("Lift")
```

The output is as follows:

```
Text(0.5, 1.0, 'Lift')
```

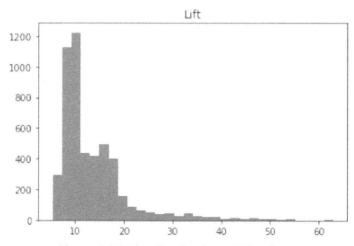

Figure 8.32: The distribution of lift values

As mentioned previously, this plot shows that 50 is a high threshold value in that there are not many points above that value.

8. Now, look at the distribution of leverage:

```
rules.hist("leverage", grid=False, bins=30)
plt.title("Leverage")
```

The output is as follows:

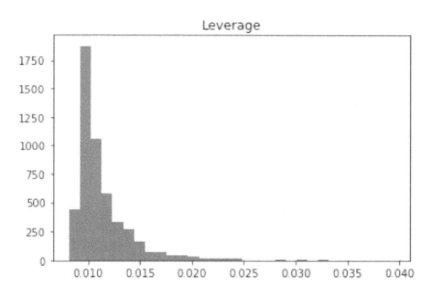

Figure 8.33: The distribution of leverage values

9. Now, look at the distribution of conviction:

```
plt.hist(
    rules[numpy.isfinite(rules['conviction'])].conviction.values,
    bins = 30
)
plt.title("Conviction")
```

The output is as follows:

```
Text(0.5, 1.0, 'Conviction')
```

Figure 8.34: The distribution of conviction values

What is interesting about the four distributions is that spikes of varying sizes appear at the upper ends of the plots, implying that there are a few very strong association rules. The distribution of confidence tails off as the confidence values get larger, but, at the very end, around the highest values, the distribution jumps up a little. The lift distribution has the most obvious spike. The conviction distribution plot shows a small spike, perhaps more accurately described as a bump, around 50. Lastly, the leverage distribution does not really show any spike in the higher values, but it does feature a long tail with some very high leverage values.

Take some time to explore the association rules found by the model. Do the product pairings make sense to you? What happened to the number of association rules when you changed the model parameter values? Do you appreciate the impact that these rules would have when attempting to improve any retail business?

Activity 20: Finding the Association Rules on the Complete Online Retail Dataset

Let's pick up the scenario set out in *Activity 19 Apriori on the Complete Online Retail Dataset*. The company leadership comes back to you and says it is great that we know how frequently each item set occurs in the dataset, but which item sets can we act upon? Which item sets can we use to change the store layout or adjust pricing? To find these answers, we derive the full association rules.

In this activity, let's derive association rules from the complete online retail transaction dataset. Ensure that you complete this activity in the notebook that uses the full dataset (in other words, the notebook with the complete retail dataset, not the notebook from the exercises that uses the 5,000-item subset).

These steps will help us to perform the activity:

1. Fit the association rule model on the full dataset. Use metric confidence and a minimum threshold of 0.6.

2. Count the number of association rules. Is the number different to that found in *step* 1 of Exercise 45, *Deriving Association Rules*?

3. Plot confidence against support.

4. Look at the distributions of confidence, lift, leverage, and conviction.

> **Note**
>
> The solution for this activity can be found on page 370.

By the end of this activity, you will have a plot of lift, leverage, and conviction.

Summary

Market basket analysis is used to analyze and extract insights from transaction or transaction-like data that can be used to help drive growth in many industries, most famously the retail industry. These decisions can include how to layout the retail space, what products to discount, and how to price products. One of the central pillars of market basket analysis is the establishment of association rules. Association rule learning is a machine learning approach to uncovering the associations between the products individuals purchase that are strong enough to be leveraged in business decisions. Association rule learning relies on the Apriori algorithm to find frequent item sets in a computationally efficient way. These models are atypical of machine learning models because no prediction is being done, the results cannot really be evaluated using any one metric, and the parameter values are selected not by grid search, but by domain requirements specific to the question of interest. That being said, the goal of pattern extraction that is at the heart of all machine learning models is most definitely present here. At the conclusion of this chapter, you should feel comfortable evaluating and interpreting the probabilistic metrics, be able to run and adjust the Apriori algorithm and association rule learning model using `mlxtend`, and know how these models are applied in business. Know that there is a decent chance the positioning and pricing of items in your neighborhood grocery store were chosen based on the past actions made by you and many other customers in that store!

In the next chapter, we explore hotspot analysis using kernel density estimation, arguably one of the most frequently used algorithms in all of statistics and machine learning.

9

Hotspot Analysis

Learning Objectives

By the end of this chapter, you will be able to:

- Understand some of the applications of spatial modeling
- Deploy hotspot models in the appropriate context
- Build kernel density estimation models
- Perform hotspot analysis and visualize the results

In this chapter, we will learn about kernel density estimation and learn how to perform hotspot analysis.

Introduction

Let's consider an imaginary scenario: a new disease has begun spreading through numerous communities in the country that you live in and the government is trying to figure out how to confront this health emergency. Critical to any plan to confront this health emergency is epidemiological knowledge, including where the patients are located and how the disease is moving. The ability to locate and quantify problem areas (which are classically referred to as hotspots) can help health professionals, policy makers, and emergency response teams craft the most effective and efficient strategies for combating the disease. This scenario highlights one of the many applications of hotspot modeling.

Hotspot modeling is an approach that is used to identify how a population is distributed across a geographical area; for example, how the population of individuals infected with the previously mentioned disease is spread across the country. The creation of this distribution relies on the availability of representative sample data. Note that the population can be anything definable in geographical terms, which includes, but is not limited to, crime, disease-infected individuals, people with certain demographic characteristics, or hurricanes:

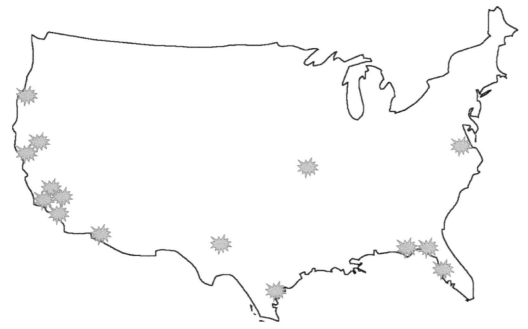

Figure 9.1: A fabricated example of fire location data showing some potential hotspots

Hotspot analysis is incredibly popular, and this is mainly because of how easy it is to visualize the results and to read and interpret the visualizations. Newspapers, websites, blogs, and TV shows all leverage hotspot analysis to support the arguments, chapters, and topics included in them or on them. While it might not be as well-known as the most popular machine learning models, the main hotspot analysis algorithm, known as **kernel density estimation**, is arguably one of the most widely used analytical techniques. Kernel density estimation is a hotspot analysis technique that is used to estimate the true population distribution of specific geographical events.

Spatial Statistics

Spatial statistics is a branch of statistics that focuses on the analysis of data that has spatial properties, including geographic or topological coordinates. It is similar to time series analysis in that the goal is to analyze data that changes across some dimension. In the case of time series analysis, the dimension across which the data changes is time, whereas in the spatial statistics case, the data changes across the spatial dimension. There are a number of techniques that are included under the spatial statistics umbrella, but the technique we are concerned with here is kernel density estimation.

As is the goal of most statistical analyses, in spatial statistics, we are trying to take samples of geographic data and use them to generate insights and make predictions. The analysis of earthquakes is one arena in which spatial statistical analyses are commonly deployed. By collecting earthquake location data, maps that identify areas of high and low earthquake likelihood can be generated, which can help scientists determine both where future earthquakes are likely to occur and what to expect in terms of intensity.

Probability Density Functions

Kernel density estimation uses the idea of the **probability density function** (**PDF**), which is one of the foundational concepts in statistics. The probability density function is a function that describes the behavior of a continuous **random variable**. That is, it expresses the likelihood, or probability, that the random variable takes on some range of values. Consider the heights of males in the United States as an example. By using the probability density function of the heights of males in the United States, we can determine the probability that some United States-based male is between 1.9 and 1.95 meters tall:

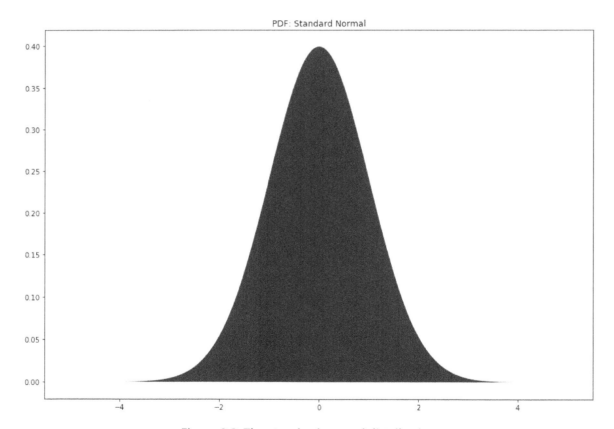

Figure 9.2: The standard normal distribution

Possibly the most popular density function in statistics is the standard normal distribution, which is simply the normal distribution centered at zero with the standard deviation equal to one.

Instead of the density function, what is typically available to statisticians or data scientists are randomly collected sample values coming from a population distribution that is unknown. This is where kernel density estimation comes in; it is a technique that is used for estimating the unknown probability density function of a random variable using sample data:

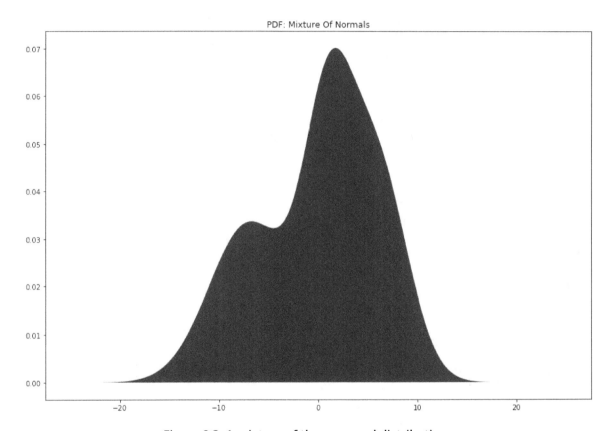

Figure 9.3: A mixture of three normal distributions

Using Hotspot Analysis in Business

We have already mentioned some of the ways in which hotspot modeling can be leveraged to meaningfully impact industry. The following use cases are common applications of hotspot modeling.

When reporting on infectious diseases, health organizations and media companies typically use hotspot analysis to communicate where the diseases are located and the likelihood of contracting the disease based on geographic location. Using hotspot analysis, this information could be reliably computed and disseminated. Hotspot analysis is great for dealing with health data because the visualizations are very straightforward. This means that the chances of data being misinterpreted either intentionally or unintentionally are relatively low.

Hotspot analysis can also be used to predict where certain events are likely to occur geographically. One research area that is leveraging the predictive capabilities of hotspot analysis more and more is the environmental sciences, which includes the study of natural disasters and extreme weather events. Earthquakes, for example, are notorious for being difficult to predict, because the time between significant earthquakes can be large, and the machinery needed to track and measure earthquakes to the degree required to make these predictions is relatively new.

In terms of public policy and resource deployment, hotspot analysis can be very impactful when dealing with the analysis of population demographics. Determining where resources, both monetary and personnel, should be deployed can be challenging; however, given that resources are often demographic-specific, hotspot analysis is a useful technique since it can be used to determine the distribution of certain demographic characteristics. By demographic characteristics we mean that we could find the geographic distribution of high school graduates, immigrants from a specific global region, or individuals making $100,000 or more annually.

Kernel Density Estimation

One of the main methodological approaches to hotspot analysis is kernel density estimation. Kernel density estimation builds an estimated density using sample data and two parameters known as the **kernel function** and the **bandwidth value**. The estimated density is, like any distribution, essentially a guideline for the behavior of a random variable. Here, we mean how frequently the random variable takes on any specific value, $x_1, \ldots, x_n$. When dealing with hotspot analysis where the data is typically geographic, the estimated density answers the question *How frequently do specific longitude and latitude pairs appear?*. If a specific longitude and latitude pair, $\{x_{longitude}, \ldots, x_{latitude}\}$, and other nearby pairs occur with high frequency, then the estimated density built using the sample data will be expected to show that the area around the longitude and latitude pair has a high likelihood.

Kernel density estimation is referred to as a smoothing algorithm, because the process of estimating a density is the process of estimating the underlying shape of the data by disregarding the eccentricities and anomalies in the sample data. Stated another way, kernel density estimation removes the noise from the data. The only assumption of the model is that the data truly belongs to some interpretable and meaningful density from which insights can be derived and acted upon. That is, there exists a true underlying distribution.

Arguably, more than any other topic in this book, kernel density estimation embodies the basic idea of statistics, which is to use sample data of finite size to make inferences about the population. We assume that the sample data contains clusters of data points and that these clusters imply regions of high likelihood in the true population. A benefit of creating a quality estimate of the true population density is that the estimated density can then be used to sample more data from the population.

Following this brief introduction, you probably have the following two questions:

- What is the bandwidth value?

- What is the kernel function?

We answer both of these questions next.

The Bandwidth Value

The most crucial parameter in kernel density estimation is called the **bandwidth value** and its impact on the quality of the estimate cannot be overestimated. A high-level definition of the bandwidth value is that it is a value that determines the degree of smoothing. If the bandwidth value is low, then the estimated density will feature limited smoothing, which means that the density will capture all the noise in the sample data. If the bandwidth value is high, then the estimated density will be very smooth. An overly smooth density will remove characteristics of the true density from the estimated density, which are legitimate and not simply noise.

In more statistical or machine learning languages, the bandwidth parameter controls the bias-variance trade-off. That is, high variance is the result of low bandwidth values because the density is sensitive to the variance of the sample data. Low bandwidth values limit any ability the model may have had to adapt to and work around gaps in the sample data that are not present in the population. Densities estimated using low bandwidth values tend to overfit the data (this is also known as under-smoothed densities). When high bandwidth values are used, then the resulting density is underfit and the estimated density has a high bias (this is also known as over-smoothed densities).

Exercise 46: The Effect of the Bandwidth Value

In this exercise, we will fit nine different models with nine different bandwidth values to sample data created in the exercise. The goal here is to solidify our understanding of the impact the bandwidth parameter can have and make clear that if an accurate estimated density is sought, then the bandwidth value needs to be selected with care. Note that finding an optimal bandwidth value will be the topic of the next section. All exercises will be done in a Jupyter notebook utilizing Python 3; ensure that all package installation is done using **pip**. The easiest way to install the **basemap** module from **mpl_toolkits** is by using *Anaconda*. Instructions for downloading and installing *Anaconda* can be found at the beginning of this book:

1. Load all of the libraries that are needed for the exercises in this chapter. Here, the **matplotlib** library is used to create basic graphics; the **basemap** library is used to create graphics involving location data; the **numpy** library is used for working with arrays and matrices; the **pandas** library is used for working with DataFrames; the **scipy** library is used for scientific computing in Python; the **seaborn** library is used for creating much more attractive and complicated graphics; and the **sklearn** library is used to access data, manipulate the data, and run models. Additionally, ensure that the graphics be run inline and set to **seaborn**, so that all graphics appear as **seaborn** graphics:

    ```
    get_ipython().run_line_magic('matplotlib', 'inline')

    import matplotlib.pyplot as plt
    import mpl_toolkits.basemap
    import numpy
    import pandas
    import scipy.stats
    import seaborn
    import sklearn.datasets
    import sklearn.model_selection
    import sklearn.neighbors

    seaborn.set()
    ```

2. Create some sample data (**vals**) by mixing three normal distributions. In addition to the sample data, define the true density curve (**true_density**) and the range over which the data will be plotted (**x_vec**):

    ```
    x_vec = numpy.linspace(-30, 30, 10000)[:, numpy.newaxis]

    vals = numpy.concatenate((
        numpy.random.normal(loc=1, scale=2.5, size=500),
    ```

```
        numpy.random.normal(loc=10, scale=4, size=500),
        numpy.random.normal(loc=-12, scale=5, size=500)
    ))[:, numpy.newaxis]

    true_density = (
        (1 / 3) * scipy.stats.norm(1, 2.5).pdf(x_vec[:, 0]) +
        (1 / 3) * scipy.stats.norm(10, 4).pdf(x_vec[:, 0]) +
        (1 / 3) * scipy.stats.norm(-12, 5).pdf(x_vec[:, 0])
    )
```

3. Define a list of tuples that will guide the creation of the multiplot graphic. Each tuple contains the row and column indices of the specific subplot, and the bandwidth value used to create the estimated density in that particular subplot:

```
position_bandwidth_vec = [
    (0, 0, 0.1), (0, 1, 0.4), (0, 2, 0.7),
    (1, 0, 1.0), (1, 1, 1.3), (1, 2, 1.6),
    (2, 0, 1.9), (2, 1, 2.5), (2, 2, 5.0)
]
```

4. Create nine plots each using a different bandwidth value. The first plot, with the index of (0, 0), will have the lowest bandwidth and the last plot, with the index of (2, 2), will have the highest bandwidth. These values are not the absolute lowest or absolute highest bandwidth values, rather they are only the minimum and maximum of the list defined in the previous step:

```
fig, ax = plt.subplots(3, 3, sharex=True, sharey=True, figsize=(12, 9))
fig.suptitle('The Effect of the Bandwidth Value', fontsize=16)

for r, c, b in position_bandwidth_vec:
    kde = sklearn.neighbors.KernelDensity(bandwidth=b).fit(vals)
    log_density = kde.score_samples(x_vec)

    ax[r, c].hist(vals, bins=50, density=True, alpha=0.5)
    ax[r, c].plot(x_vec[:, 0], numpy.exp(log_density), '-', linewidth=2)
    ax[r, c].set_title('Bandwidth = {}'.format(b))
```

The output is as follows:

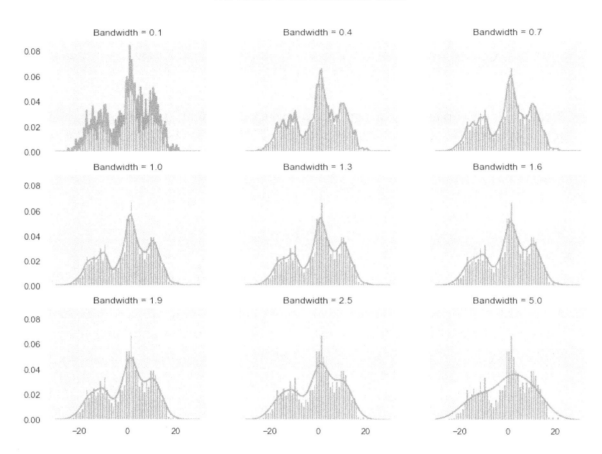

Figure 9.4: A 3 x 3 matrix of subplots; each of which features an estimated density created using one of nine bandwidth values

Notice that on the lower end, the density curves clearly overfit the data. As the bandwidth values increase, the estimated density becomes smoother until it noticeably underfits the data. Visually, it looks like the optimal bandwidth may be around 1.6.

The next step is to design an algorithm to identify the optimal bandwidth value, so that the estimated density is the most reasonable and, therefore, the most reliable and actionable.

Selecting the Optimal Bandwidth

As mentioned in the previous exercise, we can come quite close to selecting the optimal bandwidth by simply comparing several densities visually. However, this is neither the most efficient method of selecting parameter values nor the most reliable.

There are two standard approaches to optimizing the bandwidth value, and both of these will appear in future exercises and activities. The first approach is a plug-in method (or a formulaic approach) that is deterministic and not optimized on the sample data. Plug-in methods are generally much faster to implement, simpler to code, and easier to explain. However, these methods have one big downside, which is that their accuracy tends to suffer compared to approaches that are optimized on the sample data. These methods also have distributional assumptions. The most popular plug-in methods are Silverman's Rule and Scott's Rule. By default, the **seaborn** package (which will be used in future exercises) uses Scott's Rule as the method to determine the bandwidth value.

The second, and arguably the more robust, approach to finding an optimal bandwidth value is by searching a predefined grid of bandwidth values. Grid search is an empirical approach that is used frequently in machine learning and predictive modeling to optimize model hyperparameters. The process starts by defining the bandwidth grid, which is simply the collection of bandwidth values to be evaluated. Use each bandwidth value in the grid to create an estimated density; then, score the estimated density using the pseudo-log-likelihood value. The optimal bandwidth value is that which has the maximum pseudo-log-likelihood value. Think of the pseudo-log-likelihood value as the result of the probability of getting data points where we did get data points and the probability of not getting points where we did not get any data points. Ideally, both of these probabilities would be large. Consider the case where the probability of getting data points where we did get points is low. In this situation, the implication would be that the data points in the sample were anomalous because, under the true distribution, getting points where we did would not be expected with a high likelihood value.

Let's now implement the grid search approach to optimize the bandwidth value.

Exercise 47: Selecting the Optimal Bandwidth Using Grid Search

In this exercise, we will create an estimated density for the sample data created in *Exercise 46*, *The Effect of the Bandwidth Value* with an optimal bandwidth value identified using grid search and cross-validation. To run the grid search with cross-validation, we will leverage **sklearn**, which we have used throughout this book. This exercise is a continuation of Exercise 1 as we are using the same sample data and continuing our exploration of the bandwidth value:

1. Define a grid of bandwidth values and the grid search cross-validation model. Ideally, the leave-one-out approach to cross-validation should be used, but for the sake of having the model run in a reasonable amount of time, we will do a 10-fold cross-validation. Fit the model on the sample data, as follows:

```
bandwidths = 10 ** numpy.linspace(-1, 1, 100)

grid = sklearn.model_selection.GridSearchCV(
    estimator=sklearn.neighbors.KernelDensity(kernel="gaussian"),
    param_grid={"bandwidth": bandwidths},
    cv=10 #sklearn.model_selection.LeaveOneOut().get_n_splits(vals)
)
grid.fit(vals)
```

2. Extract the optimal bandwidth value from the model, as follows:

```
best_bandwidth = grid.best_params_["bandwidth"]

print(
    "Best Bandwidth Value: {}"
    .format(best_bandwidth)
)
```

The optimal bandwidth value should be approximately two. We can interpret the optimal bandwidth value as the bandwidth value producing the maximum pseudo-log-likelihood value. Note that depending on the values included in the grid, the optimal bandwidth value can change.

3. Plot the histogram of the sample data overlaid by both the true and estimated densities. In this case, the estimated density will be the optimal estimated density:

```
fig, ax = plt.subplots(figsize=(14, 10))

ax.hist(vals, bins=50, density=True, alpha=0.5, label='Sampled Values')
ax.fill(
        x_vec[:, 0], true_density,
        fc='black', alpha=0.3, label='True Distribution'
```

```
        )

    log_density = numpy.exp(grid.best_estimator_.score_samples(x_vec))
    ax.plot(
            x_vec[:, 0], log_density,
            '-', linewidth=2, label='Kernel = Gaussian'
            )

    ax.legend(loc='upper right')
```

The output is as follows:

Figure 9.5: A histogram of the random sample with the true density and the optimal estimated density overlaid

The estimated density is neither overfit or underfit to any noticeable degree and it definitely captures the three clusters. Arguably, it could map to the true density better, but this is just an estimated density generated by a model that has limitations.

Let's now move onto the second question: what is the kernel function and what role does it play?

Kernel Functions

The other parameter to be set is the kernel function. The kernel is a non-negative function that controls the shape of the density. Like topic models, we are working in a non-negative environment because it does not make sense to have negative likelihoods or probabilities.

The kernel function controls the shape of the estimated density by weighting the points in a systematic way. This systematic methodology for weighting is fairly simple; data points that are in close proximity to many other data points are up-weighted, whereas data points that are alone or far away from any other data points are down-weighted. Up-weighted data points will correspond to points of higher likelihood in the final estimated density.

Many functions can be used as kernels, but six frequent choices are Gaussian, Tophat, Epanechnikov, Exponential, Linear, and Cosine. Each of these functions represents a unique distributional shape. Note that in each of the formulas the parameter, h, represents the bandwidth value:

- Gaussian:

$$K(x;h) \propto exp - \left(\frac{x^2}{2h^2} \right)$$

Figure 9.6: The formula for the Gaussian kernel

- Tophat:

$$K(x;h) \propto \begin{cases} 0 \ if \ |x| \geq h \\ 1 \ if \ |x| < h \end{cases}$$

Figure 9.7: The formula for the Tophat kernel

- Epanechnikov:

$$K(x;h) \propto 1 - \frac{x^2}{h^2}$$

Figure 9.8: The formula for the Epanechnikov kernel

- Exponential:

$$K(x; h) \propto exp\left(-\frac{|x|}{h}\right)$$

Figure 9.9: The formula for the Exponential kernel

- Linear:

$$K(x; h) \propto \left\{1 - \frac{x}{h} \begin{array}{l} 0 \; if \; |x| \geq h \\ if \; |x| < h \end{array}\right\}$$

Figure 9.10: The formula for the Linear kernel

- Cosine:

$$K(x; h) \propto \left\{ \begin{array}{l} 0 \; if \; |x| \geq h \\ cos\frac{\pi x}{2h} \; if \; |x| < h \end{array}\right\}$$

Figure 9.11: The formula for the Cosine kernel

Here are the distributional shapes of the six kernel functions:

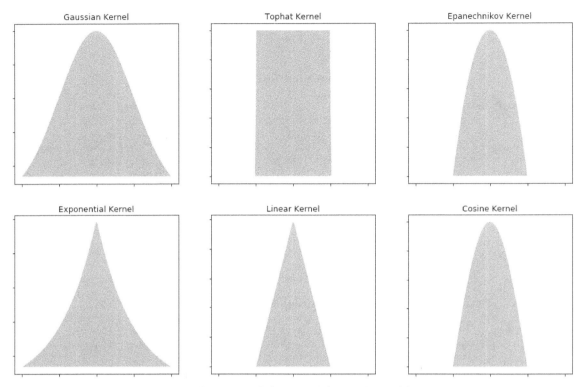

Figure 9.12: The general shapes of the six kernel functions

The choice of kernel function is not completely insignificant, but it is definitely not nearly as important as the choice of bandwidth value. A reasonable book of action would be to use the gaussian kernel for all density estimation problems, which is what we will do in the following exercises and activities.

Exercise 48: The Effect of the Kernel Function

The goal of this exercise is to understand how the choice of kernel function affects the quality of the density estimation. Like we did when exploring the bandwidth value effect, we will hold all other parameters constant, use the same data generated in the first two exercises, and run six different kernel density estimation models using the six kernel functions previously specified. Clear differences should be noticeable between the six estimated densities, but these differences should be slightly less dramatic than the differences between the densities estimated using the different bandwidth values:

1. Define a list of tuples along the same lines as the one defined previously. Each tuple includes the row and column indices of the subplot, and the kernel function to be used to create the density estimation:

    ```
    position_kernel_vec = [
        (0, 0, 'gaussian'), (0, 1, 'tophat'),
        (1, 0, 'epanechnikov'), (1, 1, 'exponential'),
        (2, 0, 'linear'), (2, 1, 'cosine'),
    ]
    ```

    Fit and plot six kernel density estimation models using a different kernel function for each. To truly understand the differences between the kernel functions, we will set the bandwidth value to the optimal bandwidth value found in Exercise 2 and not adjust it:

    ```
    fig, ax = plt.subplots(3, 2, sharex=True, sharey=True, figsize=(12, 9))
    fig.suptitle('The Effect of Different Kernels', fontsize=16)

    for r, c, k in position_kernel_vec:
        kde = sklearn.neighbors.KernelDensity(
            kernel=k, bandwidth=best_bandwidth
            ).fit(vals)
        log_density = kde.score_samples(x_vec)

        ax[r, c].hist(vals, bins=50, density=True, alpha=0.5)
        ax[r, c].plot(x_vec[:, 0], numpy.exp(log_density), '-', linewidth=2)
        ax[r, c].set_title('Kernel = {}'.format(k.capitalize()))
    ```

The output is as follows:

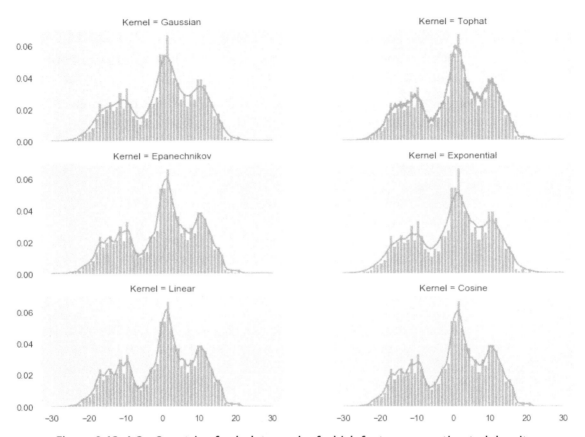

Figure 9.13: A 3 x 2 matrix of subplots, each of which features an estimated density created using one of six kernel functions

Out of the six kernel functions, the gaussian kernel produced the most reasonable estimated density. Beyond that, notice that the difference between the estimated densities with different kernels is less than the difference between the estimated densities with different bandwidth values. This goes to the previously made claim that the bandwidth value is the more important parameter and should be the focus during the model building process.

With our understanding mostly formed, let's discuss the derivation of kernel density estimation in a high-level fashion.

Kernel Density Estimation Derivation

Let's skip the formal mathematical derivation in favor of the popular derivation by intuition. Kernel density estimation turns each data point in the sample into its own distribution whose width is controlled by the bandwidth value. The individual distributions are then summed to create the desired density estimate. This concept is fairly easy to demonstrate; however, before doing that in the next exercise, let's try to think through it in an abstract way. For geographic regions containing many sample data points, the individual densities will overlap and, through the process of summing those densities, will create points of high likelihood in the estimated density. Similarly, for geographic regions containing few to no sample data points, the individual densities will not overlap and, therefore, will correspond to points of low likelihood in the estimated density.

Exercise 49: Simulating the Derivation of Kernel Density Estimation

The goal here is to demonstrate the concept of summing individual distributions to create an overall estimated density for a random variable. We will establish the concept incrementally by starting with one sample data point and then work up to many sample data points. Additionally, different bandwidth values will be applied, so our understanding of the effect of the bandwidth value on these individual densities will solidify further:

1. Define a function that will evaluate the normal distribution. The input values are the grid representing the range of the random variable, X, the sampled data point, m, and the bandwidth, b:

```
def eval_gaussian(x, m, b):
    numerator = numpy.exp(
        -numpy.power(x - m, 2) / (2 * numpy.power(b, 2))
    )
    denominator = b * numpy.sqrt(2 * numpy.pi)
    return numerator / denominator
```

2. Plot a single sample data point as a histogram and as an individual density with varying bandwidth values:

```
m = numpy.array([5.1])
b_vec = [0.1, 0.35, 0.8]

x_vec = numpy.linspace(1, 10, 100)[:, None]

fig, ax = plt.subplots(2, 3, sharex=True, sharey=True, figsize=(15, 10))

for i, b in enumerate(b_vec):
```

```
ax[0, i].hist(m[:], bins=1, fc='#AAAAFF', density=True)
ax[0, i].set_title("Histogram: Normed")

evaluation = eval_gaussian(x_vec, m=m[0], b=b)

ax[1, i].fill(x_vec, evaluation, '-k', fc='#AAAAFF')
ax[1, i].set_title("Gaussian Dist: b={}".format(b))
```

The output is as follows:

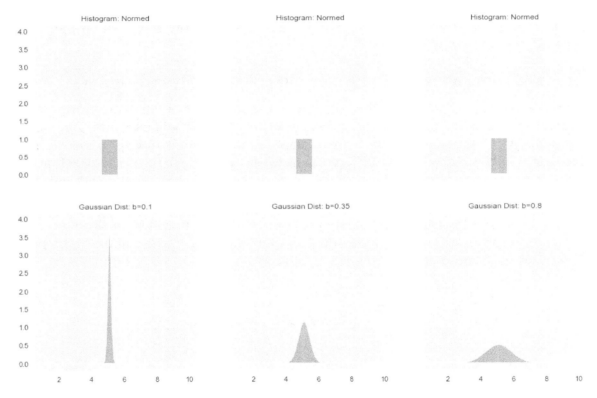

Figure 9.14: Showing one data point and its individual density at various bandwidth values

Here, we see what has already been established, which is that lower bandwidth values produce very narrow densities that tend to overfit the data.

3. Reproduce the work done in *Step 2*, but now scale up to 16 data points:

```python
m = numpy.random.normal(4.7, 0.88, 16)
n = len(m)

b_vec = [0.1, 0.35, 1.1]

x_vec = numpy.linspace(-1, 11, 100)[:, None]

fig, ax = plt.subplots(2, 3, sharex=True, sharey=True, figsize=(15, 10))

for i, b in enumerate(b_vec):
    ax[0, i].hist(m[:], bins=n, fc='#AAAAFF', density=True)
    ax[0, i].set_title("Histogram: Normed")

    sum_evaluation = numpy.zeros(len(x_vec))

    for j in range(n):
        evaluation = eval_gaussian(x_vec, m=m[j], b=b) / n
        sum_evaluation += evaluation[:, 0]

        ax[1, i].plot(x_vec, evaluation, '-k', linestyle="dashed")

    ax[1, i].fill(x_vec, sum_evaluation, '-k', fc='#AAAAFF')
    ax[1, i].set_title("Gaussian Dist: b={}".format(b))
```

The output is as follows:

Figure 9.15: Showing 16 data points, their individual densities at various bandwidth values, and the sum of their individual densities

Again, unsurprisingly, the plot utilizing the smallest bandwidth value features a wildly overfitted estimated density. That is, the estimated density captures all the noise in the sample data. Of these three densities, the second one, where the bandwidth value was set to 0.35, is the most reasonable.

Activity 21: Estimating Density in One Dimension

In this first activity, we will be generating some fake sample data and estimating the density function using kernel density estimation. The bandwidth value will be optimized using grid search cross-validation. The goal is to solidify our understanding of this useful methodology by running the model in a simple one-dimension case. We will once again leverage Jupyter notebooks to do our work.

Imagine that the sample data we will be creating describes the price of homes in a state in the United States. Momentarily ignore the values in the following sample data. The question is, *What does the distribution of home prices look like, and can we extract the probability of a house having a price that falls in some specific range?* These questions and more are answerable using kernel density estimation.

Here are the steps to complete the activity:

1. Open a new notebook and install all the necessary libraries.

2. Sample 1,000 data points from the standard normal distribution. Add 3.5 to each of the last 625 values of the sample (that is, the indices between 375 and 1,000). Set a random state of 100. To do this, set a random state of 100 using `numpy.random.RandomState` to guarantee the same sampled values, and then randomly generate the data points using the `randn(1000)` call.

3. Plot the 1,000-point sample data as a histogram and add a scatterplot below it.

4. Define a grid of bandwidth values. Then, define and fit a grid search cross-validation algorithm.

5. Extract the optimal bandwidth value.

6. Replot the histogram from *Step* 3 and overlay the estimated density.

The output will be as follows:

Figure 9.16: A histogram of the random sample with the optimal estimated density overlaid

> **Note**
>
> The solution for this activity can be found on page 374.

Hotspot Analysis

To start, hotspots are areas of higher concentrations of data points, such as particular neighborhoods where the crime rate is abnormally high or swaths of the country that are impacted by an above-average number of tornadoes. Hotspot analysis is the process of finding these hotspots, should any exist, in a population using sampled data. This process is generally done by leveraging kernel density estimation.

Hotspot analysis can be described in four high-level steps:

1. **Collect the data**: The data should include the locations of the objects or events. As we have briefly mentioned, the amount of data needed to run and achieve actionable results is relatively flexible. The optimal state is to have a sample dataset that is representative of the population.

2. **Identify the base map**: The next step is to identify which base map would best suit the analytical and presentational needs of the project. On this base map, the results of the model will be overlaid, so that the locations of the hotspots can be easily articulated in much more digestible terms, such as city, neighborhood, or region.

3. **Execute the model**: In this step, you select and execute one or multiple methodologies of extracting spatial patterns to identify hotspots. For us, this method will be – no surprise – kernel density estimation.

4. **Create the visualization**: The hotspot maps are generated by overlaying the model results on the base map to support whatever business questions are outstanding.

One of the principal issues with hotspot analysis from a usability standpoint is that the statistical significance of a hotspot is not particularly easy to ascertain. Most questions about statistical significance revolve around the existence of the hotspots. That is, do the fluctuations in likelihood of occurrence actually amount to statistically significant fluctuations? It is important to note that statistical significance is not required to perform kernel density estimation and that we will not be dealing with significance at all going forward.

While the term hotspot is traditionally reserved to describe a cluster of location data points, it is not limited to location data. Any data type can have hotspots regardless of whether or not they are referred to as hotspots. In one of the following exercises, we will model some non-location data to find hotspots, which will be regions of feature space having a high or low likelihood of occurrence.

Exercise 50: Loading Data and Modeling with Seaborn

In this exercise, we will work with the **seaborn** library to fit and visualize kernel density estimation models. This is done on both location and non-location data. Before getting into the modeling, we load the data, which is the California housing dataset that is automatically loaded with **sklearn**. Taken from the United States census in 1990, this dataset describes the housing situation in California during that time. One row of data describes one census block group. The definition of a census block group is irrelevant to this exercise, so we will bypass the definition here in favor of more hands-on coding and modeling. It is important to mention that all the variables are aggregated to the census block. For example, **MedInc** is the median income of households in each census block. Additional information on this dataset is available at https://scikit-learn.org/stable/datasets/index.html#california-housing-dataset:

1. Load the California housing dataset using **fetch_california_housing()**. Convert the data to a DataFrame using **pandas** and print the first five rows of the DataFrame:

   ```
   housing = sklearn.datasets.fetch_california_housing()

   df = pandas.DataFrame(housing['data'], columns=housing['feature_names'])
   print("Dataframe Dimensions: {dims}".format(dims=df.shape))

   df.head()
   ```

   The output is as follows:

	MedInc	HouseAge	AveRooms	AveBedrms	Population	AveOccup	Latitude	Longitude
0	8.3252	41.0	6.984127	1.023810	322.0	2.555556	37.88	-122.23
1	8.3014	21.0	6.238137	0.971880	2401.0	2.109842	37.86	-122.22
2	7.2574	52.0	8.288136	1.073446	496.0	2.802260	37.85	-122.24
3	5.6431	52.0	5.817352	1.073059	558.0	2.547945	37.85	-122.25
4	3.8462	52.0	6.281853	1.081081	565.0	2.181467	37.85	-122.25

Figure 9.17: The first five rows of the California housing dataset from sklearn

2. Filter the DataFrame based on the **HouseAge** feature, which is the median home age of each census block. Keep only the rows with **HouseAge** less than or equal to 15 and name the DataFrame **dfLess15**. Print out the first five rows of the DataFrame; Then, reduce the DataFrame down to just the longitude and latitude features:

```
dfLess15 = df[df['HouseAge'] <= 15.0]
dfLess15 = dfLess15[['Latitude', 'Longitude']]
print(
    "Less Than Or Equal To 15 Years Dataframe Dimensions: {dims}"
    .format(dims=dfLess15.shape)
)

dfLess15.head()
```

The output is as follows:

	Latitude	Longitude
59	37.82	-122.29
87	37.81	-122.27
88	37.80	-122.27
391	37.90	-122.30
437	37.87	-122.30

Figure 9.18: The first five rows of the dataset filtered down to those rows that have a value of 15 or less in the HouseAge column

3. Use **seaborn** to fit and visualize the kernel density estimation model built on the longitude and latitude data points. The **seaborn** approach to fitting these models uses Scott's Rule. There are four inputs to the model, which are the names of the two columns over which the estimated density is sought (that is, the longitude and latitude), the DataFrame to which those columns belong, and the method of density estimation (that is, the **kde** or kernel density estimation):

```
seaborn.jointplot("Longitude", "Latitude", dfLess15, kind="kde")
```

The output is as follows:

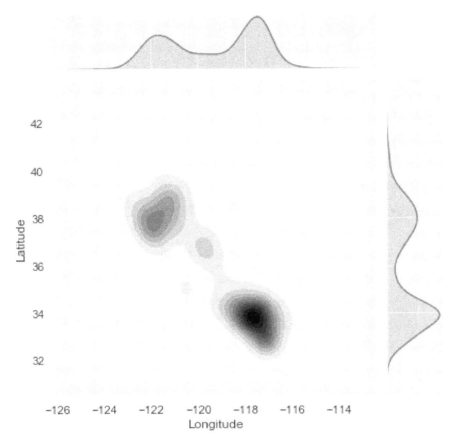

Figure 9.19: A joint plot containing both the two-dimensional estimated density plus the marginal densities for the dfLess15 dataset

If we overlay these results on a map of California, we will see that the hotspots are southern California, including Los Angeles and San Diego, the bay area, including San Francisco, and to a small degree the area known as the central valley. A benefit of this **seaborn** graphic is that we get the two-dimensional estimated density and the marginal densities for both longitude and latitude.

4. Create another filtered DataFrame based on the **HouseAge** feature; this time keep only the rows with **HouseAge** greater than 40 and name the DataFrame **dfMore40**. Additionally, remove all the columns except for longitude and latitude. Then, print the first five rows of the DataFrame:

```
dfMore40 = df[df['HouseAge'] > 40.0]
dfMore40 = dfMore40[['Latitude', 'Longitude']]
print(
    "More Than 40 Years Dataframe Dimensions: {dims}"
    .format(dims=dfMore40.shape)
)

dfMore40.head()
```

The output is as follows:

	Latitude	Longitude
0	37.88	-122.23
2	37.85	-122.24
3	37.85	-122.25
4	37.85	-122.25
5	37.85	-122.25

Figure 9.20: The top of the dataset filtered to the rows containing values greater than 40 in the HouseAge column

5. Repeat the process from *Step 3*, but now using this new filtered DataFrame:

```
seaborn.jointplot("Longitude", "Latitude", dfMore40, kind="kde")
```

The output is as follows:

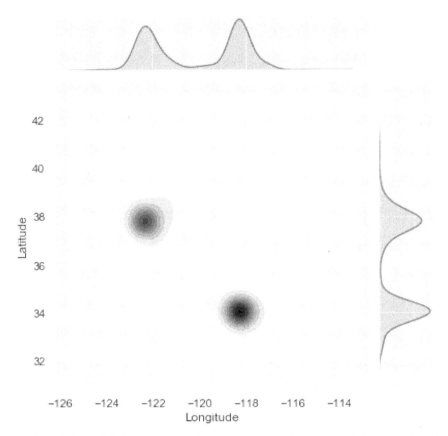

Figure 9.21: A joint plot containing both the two-dimensional estimated density plus the marginal densities for the dfMore40 dataset

This estimated density is much more compact in that the data is clustered almost entirely in two areas. Those areas are Los Angeles and the bay area. Comparing this to the plot in *Step* 3, we notice that housing development has spread out across the state. Additionally, newer housing developments occur with much higher frequencies in a larger number of census blocks.

6. Let's again create another filtered DataFrame. This time only keeping rows where **HouseAge** is less than or equal to five and name the DataFrame **dfLess5**. Plot **Population** and **MedInc** as a scatterplot, as follows:

```
dfLess5 = df[df['HouseAge'] <= 5]

x_vals = dfLess5.Population.values
```

```
y_vals = dfLess5.MedInc.values

fig = plt.figure(figsize=(10, 10))
plt.scatter(x_vals, y_vals, c='black')
plt.xlabel('Population', fontsize=18)
plt.ylabel('Median Income', fontsize=16)
```

The output is as follows:

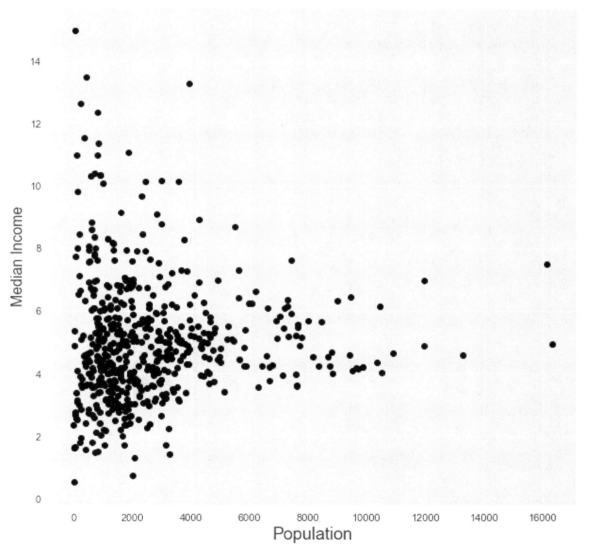

Figure 9.22: A scatterplot of the median income against population for values
of five or less in the HouseAge column

7. Use yet another **seaborn** function to fit a kernel density estimation model. Again, the optimal bandwidth is found using Scott's Rule. Replot the histogram and overlay the estimated density, as follows:

```python
fig = plt.figure(figsize=(10, 10))
ax = seaborn.kdeplot(
    x_vals,
    y_vals,
    kernel='gau',
    cmap='Blues',
    shade=True,
    shade_lowest=False
)
plt.scatter(x_vals, y_vals, c='black', alpha=0.05)
plt.xlabel('Population', fontsize=18)
plt.ylabel('Median Income', fontsize=18)
plt.title('Density Estimation With Scatterplot Overlay', size=18)
```

The output is as follows:

Figure 9.23: The same scatterplot as created in Step 6 with the estimated density overlaid

Here, the estimated density shows that census blocks with smaller populations have lower median incomes at higher likelihoods than they have high median incomes. The point of this step is to showcase how kernel density estimation can be used on non-location data.

When presenting the results of hotspot analysis, some type of map should be involved since hotspot analysis is generally done on location data. Acquiring maps on which estimated densities can be overlaid is not an easy process. Due to copyright issues, we will use very basic maps, called basemaps, on which we can overlay our estimated densities. It will be left to you to extend the knowledge you acquire in this chapter to fancier and more detailed maps. Mapping environments can also be complicated and time-consuming to download and install.

Exercise 51: Working with Basemaps

This exercise leverages the **basemap** module of **mpl_toolkits**. **basemap** is a mapping library, which can be used to create basic maps or outlines of geographic regions. These maps can have the results of kernel density estimation overlaid, so that we can clearly see where the hotspots are located.

First, check whether **basemap** is installed by running **import mpl_toolkits.basemap** in a Jupyter notebook. If it loads without error, then you are ready and need to take no further action. If the call fails, then install **basemap** using **pip** by running **python3 -m pip install basemap**. You should be good to go after restarting any already-open notebooks. Note that the **pip** installation will only work if Anaconda is installed.

The goal of this exercise is to remodel and replot the location data from *Exercise 50, Loading Data and Modeling with Seaborn*, using the kernel density estimation functions of **sklearn** and the mapping capabilities of **basemap**. Extract the longitude and latitude values from the filtered DataFrame called **dfLess15**, as follows:

1. Form the grid of locations over which the estimated density will be laid. The grid of locations is the two-dimensional location equivalent of the one-dimensional vector defining the range of the random variable in Exercise 1:

```
xgrid15 = numpy.sort(list(dfLess15['Longitude']))
ygrid15 = numpy.sort(list(dfLess15['Latitude']))
x15, y15 = numpy.meshgrid(xgrid15, ygrid15)
print("X Grid Component:\n{}\n".format(x15))
print("Y Grid Component:\n{}\n".format(y15))

xy15 = numpy.vstack([y15.ravel(), x15.ravel()]).T
print("Grid:\n{}\n".format(xy15))
```

The output is as follows:

```
X Grid Component:
[[-124.23 -124.19 -124.17 ... -114.63 -114.57 -114.31]
 [-124.23 -124.19 -124.17 ... -114.63 -114.57 -114.31]
 [-124.23 -124.19 -124.17 ... -114.63 -114.57 -114.31]
 ...
 [-124.23 -124.19 -124.17 ... -114.63 -114.57 -114.31]
 [-124.23 -124.19 -124.17 ... -114.63 -114.57 -114.31]
 [-124.23 -124.19 -124.17 ... -114.63 -114.57 -114.31]]

Y Grid Component:
[[32.54 32.54 32.54 ... 32.54 32.54 32.54]
 [32.55 32.55 32.55 ... 32.55 32.55 32.55]
 [32.55 32.55 32.55 ... 32.55 32.55 32.55]
 ...
 [41.74 41.74 41.74 ... 41.74 41.74 41.74]
 [41.75 41.75 41.75 ... 41.75 41.75 41.75]
 [41.78 41.78 41.78 ... 41.78 41.78 41.78]]
```

Figure 9.24: The x and y components of the grid representing the dfLess15 dataset

2. Define and fit a kernel density estimation model. Set the bandwidth value to 0.05 in order to save runtime; then, create likelihood values for each point on the location grid:

```
kde = sklearn.neighbors.KernelDensity(
    bandwidth=0.05,
    metric='minkowski',
    kernel='gaussian',
    algorithm='ball_tree'
)
kde.fit(dfLess15.values)

log_density = kde.score_samples(xy15)
density = numpy.exp(log_density)
density = density.reshape(x15.shape)
print("Shape of Density Values:\n{}\n".format(density.shape))
```

Notice that if you print out the shape of the likelihood values, it is 3,287 rows by 3,287 columns, which is 10,804,369 likelihood values. This is the same number of values in the preestablished longitude and latitude grid, called **xy15**.

3. Create an outline of California and overlay the estimated density computed in *Step 2*:

```
fig = plt.figure(figsize=(10, 10))
fig.suptitle(
    """
    Density Estimation:
    Location of Housing Blocks
    Where the Median Home Age <= 15 Years
    """,
    fontsize=16
)

the_map = mpl_toolkits.basemap.Basemap(
    projection='cyl',
    llcrnrlat=y15.min(), urcrnrlat=y15.max(),
    llcrnrlon=x15.min(),urcrnrlon=x15.max(),
    resolution='c'
)

the_map.drawcoastlines(linewidth=1)
the_map.drawcountries(linewidth=1)
the_map.drawstates(linewidth=1)

levels = numpy.linspace(0, density.max(), 25)
plt.contourf(x15, y15, density, levels=levels, cmap=plt.cm.Reds)

plt.show()
```

The output is as follows:

Figure 9.25: The estimated density of dfLess15 overlaid onto an outline of California

The 0.05 value was set to purposefully overfit the data slightly. You'll notice that instead of the larger clusters that make up the density in *Exercise 50, Loading Data and Modeling with Seaborn* the estimated density here is made up of much smaller clusters. This slightly overfit density might be a bit more helpful than the previous version of the density because it gives you a clearer view of where the high likelihood census blocks are truly located. One of the high-likelihood areas in the previous density was southern California, but southern California is a huge area with an enormous population and many municipalities. Bear in mind that when using the results for business decisions, certain levels of specificity might be required and should be provided if the sample data can support results with that level of specificity or granularity.

4. Repeat *Step 1*, but with the **dfMore40** DataFrame:

```
xgrid40 = numpy.sort(list(dfMore40['Longitude']))
ygrid40 = numpy.sort(list(dfMore40['Latitude']))
x40, y40 = numpy.meshgrid(xgrid40, ygrid40)
print("X Grid Component:\n{}\n".format(x40))
print("Y Grid Component:\n{}\n".format(y40))

xy40 = numpy.vstack([y40.ravel(), x40.ravel()]).T
print("Grid:\n{}\n".format(xy40))
```

The output is as follows:

```
X Grid Component:
[[-124.35 -124.26 -124.23 ... -114.61 -114.6  -114.59]
 [-124.35 -124.26 -124.23 ... -114.61 -114.6  -114.59]
 [-124.35 -124.26 -124.23 ... -114.61 -114.6  -114.59]
 ...
 [-124.35 -124.26 -124.23 ... -114.61 -114.6  -114.59]
 [-124.35 -124.26 -124.23 ... -114.61 -114.6  -114.59]
 [-124.35 -124.26 -124.23 ... -114.61 -114.6  -114.59]]

Y Grid Component:
[[32.64 32.64 32.64 ... 32.64 32.64 32.64]
 [32.66 32.66 32.66 ... 32.66 32.66 32.66]
 [32.66 32.66 32.66 ... 32.66 32.66 32.66]
 ...
 [41.43 41.43 41.43 ... 41.43 41.43 41.43]
 [41.73 41.73 41.73 ... 41.73 41.73 41.73]
 [41.78 41.78 41.78 ... 41.78 41.78 41.78]]
```

Figure 9.26: The x and y components of the grid representing the dfMore40 dataset

5. Repeat *Step 2* using the grid established in *Step 4*:

```
kde = sklearn.neighbors.KernelDensity(
    bandwidth=0.05,
    metric='minkowski',
    kernel='gaussian',
    algorithm='ball_tree'
)
kde.fit(dfMore40.values)

log_density = kde.score_samples(xy40)
density = numpy.exp(log_density)
density = density.reshape(x40.shape)
print("Shape of Density Values:\n{}\n".format(density.shape))
```

6. Repeat *Step* 3 using the estimated density computed in *Step* 5:

```python
fig = plt.figure(figsize=(10, 10))
fig.suptitle(
    """
    Density Estimation:
    Location of Housing Blocks
    Where the Median Home Age > 40 Years
    """,
    fontsize=16
)

the_map = mpl_toolkits.basemap.Basemap(
    projection='cyl',
    llcrnrlat=y40.min(), urcrnrlat=y40.max(),
    llcrnrlon=x40.min(),urcrnrlon=x40.max(),
    resolution='c'
)

the_map.drawcoastlines(linewidth=1)
the_map.drawcountries(linewidth=1)
the_map.drawstates(linewidth=1)

levels = numpy.linspace(0, density.max(), 25)
plt.contourf(x40, y40, density, levels=levels, cmap=plt.cm.Reds)

plt.show()
```

The output is as follows:

Density Estimation:
Location of Housing Blocks
Where the Median Home Age > 40 Years

Figure 9.27: The estimated density of dfMore40 overlaid onto an outline of California

This estimated density is again a redo of the one that we did in *Exercise 50, Loading Data and Modeling with Seaborn*. While the density from *Step 3* will provide more detail for a person interested in real estate or the census, this density does not actually look that different from its corollary density in *Exercise 50, Loading Data and Modeling with Seaborn*. The clusters are primarily around Los Angeles and San Francisco with almost no points anywhere else.

Activity 22: Analyzing Crime in London

In this activity, we will perform hotspot analysis with kernel density estimation on London crime data from https://data.police.uk/data/. Due to the difficulties of working with map data, we will visualize the results of the analysis using **seaborn**. However, if you feel brave and were able to run all the plots in *Exercise 51, Working with Basemaps* you are encouraged to try using maps.

The motivation for performing hotspot analysis on this crime data is two-fold. We are asked first to determine where certain types of crimes are occurring in high likelihood, so that police resources can be allocated for maximum impact. Then, as a follow up, we are asked to ascertain whether the hotspots for certain types of crime are changing over time. Both of these questions are answerable using kernel density estimation.

> **Note**
>
> This dataset is downloaded from https://data.police.uk/data/.
>
> You can download it from the Packt GitHub at https://github.com/TrainingByPackt/Applied-Unsupervised-Learning-with-Python/tree/master/Lesson09/Activity21-Activity22.
>
> Alternatively, to download the data directly from the source, go to the preceding police website, check the box for **Metropolitan Police Service**, and then set the date range to **July 2018** to **Dec 2018**. Next, click **Generate file** followed by **Download now** and name the downloaded file **metro-jul18-dec18**. Make sure that you know how or can retrieve the path to the downloaded directory.
>
> This dataset contains public sector information licensed under the Open Government License v3.0.

Here are the steps to complete the activity:

1. Load the crime data. Use the path where you saved the downloaded directory, create a list of the year-month tags, use the **read_csv** command to load the individual files iteratively, and then concatenate these files together.

2. Print diagnostics of the complete (six months) and concatenated dataset.

3. Subset the DataFrame down to four variables (**Longitude**, **Latitude**, **Month**, and **Crime type**).

4. Using the **jointplot** function from **seaborn**, fit and visualize three kernel density estimation models for bicycle theft in July, September, and December 2018.

5. Repeat *Step 4*; this time, use shoplifting crimes for the months of August, October, and November 2018.

6. Repeat *Step 5*; this time, use burglary crimes for the months of July, October, and December 2018.

   The output from the last part of *Step 6* will be as follows:

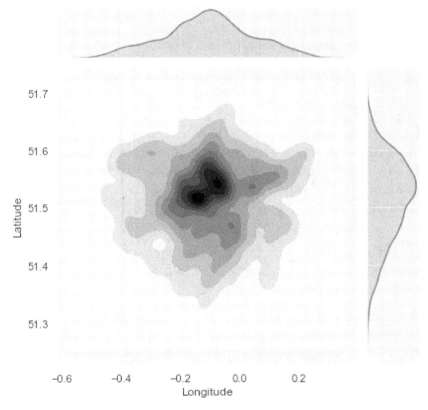

Figure 9.28: The estimated joint and marginal densities for burglaries in December 2018

To clarify one more time, the densities found in this activity should have been overlaid on maps so that we could see exactly what areas these densities cover. Attempting to overlay the results on maps on your own would be encouraged if you have the appropriate mapping platforms at your disposal. If not, you could go to the mapping services available online and use the longitude and latitude pairs to gain insight into the specific locations.

> **Note**
>
> The solution for this activity can be found on page 377.

Summary

Kernel density estimation is a classic statistical technique that is in the same family of techniques as the histogram. It allows the user to extrapolate out from sample data to make insights and predictions about the population of particular objects or events. This extrapolation comes in the form of a probability density function, which is nice because the results read as likelihoods or probabilities. The quality of this model is dependent on two parameters: the bandwidth value and the kernel function. As discussed, the most crucial component of leveraging kernel density estimation successfully is the setting of an optimal bandwidth. Optimal bandwidths are most frequently identified using grid search cross-validation with pseudo-log-likelihood as the scoring metric. What makes kernel density estimation great is both its simplicity and its applicability to so many fields.

It is routine to find kernel density estimation models in criminology, epidemiology, meteorology, and real estate to only name a few. Regardless of your area of business, kernel density estimation should be applicable.

In this book, we explored the best practices for using unsupervised learning techniques in tandem with Python libraries and extracting meaningful information from unstructured data. Now you can confidently build your own models using Python.

Appendix

Chapter 1: Introduction to Clustering

Activity 1: Implementing k-means Clustering

Solution:

1. Load the Iris data file using pandas, a package that makes data wrangling much easier through the use of DataFrames:

```
import pandas as pd
import numpy as np
import matplotlib.pyplot as plt
from sklearn.metrics import silhouette_score
from scipy.spatial.distance import cdist

iris = pd.read_csv('iris_data.csv', header=None)
iris.columns = ['SepalLengthCm', 'SepalWidthCm', 'PetalLengthCm',
'PetalWidthCm', 'species']
```

2. Separate out the **X** features and the provided **y** species labels, since we want to treat this as an unsupervised learning problem:

```
X = iris[['SepalLengthCm', 'SepalWidthCm', 'PetalLengthCm',
'PetalWidthCm']]
y = iris['species']
```

3. Get an idea of what our features look like:

```
X.head()
```

The output is as follows:

	SepalLengthCm	SepalWidthCm	PetalLengthCm	PetalWidthCm
0	5.1	3.5	1.4	0.2
1	4.9	3.0	1.4	0.2
2	4.7	3.2	1.3	0.2
3	4.6	3.1	1.5	0.2
4	5.0	3.6	1.4	0.2

Figure 1.22: First five rows of the data

4. Bring back the **k_means** function we made earlier for reference:

```
def k_means(X, K):
#Keep track of history so you can see k-means in action
    centroids_history = []
    labels_history = []
    rand_index = np.random.choice(X.shape[0], K)
    centroids = X[rand_index]
    centroids_history.append(centroids)
    while True:
# Euclidean distances are calculated for each point relative to centroids,
#and then np.argmin returns
# the index location of the minimal distance - which cluster a point     is
#assigned to
        labels = np.argmin(cdist(X, centroids), axis=1)
        labels_history.append(labels)
#Take mean of points within clusters to find new centroids:
        new_centroids = np.array([X[labels == i].mean(axis=0)
                            for i in range(K)])
        centroids_history.append(new_centroids)

        # If old centroids and new centroids no longer change, k-means is
complete and end. Otherwise continue
        if np.all(centroids == new_centroids):
            break
        centroids = new_centroids

    return centroids, labels, centroids_history, labels_history
```

5. Convert our Iris **X** feature DataFrame to a **NumPy** matrix:

```
X_mat = X.values
```

6. Run our **k_means** function on the Iris matrix:

```
centroids, labels, centroids_history, labels_history = k_means(X_mat, 3)
```

7. See what labels we get by looking at just the list of predicted species per sample:

    ```
    print(labels)
    ```

    The output is as follows:

    ```
    [2 2 2 2 2 2 2 2 2 2 2 2 2 2 2 2 2 2 2 2 2 2 2 2 2 2 2 2 2 2 2 2 2 2 2
     2 2 2 2 2 2 2 2 2 2 2 2 1 1 0 1 1 1 1 1 1 1 1 1 1 1 1 1 1 1 1 1 1 1 1
     1 1 1 0 1 1 1 1 1 1 1 1 1 1 1 1 1 1 1 1 1 1 1 1 1 1 1 0 1 0 0 0 0 1 0 0 0 0
     0 0 1 1 0 0 0 0 1 0 1 0 1 0 0 1 1 0 0 0 0 0 1 0 0 0 0 1 0 0 0 1 0 0 0 1 0
     0 1]
    ```

    Figure 1.23: List of predicted species

8. Visualize how our k-means implementation performed on the dataset:

    ```
    plt.scatter(X['SepalLengthCm'], X['SepalWidthCm'])
    plt.title('Iris - Sepal Length vs Width')
    plt.show()
    ```

    The output is as follows:

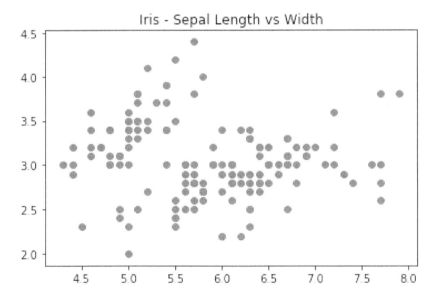

Figure 1.24: Plot of performed k-means implementation

Visualize the clusters of Iris species as follows:

```
plt.scatter(X['SepalLengthCm'], X['SepalWidthCm'], c=labels,
cmap='tab20b')
plt.title('Iris - Sepal Length vs Width - Clustered')
plt.show()
```

The output is as follows:

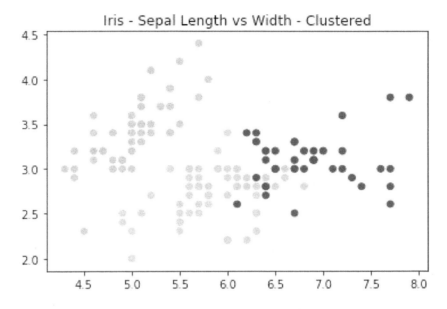

Figure 1.25: Clusters of Iris species

9. Calculate the Silhouette Score using scikit-learn implementation:

```
# Calculate Silhouette Score

silhouette_score(X[['SepalLengthCm','SepalWidthCm']], labels)
```

You will get an SSI roughly equal to 0.369. Since we are only using two features, this is acceptable, combined with the visualization of cluster memberships seen in the final plot.

Chapter 2: Hierarchical Clustering

Activity 2: Applying Linkage Criteria

Solution:

1. Visualize the **x** dataset that we created in *Exercise 7, Building a Hierarchy*:

```
from scipy.cluster.hierarchy import linkage, dendrogram, fcluster
from sklearn.datasets import make_blobs
import matplotlib.pyplot as plt
%matplotlib inline
# Generate a random cluster dataset to experiment on. X = coordinate
points, y = cluster labels (not needed)
X, y = make_blobs(n_samples=1000, centers=8, n_features=2, random_
state=800)
# Visualize the data
plt.scatter(X[:,0], X[:,1])
plt.show()
```

The output is as follows:

```
# Generate a random cluster dataset to experiment on. X = coordinate points, y = cluster labels
X, y = make_blobs(n_samples=1000, centers=8, n_features=2, random_state=800)
```

```
# Visualize the data
plt.scatter(X[:,0], X[:,1])
plt.show()
```

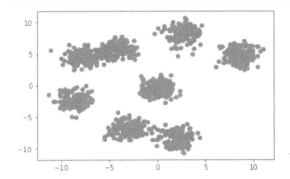

Figure 2.20: A scatter plot of the generated cluster dataset

2. Create a list with all the possible linkage method hyperparameters:

    ```
    methods = ['centroid', 'single', 'complete', 'average', 'weighted']
    ```

3. Loop through each of the methods in the list that you just created and display the effect that they have on the same dataset:

    ```
    for method in methods:
        distances = linkage(X, method=method, metric="euclidean")
        clusters = fcluster(distances, 3, criterion="distance")
        plt.title('linkage: ' + method)
        plt.scatter(X[:,0], X[:,1], c=clusters, cmap='tab20b')
        plt.show()
    ```

The output is as follows:

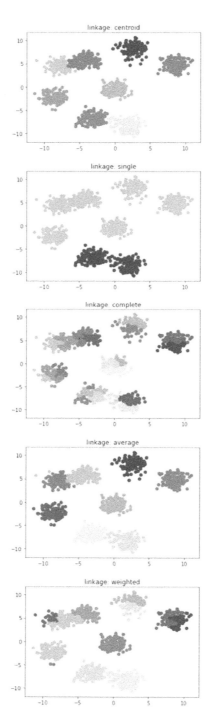

Figure 2.21: A scatter plot for all the methods

Analysis:

As you can see from the preceding plots, by simply changing the linkage criteria, you can dramatically change the efficacy of your clustering. In this dataset, centroid and average linkage work best at finding discrete clusters that make sense. This is clear from the fact that we generated a dataset of eight clusters, and centroid and average linkage are the only ones that show the clusters that are represented using eight different colors. The other linkage types fall short – most noticeably, single linkage.

Activity 3: Comparing k-means with Hierarchical Clustering

Solution:

1. Import the necessary packages from scikit-learn (**KMeans**, **AgglomerativeClustering**, and **silhouette_score**), as follows:

```
from sklearn.cluster import KMeans
from sklearn.cluster import AgglomerativeClustering
from sklearn.metrics import silhouette_score
import pandas as pd
import matplotlib.pyplot as plt
```

2. Read the wine dataset into the pandas DataFrame and print a small sample:

```
wine_df = pd.read_csv("wine_data.csv")
print(wine_df.head)
```

The output is as follows:

```
<bound method NDFrame.head of      OD_read   Proline
0            3.92   1065.0
1            3.40   1050.0
2            3.17   1185.0
3            3.45   1480.0
4            2.93    735.0
5            2.85   1450.0
```

Figure 2.22: The output of the wine dataset

3. Visualize the wine dataset to understand the data structure:

```
plt.scatter(wine_df.values[:,0], wine_df.values[:,1])
plt.title("Wine Dataset")
plt.xlabel("OD Reading")
plt.ylabel("Proline")
plt.show()
```

The output is as follows:

Figure 2.23: A plot of raw wine data

4. Use the sklearn implementation of k-means on the wine dataset, knowing that there are three wine types:

```
km = KMeans(3)
km_clusters = km.fit_predict(wine_df)
```

5. Use the sklearn implementation of hierarchical clustering on the wine dataset:

```
ac = AgglomerativeClustering(3, linkage='average')
ac_clusters = ac.fit_predict(wine_df)
```

6. Plot the predicted clusters from k-means, as follows:

```
plt.scatter(wine_df.values[:,0], wine_df.values[:,1], c=km_clusters)
plt.title("Wine Clusters from Agglomerative Clustering")
plt.xlabel("OD Reading")
plt.ylabel("Proline")
plt.show()
```

The output is as follows:

Figure 2.24: A plot of clusters from k-means clustering

7. Plot the predicted clusters from hierarchical clustering, as follows:

```
plt.scatter(wine_df.values[:,0], wine_df.values[:,1], c=ac_clusters)
plt.title("Wine Clusters from Agglomerative Clustering")
plt.xlabel("OD Reading")
plt.ylabel("Proline")
plt.show()
```

The output is as follows:

Figure 2.25: A plot of clusters from agglomerative clustering

8. Compare the silhouette score of each clustering method:

```
print("Silhouette Scores for Wine Dataset:\n")
print("k-means Clustering: ", silhouette_score(X[:,11:13], km_clusters))
print("Agg Clustering: ", silhouette_score(X[:,11:13], ac_clusters))
```

The output will be as follows:

```
Silhouette Scores for Wine Dataset:

K-Means Clustering:   0.5809421087616886
Agg Clustering:   0.5988495817462
```

Figure 2.26: Silhouette scores for the wine dataset

As you can see from the preceding silhouette metric, agglomerative clustering narrowly beats k-means clustering when it comes to separating the clusters by mean intra-cluster distance. This is not the case for every version of agglomerative clustering, however. Instead, try different linkage types and examine how the silhouette score and clustering changes between each!

Chapter 3: Neighborhood Approaches and DBSCAN

Activity 4: Implement DBSCAN from Scratch

Solution:

1. Generate a random cluster dataset as follows:

    ```
    from sklearn.cluster import DBSCAN
    from sklearn.datasets import make_blobs
    import matplotlib.pyplot as plt
    import numpy as np
    %matplotlib inline

    X_blob, y_blob = make_blobs(n_samples=500, centers=4, n_features=2,
    random_state=800)
    ```

2. Visualize the generated data:

    ```
    plt.scatter(X_blob[:,0], X_blob[:,1])
    plt.show()
    ```

    The output is as follows:

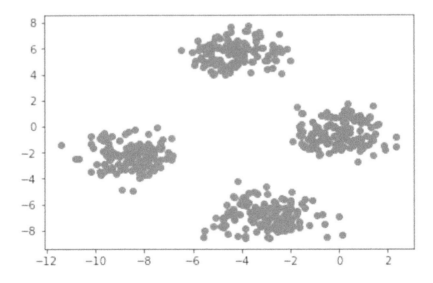

Figure 3.14: Plot of generated data

3. Create functions from scratch that allow you to call DBSCAN on a dataset:

```python
def scratch_DBSCAN(x, eps, min_pts):
    """
    param x (list of vectors): your dataset to be clustered
    param eps (float): neigborhood radius threshold
    param min_pts (int): minimum number of points threshold for a
    nieghborhood to be a cluster
    """

    # Build a label holder that is comprised of all 0s
    labels = [0]* x.shape[0]

    # Arbitrary starting "current cluster" ID
    C = 0

    # For each point p in x...
    # ('p' is the index of the datapoint, rather than the datapoint
    itself.)
    for p in range(0, x.shape[0]):

        # Only unvisited points can be evaluated as neighborhood centers
        if not (labels[p] == 0):
            continue

        # Find all of p's neighbors.
        neighbors = neighborhood_search(x, p, eps)

        # If there are not enough neighbor points, then it is classified as
    noise (-1).
        # Otherwise we can use this point as a neighborhood cluster
        if len(neighbors) < min_pts:
            labels[p] = -1
        else:
            C += 1
            neighbor_cluster(x, labels, p, neighbors, C, eps, min_pts)

    return labels


def neighbor_cluster(x, labels, p, neighbors, C, eps, min_pts):
```

```
    # Assign the cluster label to original point
    labels[p] = C

    # Look at each neighbor of p (by index, not the points themselves) and
evaluate
    i = 0
    while i < len(neighbors):

        # Get the next point from the queue.
        potential_neighbor_ix = neighbors[i]

        # If potential_neighbor_ix is noise from previous runs, we can
assign it to current cluster
        if labels[potential_neighbor_ix] == -1:
            labels[potential_neighbor_ix] = C

        # Otherwise, if potential_neighbor_ix is unvisited, we can add it
to current cluster
        elif labels[potential_neighbor_ix] == 0:
            labels[potential_neighbor_ix] = C

            # Further find neighbors of potential neighbor
            potential_neighbors_cluster = neighborhood_search(x,
potential_neighbor_ix, eps)

            if len(potential_neighbors_cluster) >= min_pts:
                neighbors = neighbors + potential_neighbors_cluster

        # Evaluate next neighbor
        i += 1

def neighborhood_search(x, p, eps):
    neighbors = []

    # For each point in the dataset...
    for potential_neighbor in range(0, x.shape[0]):

        # If a nearby point falls below the neighborhood radius threshold,
add to neighbors list
```

```
    if np.linalg.norm(x[p] - x[potential_neighbor]) < eps:
        neighbors.append(potential_neighbor)

return neighbors
```

4. Use your created DBSCAN implementation to find clusters in the generated dataset. Feel free to use hyperparameters as you see fit, tuning them based on their performance in step five:

    ```
    labels = scratch_DBSCAN(X_blob, 0.6, 5)
    ```

5. Visualize the clustering performance of your DBSCAN implementation from scratch:

    ```
    plt.scatter(X_blob[:,0], X_blob[:,1], c=labels)
    plt.title("DBSCAN from Scratch Performance")
    plt.show()
    ```

    The output is as follows:

Figure 3.15: Plot of DBSCAN implementation

As you may have noticed, it takes quite some time for a custom implementation to run. This is because we explored the non-vectorized version of this algorithm for the sake of clarity. Moving forward, you should aim to use the DBSCAN implementation provided by scikit-learn, as it is highly optimized.

Activity 5: Comparing DBSCAN with k-means and Hierarchical Clustering

Solution:

1. Import the necessary packages:

```
from sklearn.cluster import KMeans, AgglomerativeClustering, DBSCAN
from sklearn.metrics import silhouette_score
import pandas as pd
import matplotlib.pyplot as plt
%matplotlib inline
```

2. Load the wine dataset from *Chapter 2, Hierarchical Clustering* and familiarize yourself again with what the data looks like:

```
# Load Wine data set
wine_df = pd.read_csv("../CH2/wine_data.csv")

# Show sample of data set
print(wine_df.head())
```

The output is as follows:

```
   OD_read   Proline
0    3.92    1065.0
1    3.40    1050.0
2    3.17    1185.0
3    3.45    1480.0
4    2.93     735.0
```

Figure 3.16: First five rows of wine dataset

3. Visualize the data:

```
plt.scatter(wine_df.values[:,0], wine_df.values[:,1])
plt.title("Wine Dataset")
plt.xlabel("OD Reading")
plt.ylabel("Proline")
plt.show()
```

The output is as follows:

Figure 3.17: Plot of the data

4. Generate clusters using k-means, agglomerative clustering, and DBSCAN:

```
# Generate clusters from K-Means
km = KMeans(3)
km_clusters = km.fit_predict(wine_df)


# Generate clusters using Agglomerative Hierarchical Clustering
ac = AgglomerativeClustering(3, linkage='average')
ac_clusters = ac.fit_predict(wine_df)
```

5. Evaluate a few different options for DSBSCAN hyperparameters and their effect on the silhouette score:

```
db_param_options = [[20,5],[25,5],[30,5],[25,7],[35,7],[35,3]]


for ep,min_sample in db_param_options:
    # Generate clusters using DBSCAN
    db = DBSCAN(eps=ep, min_samples = min_sample)
    db_clusters = db.fit_predict(wine_df)
    print("Eps: ", ep, "Min Samples: ", min_sample)
    print("DBSCAN Clustering: ", silhouette_score(wine_df, db_clusters))
```

The output is as follows:

```
Eps:   20 Min Samples:   5
DBSCAN Clustering:   0.3997987919957757
Eps:   25 Min Samples:   5
DBSCAN Clustering:   0.35258611037074095
Eps:   30 Min Samples:   5
DBSCAN Clustering:   0.43763797761597306
Eps:   25 Min Samples:   7
DBSCAN Clustering:   0.2711660466706248
Eps:   35 Min Samples:   7
DBSCAN Clustering:   0.4600630149335495
Eps:   35 Min Samples:   3
DBSCAN Clustering:   0.5368842164535846
```

Figure 3.18: Printing the silhouette score for clusters

6. Generate the final clusters based on the highest silhouette score
   (**eps**: 35, **min_samples**: 3):

```
# Generate clusters using DBSCAN
db = DBSCAN(eps=35, min_samples = 3)
db_clusters = db.fit_predict(wine_df)
```

7. Visualize clusters generated using each of the three methods:

```
plt.title("Wine Clusters from K-Means")
plt.scatter(wine_df['OD_read'], wine_df['Proline'], c=km_clusters,s=50,
cmap='tab20b')
plt.show()

plt.title("Wine Clusters from Agglomerative Clustering")
plt.scatter(wine_df['OD_read'], wine_df['Proline'], c=ac_clusters,s=50,
cmap='tab20b')
plt.show()

plt.title("Wine Clusters from DBSCAN")
plt.scatter(wine_df['OD_read'], wine_df['Proline'], c=db_clusters,s=50,
cmap='tab20b')
plt.show()
```

The output is as follows:

Figure 3.19: Plot of clusters using different algorithms

8. Evaluate the silhouette score of each approach:

```
# Calculate Silhouette Scores
print("Silhouette Scores for Wine Dataset:\n")
print("K-Means Clustering: ", silhouette_score(wine_df, km_clusters))
print("Agg Clustering: ", silhouette_score(wine_df, ac_clusters))
print("DBSCAN Clustering: ", silhouette_score(wine_df, db_clusters))
```

The output is as follows:

```
Silhouette Scores for Wine Dataset:

K-Means Clustering:  0.5809421087616886
Agg Clustering:  0.5988495817462
DBSCAN Clustering:  0.5368842164535846
```

Figure 3.20: Silhouette score

As you can see, DBSCAN isn't automatically the best choice for your clustering needs. One key trait that makes it different form other algorithms is the use of noise as a potential clustering. In some cases, this is great, as it removes outliers, however, there may be situations where it is not tuned well enough and classifies too many points as noise. Can you improve the silhouette score by tuning the hyperparameters?

Chapter 4: Dimension Reduction and PCA

Activity 6: Manual PCA versus scikit-learn

Solution

1. Import the **pandas**, **numpy**, and **matplotlib** plotting libraries and the scikit-learn **PCA** model:

   ```
   import pandas as pd
   import numpy as np
   import matplotlib.pyplot as plt
   from sklearn.decomposition import PCA
   ```

2. Load the dataset and select only the sepal features as per the previous exercises. Display the first five rows of the data:

   ```
   df = pd.read_csv('iris-data.csv')
   df = df[['Sepal Length', 'Sepal Width']]
   df.head()
   ```

   The output is as follows:

	Sepal Length	Sepal Width
0	5.1	3.5
1	4.9	3.0
2	4.7	3.2
3	4.6	3.1
4	5.0	3.6

   Figure 4.43: The first five rows of the data

3. Compute the **covariance** matrix for the data:

```
cov = np.cov(df.values.T)
cov
```

The output is as follows:

```
array([[ 0.68569351, -0.03926846],
       [-0.03926846,  0.18800403]])
```

Figure 4.44: The covariance matrix for the data

4. Transform the data using the scikit-learn API and only the first principal component. Store the transformed data in the **sklearn_pca** variable:

```
model = PCA(n_components=1)
sklearn_pca = model.fit_transform(df.values)
```

5. Transform the data using the manual PCA and only the first principal component. Store the transformed data in the **manual_pca** variable.

```
eigenvectors, eigenvalues, _ = np.linalg.svd(cov, full_matrices=False)
P = eigenvectors[0]
manual_pca = P.dot(df.values.T)
```

6. Plot the **sklearn_pca** and **manual_pca** values on the same plot to visualize the difference:

```
plt.figure(figsize=(10, 7));
plt.plot(sklearn_pca, label='Scikit-learn PCA');
plt.plot(manual_pca, label='Manual PCA', linestyle='--');
plt.xlabel('Sample');
plt.ylabel('Transformed Value');
plt.legend();
```

The output is as follows:

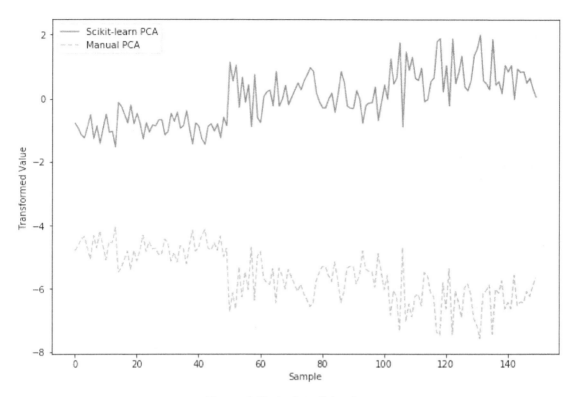

Figure 4.45: A plot of the data

7. Notice that the two plots look almost identical, except that one is a mirror image of another and there is an offset between the two. Display the components of the **sklearn_pca** and **manual_pca** models:

```
model.components_
```

The output is as follows:

```
array([[ 0.99693955, -0.07817635]])
```

Now print **P**:

```
P
```

The output is as follows:

```
array([-0.99693955,  0.07817635])
```

Notice the difference in the signs; the values are identical, but the signs are different, producing the mirror image result. This is just a difference in convention, nothing meaningful.

8. Multiply the `manual_pca` models by `-1` and re-plot:

```
manual_pca *= -1
plt.figure(figsize=(10, 7));
plt.plot(sklearn_pca, label='Scikit-learn PCA');
plt.plot(manual_pca, label='Manual PCA', linestyle='--');
plt.xlabel('Sample');
plt.ylabel('Transformed Value');
plt.legend();
```

The output is as follows:

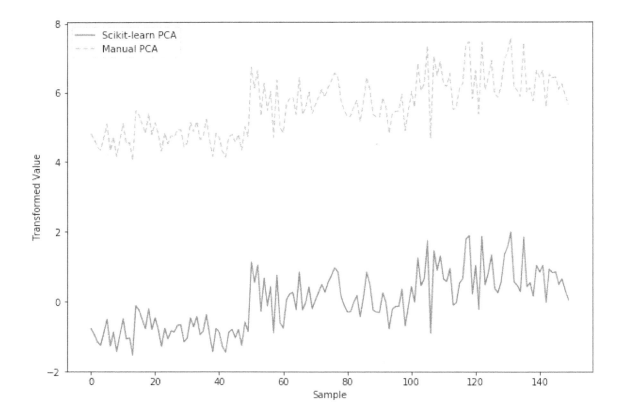

Figure 4.46: Re-plotted data

9. Now, all we need to do is deal with the offset between the two. The scikit-learn API subtracts the mean of the data prior to the transform. Subtract the mean of each column from the dataset before completing the transform with manual PCA:

```
mean_vals = np.mean(df.values, axis=0)
offset_vals = df.values - mean_vals
manual_pca = P.dot(offset_vals.T)
```

10. Multiply the result by **-1**:

```
manual_pca *= -1
```

11. Re-plot the individual **sklearn_pca** and **manual_pca** values:

```
plt.figure(figsize=(10, 7));
plt.plot(sklearn_pca, label='Scikit-learn PCA');
plt.plot(manual_pca, label='Manual PCA', linestyle='--');
plt.xlabel('Sample');
plt.ylabel('Transformed Value');
plt.legend();
```

The output is as follows:

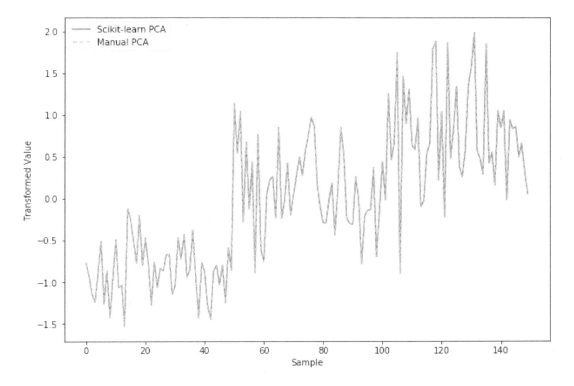

Figure 4.47: Re-plotting the data

The final plot will demonstrate that the dimensionality reduction completed by the two methods are, in fact, the same. The differences lie in the differences in the signs of the **covariance** matrices, as the two methods simply use a different feature as the baseline for comparison. Finally, there is also an offset between the two datasets, which is attributed to the mean samples being subtracted before executing the transform in the scikit-learn PCA.

Activity 7: PCA Using the Expanded Iris Dataset

Solution:

1. Import **pandas** and **matplotlib**. To enable 3D plotting, you will also need to import **Axes3D**:

   ```
   import pandas as pd
   import numpy as np
   import matplotlib.pyplot as plt
   from sklearn.decomposition import PCA
   from mpl_toolkits.mplot3d import Axes3D # Required for 3D plotting
   ```

2. Read in the dataset and select the columns **Sepal Length**, **Sepal Width**, and **Petal Width**:

   ```
   df = pd.read_csv('iris-data.csv')[['Sepal Length', 'Sepal Width', 'Petal Width']]
   df.head()
   ```

   The output is as follows:

	Sepal Length	Sepal Width	Petal Width
0	5.1	3.5	0.2
1	4.9	3.0	0.2
2	4.7	3.2	0.2
3	4.6	3.1	0.2
4	5.0	3.6	0.2

   Figure 4.48: Sepal Length, Sepal Width, and Petal Width

3. Plot the data in three dimensions:

```
fig = plt.figure(figsize=(10, 7))
ax = fig.add_subplot(111, projection='3d')
ax.scatter(df['Sepal Length'], df['Sepal Width'], df['Petal Width']);
ax.set_xlabel('Sepal Length (mm)');
ax.set_ylabel('Sepal Width (mm)');
ax.set_zlabel('Petal Width (mm)');
ax.set_title('Expanded Iris Dataset');
```

The output is as follows:

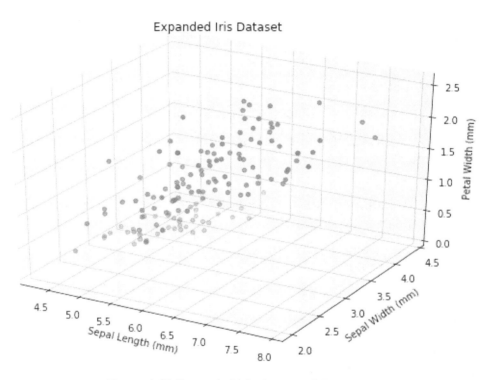

Figure 4.49: Expanded Iris dataset plot

4. Create a **PCA** model without specifying the number of components:

```
model = PCA()
```

5. Fit the model to the dataset:

```
model.fit(df.values)
```

The output is as follows:

```
PCA(copy=True, iterated_power='auto', n_components=None, random_state=None,
    svd_solver='auto', tol=0.0, whiten=False)
```

Figure 4.50: The model fitted to the dataset

6. Display the eigenvalues or **explained_variance_ratio_**:

```
model.explained_variance_ratio_
```

The output is as follows:

```
array([0.8004668 , 0.14652357, 0.05300962])
```

7. We want to reduce the dimensionality of the dataset, but still keep at least 90% of the variance. What are the minimum number of components required to keep 90% of the variance?

The first two components are required for at least 90% variance. The first two components provide 94.7% of the variance within the dataset.

8. Create a new **PCA** model, this time specifying the number of components required to keep at least 90% of the variance:

```
model = PCA(n_components=2)
```

9. Transform the data using the new model:

```
data_transformed = model.fit_transform(df.values)
```

10. Plot the transformed data:

```
plt.figure(figsize=(10, 7))
plt.scatter(data_transformed[:,0], data_transformed[:,1]);
```

The output is as follows:

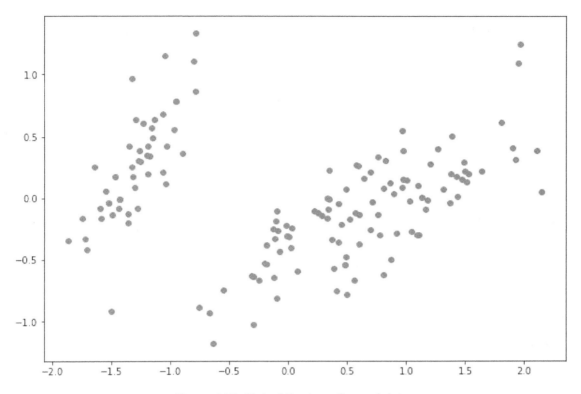

Figure 4.51: Plot of the transformed data

11. Restore the transformed data to the original dataspace:

```
data_restored = model.inverse_transform(data_transformed)
```

12. Plot the restored data in three dimensions in one subplot and the original data in a second subplot to visualize the effect of removing some of the variance:

```
fig = plt.figure(figsize=(10, 14))

# Original Data
ax = fig.add_subplot(211, projection='3d')
ax.scatter(df['Sepal Length'], df['Sepal Width'], df['Petal Width'],
label='Original Data');
ax.set_xlabel('Sepal Length (mm)');
ax.set_ylabel('Sepal Width (mm)');
ax.set_zlabel('Petal Width (mm)');
ax.set_title('Expanded Iris Dataset');
```

```
# Transformed Data
ax = fig.add_subplot(212, projection='3d')
ax.scatter(data_restored[:,0], data_restored[:,1], data_restored[:,2],
label='Restored Data');
ax.set_xlabel('Sepal Length (mm)');
ax.set_ylabel('Sepal Width (mm)');
ax.set_zlabel('Petal Width (mm)');
ax.set_title('Restored Iris Dataset');
```

The output is as follows:

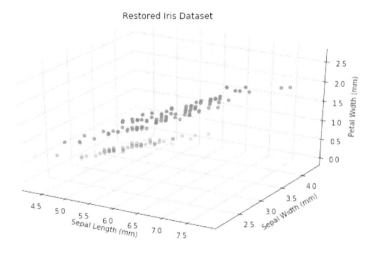

Figure 4.52: Plot of the expanded and the restored Iris datasets

Looking at *Figure* 4.52, we can see that, as we did with the 2D plots, we have removed much of the noise within the data, but retained the most important information regarding the trends within the data. It can be seen that in general, the sepal length increases with the petal width and that there seems to be two clusters of data within the plots, one sitting above the other.

> **Note**
>
> When applying PCA, it is important to keep in mind the size of the data being modelled, as well as the available system memory. The singular value decomposition process involves separating the data into the eigenvalues and eigenvectors, and can be quite memory intensive. If the dataset is too large, you may either be unable to complete the process, suffer significant performance loss, or lock up your system.

Chapter 5: Autoencoders

Activity 8: Modeling Neurons with a ReLU Activation Function

Solution:

1. Import **numpy** and matplotlib:

    ```
    import numpy as np
    import matplotlib.pyplot as plt
    ```

2. Allow latex symbols to be used in labels:

    ```
    plt.rc('text', usetex=True)
    ```

3. Define the ReLU activation function as a Python function:

    ```
    def relu(x):
        return np.max((0, x))
    ```

4. Define the inputs (**x**) and tunable weights (**theta**) for the neuron. In this example, the inputs (**x**) will be 100 numbers linearly spaced between –5 and 5. Set **theta** = 1:

    ```
    theta = 1
    x = np.linspace(-5, 5, 100)
    x
    ```

    The output is as follows:

    ```
    array([-5.        , -4.8989899 , -4.7979798 , -4.6969697 , -4.5959596 ,
           -4.49494949, -4.39393939, -4.29292929, -4.19191919, -4.09090909,
           -3.98989899, -3.88888889, -3.78787879, -3.68686869, -3.58585859,
           -3.48484848, -3.38383838, -3.28282828, -3.18181818, -3.08080808,
           -2.97979798, -2.87878788, -2.77777778, -2.67676768, -2.57575758,
           -2.47474747, -2.37373737, -2.27272727, -2.17171717, -2.07070707,
           -1.96969697, -1.86868687, -1.76767677, -1.66666667, -1.56565657,
    ```

    Figure 5.35: Printing the inputs

5. Compute the output (**y**):

    ```
    y = [relu(_x * theta) for _x in x]
    ```

6. Plot the output of the neuron versus the input:

    ```
    fig = plt.figure(figsize=(10, 7))
    ax = fig.add_subplot(111)

    ax.plot(x, y)
    ```

```
ax.set_xlabel('$x$', fontsize=22);
ax.set_ylabel('$h(x\Theta)$', fontsize=22);
ax.spines['left'].set_position(('data', 0));
ax.spines['top'].set_visible(False);
ax.spines['right'].set_visible(False);
ax.tick_params(axis='both', which='major', labelsize=22)
```

The output is as follows:

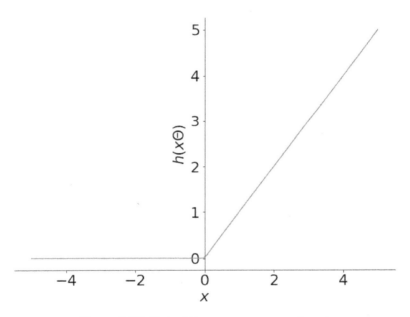

Figure 5.36: Plot of the neuron versus input

7. Now, set **theta** = **5** and recompute and store the output of the neuron:

   ```
   theta = 5
   y_2 = [relu(_x * theta) for _x in x]
   ```

8. Now, set **theta** = **0.2** and recompute and store the output of the neuron:

   ```
   theta = 0.2
   y_3 = [relu(_x * theta) for _x in x]
   ```

9. Plot the three different output curves of the neuron (**theta** = 1, **theta** = 5, **theta** = 0.2) on one graph:

   ```
   fig = plt.figure(figsize=(10, 7))
   ax = fig.add_subplot(111)

   ax.plot(x, y, label='$\Theta=1$');
   ```

```
ax.plot(x, y_2, label='$\Theta=5$', linestyle=':');
ax.plot(x, y_3, label='$\Theta=0.2$', linestyle='--');
ax.set_xlabel('$x\Theta$', fontsize=22);
ax.set_ylabel('$h(x\Theta)$', fontsize=22);
ax.spines['left'].set_position(('data', 0));
ax.spines['top'].set_visible(False);
ax.spines['right'].set_visible(False);
ax.tick_params(axis='both', which='major', labelsize=22);
ax.legend(fontsize=22);
```

The output is as follows:

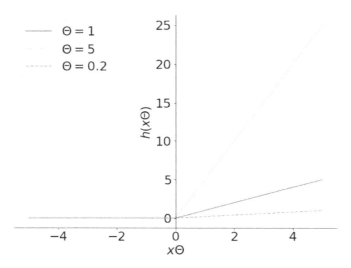

Figure 5.37: Three output curves of the neuron

In this activity, we created a model of a ReLU-based artificial neural network neuron. We can see that the output of this neuron is very different to the sigmoid activation function. There is no saturation region for values greater than 0 because it simply returns the input value of the function. In the negative direction, there is a saturation region where only 0 will be returned if the input is less than 0. The ReLU function is an extremely powerful and commonly used activation function that has shown to be more powerful than the sigmoid function in some circumstances. ReLU is often a good first-choice activation function.

Activity 9: MNIST Neural Network

Solution:

In this activity, you will train a neural network to identify images in the MNIST dataset and reinforce your skills in training neural networks:

1. Import **pickle**, **numpy**, **matplotlib**, and the **Sequential** and **Dense** classes from Keras:

    ```
    import pickle
    import numpy as np
    import matplotlib.pyplot as plt
    from keras.models import Sequential
    from keras.layers import Dense
    ```

2. Load the **mnist.pkl** file, which contains the first 10,000 images and corresponding labels from the MNIST dataset that are available in the accompanying source code. The MNIST dataset is a series of 28 x 28 grayscale images of handwritten digits 0 through 9. Extract the images and labels:

    ```
    with open('mnist.pkl', 'rb') as f:
        data = pickle.load(f)

    images = data['images']
    labels = data['labels']
    ```

3. Plot the first 10 samples along with the corresponding labels:

    ```
    plt.figure(figsize=(10, 7))
    for i in range(10):
        plt.subplot(2, 5, i + 1)
        plt.imshow(images[i], cmap='gray')
        plt.title(labels[i])
        plt.axis('off')
    ```

The output is as follows:

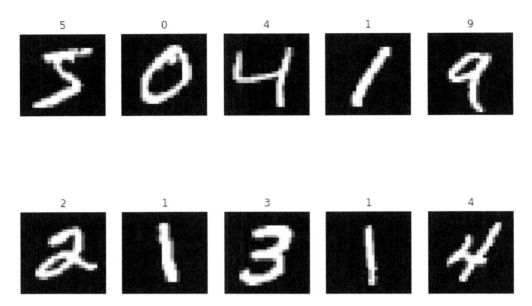

Figure 5.38: First 10 samples

4. Encode the labels using one hot encoding:

```
one_hot_labels = np.zeros((images.shape[0], 10))

for idx, label in enumerate(labels):
    one_hot_labels[idx, label] = 1

one_hot_labels
```

The output is as follows:

```
array([[0., 0., 0., ..., 0., 0., 0.],
       [1., 0., 0., ..., 0., 0., 0.],
       [0., 0., 0., ..., 0., 0., 0.],
       ...,
       [0., 0., 0., ..., 0., 0., 0.],
       [0., 0., 0., ..., 0., 0., 1.],
       [0., 0., 0., ..., 1., 0., 0.]])
```

Figure 5.39: Result of one hot encoding

5. Prepare the images for input into a neural network. As a hint, there are two separate steps in this process:

    ```
    images = images.reshape((-1, 28 ** 2))
    images = images / 255.
    ```

6. Construct a neural network model in Keras that accepts the prepared images, has a hidden layer of 600 units with a ReLU activation function, and an output of the same number of units as classes. The output layer uses a **softmax** activation function:

    ```
    model = Sequential([
        Dense(600, input_shape=(784,), activation='relu'),
        Dense(10, activation='softmax'),
    ])
    ```

7. Compile the model using multiclass cross-entropy, stochastic gradient descent, and an accuracy performance metric:

    ```
    model.compile(loss='categorical_crossentropy',
                  optimizer='sgd',
                  metrics=['accuracy'])
    ```

8. Train the model. How many epochs are required to achieve at least 95% classification accuracy on the training data? Let's have a look:

    ```
    model.fit(images, one_hot_labels, epochs=20)
    ```

    The output is as follows:

    ```
    10000/10000 [==============================] - 2s 152us/step - loss: 0.1963 - acc: 0.9471
    Epoch 13/20
    10000/10000 [==============================] - 2s 157us/step - loss: 0.1921 - acc: 0.9479
    Epoch 14/20
    10000/10000 [==============================] - 2s 173us/step - loss: 0.1877 - acc: 0.9487
    Epoch 15/20
    10000/10000 [==============================] - 2s 157us/step - loss: 0.1836 - acc: 0.9507
    Epoch 16/20
    10000/10000 [==============================] - 2s 156us/step - loss: 0.1791 - acc: 0.9522
    Epoch 17/20
    10000/10000 [==============================] - 2s 157us/step - loss: 0.1754 - acc: 0.9532
    Epoch 18/20
    10000/10000 [==============================] - 2s 158us/step - loss: 0.1714 - acc: 0.9538
    Epoch 19/20
    10000/10000 [==============================] - 2s 156us/step - loss: 0.1681 - acc: 0.9544
    Epoch 20/20
    10000/10000 [==============================] - 2s 160us/step - loss: 0.1638 - acc: 0.9559

    <keras.callbacks.History at 0x7f60f7011f60>
    ```

Figure 5.40: Training the model

15 epochs are required to achieve at least 95% classification accuracy on the training set.

In this example, we have measured the performance of the neural network classifier using the data that the classifier was trained with. In general, this method should not be used as it typically reports a higher level of accuracy than one should expect from the model. In supervised learning problems, there are a number of **cross-validation** techniques that should be used instead. As this is a book on unsupervised learning, cross-validation lies outside the scope of this book.

Activity 10: Simple MNIST Autoencoder

Solution:

1. Import **pickle**, **numpy**, and **matplotlib**, and the **Model**, **Input**, and **Dense** classes from Keras:

   ```
   import pickle
   import numpy as np
   import matplotlib.pyplot as plt
   from keras.models import Model
   from keras.layers import Input, Dense
   ```

2. Load the images from the supplied sample of the MNIST dataset that is provided with the accompanying source code (**mnist.pkl**):

   ```
   with open('mnist.pkl', 'rb') as f:
       images = pickle.load(f)['images']
   ```

3. Prepare the images for input into a neural network. As a hint, there are **two** separate steps in this process:

   ```
   images = images.reshape((-1, 28 ** 2))
   images = images / 255.
   ```

4. Construct a simple autoencoder network that reduces the image size to 10 x 10 after the encoding stage:

   ```
   input_stage = Input(shape=(784,))
   encoding_stage = Dense(100, activation='relu')(input_stage)
   decoding_stage = Dense(784, activation='sigmoid')(encoding_stage)
   autoencoder = Model(input_stage, decoding_stage)
   ```

5. Compile the autoencoder using a binary cross-entropy loss function and **adadelta** gradient descent:

```
autoencoder.compile(loss='binary_crossentropy',
                optimizer='adadelta')
```

6. Fit the encoder model:

```
autoencoder.fit(images, images, epochs=100)
```

The output is as follows:

```
Epoch 96/100
10000/10000 [==============================] - 1s 130us/step - loss: 0.0755
Epoch 97/100
10000/10000 [==============================] - 1s 127us/step - loss: 0.0754
Epoch 98/100
10000/10000 [==============================] - 1s 126us/step - loss: 0.0754
Epoch 99/100
10000/10000 [==============================] - 1s 125us/step - loss: 0.0753
Epoch 100/100
10000/10000 [==============================] - 1s 128us/step - loss: 0.0752

<keras.callbacks.History at 0x7f5e9d2f0860>
```

Figure 5.41: Training the model

7. Calculate and store the output of the encoding stage for the first five samples:

```
encoder_output = Model(input_stage, encoding_stage).predict(images[:5])
```

8. Reshape the encoder output to 10 x 10 (10 x 10 = 100) pixels and multiply by 255:

```
encoder_output = encoder_output.reshape((-1, 10, 10)) * 255
```

9. Calculate and store the output of the decoding stage for the first five samples:

```
decoder_output = autoencoder.predict(images[:5])
```

10. Reshape the output of the decoder to 28 x 28 and multiply by 255:

```
decoder_output = decoder_output.reshape((-1, 28, 28)) * 255
```

11. Plot the original image, the encoder output, and the decoder:

```
images = images.reshape((-1, 28, 28))
plt.figure(figsize=(10, 7))
for i in range(5):
    plt.subplot(3, 5, i + 1)
    plt.imshow(images[i], cmap='gray')
    plt.axis('off')
```

```
plt.subplot(3, 5, i + 6)
plt.imshow(encoder_output[i], cmap='gray')
plt.axis('off')

plt.subplot(3, 5, i + 11)
plt.imshow(decoder_output[i], cmap='gray')
plt.axis('off')
```

The output is as follows:

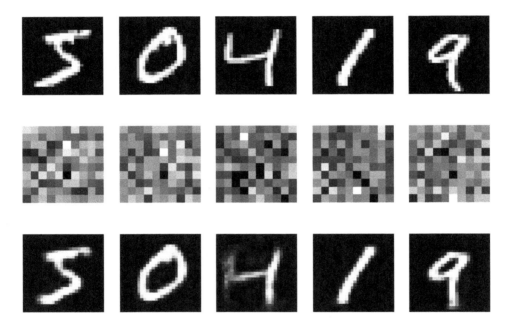

Figure 5.42: The original image, the encoder output, and the decoder

So far, we have shown how a simple single hidden layer in both the encoding and decoding stage can be used to reduce the data to a lower dimension space. We can also make this model more complicated by adding additional layers to both the encoding and the decoding stages.

Activity 11: MNIST Convolutional Autoencoder

Solution:

1. Import **pickle**, **numpy**, **matplotlib**, and the **Model** class from **keras.models** and import **Input**, **Conv2D**, **MaxPooling2D**, and **UpSampling2D** from **keras.layers**:

```
import pickle
import numpy as np
import matplotlib.pyplot as plt
from keras.models import Model
from keras.layers import Input, Conv2D, MaxPooling2D, UpSampling2D
```

2. Load the data:

```
with open('mnist.pkl', 'rb') as f:
    images = pickle.load(f)['images']
```

3. Rescale the images to have values between 0 and 1:

```
images = images / 255.
```

4. We need to reshape the images to add a single depth channel for use with convolutional stages. Reshape the images to have a shape of 28 x 28 x 1:

```
images = images.reshape((-1, 28, 28, 1))
```

5. Define an input layer. We will use the same shape input as an image:

```
input_layer = Input(shape=(28, 28, 1,))
```

6. Add a convolutional stage with 16 layers or filters, a 3 x 3 weight matrix, a ReLU activation function, and using same padding, which means the output has the same length as the input image:

```
hidden_encoding = Conv2D(
    16, # Number of layers or filters in the weight matrix
    (3, 3), # Shape of the weight matrix
    activation='relu',
    padding='same', # How to apply the weights to the images
)(input_layer)
```

7. Add a max pooling layer to the encoder with a 2 x 2 kernel:

```
encoded = MaxPooling2D((2, 2))(hidden_encoding)
```

8. Add a decoding convolutional layer:

```
hidden_decoding = Conv2D(
    16, # Number of layers or filters in the weight matrix
    (3, 3), # Shape of the weight matrix
    activation='relu',
    padding='same', # How to apply the weights to the images
)(encoded)
```

9. Add an upsampling layer:

```
upsample_decoding = UpSampling2D((2, 2))(hidden_decoding)
```

10. Add the final convolutional stage, using one layer as per the initial image depth:

```
decoded = Conv2D(
    1, # Number of layers or filters in the weight matrix
    (3, 3), # Shape of the weight matrix
    activation='sigmoid',
    padding='same', # How to apply the weights to the images
)(upsample_decoding)
```

11. Construct the model by passing the first and last layers of the network to the **Model** class:

```
autoencoder = Model(input_layer, decoded)
```

12. Display the structure of the model:

```
autoencoder.summary()
```

The output is as follows:

```
Layer (type)                 Output Shape              Param #
=================================================================
input_1 (InputLayer)         (None, 28, 28, 1)         0
_____
conv2d_1 (Conv2D)            (None, 28, 28, 16)        160
_____
max_pooling2d_1 (MaxPooling2 (None, 14, 14, 16)        0
_____
conv2d_2 (Conv2D)            (None, 14, 14, 16)        2320
_____
up_sampling2d_1 (UpSampling2 (None, 28, 28, 16)        0
_____
conv2d_3 (Conv2D)            (None, 28, 28, 1)         145
=================================================================
Total params: 2,625
Trainable params: 2,625
Non-trainable params: 0
```

Figure 5.43: Structure of model

13. Compile the autoencoder using a binary cross-entropy loss function and **adadelta** gradient descent:

```
autoencoder.compile(loss='binary_crossentropy',
                optimizer='adadelta')
```

14. Now, let's fit the model; again, we pass the images as the training data and as the desired output. Train for 20 epochs as convolutional networks take a lot longer to compute:

```
autoencoder.fit(images, images, epochs=20)
```

The output is as follows:

```
Epoch 15/20
10000/10000 [==============================] - 9s 894us/step - loss: 0.0641
Epoch 16/20
10000/10000 [==============================] - 9s 931us/step - loss: 0.0640
Epoch 17/20
10000/10000 [==============================] - 9s 890us/step - loss: 0.0639
Epoch 18/20
10000/10000 [==============================] - 9s 943us/step - loss: 0.0638
Epoch 19/20
10000/10000 [==============================] - 9s 914us/step - loss: 0.0636
Epoch 20/20
10000/10000 [==============================] - 9s 931us/step - loss: 0.0635
```

Figure 5.44: Training the model

15. Calculate and store the output of the encoding stage for the first five samples:

```
encoder_output = Model(input_layer, encoded).predict(images[:5])
```

16. Reshape the encoder output for visualization, where each image is X*Y in size:

```
encoder_output = encoder_output.reshape((-1, 14 * 14, 16))
```

17. Get the output of the decoder for the first five images:

```
decoder_output = autoencoder.predict(images[:5])
```

18. Reshape the decoder output to 28 x 28 in size:

```
decoder_output = decoder_output.reshape((-1, 28, 28))
```

19. Reshape the original images back to 28 x 28 in size:

```
images = images.reshape((-1, 28, 28))
```

20. Plot the original image, the mean encoder output, and the decoder:

```python
plt.figure(figsize=(10, 7))
for i in range(5):
    plt.subplot(3, 5, i + 1)
    plt.imshow(images[i], cmap='gray')
    plt.axis('off')

    plt.subplot(3, 5, i + 6)
    plt.imshow(encoder_output[i], cmap='gray')
    plt.axis('off')

    plt.subplot(3, 5, i + 11)
    plt.imshow(decoder_output[i], cmap='gray')
    plt.axis('off')
```

The output is as follows:

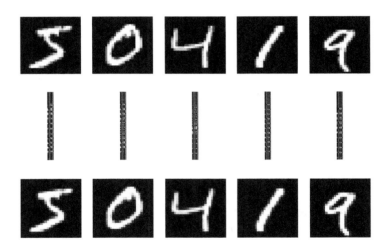

Figure 5.45: The original image, the encoder output, and the decoder

At the end of this activity, you will have developed an autoencoder comprising convolutional layers within the neural network. Note the improvements made in the decoder representations. This architecture has a significant performance benefit over fully-connected neural network layers and is extremely useful in working with image-based datasets and generating artificial data samples.

Chapter 6: t-Distributed Stochastic Neighbor Embedding (t-SNE)

Activity 12: Wine t-SNE

Solution:

1. Import **pandas**, **numpy**, **matplotlib**, and the **t-SNE** and **PCA** models from scikit-learn:

```
import pandas as pd
import numpy as np
import matplotlib.pyplot as plt
from sklearn.decomposition import PCA
from sklearn.manifold import TSNE
```

2. Load the Wine dataset using the **wine.data** file included in the accompanying source code and display the first five rows of data:

```
df = pd.read_csv('wine.data', header=None)
df.head()
```

The output is as follows:

	0	1	2	3	4	5	6	7	8	9	10	11	12	13
0	1	14.23	1.71	2.43	15.6	127	2.80	3.06	0.28	2.29	5.64	1.04	3.92	1065
1	1	13.20	1.78	2.14	11.2	100	2.65	2.76	0.26	1.28	4.38	1.05	3.40	1050
2	1	13.16	2.36	2.67	18.6	101	2.80	3.24	0.30	2.81	5.68	1.03	3.17	1185
3	1	14.37	1.95	2.50	16.8	113	3.85	3.49	0.24	2.18	7.80	0.86	3.45	1480
4	1	13.24	2.59	2.87	21.0	118	2.80	2.69	0.39	1.82	4.32	1.04	2.93	735

Figure 6.24: The first five rows of the wine dataset.

3. The first column contains the labels; extract this column and remove it from the dataset:

```
labels = df[0]
del df[0]
```

4. Execute PCA to reduce the dataset to the first six components:

```
model_pca = PCA(n_components=6)
wine_pca = model_pca.fit_transform(df)
```

5. Determine the amount of variance within the data described by these six components:

```
np.sum(model_pca.explained_variance_ratio_)
```

The output is as follows:

```
0.99999314824536
```

6. Create a t-SNE model using a specified random state and a **verbose** value of 1:

```
tsne_model = TSNE(random_state=0, verbose=1)
tsne_model
```

The output is as follows:

```
TSNE(angle=0.5, early_exaggeration=12.0, init='random', learning_rate=200.0,
    method='barnes_hut', metric='euclidean', min_grad_norm=1e-07,
    n_components=2, n_iter=1000, n_iter_without_progress=300,
    perplexity=30.0, random_state=0, verbose=1)
```

Figure 6.25: Creating t-SNE model.

7. Fit the PCA data to the t-SNE model:

```
wine_tsne = tsne_model.fit_transform(wine_pca.reshape((len(wine_pca), -1)))
```

The output is as follows:

```
[t-SNE] Computing 91 nearest neighbors...
[t-SNE] Indexed 178 samples in 0.000s...
[t-SNE] Computed neighbors for 178 samples in 0.003s...
[t-SNE] Computed conditional probabilities for sample 178 / 178
[t-SNE] Mean sigma: 9.207049
[t-SNE] KL divergence after 250 iterations with early exaggeration: 51.930435
[t-SNE] KL divergence after 900 iterations: 0.135609
```

Figure 6.26: Fitting PCA data t-SNE model

8. Confirm that the shape of the t-SNE fitted data is two dimensional:

```
wine_tsne.shape
```

The output is as follows:

```
(172, 8)
```

9. Create a scatter plot of the two-dimensional data:

```
plt.figure(figsize=(10, 7))
plt.scatter(wine_tsne[:,0], wine_tsne[:,1]);
plt.title('Low Dimensional Representation of Wine');
plt.show()
```

The output is as follows:

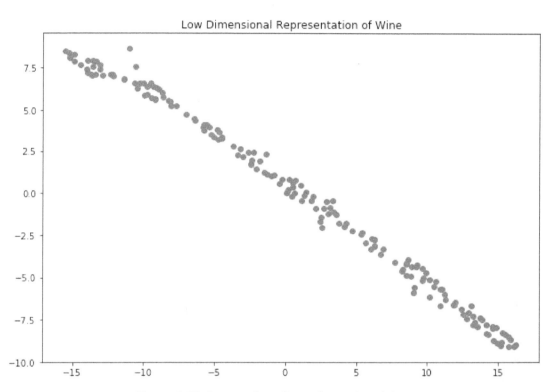

Figure 6.27: Scatterplot of two-dimensional data

10. Create a secondary scatter plot of the two-dimensional data with the class labels applied to visualize any clustering that may be present:

```
MARKER = ['o', 'v', '^',]
plt.figure(figsize=(10, 7))
plt.title('Low Dimensional Representation of Wine');
for i in range(1, 4):
    selections = wine_tsne[labels == i]
    plt.scatter(selections[:,0], selections[:,1], marker=MARKER[i-1],
label=f'Wine {i}', s=30);
    plt.legend();
plt.show()
```

The output is as follows:

Figure 6.28: Secondary plot of two-dimensional data

Note that while there is an overlap between the wine classes, it can also be seen that there is some clustering within the data. The first wine class is predominantly positioned in the top left-hand corner of the plot, the second wine class in the bottom-right, and the third wine class between the first two. This representation certainly couldn't be used to classify individual wine samples with great confidence, but it shows an overall trend and series of clusters contained within the high-dimensional data that we were unable to see earlier.

Activity 13: t-SNE Wine and Perplexity

Solution:

1. Import **pandas**, **numpy**, `matplotlib`, and the **t-SNE** and **PCA** models from scikit-learn:

```
import pandas as pd
import numpy as np
import matplotlib.pyplot as plt
from sklearn.decomposition import PCA
from sklearn.manifold import TSNE
```

2. Load the Wine dataset and inspect the first five rows:

```
df = pd.read_csv('wine.data', header=None)
df.head()
```

The output is as follows:

	0	1	2	3	4	5	6	7	8	9	10	11	12	13
0	1	14.23	1.71	2.43	15.6	127	2.80	3.06	0.28	2.29	5.64	1.04	3.92	1065
1	1	13.20	1.78	2.14	11.2	100	2.65	2.76	0.26	1.28	4.38	1.05	3.40	1050
2	1	13.16	2.36	2.67	18.6	101	2.80	3.24	0.30	2.81	5.68	1.03	3.17	1185
3	1	14.37	1.95	2.50	16.8	113	3.85	3.49	0.24	2.18	7.80	0.86	3.45	1480
4	1	13.24	2.59	2.87	21.0	118	2.80	2.69	0.39	1.82	4.32	1.04	2.93	735

Figure 6.29: The first five rows of wine data.

3. The first column provides the labels; extract them from the DataFrame and store them in a separate variable. Ensure that the column is removed from the DataFrame:

```
labels = df[0]
del df[0]
```

4. Execute PCA on the dataset and extract the first six components:

```
model_pca = PCA(n_components=6)
wine_pca = model_pca.fit_transform(df)
wine_pca = wine_pca.reshape((len(wine_pca), -1))
```

5. Construct a loop that iterates through the perplexity values (1, 5, 20, 30, 80, 160, 320). For each loop, generate a t-SNE model with the corresponding perplexity and print a scatter plot of the labeled wine classes. Note the effect of different perplexity values:

```
MARKER = ['o', 'v', '^',]
for perp in [1, 5, 20, 30, 80, 160, 320]:
    tsne_model = TSNE(random_state=0, verbose=1, perplexity=perp)
    wine_tsne = tsne_model.fit_transform(wine_pca)
    plt.figure(figsize=(10, 7))
    plt.title(f'Low Dimensional Representation of Wine. Perplexity
{perp}');
    for i in range(1, 4):
        selections = wine_tsne[labels == i]
        plt.scatter(selections[:,0], selections[:,1], marker=MARKER[i-1],
label=f'Wine {i}', s=30);
        plt.legend();
```

A perplexity value of 1 fails to separate the data into any particular structure:

Figure 6.30: Plot for perplexity value 1

Increasing the perplexity to 5 leads to a very non-linear structure that is difficult to separate, and it's hard to identify any clusters or patterns:

Figure 6.31: Plot for perplexity of 5

A perplexity of 20 finally starts to show some sort of horse-shoe structure. While visually obvious, this can still be tricky to implement:

Figure 6.32: Plot for perplexity of 20

A perplexity of 30 demonstrates quite good results. There is a linear relationship between the projected structure with some separation between the types of wine:

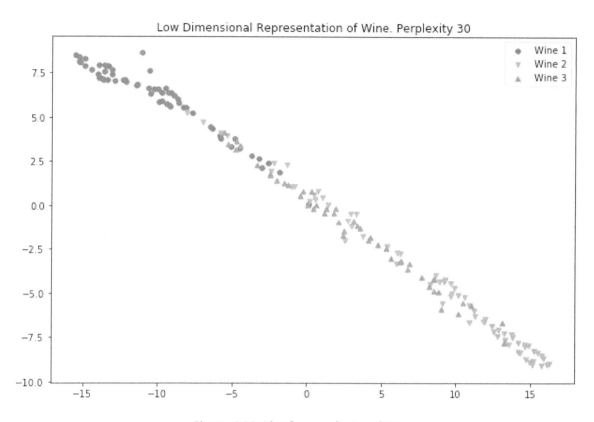

Figure 6.33: Plot for perplexity of 30

Finally, the last two images in the activity show the extent to which the plots can become increasingly complex and non-linear with increasing perplexity:

Figure 6.34: Plot for perplexity of 80

Here's the plot for a perplexity of 160:

Figure 6.35: Plot for perplexity of 160

Looking at the individual plots for each of the perplexity values, the effect perplexity has on the visualization of data is immediately obvious. Very small or very large perplexity values produces a range of unusual shapes that don't indicate the presence of any persistent pattern. The most plausible value seems to be 30, which produced the most linear plot we saw in the previous activity.

In this activity, we demonstrated the need to be careful when selecting the perplexity and that some iteration may be required to determine the correct value.

Activity 14: t-SNE Wine and Iterations

Solution:

1. Import **pandas**, **numpy**, **matplotlib**, and the **t-SNE** and **PCA** models from scikit-learn:

    ```
    import pandas as pd
    import numpy as np
    import matplotlib.pyplot as plt
    from sklearn.decomposition import PCA
    from sklearn.manifold import TSNE
    ```

2. Load the Wine dataset and inspect the first five rows:

    ```
    df = pd.read_csv('wine.data', header=None)
    df.head()
    ```

    The output is as follows:

	0	1	2	3	4	5	6	7	8	9	10	11	12	13
0	1	14.23	1.71	2.43	15.6	127	2.80	3.06	0.28	2.29	5.64	1.04	3.92	1065
1	1	13.20	1.78	2.14	11.2	100	2.65	2.76	0.26	1.28	4.38	1.05	3.40	1050
2	1	13.16	2.36	2.67	18.6	101	2.80	3.24	0.30	2.81	5.68	1.03	3.17	1185
3	1	14.37	1.95	2.50	16.8	113	3.85	3.49	0.24	2.18	7.80	0.86	3.45	1480
4	1	13.24	2.59	2.87	21.0	118	2.80	2.69	0.39	1.82	4.32	1.04	2.93	735

Figure 6.36: The first five rows of wine dataset

3. The first column provides the labels; extract these from the DataFrame and store them in a separate variable. Ensure that the column is removed from the Data-Frame:

```
labels = df[0]
del df[0]
```

4. Execute PCA on the dataset and extract the first six components:

```
model_pca = PCA(n_components=6)
wine_pca = model_pca.fit_transform(df)
wine_pca = wine_pca.reshape((len(wine_pca), -1))
```

5. Construct a loop that iterates through the iteration values (**250**, **500**, **1000**). For each loop, generate a t-SNE model with the corresponding number of iterations and identical number of iterations without progress values:

```
MARKER = ['o', 'v', '1', 'p' ,'*', '+', 'x', 'd', '4', '.']
for iterations in [250, 500, 1000]:
    model_tsne = TSNE(random_state=0, verbose=1, n_iter=iterations, n_
iter_without_progress=iterations)
    mnist_tsne = model_tsne.fit_transform(mnist_pca)
```

6. Construct a scatter plot of the labeled wine classes. Note the effect of different iteration values:

```
    plt.figure(figsize=(10, 7))
    plt.title(f'Low Dimensional Representation of MNIST (iterations =
{iterations})');
    for i in range(10):
        selections = mnist_tsne[mnist['labels'] == i]
        plt.scatter(selections[:,0], selections[:,1], alpha=0.2,
marker=MARKER[i], s=5);
        x, y = selections.mean(axis=0)
        plt.text(x, y, str(i), fontdict={'weight': 'bold', 'size': 30})
```

The output is as follows:

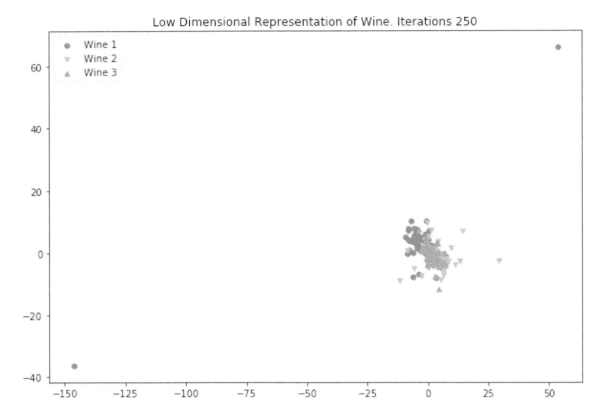

Figure 6.37: Scatterplot of wine classes with 250 iterations

Here's the plot for 500 iterations:

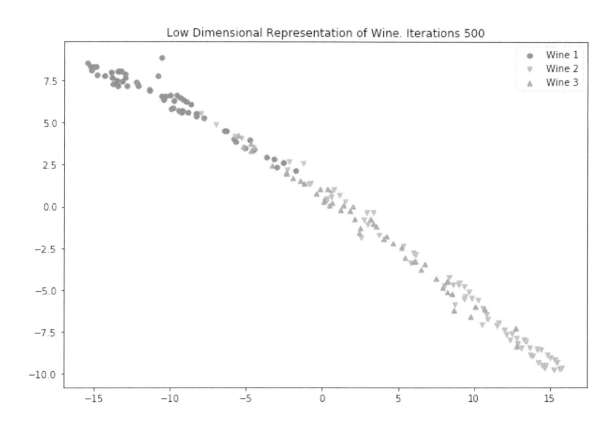

Figure 6.38: Scatterplot of wine classes with 500 iterations

Here's the plot for 1,000 iterations:

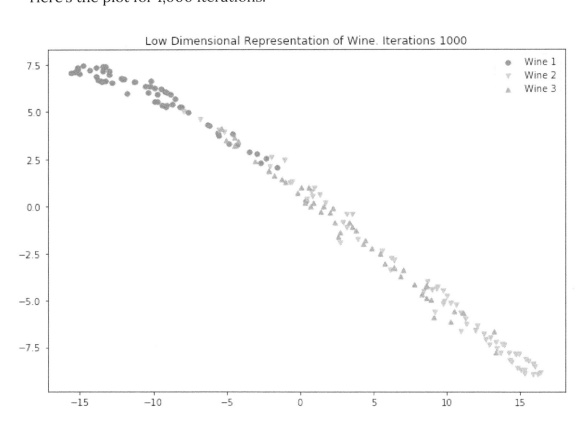

Figure 6.39: Scatterplot of wine classes with 1,000 iterations

Again, we can see the improvement in the structure of the data as the number of iterations increase. Even in a relatively simple dataset such as this, 250 iterations are not sufficient to project any structure of data into the lower-dimensional space.

As we observed in the corresponding activity, there is a balance to find in setting the iteration parameter. In this example, 250 iterations were insufficient, and at least 1,000 iterations were required for the final stabilization of the data.

Chapter 7: Topic Modeling

Activity 15: Loading and Cleaning Twitter Data

Solution:

1. Import the necessary libraries:

    ```
    import langdetect
    import matplotlib.pyplot
    import nltk
    import numpy
    import pandas
    import pyLDAvis
    import pyLDAvis.sklearn
    import regex
    import sklearn
    ```

2. Load the LA Times health Twitter data (**latimeshealth.txt**) from https://github. com/TrainingByPackt/Applied-Unsupervised-Learning-with-Python/tree/ master/Lesson07/Activity15-Activity17:

    > **Note**
    >
    > Pay close attention to the delimiter (it is neither a comma nor a tab) and double-check the header status.

    ```
    path = '<Path>/latimeshealth.txt'
    df = pandas.read_csv(path, sep="|", header=None)
    df.columns = ["id", "datetime", "tweettext"]
    ```

3. Run a quick exploratory analysis to ascertain the data size and structure:

    ```
    def dataframe_quick_look(df, nrows):
    print("SHAPE:\n{shape}\n".format(shape=df.shape))
    print("COLUMN NAMES:\n{names}\n".format(names=df.columns))
    print("HEAD:\n{head}\n".format(head=df.head(nrows)))

    dataframe_quick_look(df, nrows=2)
    ```

The output is as follows:

```
SHAPE:
(4171, 3)

COLUMN NAMES:
Index(['id', 'datetime', 'tweettext'], dtype='object')

HEAD:
                        id                        datetime  \
0   576760256031682561    Sat Mar 14 15:02:15 +0000 2015
1   576715414811471872    Sat Mar 14 12:04:04 +0000 2015


                                               tweettext
0   Five new running shoes that aim to go the extr...
1   Gym Rat: Disq class at Crunch is intense worko...
```

Figure 7.54: Shape, column names, and head of data

4. Extract the tweet text and convert it to a list object:

```
raw = df['tweettext'].tolist()
print("HEADLINES:\n{lines}\n".format(lines=raw[:5]))
print("LENGTH:\n{length}\n".format(length=len(raw)))
```

The output is as follows:

```
HEADLINES:
['Five new running shoes that aim to go the extra mile http://lat.ms/1ELp3wU', 'Gym Rat: Disq class at Crunch is intense workou
t on pulley system http://lat.ms/1EKOFdr', 'Noshing through thousands of ideas at Natural Products Expo West http://lat.ms/1EHq
ywg', 'Natural Products Expo also explores beauty, supplements and more http://lat.ms/1EHqyfE', 'Free Fitness Weekends in South
Bay beach cities aim to spark activity http://lat.ms/1EH3SMC']

LENGTH:
4171
```

Figure 7.55: Headlines and their length

5. Write a function to perform language detection, tokenization on whitespaces, and replace screen names and URLs with **SCREENNAME** and **URL**, respectively. The function should also remove punctuation, numbers, and the **SCREENNAME** and **URL** replacements. Convert everything to lowercase, except **SCREENNAME** and **URL**. It should remove all stop words, perform lemmatization, and keep words with five or more letters:

> **Note**
>
> Screen names start with the **@** symbol.

```
def do_language_identifying(txt):
    try:
        the_language = langdetect.detect(txt)
    except:
        the_language = 'none'
    return the_language
def do_lemmatizing(wrd):
    out = nltk.corpus.wordnet.morphy(wrd)
    return (wrd if out is None else out)
def do_tweet_cleaning(txt):
# identify language of tweet
# return null if language not english
    lg = do_language_identifying(txt)
    if lg != 'en':
        return None
# split the string on whitespace
    out = txt.split(' ')
# identify screen names
# replace with SCREENNAME
    out = ['SCREENNAME' if i.startswith('@') else i for i in out]
# identify urls
# replace with URL
    out = ['URL' if bool(regex.search('http[s]?://', i)) else i for i in
out]
    # remove all punctuation
    out = [regex.sub('[^\\w\\s]|\n', '', i) for i in out]
    # make all non-keywords lowercase
    keys = ['SCREENNAME', 'URL']
    out = [i.lower() if i not in keys else i for i in out]
    # remove keywords
```

```
        out = [i for i in out if i not in keys]
        # remove stopwords
        list_stop_words = nltk.corpus.stopwords.words('english')
        list_stop_words = [regex.sub('[^\\w\\s]', '', i) for i in list_stop_
    words]
        out = [i for i in out if i not in list_stop_words]
        # lemmatizing
        out = [do_lemmatizing(i) for i in out]
        # keep words 4 or more characters long
        out = [i for i in out if len(i) >= 5]
        return out
```

6. Apply the function defined in *step 5* to every tweet:

```
clean = list(map(do_tweet_cleaning, raw))
```

7. Remove elements of output list equal to **None**:

```
clean = list(filter(None.__ne__, clean))
print("HEADLINES:\n{lines}\n".format(lines=clean[:5]))
print("LENGTH:\n{length}\n".format(length=len(clean)))
```

The output is as follows:

```
HEADLINES:
[['running', 'shoes', 'extra'], ['class', 'crunch', 'intense', 'workout', 'pulley', 'system'], ['thousand', 'natural', 'produc
t'], ['natural', 'product', 'explore', 'beauty', 'supplement'], ['fitness', 'weekend', 'south', 'beach', 'spark', 'activity']]

LENGTH:
4093
```

Figure 7.56: Headline and length after removing None

8. Turn the elements of each tweet back into a string. Concatenate using white space:

```
clean_sentences = [" ".join(i) for i in clean]
print(clean_sentences[0:10])
```

The first 10 elements of the output list should resemble the following:

```
['running shoes extra', 'class crunch intense workout pulley system', 'thousand natural product', 'natural product explore beau
ty supplement', 'fitness weekend south beach spark activity', 'kayla harrison sacrifice', 'sonic treatment alzheimers disease',
'ultrasound brain restore memory alzheimers needle onlyso farin mouse', 'apple researchkit really medical research', 'warning c
hantix drink taking might remember']
```

Figure 7.57: Tweets cleaned for modeling

9. Keep the notebook open for future modeling.

Activity 16: Latent Dirichlet Allocation and Health Tweets

Solution:

1. Specify the **number_words**, **number_docs**, and **number_features** variables:

```
number_words = 10
number_docs = 10
number_features = 1000
```

2. Create a bag-of-words model and assign the feature names to another variable for use later on:

```
vectorizer1 = sklearn.feature_extraction.text.CountVectorizer(
    analyzer=»word»,
    max_df=0.95,
    min_df=10,
    max_features=number_features
)
clean_vec1 = vectorizer1.fit_transform(clean_sentences)
print(clean_vec1[0])

feature_names_vec1 = vectorizer1.get_feature_names()
```

The output is as follows:

```
(0, 320)    1
```

3. Identify the optimal number of topics:

```
def perplexity_by_ntopic(data, ntopics):
    output_dict = {
        «Number Of Topics": [],
        «Perplexity Score»: []
    }
    for t in ntopics:
        lda = sklearn.decomposition.LatentDirichletAllocation(
            n_components=t,
            learning_method="online",
            random_state=0
        )
```

```
                lda.fit(data)
                output_dict["Number Of Topics"].append(t)
                output_dict["Perplexity Score"].append(lda.perplexity(data))
            output_df = pandas.DataFrame(output_dict)
            index_min_perplexity = output_df["Perplexity Score"].idxmin()
            output_num_topics = output_df.loc[
                index_min_perplexity,  # index
                «Number Of Topics"  # column
            ]
            return (output_df, output_num_topics)
        df_perplexity, optimal_num_topics = perplexity_by_ntopic(
            clean_vec1,
            ntopics=[i for i in range(1, 21) if i % 2 == 0]
        )
        print(df_perplexity)
```

The output is as follows:

```
          Number Of Topics   Perplexity Score
       0                 2         349.004885
       1                 4         404.137619
       2                 6         440.677441
       3                 8         464.222793
       4                10         478.094739
       5                12         493.116250
       6                14         506.144776
       7                16         524.674504
       8                18         530.975575
       9                20         535.461393
```

Figure 7.58: Number of topics versus perplexity score data frame

4. Fit the LDA model using the optimal number of topics:

```
lda = sklearn.decomposition.LatentDirichletAllocation(
    n_components=optimal_num_topics,
    learning_method="online",
    random_state=0
)
lda.fit(clean_vec1)
```

The output is as follows:

```
LatentDirichletAllocation(batch_size=128, doc_topic_prior=None,
            evaluate_every=-1, learning_decay=0.7,
            learning_method='online', learning_offset=10.0,
            max_doc_update_iter=100, max_iter=10, mean_change_tol=0.001,
            n_components=2, n_jobs=None, n_topics=None, perp_tol=0.1,
            random_state=0, topic_word_prior=None,
            total_samples=1000000.0, verbose=0)
```

Figure 7.59: LDA model

5. Create and print the word-topic table:

```
def get_topics(mod, vec, names, docs, ndocs, nwords):
    # word to topic matrix
    W = mod.components_
    W_norm = W / W.sum(axis=1)[:, numpy.newaxis]
    # topic to document matrix
    H = mod.transform(vec)
    W_dict = {}
    H_dict = {}
    for tpc_idx, tpc_val in enumerate(W_norm):
        topic = «Topic{}".format(tpc_idx)
        # formatting w
        W_indices = tpc_val.argsort()[::-1][:nwords]
        W_names_values = [
            (round(tpc_val[j], 4), names[j])
            for j in W_indices
        ]
        W_dict[topic] = W_names_values
        # formatting h
        H_indices = H[:, tpc_idx].argsort()[::-1][:ndocs]
        H_names_values = [
        (round(H[:, tpc_idx][j], 4), docs[j])
            for j in H_indices
        ]
        H_dict[topic] = H_names_values
    W_df = pandas.DataFrame(
        W_dict,
        index=["Word" + str(i) for i in range(nwords)]
    )
    H_df = pandas.DataFrame(
```

```
            H_dict,
            index=["Doc" + str(i) for i in range(ndocs)]
    )
    return (W_df, H_df)

W_df, H_df = get_topics(
    mod=lda,
    vec=clean_vec1,
    names=feature_names_vec1,
    docs=raw,
    ndocs=number_docs,
    nwords=number_words
)
print(W_df)
```

The output is as follows:

```
                             Topic0                    Topic1
        Word0        (0.0417, latfit)        (0.0817, study)
        Word1        (0.0336, health)       (0.0306, cancer)
        Word2        (0.0242, people)      (0.0212, patient)
        Word3         (0.0203, could)        (0.0172, death)
        Word4         (0.0192, brain)       (0.017, obesity)
        Word5     (0.018, researcher)       (0.0168, doctor)
        Word6         (0.0176, woman)        (0.0166, heart)
        Word7         (0.016, report)      (0.0148, disease)
        Word8     (0.0143, california)      (0.0144, weight)
        Word9      (0.0125, scientist)    (0.0115, research)
```

Figure 7.60: Word-topic table for the health tweet data

6. Print the document-topic table:

```
print(H_df)
```

The output is as follows:

```
                                               Topic0  \
Doc0  (0.9443, Want your legs to look good in those ...
Doc1  (0.9442, 11% of hospital patients got care the...
Doc2  (0.9373, Spend time with dad this Father's Day...
Doc3  (0.9373, Hve fun! That's an order. It's import...
Doc4  (0.9372, Need a new challenge for your ab work...
Doc5  (0.9368, ZMapp goes 18-for-18 in treating monk...
Doc6  (0.9367, Anti-vaccination activists target hig...
Doc7  (0.9337, RT @latimesscience: @xprize pulled th...
Doc8  (0.9285, About 75% of homeless people smoke, a...
Doc9  (0.9284, Yogi crunches can give you flat abs a...


                                               Topic1
Doc0  (0.9498, Computer problems are delaying nursin...
Doc1  (0.9457, Trans fats? DONE. Will the @US_FDA go...
Doc2  (0.9414, Supplements to boost "low T" increase...
Doc3  (0.9372, Study: The 2009 H1N1 "swine flu" pand...
Doc4  (0.9363, Doctors often delay vaccines for youn...
Doc5  (0.9357, Humans eat more calories, protein and...
Doc6  (0.9356, Las Vegas: Finding the latest in bike...
Doc7  (0.9354, Soccer players' ACL injury risk may d...
Doc8  (0.9284, Men walk more slowly with a woman IF ...
Doc9  (0.9284, Do blood transfusions from Ebola surv...
```

Figure 7.61: Document topic table

7. Create a biplot visualization:

```
lda_plot = pyLDAvis.sklearn.prepare(lda, clean_vec1, vectorizer1, R=10)
pyLDAvis.display(lda_plot)
```

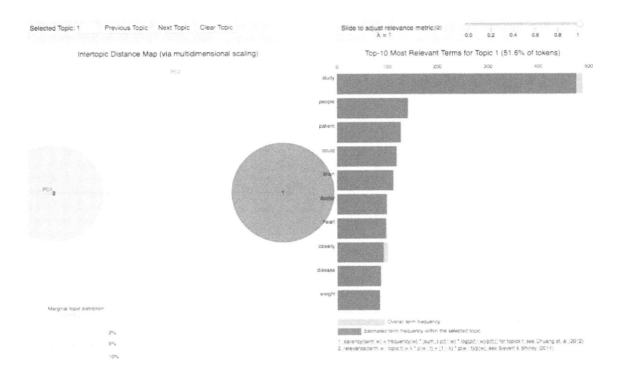

Figure 7.62: A histogram and biplot for the LDA model trained on health tweets

8. Keep the notebook open for future modeling.

Activity 17: Non-Negative Matrix Factorization

Solution:

1. Create the appropriate bag-of-words model and output the feature names as another variable:

```
vectorizer2 = sklearn.feature_extraction.text.TfidfVectorizer(
    analyzer="word",
    max_df=0.5,
    min_df=20,
    max_features=number_features,
    smooth_idf=False
)
clean_vec2 = vectorizer2.fit_transform(clean_sentences)
print(clean_vec2[0])

feature_names_vec2 = vectorizer2.get_feature_names()
```

2. Define and fit the NMF algorithm using the number of topics (**n_components**) value from activity two:

```
nmf = sklearn.decomposition.NMF(
    n_components=optimal_num_topics,
    init="nndsvda",
    solver="mu",
    beta_loss="frobenius",
    random_state=0,
    alpha=0.1,
    l1_ratio=0.5
)
nmf.fit(clean_vec2)
```

The output is as follows:

```
NMF(alpha=0.1, beta_loss='frobenius', init='nndsvda', l1_ratio=0.5,
    max_iter=200, n_components=2, random_state=0, shuffle=False, solver='mu',
    tol=0.0001, verbose=0)
```

Figure 7.63: Defining the NMF model

3. Get the topic-document and word-topic result tables. Take a few minutes to explore the word groupings and try to define the abstract topics:

```
W_df, H_df = get_topics(
    mod=nmf,
    vec=clean_vec2,
    names=feature_names_vec2,
    docs=raw,
    ndocs=number_docs,
    nwords=number_words
)

print(W_df)
```

```
                      Topic0                  Topic1
Word0      (0.3794, study)        (0.5955, latfit)
Word1     (0.0256, cancer)         (0.0487, steps)
Word2     (0.0207, people)         (0.0446, today)
Word3    (0.0183, obesity)      (0.0402, exercise)
Word4      (0.0183, brain)    (0.0273, healthtips)
Word5     (0.0182, health)      (0.0258, workout)
Word6    (0.0175, suggest)      (0.0203, getting)
Word7     (0.0167, weight)      (0.0192, fitness)
Word8      (0.0152, woman)        (0.0143, great)
Word9       (0.013, death)      (0.0131, morning)
```

Figure 7.64: The word-topic table with probabilities

4. Adjust the model parameters and rerun *step* 3 and *step* 4.

Chapter 8: Market Basket Analysis

Activity 18: Loading and Preparing Full Online Retail Data

Solution:

1. Load the online retail dataset file:

```
import matplotlib.pyplot as plt
import mlxtend.frequent_patterns
import mlxtend.preprocessing
import numpy
import pandas

online = pandas.read_excel(
    io="Online Retail.xlsx",
    sheet_name="Online Retail",
    header=0
)
```

2. Clean and prep the data for modeling, including turning the cleaned data into a list of lists:

```
online['IsCPresent'] = (
    online['InvoiceNo']
    .astype(str)
    .apply(lambda x: 1 if x.find('C') != -1 else 0)
)

online1 = (
    online
    .loc[online["Quantity"] > 0]
    .loc[online['IsCPresent'] != 1]
    .loc[:, ["InvoiceNo", "Description"]]
    .dropna()
)

invoice_item_list = []
for num in list(set(online1.InvoiceNo.tolist())):
    tmp_df = online1.loc[online1['InvoiceNo'] == num]
    tmp_items = tmp_df.Description.tolist()
    invoice_item_list.append(tmp_items)
```

3. Encode the data and recast it as a DataFrame:

```
online_encoder = mlxtend.preprocessing.TransactionEncoder()
online_encoder_array = online_encoder.fit_transform(invoice_item_list)

online_encoder_df = pandas.DataFrame(
    online_encoder_array,
    columns=online_encoder.columns_
)

online_encoder_df.loc[
    20125:20135,
    online_encoder_df.columns.tolist()[100:110]
]
```

The output is as follows:

	6 CHOCOLATE LOVE HEART T-LIGHTS	6 EGG HOUSE PAINTED WOOD	6 GIFT TAGS 50'S CHRISTMAS	6 GIFT TAGS VINTAGE CHRISTMAS	6 RIBBONS ELEGANT CHRISTMAS	6 RIBBONS EMPIRE	6 RIBBONS RUSTIC CHARM	6 RIBBONS SHIMMERING PINKS	6 ROCKET BALLOONS	60 CAKE CASES DOLLY GIRL DESIGN
20125	False	False	False	False	False	False	False	False	False	False
20126	False	False	False	False	False	False	False	False	False	False
20127	False	False	False	False	False	False	False	False	False	False
20128	False	False	False	False	False	False	False	False	False	False
20129	False	False	False	False	False	False	False	False	False	False
20130	False	False	False	False	False	False	False	False	False	False
20131	False	False	False	False	False	False	False	False	False	False
20132	False	False	False	False	False	False	False	False	False	False
20133	False	False	False	False	False	False	False	False	False	False
20134	False	False	False	False	False	False	False	False	False	False
20135	False	False	False	False	False	False	False	False	False	False

Figure 8.35: A subset of the cleaned, encoded, and recast DataFrame built from the complete online retail dataset

Activity 19: Apriori on the Complete Online Retail Dataset

Solution:

1. Run the Apriori algorithm on the full data with reasonable parameter settings:

```
mod_colnames_minsupport = mlxtend.frequent_patterns.apriori(
    online_encoder_df,
    min_support=0.01,
    use_colnames=True
)
mod_colnames_minsupport.loc[0:6]
```

The output is as follows:

	support	itemsets
0	0.013359	(SET 2 TEA TOWELS I LOVE LONDON)
1	0.015793	(10 COLOUR SPACEBOY PEN)
2	0.012465	(12 MESSAGE CARDS WITH ENVELOPES)
3	0.017630	(12 PENCIL SMALL TUBE WOODLAND)
4	0.017978	(12 PENCILS SMALL TUBE RED RETROSPOT)
5	0.017630	(12 PENCILS SMALL TUBE SKULL)
6	0.013309	(12 PENCILS TALL TUBE RED RETROSPOT)

Figure 8.36: The Apriori algorithm results using the complete online retail dataset

2. Filter the results down to the item set containing **10 COLOUR SPACEBOY PEN.** Compare the support value with that under *Exercise 44, Executing the Apriori algorithm*:

```
mod_colnames_minsupport[
    mod_colnames_minsupport['itemsets'] == frozenset(
        {'10 COLOUR SPACEBOY PEN'}
    )
]
```

The output is as follows:

	support	itemsets
1	0.015793	(10 COLOUR SPACEBOY PEN)

Figure 8.37: Result of item set containing 10 COLOUR SPACEBOY PEN

The support value does change. When the dataset is expanded to include all transactions, the support for this item set increases from 0.015 to 0.015793. That is, in the reduced dataset used for the exercises, this item set appears in 1.5% of the transactions, while in the full dataset, it appears in approximately 1.6% of transactions.

3. Add another column containing the item set length. Then, filter down to those item sets whose length is two and whose support is in the range [0.02, 0.021]. Are the item sets the same as those found in *Exercise 44, Executing the Apriori algorithm, Step 6*?

```
mod_colnames_minsupport['length'] = (
    mod_colnames_minsupport['itemsets'].apply(lambda x: len(x))
)

mod_colnames_minsupport[
    (mod_colnames_minsupport['length'] == 2) &
    (mod_colnames_minsupport['support'] >= 0.02) &
    (mod_colnames_minsupport['support'] < 0.021)
]
```

	support	itemsets	length
836	0.020759	(ALARM CLOCK BAKELIKE PINK, ALARM CLOCK BAKELI...	2
887	0.020362	(CHARLOTTE BAG SUKI DESIGN, CHARLOTTE BAG PINK...	2
923	0.020610	(CHARLOTTE BAG SUKI DESIGN, STRAWBERRY CHARLOT...	2
1105	0.020560	(JUMBO BAG PINK POLKADOT, JUMBO BAG BAROQUE B...	2
1114	0.020908	(JUMBO SHOPPER VINTAGE RED PAISLEY, JUMBO BAG...	2
1116	0.020957	(JUMBO STORAGE BAG SUKI, JUMBO BAG BAROQUE BL...	2
1129	0.020560	(JUMBO BAG RED RETROSPOT, JUMBO BAG ALPHABET)	2
1137	0.020163	(JUMBO BAG PEARS, JUMBO BAG APPLES)	2
1203	0.020709	(JUMBO SHOPPER VINTAGE RED PAISLEY, JUMBO BAG ...	2
1218	0.020560	(JUMBO STORAGE BAG SKULLS, JUMBO BAG RED RETRO...	2
1236	0.020610	(RECYCLING BAG RETROSPOT , JUMBO BAG RED RETRO...	2
1328	0.020610	(LUNCH BAG BLACK SKULL., LUNCH BAG APPLE DESIGN)	2
1390	0.020610	(LUNCH BAG SUKI DESIGN , LUNCH BAG PINK POLKADOT)	2
1458	0.020610	(WHITE HANGING HEART T-LIGHT HOLDER, NATURAL S...	2

Figure 8.38: The section of the results of filtering based on length and support

The results did change. Before even looking at the particular item sets and their support values, we see that this filtered DataFrame has fewer item sets than the DataFrame in the previous exercise. When we use the full dataset, there are fewer item sets that match the filtering criteria; that is, only 14 item sets contain 2 items and have a support value greater than or equal to 0.02, and less than 0.021. In the previous exercise, 17 item sets met these criteria.

4. Plot the **support** values:

```
mod_colnames_minsupport.hist("support", grid=False, bins=30)
plt.title("Support")
```

```
Text(0.5, 1.0, 'Support')
```

Figure 8.39: The distribution of support values

This plot shows the distribution of support values for the full transaction dataset. As you might have assumed, the distribution is right skewed; that is, most of the item sets have lower support values and there is a long tail of support values on the higher end of the spectrum. Given how many unique item sets exist, it is not surprising that no single item set appears in a high percentage of the transactions. With this information, we could tell management that even the most prominent item set only appears in approximately 10% of the transactions, and that the vast majority of item sets appear in less than 2% of transactions. These results may not support changes in store layout, but could very well inform pricing and discounting strategies. We would gain more information on how to build these strategies by formalizing some association rules.

Activity 20: Finding the Association Rules on the Complete Online Retail Dataset

Solution:

1. Fit the association rule model on the full dataset. Use metric confidence and a minimum threshold of 0.6:

```
rules = mlxtend.frequent_patterns.association_rules(
    mod_colnames_minsupport,
    metric="confidence",
    min_threshold=0.6,
    support_only=False
)
rules.loc[0:6]
```

The output is as follows:

	antecedents	consequents	antecedent support	consequent support	support	confidence	lift	leverage	conviction
0	(ALARM CLOCK BAKELIKE CHOCOLATE)	(ALARM CLOCK BAKELIKE GREEN)	0.021255	0.048669	0.013756	0.647196	13.297902	0.012722	2.696488
1	(ALARM CLOCK BAKELIKE CHOCOLATE)	(ALARM CLOCK BAKELIKE RED)	0.021255	0.052195	0.014501	0.682243	13.071023	0.013392	2.982798
2	(ALARM CLOCK BAKELIKE ORANGE)	(ALARM CLOCK BAKELIKE GREEN)	0.022100	0.048669	0.013558	0.613483	12.605201	0.012482	2.461292
3	(ALARM CLOCK BAKELIKE RED)	(ALARM CLOCK BAKELIKE GREEN)	0.052195	0.048669	0.031784	0.608944	12.511932	0.029244	2.432722
4	(ALARM CLOCK BAKELIKE GREEN)	(ALARM CLOCK BAKELIKE RED)	0.048669	0.052195	0.031784	0.653061	12.511932	0.029244	2.731908
5	(ALARM CLOCK BAKELIKE IVORY)	(ALARM CLOCK BAKELIKE RED)	0.028308	0.052195	0.018524	0.654386	12.537313	0.017047	2.742380
6	(ALARM CLOCK BAKELIKE ORANGE)	(ALARM CLOCK BAKELIKE RED)	0.022100	0.052195	0.014998	0.678652	13.002217	0.013845	2.949463

Figure 8.40: The association rules based on the complete online retail dataset

2. Count the number of association rules. Is the number different to that found in *Exercise 45, Deriving Association Rules, Step 1*?

```
print("Number of Associations: {}".format(rules.shape[0]))
```

There are **498** association rules.

3. Plot confidence against support:

```
rules.plot.scatter("support", "confidence", alpha=0.5, marker="*")
plt.xlabel("Support")
plt.ylabel("Confidence")
plt.title("Association Rules")
plt.show()
```

The output is as follows:

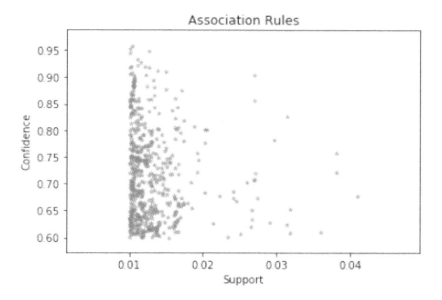

Figure 8.41: The plot of confidence against support

The plot reveals that there are some association rules featuring relatively high support and confidence values for this dataset.

4. Look at the distributions of lift, leverage, and conviction:

```
rules.hist("lift", grid=False, bins=30)
plt.title("Lift")
```

The output is as follows:

```
Text(0.5, 1.0, 'Lift')
```

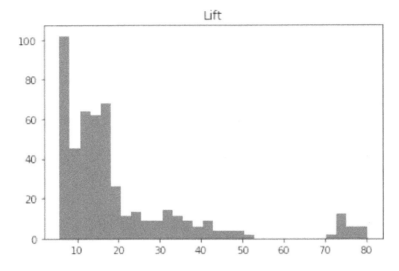

Figure 8.42: The distribution of lift values

```
rules.hist("leverage", grid=False, bins=30)
plt.title("Leverage")
```

The output is as follows:

```
Text(0.5, 1.0, 'Leverage')
```

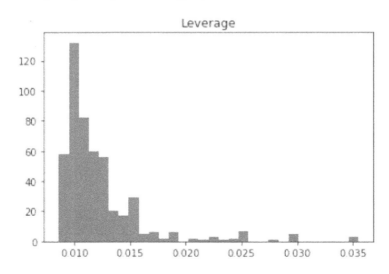

Figure 8.43: The distribution of leverage values

```
plt.hist(
    rules[numpy.isfinite(rules['conviction'])].conviction.values,
    bins = 30
)
plt.title("Conviction")
```

The output is as follows:

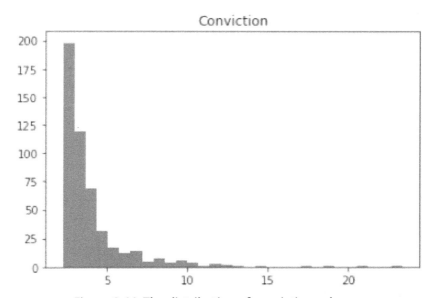

Figure 8.44: The distribution of conviction values

Having derived association rules, we can return to management with additional information, the most important of which would be that there are roughly seven item sets that have reasonably high values for both support and confidence. Look at the scatterplot of confidence against support to see the seven item sets that are separated from all the others. These seven item sets also have high lift values, as can be seen in the lift histogram. It seems that we have identified some actionable association rules, rules that we can use to drive business decisions.

Chapter 9: Hotspot Analysis

Activity 21: Estimating Density in One Dimension

Solution:

1. Open a new notebook and install all the necessary libraries.

    ```
    get_ipython().run_line_magic('matplotlib', 'inline')

    import matplotlib.pyplot as plt
    import numpy
    import pandas
    import seaborn
    import sklearn.datasets
    import sklearn.model_selection
    import sklearn.neighbors

    seaborn.set()
    ```

2. Sample 1,000 data points from the standard normal distribution. Add 3.5 to each of the last 625 values of the sample (that is, the indices between 375 and 1,000). To do this, set a random state of 100 using **numpy.random.RandomState** to guarantee the same sampled values, and then randomly generate the data points using the **randn(1000)** call:

    ```
    rand = numpy.random.RandomState(100)
    vals = rand.randn(1000)  # standard normal
    vals[375:] += 3.5
    ```

3. Plot the 1,000-point sample data as a histogram and add a scatterplot below it:

    ```
    fig, ax = plt.subplots(figsize=(14, 10))
    ax.hist(vals, bins=50, density=True, label='Sampled Values')
    ax.plot(vals, -0.005 - 0.01 * numpy.random.random(len(vals)), '+k',
    label='Individual Points')
    ax.legend(loc='upper right')
    ```

The output is as follows:

Figure 9.29: A histogram of the random sample with a scatterplot underneath

4. Define a grid of bandwidth values. Then, define and fit a grid search cross-validation algorithm:

```
bandwidths = 10 ** numpy.linspace(-1, 1, 100)

grid = sklearn.model_selection.GridSearchCV(
    estimator=sklearn.neighbors.KernelDensity(kernel="gaussian"),
    param_grid={"bandwidth": bandwidths},
    cv=10
)
grid.fit(vals[:, None])
```

5. Extract the optimal bandwidth value:

```
best_bandwidth = grid.best_params_["bandwidth"]

print(
    "Best Bandwidth Value: {}"
    .format(best_bandwidth)
)
```

6. Replot the histogram from *Step 3* and overlay the estimated density:

```
fig, ax = plt.subplots(figsize=(14, 10))

ax.hist(vals, bins=50, density=True, alpha=0.75, label='Sampled Values')

x_vec = numpy.linspace(-4, 8, 10000)[:, numpy.newaxis]
log_density = numpy.exp(grid.best_estimator_.score_samples(x_vec))
ax.plot(
    x_vec[:, 0], log_density,
    '-', linewidth=4, label='Kernel = Gaussian'
)

ax.legend(loc='upper right')
```

The output is as follows:

Figure 9.30: A histogram of the random sample with the optimal estimated density overlaid

Activity 22: Analyzing Crime in London

Solution:

1. Load the crime data. Use the path where you saved the downloaded directory, create a list of the year-month tags, use the **read_csv** command to load the individual files iteratively, and then concatenate these files together:

```
base_path = (
    "~/Documents/packt/unsupervised-learning-python/"
    "lesson-9-hotspot-models/metro-jul18-dec18/"
    "{yr_mon}/{yr_mon}-metropolitan-street.csv"
)

print(base_path)

yearmon_list = [
    "2018-0" + str(i) if i <= 9 else "2018-" + str(i)
    for i in range(7, 13)
]

print(yearmon_list)

data_yearmon_list = []

for idx, i in enumerate(yearmon_list):
    df = pandas.read_csv(
        base_path.format(yr_mon=i),
        header=0
    )

    data_yearmon_list.append(df)

    if idx == 0:
        print("Month: {}".format(i))
        print("Dimensions: {}".format(df.shape))
        print("Head:\n{}\n".format(df.head(2)))

london = pandas.concat(data_yearmon_list)
```

The output is as follows:

```
Month: 2018-07
Dimensions: (95677, 12)
Head:
                                             Crime ID    Month  \
0   e9fe81ec7a6f5d2a80445f04be3d7e92831dbf3090744e...  2018-07
1   076b796ba1e1ba3f69c9144e2aa7a7bc85b61d51bf7a59...  2018-07

                  Reported by            Falls within   Longitude  \
0   Metropolitan Police Service   Metropolitan Police Service   0.774271
1   Metropolitan Police Service   Metropolitan Police Service  -1.007293

    Latitude                   Location   LSOA code             LSOA name  \
0   51.148147   On or near Bethersden Road   E01024031           Ashford 012B
1   51.893136             On or near Prison   E01017674   Aylesbury Vale 010D

    Crime type        Last outcome category   Context
0   Other theft   Status update unavailable       NaN
1   Other crime    Awaiting court outcome        NaN
```

Figure 9.31: An example of one of the individual crime files

This printed information is just for the first of the loaded files, which will be the criminal information from the Metropolitan Police Service for July 2018. This one file has nearly 100,000 entries. You will notice that there is a great deal of interesting information in this dataset, but we will focus on **Longitude**, **Latitude**, **Month**, and **Crime type**.

2. Print diagnostics of the complete (six months) and concatenated dataset:

```
print(
    "Dimensions - Full Data:\n{}\n"
    .format(london.shape)
)
print(
    "Unique Months - Full Data:\n{}\n"
    .format(london["Month"].unique())
)
print(
    "Number of Unique Crime Types - Full Data:\n{}\n"
    .format(london["Crime type"].nunique())
)
print(
    "Unique Crime Types - Full Data:\n{}\n"
    .format(london["Crime type"].unique())
```

```
    )
print(
    "Count Occurrences Of Each Unique Crime Type - Full Type:\n{}\n"
    .format(london["Crime type"].value_counts())
)
```

The output is as follows:

```
Dimensions - Full Data:
(546032, 12)

Unique Months - Full Data:
['2018-07' '2018-08' '2018-09' '2018-10' '2018-11' '2018-12']

Number of Unique Crime Types - Full Data:
14

Unique Crime Types - Full Data:
['Other theft' 'Other crime' 'Violence and sexual offences'
 'Anti-social behaviour' 'Criminal damage and arson' 'Drugs'
 'Possession of weapons' 'Theft from the person' 'Vehicle crime'
 'Burglary' 'Public order' 'Robbery' 'Shoplifting' 'Bicycle theft']

Count Occurrences Of Each Unique Crime Type - Full Type:
Violence and sexual offences    117499
Anti-social behaviour           115448
Other theft                      61833
Vehicle crime                    58857
Burglary                         41145
Criminal damage and arson        28436
Public order                     24655
Theft from the person            22670
Shoplifting                      21296
Drugs                            17292
Robbery                          17060
Bicycle theft                    11362
Other crime                       5223
Possession of weapons             3256
Name: Crime type, dtype: int64
```

Figure 9.32: Descriptors of the full crime dataset

3. Subset the DataFrame down to four variables (**Longitude**, **Latitude**, **Month**, and **Crime type**):

```
london_subset = london[["Month", "Longitude", "Latitude", "Crime type"]]
london_subset.head(5)
```

The output is as follows:

	Month	Longitude	Latitude	Crime type
0	2018-07	0.774271	51.148147	Other theft
1	2018-07	-1.007293	51.893136	Other crime
2	2018-07	0.744706	52.038219	Violence and sexual offences
3	2018-07	0.148434	51.595164	Anti-social behaviour
4	2018-07	0.137065	51.583672	Anti-social behaviour

Figure 9.33: Crime data in DataFrame form subset down to the Longitude, Latitude, Month, and Crime type columns

4. Using the **jointplot** function from **seaborn**, fit and visualize three kernel density estimation models for bicycle theft in July, September, and December 2018:

```
crime_bicycle_jul = london_subset[
    (london_subset["Crime type"] == "Bicycle theft") &
    (london_subset["Month"] == "2018-07")
]

seaborn.jointplot("Longitude", "Latitude", crime_bicycle_jul, kind="kde")
```

The output is as follows:

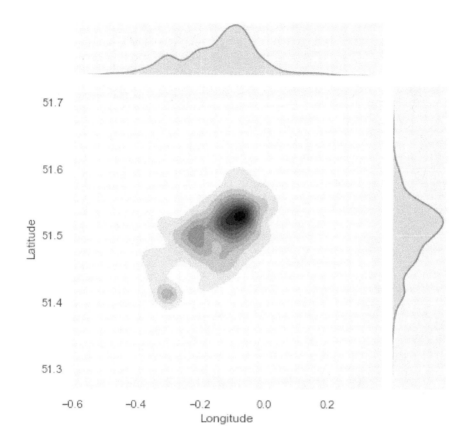

Figure 9.34: The estimated joint and marginal densities for bicycle thefts in July 2018

```
crime_bicycle_sept = london_subset[
    (london_subset["Crime type"] == "Bicycle theft") &
    (london_subset["Month"] == "2018-09")
]

seaborn.jointplot("Longitude", "Latitude", crime_bicycle_sept, kind="kde")
```

The output is as follows:

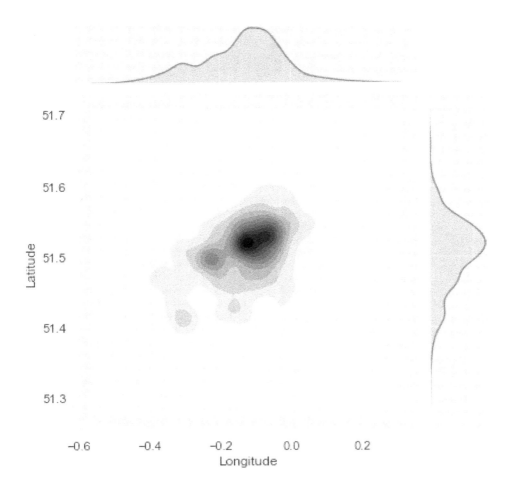

Figure 9.35: The estimated joint and marginal densities for bicycle thefts in September 2018

```
crime_bicycle_dec = london_subset[
    (london_subset["Crime type"] == "Bicycle theft") &
    (london_subset["Month"] == "2018-12")
]

seaborn.jointplot("Longitude", "Latitude", crime_bicycle_dec, kind="kde")
```

The output is as follows:

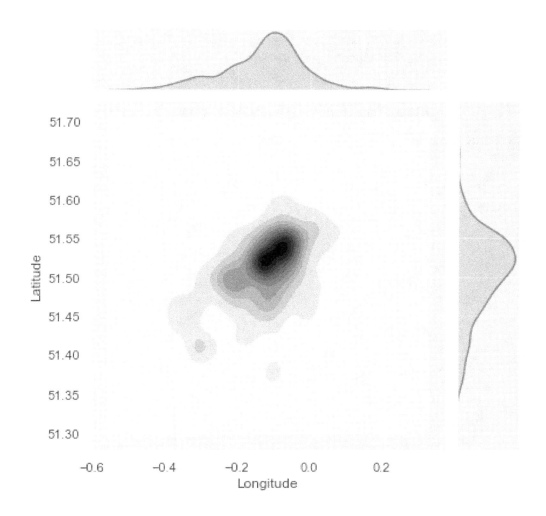

Figure 9.36: The estimated joint and marginal densities for bicycle thefts in December 2018

From month to month, the density of bicycle thefts stays quite constant. There are slight differences between the densities, which is to be expected given that the data that is the foundation of these estimated densities is three one-month samples. Given these results, police or criminologists should be confident in predicting where future bicycle thefts are most likely to occur.

5. Repeat *Step* 4; this time, use shoplifting crimes for the months of August, October, and November 2018:

```
crime_shoplift_aug = london_subset[
    (london_subset["Crime type"] == "Shoplifting") &
    (london_subset["Month"] == "2018-08")
]
```

```
seaborn.jointplot("Longitude", "Latitude", crime_shoplift_aug, kind="kde")
```

The output is as follows:

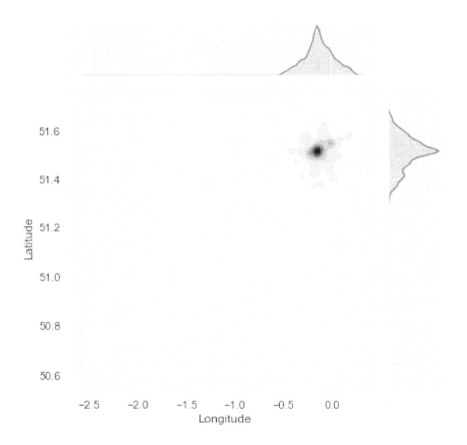

Figure 9.37: The estimated joint and marginal densities for shoplifting incidents in August 2018

```
crime_shoplift_oct = london_subset[
    (london_subset["Crime type"] == "Shoplifting") &
    (london_subset["Month"] == "2018-10")
]
```

```
seaborn.jointplot("Longitude", "Latitude", crime_shoplift_oct, kind="kde")
```

The output is as follows:

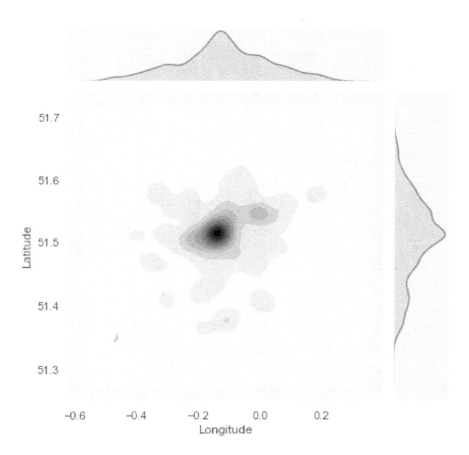

Figure 9.38: The estimated joint and marginal densities for shoplifting incidents in October 2018

```
crime_shoplift_nov = london_subset[
    (london_subset["Crime type"] == "Shoplifting") &
    (london_subset["Month"] == "2018-11")
]
```

```
seaborn.jointplot("Longitude", "Latitude", crime_shoplift_nov, kind="kde")
```

The output is as follows:

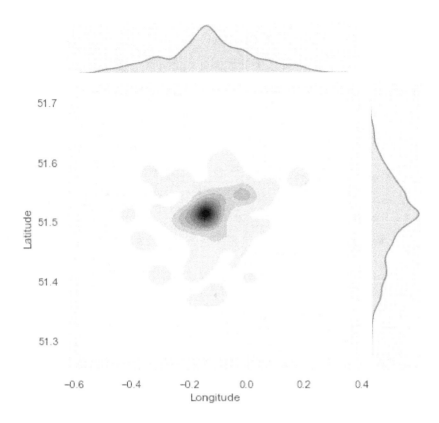

Figure 9.39: The estimated joint and marginal densities for shoplifting incidents in November 2018

Like the bicycle theft results, the shoplifting densities are quite stable across the months. The density from August 2018 looks different from the other two months; however, if you look at the longitude and latitude values, you will notice that the density is very similar, but it has just shifted and scaled. The reason for this is that there were probably a number of outliers forcing the creation of a much larger plotting region.

6. Repeat *Step 5*; this time use burglary crimes for the months of July, October, and December 2018:

```
crime_burglary_jul = london_subset[
    (london_subset["Crime type"] == "Burglary") &
    (london_subset["Month"] == "2018-07")
]
```

```
seaborn.jointplot("Longitude", "Latitude", crime_burglary_jul, kind="kde")
```

The output is as follows:

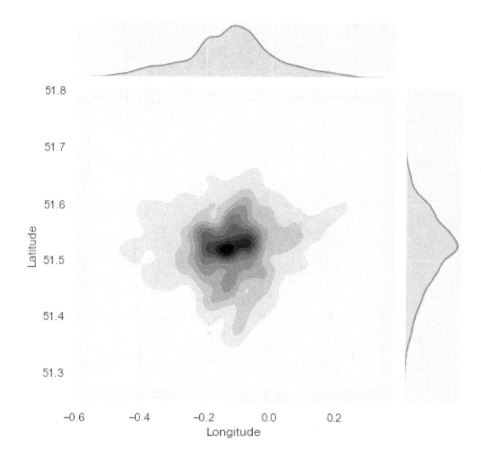

Figure 9.40: The estimated joint and marginal densities for burglaries in July 2018

```
crime_burglary_oct = london_subset[
    (london_subset["Crime type"] == "Burglary") &
    (london_subset["Month"] == "2018-10")
]


seaborn.jointplot("Longitude", "Latitude", crime_burglary_oct, kind="kde")
```

The output is as follows:

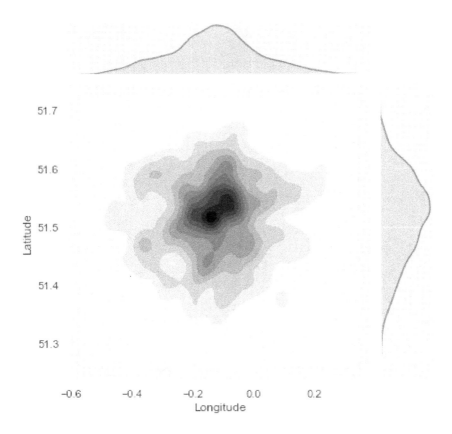

Figure 9.41: The estimated joint and marginal densities for burglaries in October 2018

```
crime_burglary_dec = london_subset[
    (london_subset["Crime type"] == "Burglary") &
    (london_subset["Month"] == "2018-12")
]

seaborn.jointplot("Longitude", "Latitude", crime_burglary_dec, kind="kde")
```

The output is as follows:

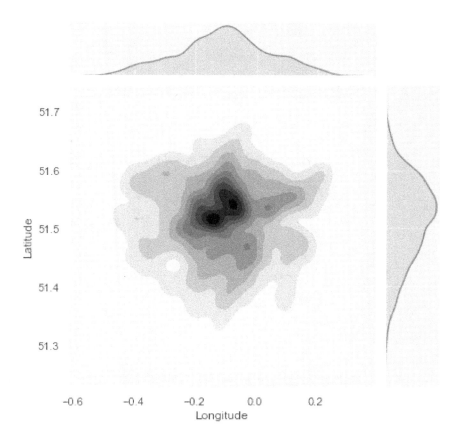

Figure 9.42: The estimated joint and marginal densities for burglaries in December 2018

Once again, we can see that the distributions are quite similar across the months. The only difference is that the densities seem to widen or spread from July to December. As always, the noise and inherent lack of information contained in the sample data is causing small shifts in the estimated densities.

Index

About

All major keywords used in this book are captured alphabetically in this section. Each one is accompanied by the page number of where they appear.